Aside from Teaching,
What in the World Can You Do?

ASIDE FROM TEACHING, WHAT IN THE WORLD CAN YOU DO?

Career Strategies for Liberal Arts Graduates

Dorothy K. Bestor

University of Washington Press
Seattle and London

To Arthur Bestor:
for surviving this revision

Aside from Teaching, What in the World Can You Do? is a revised and expanded version of *Aside from Teaching English, What in the World Can You Do?* (copyright © 1977 by the University of Washington Press). An earlier version of *Aside from Teaching English, What in the World Can You Do?* (copyright © 1976 by Dorothy K. Bestor) was published for the University of Washington Placement Center by ASUW Lecture Notes.

Library of Congress Cataloging in Publication Data

Bestor, Dorothy K.
Aside from teaching, what in the world can you
do?

Rev. ed. of: Aside from Teaching English, what
in the world can you do? c1977.
Bibliography: p.
Includes index.
1. Vocational guidance.   2. Teaching—Vocational
guidance.   3. English language—Study and teaching.
I. Title.
HF5381.B412   1982   331.7'023   82-2009
ISBN 0-295-95725-5   AACR2

Acknowledgments

In various ways I am indebted to many persons and organizations. I should like to thank Laura Horowitz for permission to reprint, in chapter 8, passages from *The Editorial Eye*, published by Editorial Experts, Inc., Alexandria, Virginia; Joanne Landesman and the editors of *Across the Board* for passages in chapter 12 which appeared in a May 1979 article by Landesman entitled "Can Humanities Academics Find Happiness with Businessmen (and Vice Versa)?"; Dale Mathews, Mary Easthope, and the editors of *Rackham Reports*, published by the Horace E. Rackham School of Graduate Studies, University of Michigan, for a few passages in chapter 2 and the summary of the Ph.D. employment crisis in Appendix A.

Several short passages in chapters 1, 6, and 12 first appeared in articles of mine in the *Association for School, College, and University Staffing* [ASCUS] *Annual*, 1980, 1981, and 1982; others in the *Black Collegian* (November-December 1978), and in the *Washington English Journal* (May 1980). The second half of chapter 8 appeared in somewhat abridged form in an article of mine in *Scholarly Publishing* (October 1981).

I am particularly grateful for the chance to use unpublished material. My greatest debt is to the Modern Language Association of America, whose staff members Ann Kirschner and Richard Brod were most helpful in arranging for me to use 160 manuscript replies to a 1978 MLA inquiry into the nonteaching careers of Ph.D.'s in English. I also want to thank Alma Kadragic of the American Broadcasting Company, who has allowed me to use in chapter 11 excerpts from a paper she originally submitted as a chapter in "Translate Yourself," a collection describing the experiences of women who have found alternatives to teaching; to Howard Shenson, the "consultant's consultant," who gave me permission to use in an appendix the questionnaire "Are You Meant to Be a Consultant?" devised by him and his colleague, Don Swartz, Director, International Institute for the Study of Systems Renewal, a Division of Organization Renewal, Inc.;

and Martin VandenAkker, Jr., for allowing to quote from his unpublished senior paper, submitted at Albion College in April 1979, "The Relevance of English Writing and Literature in Practicing Medicine."

For sharing with me the experience and the opinions which form the central core of this book, I cannot suficiently thank the over 450 job-seekers, job-holders, employers, and counselors who willingly talked with me or filled out my questionnaires, and in some cases expanded them at my request to form the two dozen first-person narratives which give an additional dimension to their ideas. I would like to give especial thanks to members of the English departments and the staffs of the Placement and Career Planning centers of ten colleges and universities that, through inviting me to talk to their student about career choices, greatly enlarged the base from which I was gathering information and opinion. From 1977 through 1981 these institutions included Albion College in Michigan; the College of St. Benedict and St. Olaf College in Minnesota; Lane Community College and Linfield College in Oregon; Miami University in Ohio; the University of Michigan; and the University of Washington, Western Washington University, and the University of Puget Sound in Washington.

For reading portions of the manuscript and offering very welcome encouragement, I continue to be grateful to Mary Coney, Robert Heilman, and Ivan Settles, all of the University of Washington, and to Rosemary VanArsdel of the University of Puget Sound, all of whom made invaluable suggestions about the manuscript of the first edition. While preparing the second edition I have also become indebted to Tina Brinson of Western Washington University, Vicki Adams, Elisabeth Case, Leila Charbonneau, and Elsa Steele of Seattle, Penny Hauser-Cram of the *Harvard Educational Review*, Ian Montagnes of the University of Toronto Press, Paul O'Dea of the National Council of Teachers of English, and Peggy Sherwood of the Princeton University Press. I would also like to thank the staff members of the University of Washington Press, all of whom have worked with me patiently and resourcefully. Most of all I am indebted to my husband, Arthur Bestor, who thought up the title for the first edition and who, during the apparently never-ending process of revision, has often cheerfully interrupted his own writing to help me find a better word or to cook the meals.

Contents

To the Reader

This book stems in part from questions asked by students during my thirteen years of teaching college English. "If I major in English, what can I do with it after I graduate?" many of them wondered. My search for answers was intensified in 1974 and 1975 when, as a counselor in the Placement Center of the University of Washington, I tried hard to help qualified candidates find either college teaching positions or alternative ones. One of the typical questions I heard was, "I have these advanced degrees, but how do I find anyone to hire me?" Partly because so many candidates who were well prepared to teach English came in with such questions, and partly because my own teaching experience had been in English, I began to put together a bibliography and a few suggestions about finding alternatives to teaching English.

When Professor Robert Heilman of the English Department at the University of Washington urged that I write to publishing and business firms to ask how people with backgrounds in English could be useful to them, I was glad to do so. But I had no sooner begun to look into these fields than other areas, such as government agencies, university nonacademic staffs, continuing education programs, and the media, seemed to demand investigation as well. The flood of questions from job candidates coming to my office led to provisional answers, and these in turn to still more questions. The further one goes in exploring paths of entry into these fields, the more one realizes the impossibility of definitive answers.

The problem of finding employment in teaching, traditionally the primary career choice of graduates in English, was serious enough when the 1977 edition of this book, *Aside from Teaching English, What in the World Can You Do?* was published. Since then the situation has become graver still, until now, in the winter of 1981-82, slashing budget cuts at federal, state, and local levels threaten even more widespread academic unemployment, particularly in humanities fields.

Increasingly as other liberal arts graduates—in history, philosophy, modern languages, history of art, and classics—share the employment problems of graduates in English, it has become evident that they can share many of the solutions. Accordingly this new edition, with its broader title, although still focusing mainly on English majors, may also be useful to a wider audience. I hope that it can demonstrate and illustrate for graduates in other humanistic fields the possibility of applying what they have learned to tasks, both those recognized and those not yet recognized, in a wider world than the academic one.

The earlier edition was based largely on interviews with or questionnaire responses from over 350 employers and successful job-seekers in fields where people with backgrounds in English could fill a need. Material for this new edition has come in large part from the over 450 additional interviews held or questionnaire responses received, among them from placement counselors across the country, from freelance editors, institutional staff editors, persons in book publishing and the media, former liberal arts majors in business and government, a group of 160 unpublished responses surveyed recently by the Modern Language Association, and from a smaller, parallel survey of my own. Gaps in what I could learn from these lively and willing informants I have filled in through attending conferences on careers, on consulting, on editing, and on women in business, as well as by reading in the burgeoning literature of career planning and job-hunting. Because of the inevitable time lag between finishing a manuscript and seeing it in print, some names, positions, regulations, or policies described here may have changed by the time you read this book. The underlying thesis they illustrate—namely that the world is wide and there are many uses to which one can put a degree in the humanities other than by following in the footsteps of one's college instructors and trying eventually to replace them in the classroom—should, however, remain true for some time to come.

In revising this book for a second edition, I am more convinced than ever that this principle holds true; but I realize that changes are occurring in some jobs, in employers' and employees' expectations, and in the whole economy. Several "alternative" fields have become almost as crowded as teaching; state and federal budget cuts have made some other areas less appealing than they were three years ago; and new technologies are often said to be on the verge of revolutionizing all communications fields.

Yet in order to complete this revision I have had to adopt some arbitrary cut-off points and to decide upon a modestly pragmatic plan: to replace those statements in the 1977 edition which have become obsolete, to leave in place those that are still valid, and to add just as much new material as necessary to give readers some guidelines for the 1980s. In doing so I have written six new chapters: chapter 2, directed to the concerns of readers with doctoral degrees in English or related subjects; chapter 3, on self-assessment; chapter 4, on ways of presenting yourself, on paper or in person, to future employers; chapter 13, for those hoping to start their own business enterprises; chapter 15, directed particularly toward the career problems of women; and chapter 16, a new summary and conclusion. I have also gathered new material for and largely rewritten chapter 1, which lays out the whole problem, chapter 8, on freelance editing, chapter 10, on book publishing, chapter 11, on entering the media, chapter 12, on business, and chapter 14, on working for the government. The four remaining chapters have been reviewed and some additions made.

My own interest in this whole subject comes from both professional and personal involvement. As a graduate student, a Ph.D. in British studies, and then a college and university English teacher for nine years, I shared the tunnel vision of many academics who consider alternatives to teaching careers as remote possibilities for others to investigate. After a hiatus of some years to bring up my family (meanwhile doing part-time work as editor, research assistant, and oral history interviewer), I returned in 1969 to teaching—though not in the same kind of setting in which I had taught before my long vacation from the job market. Instead I discovered that teaching community college students offered unexpected challenges and satisfactions.

Eventually, however, the discrepancy between time spent and salary received in part-time community college teaching aroused my interest in the whole problem of career qualifications, choices, and changes; this concern led in turn to my experience as placement counselor for higher education at the University of Washington. While in that position I began to write what was to have been a small pamphlet to be issued to the many liberal arts majors who came to see me wondering what in the world they could do with as "impractical" a course of study as the ones on which they had embarked. The pamphlet grew and grew—to 105 pages—and was published in 1976 by the ASUW Lecture Notes Office for the University of Washington Placement Center. After I had left the placement center to help found a freelance editing firm and to teach continuing education courses in writing and literature at the university, I kept working on this project and collecting the material which resulted in the first University of Washington Press edition of 1977.

In recent years I have constantly had it brought home to me that career choices and job searches are not merely interesting topics for books, articles, and talks; they involve hard decisions made by people very close to me. My sons, my daughters-in-law, and many of my friends are in the throes of the various career changes described in this book. I realize, therefore, when in this book I urge flexibility, geographical mobility, and willingness to consider unlikely-seeming options, that what I suggest is often easier urged than done; and I sympathize with the initial resistance to a change of goals on the part of those who have invested time, money, and hope in their preparation for teaching.

A few points made in the preface to the 1977 edition bear repeating. As in the earlier edition, I am writing for seven groups of readers: college students wondering whether to major in any of the humanities; recent B.A.'s in these fields; graduate students looking ahead; M.A.'s or Ph.D.'s looking for their first job; Ph.D.'s from other years, especially those who have been teaching, trying to change jobs or start new careers; college-educated women returning to work; and counselors of any of these job-seekers.

Aside from the two chapters (2 and 15) whose audiences are apparent from their titles, all the other chapters could be helpful to anyone reading this book. One of the ironies of the current job crisis is that job-seekers with B.A.'s, M.A.'s, and Ph.D.'s (and indeed—as one of the case histories in chapter 11 shows—sometimes those without four-year degrees) occasionally compete for the same kinds of entry-level positions—as information specialists, editors, writers, reporters, management trainees, or political aides. Each group, however, has its own strong points, and whatever your stage of formal education, you can learn to develop them to your advantage. The points in favor of job candidates with B.A.'s are that they are usually not considered "overqualified"; they do not have years of academic habits built up through teaching or independent research to unlearn; and, moreover, employers feel comfortable in offering them entry-level salaries. Job-seekers with M.A.'s can be glad that they have an added qualification, without having made such a great investment of time and money in an academic career that a nonacademic employer hesitates to hire them. Candidates with Ph.D.'s have something of a negative image to overcome in the minds of employers who may consider them overspecialized. As later chapters will show, however, Ph.D.'s have learned much that can serve them well outside of academia; sometimes, too, by backtracking and picking up certain skills that they did not have time to learn along the way, they may make more rapid progress in business, publishing, or government employment than they otherwise would.

Let me point out first certain things that this book does *not* undertake to do and then indicate what you can expect to find in it. It does not purport to give lists of specific job vacancies: openings come and go too rapidly. It does not offer statistics and projections showing exactly how many hundred editors, reporters, information specialists, technical writers, and public relations persons will be needed in this country in the next ten years: this is the function of the latest volume of the *Occupational Outlook Handbook*, published by the U.S. Department of Labor.

Nor does this volume attempt to be a comprehensive state-by-state guidebook, with good, better, and best places to apply in each region. The original 1976 pamphlet used as its starting point, Seattle, the University of Washington, and surrounding areas in the Pacific Northwest. In each of the two subsequent University of Washington Press editions I have balanced this local emphasis as much as possible with examples from other parts of the country, though not striving for equal geographical distribution of evidence. I hope, however, that all readers using this book will freely translate, apply, and extrapolate from what they find here. If a government agency or a group of editors or a handbook of vocational information is mentioned as originating in Washington or Oregon, I hope that you will automatically ask yourself, wherever you may be as you read, "Do we have anything like that here? If not, why not? What's the nearest thing to it? If we do have something like it, what use can I make of it in my own job search?"

Although *Aside from Teaching* . . . deals mainly with how and where to look for nonteaching positions, I have often deliberately discussed not only the strategies of the job search but what duties and opportunities certain relatively unpublished jobs involve. Many of you with degrees in English have only a generalized notion that somewhere out in the world people *do* edit, work on university and hospital publications, make indexes, design and teach courses for adults, or do research and writing for government agencies. Since there are few hard-and-fast job descriptions for some of these posts, you tend to approach job counselors with the knowledge that such work exists but with no sense of what it involves or whether indeed you are already qualified to do it. I have tried therefore to give just enough of a picture of what people do in these and other jobs so that those interested will follow up by reading the fuller treatments of them listed in the Bibliography.

As you read, please bear in mind that although some of the persons I quote have made a successful transition from being a graduate student or teacher to becoming a continuing education specialist, ad-

ministrative assistant, freelance editor, university information specialist or editor, city editor of a daily paper, editor of a publishing
house, director of a management training program for a chain of
stores, or government analyst, other people whom I consulted went
directly to these fields as their first choice. I can hardly emphasize
enough that many of these people, although they have advice for you
who may want to get into these fields from the now overcrowded one
of teaching in the humanities, did not themselves seek out their jobs
as "alternative careers." Teachers and students of English, book publishers, writers, reporters, technical editors, columnists, critics—all
of them members of professions dealing in words and ideas in an attempt to influence people—tend to operate on different hypotheses
about what is central and what is alternative. It is easy to forget how
closely a job-seeker's notion of "alternatives" depends on where his
or her job search first led.

Yet wherever your particular starting place, I hope that these comments from interviewees, and especially these suggestions from
other job-seekers, will be a stimulus to your self-assessment and then
to your own imaginative plan of action.

ASIDE FROM TEACHING,
WHAT IN THE WORLD CAN YOU DO?

1. Liberal Arts Graduates in the 1980s—Who Needs Them?

Liberal arts graduates have qualities that companies look for in potential employees: analytical skills and the ability to express themselves effectively, or what Richard Thain, the president of the Midwest College Placement Officers Association, called "the classic benefits of a classic education."

—Christopher Wellisz, "Darker Days for College Grads," *New York Times*, October 11, 1981

According to the conventional wisdom of the 1980s, society is so beleaguered by environmental problems, economic crises, and international tensions that only natural scientists, engineers, economists, political scientists, and military experts—along with the statisticians and computer experts who keep track of their activities—are of much use. In difficult times, many people hunger for solid, quantifiable information and for the disciplines that offer it. As employment experts announce today, "There is a need for scientific types, engineering people . . . managers and marketing and financial executives."[1] Employers and job-seekers alike sometimes appear to be reverting to that uncritical reliance on verifiable data satirized by Dickens in *Hard Times* through the character of Thomas Gradgrind, a man who kept saying, "Facts alone are wanted in life. . . . Stick to Facts, Sir!" Of what possible use, we sometimes wonder today, are the liberal arts majors—those bookish students and teachers who deal with literature and the other liberal arts, with beliefs and values and imagination? Humanities majors and the works they study and teach are therefore often in danger of being dismissed as luxuries, appropriate only to happier times.

Meanwhile job-seekers—recent or past graduates with degrees in the liberal arts—tend too often to accept the picture of their fields of study as irrelevant or useless. I "graduated with a degree in English Lit, qualifying me for absolutely nothing," writes Marcia Carsey, a woman who has become one of the vice-presidents of a major TV network.[2] Too many other liberal arts majors would echo Carsey's assertion uncritically. They have become accustomed to such headlines as "Programmers: Writing Their Own Ticket," "Electronic Experts Have System Wired," "Outlook Bright for Engineers, Dim for Others."[3] Often they become too cowed to read beyond the headlines, or to look around at the world and remind themselves how many people (including those who collect such information and compose such headlines) work at nontechnical, nonscientific jobs.

One must admit, of course, that currently there appears to be a saturated market for all college graduates. The Bureau of Labor Statistics estimates that, by 1990, the number of college graduates will have exceeded the available technical and professional jobs by more than three million.[4] In connection with these three million jobs, Christopher Wellisz points out in the New York Times, "A declining birthrate has affected the market for fields like education, a traditional source of employment for graduates, particularly in the liberal arts."[5]

Yet before you, as an undergraduate, recent graduate, graduate student, or college teacher of the humanities conclude that you have made a hopeless career choice, it is time to take an objective look at your major field and what it can enable you to do. Going beyond the pieties of those commencement orations wherein speakers continually invoke "our priceless heritage of the liberal arts and the humanities," one must ask what in fact the humanities are, and what studying them is "good for."

In current usage, the "humanities" include English language and literature, other modern languages and their literatures, linguistics, history (including the history of art and music), classical languages and literature, and philosophy.[6] If you are one of the 250,000 new humanities B.A.'s who graduate each year, or a newly qualified teacher in one of these fields looking for a position, perhaps it is time to stop thinking of yourself according to an academic category ("an English major," "an M.A. in American history," "a Ph.D. in French looking for a tenure-track job"). Instead, this may be the time to look back over your courses and seminars, to analyze them and abstract from them not what authors you "covered" or what historical periods you became at home in, but what kinds of intellectual functions you learned to perform.

Of course not everyone studying literature, history, or philosophy will gain exactly the same capabilities from them; differences in students' temperament and variations in emphasis from one instructor to another will lead some students to graduate from humanistic programs with highly developed writing skills while others will tend to be best at critical analysis or original research. Nonetheless, on thinking over the work you did as an undergraduate major in one of the humanities disciplines, you will probably find that you developed, or at least were encouraged to develop, most of the capabilities listed below. Some of them are fairly specific and measurable ones; some are broader and less tangible habits of mind. In any case, however one wants to label them, there are certain abilities that majors in English and other humanities disciplines presumably have developed:

You've learned to read carefully and thoughtfully, paying close attention to words, to their exact meanings, and to their connotations.

You've learned to respond to, and to formulate and defend your responses to, what you read and what you experience.

You've learned how to use a library, both to find reference information quickly and to use a wide range of sources for research.

Once you find the information you need, you can analyze it and compare contradictory pieces of evidence; you don't uncritically seize upon the first set of facts you find in print.

Having dug out the information you're looking for, you can organize it so that it can shed light upon a problem.

Your wide reading experience should have led you to an awareness of alternative interpretations and solutions of problems.

Through the study of literature and history, you should have learned to empathize with the feelings, aspirations, and limitations of persons drastically different from yourself. Although it would be impossible to document a specific carryover, it seems likely that the more you come to identify with a wide range of characters through your reading, the more you develop the habit of trying to understand rather than judge the people you meet in everyday life.

As a humanities major, you have learned or are in the process of learning to write clearly and interestingly about your ideas, your findings, and your conclusions. Through your varied reading you should have developed a sensitivity to your audience and their needs. And (extremely important), you have learned to get your papers into final form, to finish and let go of them, working under pressure all the while.

Finally, you may have learned to make not only written presentations of your ideas but oral ones—in a class, a small seminar group, or a one-to-one conference.

Reading this list, not every humanities major will feel brimming over with all these capabilities. Probably the kind of expertise that a great many of you, not excluding English majors, will be most hesitant to claim is writing ability. Fortunately, however, it is seldom too late to work at improving your writing. No matter what your stage of education or professional advancement, you can either work on your writing by yourself or find courses that will help. Whether they are for academic credit or not, whether they are in departments of English, philosophy, history, communications, or continuing education, doesn't matter so long as you have to hand in papers frequently to an instructor who cares about writing, reads your work attentively, makes constructive comments, and establishes a classroom atmosphere conducive to open discussion of class members' papers by one another.[7]

Once you have decided to improve your writing skills by constant practice, you should begin to find that such ability, in combination with the research, organizational, analytical, and other skills of the humanities major, is useful, even valued, more widely than you have realized. "Major in English," urges Dr. Robert Batscha, director of the Center for Communication in New York. "Employers everywhere, always, need people who can write."[8] Some employers, aware of this need, make a deliberate effort to hire liberal arts majors; according to an executive of the J. C. Penney Company, writing in a recent *New York Times* special section on careers, such companies include "retailers, bankers, insurance companies, ad agencies, government, nonprofit organizations, publishing houses, loan companies, the military, and airlines."[9] (Later chapters of this book report on other categories of possible employers of liberal arts graduates.)

Members of the professions, too, are becoming increasingly vocal about the usefulness in their fields of a liberal arts background and one of its end results, a skill in communication. Frank Harper, legal counsel for a nationwide chemical company, emphasizes the need for both oral and written communication in the practice of law: "A degree in communication—called English—has proved in the two years since I graduated from law school to have been a perfect choice for preparing me . . . to be the best attorney possible for my clients, for my corporation, and for myself."[10] Many members of the medical profession, turning away from the traditional advice to premedical students to take as much science as possible while undergraduates, now encourage such students to major in the humanities. In a study in which Martin VandenAkker, Jr., of Albion College surveyed the opinions of some of the medical profession on the value of undergraduate English courses for premedical students, four-fifths of them arrived at this consensus, "Learning writing skills helps the student, and later the physician, organize, synthesize, classify, and associate;" moreover, "the study of literature should be part of the training of every clinician, as a way of sharpening both his analytic and his empathetic powers."[11] In somewhat the same vein, a Chicago surgeon, Ernestine Hambrick, M.D., writes on the value of the liberal arts in a medical career: "Communication is the key, whether it be used to express feelings, convey instructions, direct actions, share knowledge, or influence reactions. . . . A knowledge of the structure and proper manipulation of the language combined with the effective and attractive verbal and written transfer of thoughts, concepts, and ideas are the essentials of success. . . ."[12]

Whatever the company, industry, or profession, a need for persons who use language well may surface in various ways. As Linwood E. Orange has shown in *English, The Pre-Professional Major*, an increasing number of employers realize how much they "need people who can write," and are anxious to hire those who show evidence of being able to do so.[13] Other employers, whose offices turn out gobbledegook and jargon of the kind currently under fire by Joseph Mitchell, Edwin Newman, Malcolm Baldrige, William Safire, and kindred supporters of plain, clear language, are unaware of their needs yet sometimes responsive to reeducation and persuasion.[14]

If you have the chance—either as a teacher of continuing education courses, a writing consultant, or an editor—to work with business and professional persons whose language needs improvement, you will find that what is involved is not mere "remedial English." Most writing-related work touched upon in this book involves far more than simply showing people their mistakes and how to correct them. Instead you can expect to be teaching, writing, or editing in areas extending far beyond textbook rules. How, for instance, would you describe in four pages, in terms that might keep it from being wiped out by budget cuts, a neighborhood social agency serving 320 minority families? How would you help a biologist whose grant proposal had been rejected with the comment, "This may be good science, but the writing is so bad we can't tell"? What would you include in a museum newsletter or alumni magazine to ensure its being read instead of pitched into the wastebasket? How would you design a writing course for a group of urban planners who see that their reports are too wordy and abstract but can't come up with a remedy by themselves?

If you can draw from and build upon your experience in doing research and in organizing, rewriting, and editing your college or graduate school papers, if you keep your audience in mind, and if you aren't overawed by new subject matter, you may find yourself doing all kinds of work that is not only needed but valued. It will be far from routine, and will represent an intellectual challenge as you adapt to new situations many of the techniques you have learned as a student of English or the other humanities subjects.

If, in addition to having been a student of the humanities, you have also handled teaching responsibilities, you will have developed additional abilities transferable to other careers. You may have taken these abilities for granted. "Too many people in education have a narrow vision; they see themselves only as teachers," writes a former teacher who is now a public information officer at a Midwestern university. Yet if you have taught, you have probably as a matter of course developed many skills and attitudes that are valuable outside the classroom:

You can work under pressure. Each class session represents a deadline met. Hardly any other profession that humanities majors enter (except journalism) demands so great an ability to keep producing and performing on schedule.

You can keep exact records. Knowing that at any time you may have to justify a grade to a student or show a student teacher what the class has covered and where it is heading, you make yourself write out your syllabi and record the classes' progress in detail.

In addition to organizing information, you have learned to organize time—to make both long-range plans (for a quarter, a semester, or a year) and short-range ones (for the fifty minutes of each class hour).

Your library and research skills have probably extended to audiovisual resources. You know the advantages and limitations of films, filmstrips, videotapes, slides, reel-to-reel and cassette tapes, as well as overhead and opaque projectors. (You can use any or all of them to help bring a subject to life, but you resist turning each class session into a multimedia production.)

You have discovered something about motivating people to learn. Through the atmosphere you establish in your classroom and through individualizing your instruction, you can often lead students to undertake independent projects or to see the excitement in a subject they thought they didn't like.

You are willing to make decisions, and you make them many times a day without trying to avoid responsibility.

You are flexible. You can come up with alternative ideas in almost any situation. If you find that the audiovisual equipment has blown a fuse or that your new textbooks will arrive four weeks late, you have a contingency plan and you carry it out.

Whether you are a teacher casting about for an alternative career or you are wondering about nonteaching options as you complete a bachelor's or graduate degree in the liberal arts, your flexibility will be constantly drawn upon. A shift in the kind of work you are looking for will probably not come about easily. There is reason enough to hesitate at the beginning. Your daily schedule, your summer vacations, most of your work habits, the kind of accountability you are subject to, possibly even your friends and the area you live in—all these may change if you decide to change your work. Then too, there is the question of "what people really *do*" in some of the jobs that you have heard of but not watched at first hand the way we all from our early childhood watch teachers teaching. "People sometimes resist alternative jobs out of ignorance," William Bliss of the Yale Alumni Placement Service once told me. "They do not know what the editor of a house organ does."[15] And there are personal reasons, too, for resisting the idea of nonteaching jobs. Some candidates have focused for so long on what Donna Martyn, director of the office of Placement Services at Harvard University, calls "the personal and social expectations of an academic position"[16] that they drop into their campus placement center, ask perfunctorily about alternatives to teaching positions, and then play what Eric Berne calls the "game of 'Yes, but. . . .'"[17] Objections and excuses abound: "But I'm too inexperienced; nobody would hire me." "But I'm too *old* to change." "I can't find any business or government jobs being advertised for anyone with my background." "I didn't major in science, so how could I ever do technical writing?" "There's not enough money in teaching continuing education courses—I can't afford to do it after all I've invested in getting my degrees." "I wouldn't want to be stuck in an office from nine to five."

Although asking for advice and then objecting to counsel received is a common human reaction, it is self-defeating for the job-hunter. It can seduce you into apathy, or it can tempt those of you who want to teach to comb once more the list of teaching vacancies published by the Modern Language Association or by regional agencies to mail out yet another hundred inquiries, and to do little or nothing while awaiting replies. Those who fall into this trap are not unlike the compulsive ditchdiggers mentioned in a book on problem-solving by James L. Adams of Stanford University. These people, as Adams points out, quoting Edward deBono, tend to keep working harder and harder at the same solution to their problem, like post-hole diggers who try "to dig holes deeper and bigger, to make them altogether better holes. But if the hole is in the wrong place, then no amount of improvement is going to put it in the right place. No matter how obvious this may seem to every digger, it is still easier to go on digging in the same place than to start all over again in a new place. Vertical thinking is digging the same hole deeper; lateral thinking is trying again elsewhere." [18]

A few brief examples may demonstrate some of the discoveries you may make when you look freshly at your humanities education as a possible entry to satisfying and well-paid work.

A woman with a B.A. in English, an M.A. in linguistics, and six years' experience teaching English as a second language, now plans and directs the programs of a university noncredit studies division. "Until I was interviewed for this job," she reports, "I didn't know that any positions like it existed. Now I wouldn't want to do anything else."

A radio news commentator with a B.A. in English found, despite having put considerable effort into writing résumés and letters of application, that actually the best way to get into public affairs broadcasting was to be able to "talk yourself into someone's office for an interview, to be willing to start as a disc jockey or a switchboard manager to get to know people."

A woman with a Ph.D. in English found in the Sunday papers an advertisement directed *toward students, not teachers*, in which a four-year college invited adults with unfinished B.A.'s in business or the social sciences to complete their graduation requirements at a new branch of the school. She saw that although many of the courses listed would involve writing papers, no English offerings were mentioned. The next day she visited the program's administrators, showed them syllabi of writing courses for adults she had given elsewhere, and offered to adapt them for the school's new clientele. She was hired, and soon found herself in charge of designing and teaching courses in both writing and literature to various groups of adult students.

A university teaching assistant in English whose position was about to be phased out succeeded in creating her own job as writing associate of a law school. As she explains, she went with her husband, an attorney, to a legal convention, where, she says: "I picked up a little book about the language of the law, saw the problems lawyers have in their writing, drew up a course proposal, and asked to see the dean of the Law School. After several conversations with him, and one trial set of lectures which I volunteered to give to new law students, I convinced him that he needed me." Since being hired she has expanded her course offerings considerably; she reports that both students and faculty are responsive to her efforts.

A former secondary school admissions officer, moving to a new community and unable to find a position in a school or college admissions office, set up her own freelance advisory service as a "college admission counselor." She now advises high school students and their parents about the college application process, and is successful enough that she is glad not to have been hired for one of the nine-to-five positions in a school or college for which she had applied.

Several former teachers have set up as "writing consultants" to banks, insurance companies, and government agencies. They report financial success and personal satisfaction.

As these examples suggest, there may be pathways that only you can open up and explore, and they may lead to work you scarcely knew existed. Often it is up to you to invent or create your own job. Read ads imaginatively. Pick out and prepare yourself for the kind of position you would like. Realize that some jobs have much simpler application procedures than teaching positions have. Consider starting out as a consultant to perform needed services. Be willing, if necessary, to offer an employer without charge a brief sample of what you can do (but don't let yourself get stuck in a volunteer spot beyond an agreed-upon time). Finally, don't overlook the possibility of demonstrating to a firm or agency that you are the person to fill a need they were only beginning to perceive.

Above all, the successful job-seekers quoted throughout this book urge you not to be discouraged. They—and I—hope that you will test for yourself rather than swallow whole the generalizations made in the media and elsewhere as to the current uselessness of humanistic training. You may find that the prophets of doom have somewhat overstated the case. Those of you who have been working toward advanced degrees should see the promise—and not just the warning—in the conclusion reached over a decade ago in a study of academic career opportunities made by the economists Dael Wolfle and Charles Kidd: "Many new doctorates will enter nontraditional jobs and will do work that has not attracted many of their predecessors. . . . Few of them will be unemployed, but few will be employed in college and university teaching and research."[19]

In a broadened horizon one can often find hope. Somewhere—perhaps in a place where you little expect to find it—there exists an interesting career that can engage your writing ability, your experience in collecting, organizing, and analyzing material, your ability to enter into the mind of a person unlike yourself, and your ability to interpret ideas to others.

2. "The Rules Have Changed": Considerations for Ph.D.'s

A lot of people in America feel that they have had the rules changed on them right in the middle of the game. . . . The problem confronting people who received their doctorates in the early seventies . . . is not where they teach or what sort of students they teach but whether they teach at all.
—Calvin Trillin, "Thoughts on Changes in the Rules," *New Yorker*

Visiting as a reporter an annual meeting of the Modern Language Association in New York City not long ago, Calvin Trillin was struck by the predicament of hundreds of young men and women who, having entered graduate school to study English or foreign languages with the hope of teaching them, emerged several years later to find themselves in a world where their talents seemed redundant because the rules had changed. As Trillin noted with concern, a professor in his late thirties "may have gone through four years of graduate school, specializing in the poetry of Thomas Carew," thinking that promotion and "tenure and a graduate seminar followed a doctorate as surely as pentameter followed iambic." Yet he may now be thankful to be teaching mainly composition courses, or to be teaching at all. "The rules have changed. . . . This is not the game he signed up to play."[1]

The shrinking job market for college and university teachers of English has been discussed ever since the 1969 MLA meeting in Denver, and predictions for a similarly shrinking market for Ph.D.'s in nearly all fields have been in the news since the spring of 1972, when economists Dael Wolfle and Charles Kidd dropped a bombshell in an *AAUP Bulletin* article: "From 1861 . . . through 1970, American universities awarded 340,000 doctor's degrees. Half of these degrees were awarded in the last nine years of the period."[2] Although this statement—with its implications of crisis if the number of Ph.D.'s awarded were to continue accelerating at such a rate—appears not to have cut back significantly on the graduate student population in hu-

12

manities programs, there has since the early 1970s been growing concern (see Appendix A).

The uneven ratio of well-qualified academic job-seekers to available academic positions is not just a problem of Ph.D.'s in the humanities; anthropologists, astronomers, clinical psychologists, biologists, and mathematicians, among others, are finding teaching posts hard to come by. Nor is it just a problem of job-seekers in the United States and Canada; reports from the media and conversations with teachers in other countries confirm that an academic job crisis is occurring in most Western countries and in Japan. For the purposes of this chapter, however, it is necessary to focus on the employment problems of American and Canadian Ph.D.'s in the humanities—that is, English, classical and modern languages and literature, history (including the history of art), and philosophy.

At present the question before those of you who hold advanced degrees in such fields is this: once you have gone far enough into graduate work in the humanities to be near completing requirements for a Ph.D., have you entered a one-way, dead-end street? If you want or need to make a career change, is there a chance that you can do so? If the rules of job-seeking inside your field have changed, have you investigated the rules outside it?

Since the early 1970s, increasing numbers of you *have* needed or wanted to make such a change, and since then societies of scholars like the Modern Language Association, the American Historical Association, the American Classical Association, the American Philosophical Association, as well as various academic departments and university placement centers, have been paying increasing attention to Ph.D.'s in English, or the various other humanities disciplines, who want to do something other than teach. In particular the MLA and English departments across the country have worked to establish liaison with possible nonacademic employers to encourage businesses, foundations, and government agencies to look to graduate schools and college faculties as new sources of recruits (see chapter 12); and the American Historical Association has sponsored similar liaison attempts, along with new courses and graduate programs to prepare history Ph.D.'s for alternative employment.

Emerging from these efforts are, for example, recommendations originating in a conference at Princeton University in 1977 on the topic "Alternative Careers for Ph.D.'s in the Humanities." At this meeting, discussion between academics and insurance executives produced the suggestion, made by a Ph.D. in German, that humanities Ph.D.'s, most of whom have also been teaching assistants, exhibit such capabilities as these:

Demonstrated ability in teaching, reading, writing, and research
Experience in counseling and advising
Administrative background (course organization, grading, committee participation)
Capacity to see problems from different angles
Ability to argue logically
Familiarity with a product (the subject matter and the students)
Accountability to students and administration.[3]

Given such capacities, graduate students would do well, the members of the conference suggested, to "(1) cope with their personal disappointment and bitterness" about graduate work or the shortage of jobs "*before* entering the job market; (2) reassess skills and interests, strengths and weaknesses; (3) capitalize on wider areas of education and concern, transferable skills, and useful experiences . . . ; (4) present abilities in language that the business world can understand; (5) prepare a functional résumé, reflecting their redefinition, and learn the art of interviews; (6) learn auxiliary skills to give an aura of practicality and exhibit a willingness to deal with routine job-oriented problems; (7) be attuned to growth areas, such as accounting, computer science, investment analysis."[4]

The same year, another set of proposals appeared in *The Useful Humanists: Alternative Careers for Ph.D.'s in the Humanities.* Dealing with the possibility of restructuring graduate education so that students will not automatically try to pattern themselves after their professors and thus think of college teaching as their only possible career, Rita Jacobs envisioned a less narrow graduate training than our present one. According to her plan, "attention would be paid to preparing certain students to teach; others could be prepared to function on industrial-research teams, in corporate responsibility and planning departments, in public policy areas, in health-care delivery services, etc. It is with these questions that we have to grapple when it comes to reenvisioning a future for the humanities."[5]

The journals and bulletins in which members of the English teaching profession talk to one another are full of articles suggesting improvements in the graduate school English curriculum, as well as closer relations between graduates of English programs and the world of employment. For the past several years such publications as *College English,* the *Journal of College Composition and Communication,* the *Associated Departments of English Bulletin (ADE Bulletin),* the *Southern Humanities Bulletin,* and the annual collection of essays issued by the MLA as *Profession 76, 77, 78, 79, 80,* and *81,* have carried essays proposing ingenious and urgently phrased remedies for the current overproduction of Ph.D.'s in English. Broaden the English curriculum, both graduate and undergraduate, some writers propose; make contacts with business and government; develop internships, traineeships, and double majors. Keep the curriculum the way it is, other writers urge: concentrate on doing what traditional departments of English already do well, but be more selective in admitting students to graduate school.[6] Such improvements and many more are often described so persuasively that as one reads one feels that they must be on the verge of being implemented—in a few institutions if not yet widely.

Yet all academic reforms take time, funding, and the approval of departmental committees and university administrators. Meanwhile, you as a job-seeker cannot wait until reforms have taken place, nor can you begin your education all over again according to a more rational plan. What then can you do?

If you are a graduate student or Ph.D. hoping to teach but beginning to explore the possibility of other careers, you probably are asking some such questions as these: *Are there any positions waiting for me "out there in the real world"? If so, what are they? And will they give me a chance to draw upon some of the things I've worked so hard on during the past four to six years? What would I have to give up if I took one of these jobs? And if I wanted one, how could I find one?*

The transition from the academic to the unacademic job market does present hurdles. Going to graduate school raises certain expectations, some positive, some negative. A person obtaining a Ph.D. will usually have invested as much time and money as it takes to graduate from law or medical school. After such commitments, it seems reasonable to expect some reward. Then too, the atmosphere of graduate school tends to foster the idea of going on and on in one's field of growing expertise. The highest praise a professor can give a graduate student is that he or she "shows promise of becoming one of the next generation of scholars who will make an outstanding contribution to the field." As Dean Victor Lindquist of Northwestern University puts it bluntly, "The further you get in education, the more you're tied in with the politics of the department, the discipline, the university. Hardly one professor in twenty-five can give students objective career advising when it comes to considering careers outside of his or her own academic field. Too many faculty members view their graduate students as potential clones."[7]

As for negative expectations, graduate students too often begin after a few years to think that their abilities to do anything else but study, teach, and write in their special fields have atrophied. Duncan

Brown, the hero of Margaret Atwood's novel, *The Edible Woman*, and a graduate student in English, is a spokesman for this view: "Once you've gone this far you aren't fit for anything else. Something happens to your mind. You're overqualified, overspecialized, and everybody knows it. Nobody in any other game would be crazy enough to hire me. I wouldn't even make a good ditchdigger. . . . No, no, I'll have to be a slave in the paper mines for all time."[8]

Fortunately, however, Duncan Brown was wrong. Reports coming in to placement centers and to professional societies suggest that not all humanities graduate students and Ph.D.'s ignore the wider applicability of their education, and that not all employers are skeptical about hiring them. Having talked and corresponded with many graduate students and Ph.D.'s in the humanities during the past few years, I have learned that a surprising number are indeed making a start in alternative careers, often to their great satisfaction.

Some job-seekers would find it reassuring if there were a quantitative survey that could show exactly how many American and Canadian Ph.D.'s in the various branches of academia had made such transitions, and with what degree of satisfaction. Although attempts to make a survey have been under way for several years, conclusive data are not yet forthcoming.[9] Other readers may ask, "Just what non-teaching positions are there for a Ph.D. in classics? In philosophy? In French literature? How do these positions differ from one another?" One of the findings of this book, however, is that careers for holders of advanced degrees tend not to depend so much on the subject matter studied as upon skills used—analysis, writing and research, and ability to deal with archives and artifacts.

It is true, however, that a few career fields are more easily entered by graduates of specific humanities disciplines. History Ph.D.'s, for example, will find it easier to attain positions as archivists or historic preservationists, and Ph.D.'s in classics, modern languages, and English will usually find it easier to attain positions as editors. But there are many crossovers from one humanities field to another; just as the problem of the shortage of teaching positions cuts across departmental and disciplinary lines, many of the solutions being arrived at are interdisciplinary too.

A PROGRAM IN HISTORICAL EDITING

Among the attempts at innovative solutions are courses designed to prepare persons with doctoral training to become scholarly editors, condensed versions of the M.B.A. program set up as special summer seminars for humanists (see chapter 12), and programs such as "Public History" developed in the late 1970s and early 1980s at several universities.

The first academic program in editing was established in January 1980 by the History Department of Arizona State University. It was conceived of as a "specialization in historical editing and publishing to train graduate students in history for careers in the book publishing industry. . . . [It] adds to the existing master's degree requirements four courses in editing and publishing and a summer internship with a university press, historical papers project, or scholarly journal publisher." The coordinator of the program, Beth Luey, points out that while other institutions have tended to deal with the problem of unemployed Ph.D.'s in a "remedial way, 'retooling' Ph.D.'s for non-teaching employment," such a concept suggests that the "most legitimate career for a historian, a literary scholar, or a philosopher is teaching, and only when one has failed to find such employment should other alternatives be sought." [10]

PROGRAMS FOR THE PUBLIC HISTORIAN

The Arizona State program offers one way of enlarging nonteaching opportunities for historians. Across the country, other university departments of history have heeded the paradox pointed out in 1976 by Professor Frank Freidel of Harvard: "There never has been a greater need for professionally trained historians than today, and never has there been a time when so many historians were seeking employment." [11] In an effort to correct this anomaly, the Public History program has been developed at several universities throughout the country.

The program's title may not make immediately apparent the variety of work that it can include. Public history is not simply governmental or administrative history. As Ellen Coughlin wrote in the *Chronicle of Higher Education* in 1979, "public history is the practice of history outside an academic setting—the application of historical perceptions and techniques to something other than classroom teaching and scholarly research." Such training "can be used in the management of industrial corporations, the formation of public policy, the preservation of cultural resources, . . . and [the operation of] government, business, museums, archives, libraries, newspapers, or broadcasting organizations." [12]

Courses leading to qualification for this work are many and often interdisciplinary or interinstitutional. For example, at two closely situated universities, Washington State University at Pullman and, eight miles away, the University of Idaho at Moscow, there is a combined offering of more than one hundred related courses, among them architecture, regional planning, cultural resource management, environmental studies, museology, and public administration.[13]

Among many career options to which such programs can lead are archival work, continuing education teaching and administration, consulting for business and governmental agencies, curatorial work in history museums, editing historical journals, environmental research, historical society administration, oral history research, park service administration and development, records management and records preservation (for government agencies or private industry), and writing as a "contract historian" for business, government, and nonprofit organizations.[14] It is reassuring to note that private business is beginning to see the value of the abilities of scholars with some of this specialized training. To cite one example mentioned by Professor Robert Burke of the University of Washington, a Ph.D. in history who had gone through one of these programs was hired to write the history of a large aircraft corporation. Despite initial wariness on both sides, the aircraft executives are finding his archival and analytical skills enormously helpful in showing them how and on what basis various crucial company decisions were arrived at. Problems of mutual skepticism that surfaced at the beginning of the historian's work for the company were inevitable, Burke says, until the company officials realized what the historian's training involved, that it was applicable to their corporation's needs, and that the historian was somewhat familiar with their language and their way of conceptualizing problems. "At first," says Burke, "the historian's biggest problem is learning and using the industry's jargon. Once he or she has done that, there's a good groundwork for cooperation."[15]

AN MLA SURVEY OF PH.D.'S IN NONTEACHING POSITIONS

These programs in historical editing and in public history offer real possibilities. As yet, however, there is little data on how many history Ph.D.'s, having gone through such programs, have found employment to match their training, nor is there a body of subjective opinion indicating their degree of satisfaction with their new careers. The largest body of material I have come upon dealing with successful transitions of Ph.D.'s from academia to the world outside comes from a Modern Language Association survey in 1978. In the spring of that year the MLA distributed a questionnaire to Ph.D.'s in English working outside academia. Since the results were tabulated by the MLA but never analyzed in detail, I obtained permission to read and discuss these anonymous responses.[16] If you have done graduate work, whether in English or another humanities field, you may find it helpful to read the following sampling from and analysis of their opinions. Much of what they say applies across the board to nearly anyone educated in a humanistic field of graduate work.

Statements taken from questionnaire responses such as these must, of course, be read with caution: they may show how a respondent feels during twenty minutes of a particularly good or bad week rather than representing reflective judgment over a span of years. Only in truly longitudinal studies, such as *The Seasons of a Man's Life* by Daniel J. Levinson or the various "life cycle" studies by Erik Erikson,[17] can one even approach scientific accuracy about the career satisfactions of groups of people. Nevertheless, impressionistic though this chapter must be, I hope it will be helpful in showing the range of attitudes felt by humanities advanced-degree holders in transition to other careers and in summarizing the advice they offer.

Despite the stereotype that Ph.D.'s in any field, not to mention English, are too dreamy and bookish to do well in business, the Ph.D.'s in the MLA survey are successfully filling a wide variety of positions, for example those of technical writer for a computer company, public relations writer/editor for a large manufacturing firm, account executive for an advertising agency, and speech writer for an insurance company. Those in academic administration hold, among others, such positions as assistant editor in a university communications office, director of communications skills in a graduate school of business, assistant director of admissions at a university, president of a community college, and vice-chancellor of a university. The Ph.D.'s in English now working for the government include, for example, an editor in the science and education department of the U.S. Department of Agriculture, a director of correspondence for the speaker of a state assembly, an energy coordinator for a state public housing program, and the staff assistant for the school policy commission in the mayor's office of a major city. Among the Ph.D.'s in publishing or journalism are the editor of a museum magazine, an associate editor of the college department of a national publishing house, the senior copy editor, medical books division, of a national publishing house, and the editor of a daily newspaper in a small city. Those who have gone into other professions include two clergymen, a legal clerk who went to law school after getting his Ph.D., and several librarians who have taken M.L.S. degrees to qualify for such positions as head of special collections in a university library or technical services librarian in a liberal arts college.

Those running their own businesses include a woman who has set up an editorial service, a man who owns and runs an antiquarian bookshop, and another who is the proprietor of a philatelic shop. Those working for foundations and other nonprofit organizations include an assistant director of programs in a large museum, the staff director/editor of humanities projects in a national research academy, and the literature officer, national headquarters of a Protestant church.

Looking at the range of positions held by the 160 Ph.D.'s in the MLA survey and the 40 Ph.D.'s and Ph.D. candidates in my own, one finds the distribution shown in Table 1.

Few of these career changers reported that the shift they made was easy. In fact, one of them warns that "anyone who goes through a true change must forge a new self—an experience fraught with dangers, though it promises great rewards. . . . Kurt Lewin and his followers have outlined the change process: the individual goes through 'un-

TABLE 1

	MLA Survey (160 responses)	Bestor survey (40 responses)
Noncollege teaching	15	5
Campus staff-administrative positions	23	6
Freelance editor/writers	6	8
Institutional editors (for colleges, universities, museums, and hospitals)	10	3
Media positions (print and broadcasting)	8	3
Publishing (book and magazine)	15	7
Business positions		
As employees	27	5
As owners of own firms	18	2
Government	32	7
New profession, requiring new degree (library, law, or the clergy)	13	3
Miscellaneous occupations (nurse's aid, fabric cutter, dancer)	3	
Total	170*	49*

*Each of these samples, when broken down by categories of positions, has a total larger than the number of persons surveyed, because in several cases the respondents had two occupations simultaneously.

freezing, changing, and refreezing'—it involves the physical removal of the individual from his accustomed routines, sources of information, and social relationships; a period of humiliation in which the old way is seen to be unworthy; and the consistent linking of reward to the willingness to change. My own experiences confirm this. I would advise the career-changing academic to read Lewin, Abraham Maslow, Erikson, anyone who writes about growth and change."[18]

WAYS OF ADJUSTING TO CAREER CHANGE

But though such change has not been easy, it has in many cases been possible. Five main patterns appear into which humanities Ph.D.'s or near-Ph.D.'s making a shift into noncollege-teaching careers tend to group themselves. These groups I have termed the deniers, the protesters, the reluctant pragmatists, the satisfied pragmatists, and the discoverers.

The deniers do not appear in the questionnaire responses because they have not started actively looking for alternative positions, much less found them. They have heard and read the employment statistics for job-seekers with advanced degrees in the liberal arts, but each one continues to believe that he or she will be the one in ten who will not only receive a college teaching post but will eventually be able to make a lifelong career in such teaching. Haven't they received A's in all their graduate courses, as well as prizes, fellowships, faculty approval? Haven't they sometimes in their first few years of teaching published scholarly articles and received "best teaching" awards? So these job-seekers continue to mail out their letters and *curricula vitae* to several hundred colleges and universities, hoping for interviews and offers which seldom come. They insist that they will dig in their heels and wait for a tenure-track teaching job no matter what the consequences; if they must accept other work, they consider it interim employment, in which they cannot bring themselves to make a real investment of their minds or imaginations.

There appear to be fewer representatives of this pattern in 1981 than there were in the mid-1970s, when as a placement counselor at the University of Washington I saw many of them in my office. Yet there have been enough of them in the past few years applying half-heartedly for nonteaching jobs to reinforce a stereotype in the minds of business employers, many of whom fear that any Ph.D. "really wants only to teach, and will leave us as soon as he or she hears of a good academic job." Convinced as many of these Ph.D.'s are (those of them who really *do* want only to teach) that any kind of employment aside from teaching would be "second rate or second best," **they** sometimes develop a defensive arrogance that is just as unfortunate and unnecessary as Duncan Brown's excessive humility.

A second group can be called the protesters. Even if they have found and are actually enjoying alternative jobs, they are still explosively vehement against "the system." "I wish I had quit after the M.A.," writes a Ph.D. now supporting himself by freelance writing and editing. "I am still bitter about the total absence of any help, or even sympathy, rendered by my department or my adviser (who is nationally known) in obtaining a teaching job or preparing for the lack of one. . . . To pretend that the Ph.D. . . . is of any real value to anything other than a university position . . . is to ignore reality and perpetuate a system of misery and waste." Writes another (who has a job as budget analyst which he actually prefers to college teaching), "If the MLA encourages the training of Ph.D.'s, it implicitly has the moral and ethical *duty*" to place them. Of the 160 MLA questionnaires and the 40 from my own survey, there were 15 persons who bitterly attacked their professors, the academic tenure system, the professional societies, or the dwindling legislative support of state universities in similar terms.

One must sympathize with many of these complaints. Most thoughtful members of the academic professions do agree that the tenure system needs rethinking, that teaching assistants are sometimes exploited, and that graduate school enrollments should be more severely limited than they have been. As Professor Ward Hellstrom, chairman of the MLA Advisory Committee on the Job Market, said in December 1980, "It seems . . . that as a profession we have much in common with American farmers, who overproduce in a disorganized fashion and then suffer the results of a depressed market." [19]

It is important, most placement counselors agree, that when jobseekers feel that they have reason for bitterness about their chances for employment, they have an opportunity to voice their feelings and to realize that many others in their situation share them. June Millet of the University of California at Los Angeles and Janice Lewis of the University of Arizona are among the counselors who, in conducting workshops on "Nonacademic Job Search Strategies," begin their opening sessions by encouraging the participants to express their negative feelings. "It is necessary," says Millet, "to get out into the open as soon as possible all the hostility, the resentment, and the discouragement that academic career shifters are feeling. Only by verbalizing it and realizing that they are not alone can they get beyond such feelings and start taking stock of their assets and their options." [20]

Another group of academic career changers might be called the reluctant pragmatists. They have found positions, often new careers, which in some respect they consider better than teaching; yet they still resent having had to make such a change. A worker for the city government of a large West Coast city speaks glowingly of her high salary but confesses boredom with her job; a woman working for an East Coast advertising firm enjoys her job yet feels that she's "not fully utilizing [her] skills, talents, and training." There were 45 MLA questionnaires making similar points, and 8 from the smaller group with whom I have been in direct contact.

A different—and happier—kind of adjustment was the lot of 54 of the MLA group and 15 of my own sample: these are the satisfied pragmatists, who, though probably they would not have initiated a career shift had circumstances not pushed them into it, are now pleased with the results. Such are, for example, the director of editorial services at one of the world's largest public affairs consulting firms, the recruiter of professional staff for a university medical center, the staff assistant in the mayor's office of a West Coast city, the legal clerk for a large law firm, a person working in the Office of University Relations at a private university in Pennslyvania, several persons connected with publishing, several who run their own businesses, and some 55 others.

In explaining why they feel satisfied, they cite many different reasons. A good many of the Ph.D.'s who have gone into business or into the higher levels of administration mention their salaries as being "about twice what I'd be paid as an assistant professor." Others proclaim their relief at being free from "the tortured syntax of freshman themes." Many find it a joy to be rid not only of grading papers but also of preparing lectures, so that evening and weekend "free" time is really free—for writing fiction or poetry, keeping up with scholarship, or doing wide general reading. Several career changers report experiencing "an incredible amount of released energy" once they had made the transition to a job that started and stopped at definite hours.

Another bonus that—unexpectedly—many of those who have left academia report is finding "interesting people and a hospitable atmosphere." A staff member of a large firm that devises and administers college admissions tests finds his work "congenial to academics and rather more satisfying than teaching these days." An English Ph.D. now in business advises job-seekers, "Don't believe all the myths perpetuated in academic circles about the low level of intelligence in the business community." An editor has discovered that the scientists she now works with are "very like the academics I was used to as a teacher"; a man who has entered New York publishing believes that in it "the intellectual rewards are greater, the internal politics are not nearly so vicious, and you deal with a better class of people on a day-to-day basis"; and a humanities Ph.D. now in marketing urges nonacademic job-seekers to realize, "There are thousands of people 'out there' leading happy and productive lives even though they may know nothing about *Middlemarch*, or that their sensibilities are dissociated."

Several other Ph.D.'s in English comment on the new variety in their work days and weeks. "No situation I meet is just like another one," they say, or "I meet a wider range of people in one week through my present job in sales than I used to in a semester of teaching." One woman, whose position with a medium-size corporation involves speaking, training, public relations, and sales, writes: "I deal with completely new and different situations every day, get to travel frequently but not too often, and am learning how the business world works."

Finally, a number of respondents point out that the business world, despite all that one hears of its cutthroat atmosphere, is actually fairer than academia: they contend that promotions come more often and that there is more reward for genuine effort and less chance of six to eight years of work all going for nothing. Says a staff member of a large testing corporation: "Be prepared for a pleasant surprise once you find a job. In looking back on my academic life, I enjoyed it, but I don't miss the rotten treatment that departments and university administrators inflict on professors and graduate students. I also don't miss having my job depend upon enrollment."

A woman who has gone into publishing carries a similar point still further: "Some academics tend to distrust the business world *a priori*, which isn't useful. After venturing out into it, one finds that there are thousands of rewarding, honorable jobs 'out there.' And many of them give you a chance to agitate quietly or not so quietly within your own company or industry for favorite causes—equal opportunity, nonsexist language, freedom of information, environmental safeguards, or whatever."

Last of the five main patterns of adjustment is a very fortunate group, barely smaller than the "satisfied pragmatists" and considerably larger than that of the deniers and the protesters (52 out of the MLA sample, and 10 out of mine). One might call them the discoverers, for they have learned things about the world and about themselves that lead them to feel very positive about their job changes. In their responses to the MLA question: "Are you satisfied with your present job?" their answers read: "Yes!" "Very much so." "Extremely." "Definitely." "Love it." "I couldn't ask for a better job." One of the Ph.D.'s most emphatic on this point, who now is head of a university library's Special Collections Department, says he is "extremely fulfilled, and stretched in exciting ways."

Among the discoveries that particularly please such career changers is the recognition of new talents that they were hardly aware of before beginning to switch careers—talents such as the abilities to speak to and hold the interest of varied groups of adults rather than just the captive undergraduate audiences of the classroom, to write quickly and effectively, and sometimes to make policy decisions and get them implemented without their needing the approval of a committee.

Another discovery is of worlds "out there, beyond the classroom" that they had known very little about—such as politics, management, and publishing. "I've been surprised . . . at how interesting the *business* end of publishing is" writes a woman Ph.D. in English now publicity coordinator for a large New York educational and scientific publishing house. The public information officer of a university-based music conservatory says that his job suits him perfectly "because I am around creative musicians and artists. My ideal job would be reviewing films or books, but I'll never achieve that, so this is second best and certainly superior to teaching English 101."

There is often the discovery, too, that even Ph.D.'s in English can find positions in which they draw on all their skills and use them in the furtherance of goals important to them personally. Says a woman who left full-time teaching to found her own editorial service in the Southwest, "I'm so busy that currently I hardly have time to read the daily paper, but I'm very satisfied. I have minimum security, but maximum freedom, and the feeling that I'm doing something meaningful." Comments a man who after getting his Ph.D. in English and teaching full-time has become an assistant director of Graduate, Professional, and Foreign Admissions at a Midwestern state university: "Satisfied? Very much so. I do what amounts to liaison work with 110 graduate departments and some eight professional programs. I am chiefly responsible for seeing that university admissions policies are observed in the admission of graduate, professional, and foreign students. Providing a needed service and doing it very well can be satisfying. Contacts with faculty and students from all disciplines are rewarding."

A woman who received her Ph.D. in English literature and theology says of her position (as literary editor for the Board of Global Ministries of a worldwide Protestant church), "I edit material—sometimes rewriting it; I write on request for the magazines, I help plan material, I teach in 'lab schools' and speak, I lay out material, I work with artists, and keep informed on religion and women's concerns—this job requires everything I trained for." Another woman, working for an academic testing service, reports: "My work here directly involves both the general skills and the specific information derived from my graduate studies. I 'invent' questions about language, literature, and reasoning. I use my training daily, do not have to contend with university policies or administration or with unresponsive and uninterested students." And an assistant book editor of a large East Coast suburban daily, whose job it is to "lay out, edit, and supervise the production of a five-page Sunday book review section and write as many book reviews as I have time for" says that she's satisfied because not only is the pay good (about $28,000 a year) but "I feel that I am both using my academic background and continuing to learn." Like her, a number of the people in the MLA survey convey a sense of at last having found themselves, in somewhat the spirit that one Ph.D. in history, now turned university librarian, whom I interviewed said that he feels now that he "was always *meant* to become a librarian, of the archival variety."

How and Where to Look for Nonteaching Positions

Those in the group I see as being discoverers often say that their jobs involve most of the advantages of college teaching and few or none of the disadvantages. You may be wondering how they came upon such positions and where you could expect to find comparable ones. Many of the questionnaire responses offer copious advice to graduate students and Ph.D.'s; in so doing, they deal first with necessary attitudinal changes and then with more specific measures to take in job-seeking.

In telling what changes in point of view they had to make, many Ph.D.'s say that they had to deal first with a feeling of failure at not finding a teaching job, or not remaining in it once they'd found one. A woman who couldn't find one said that she had had problems "in accepting that something I had trained for and wanted for six years was not to be." Others who easily acquired good nonteaching positions said that it took them some time to get over certain guilt feelings—to the effect that they were "wasting their talents," "throwing away all their education," or letting down their families or their major professors. One person—though only one—said: "The people with whom I work may be threatened by my degree; at any rate, they make special efforts to 'keep me in my place.' It requires a great deal of adjustment to their attitude and to my having to work under people less skilled and less well organized than I am." Several others commented that through leaving college teaching and its structured career ladder, they found it frightening at first to have to decide what their goals were and how to define success.

On the positive side, respondents pointed out that the Ph.D. career changer must widen her or his horizons, must get outside of what can be the "closed belief system" of academia—a system which some see as analogous to certain highly structured religious, economic, or political dogmas. Above everything, Ph.D.'s must maintain their curiosity. "One thing which Ph.D.'s are demonstrably good at is learning—we shouldn't stop after graduate school! The unlikeliest bits of knowledge can help you get a job, or advance in it. Most non-academic fields, I expect, include unanticipated gains in new information and skills." Adds another teacher now working for a corporation: "A graduate education should not destroy an individual's intellectual flexibility or general broadmindedness. The individual who remains intellectually alive and responsive will find a way to adapt, or a way to apply his learning in jobs that are not strictly academic."

Predictably, many of the successful job changers urge those who want jobs like theirs to avoid elitism, or as one man puts it succinctly, "Forego snottiness." Don't flaunt your graduate degrees. One man now supervising a high school and college cooperative program develops such ideas to a point that may give some Ph.D.'s in humanities rather a jolt: "Learn that literature is an interesting but relatively minor component of human life and that knowledge *about* literature alone seldom brings wisdom, morality, or an ability to use power well. Learn to respect the intelligence and sensitivity of those outside academe and to recognize the self-protective arrogance of most academics."

Coming down to more specific advice about job-hunting, there is a sharp cleavage among the responses on one point. "Bail out now," urges one group. Leave academia immediately and search for an alternative job, whether or not you've finished your Ph.D. "I would sincerely advise anyone now enrolled in a graduate English program to drop out of the program as soon as possible unless he or she (a) wants the degree for its own sake or (b) wants to teach composition to functional illiterates for years to come," advises a man who has gone into publishing. Half a dozen other men and women Ph.D.'s agree with him that the best thing that you can do for your career is to cut your ties with your university at once and be ready for a new start, perhaps at an entry-level position in another field, realizing that you may have to prove yourself all over again. Those who follow this line of reasoning echo the suggestion made at the 1977 Princeton Conference on Alternate Careers, that your best hope is to capitalize on any nongraduate-school work experience you have, whether in business, campus publications, the Peace Corps, or the armed forces.

On the other side there are those who vehemently disagree with the idea of deemphasizing one's advanced degree and one's academic background. "Don't hide your degree, even if it's in a field 'irrelevant' to the job at hand," urges a woman working for a state government. "You really do have abilities which are worth while and which you should not play down or undervalue," urges another. "Do not be sorry about or ashamed of your background. Educated people *are* an elite," writes still another.

Obviously it is in a large part a matter of individual temperament and opportunity whether you decide to keep in touch with the academic world, drawing on and adding to what you have learned there to apply to a nonacademic career, or to leave that world entirely. Those who choose the first course may benefit from the advice of a Ph.D. in English who is now an associate examiner for a firm that devises and administers college admissions tests: "Get to know the individuals and firms with which you or your colleagues come in contact in the normal course of academic life—educational publishers, providers of various services to the academic community, and the like. I learned of my present job through a former teacher of mine who was serving as a consultant here. I am now in a position to hire other academics as consultants from time to time. . . . What I am suggesting is that one marshal one's forces on the border where business and academe meet and look especially hard and long for those people who frequently cross from one side to the other."

For those who on the other hand think they will do better by leaving their academic careers completely behind them, the questionnaire responses offer two main approaches. Both involve identifying your special skills; after that, you may want to "find a job area that interests you, such as training and development, writing, evaluation and testing, and then find out what positions exist in that area and what is needed to qualify for them. Join the relevant professional societies [for instance the American Society for Training and Development, or the Society for Technical Communication]; ask some of the [local] officers of those societies for advice on your job search. And don't be dismayed if your qualifications don't exactly match those specified when you are applying for a position. Sometimes those lists of qualifications are for an ideal candidate, and the employer will be happy to settle for a less than perfect match." Alternatively, you can identify a few business corporations that particularly interest you, and try to "sell" them the skills you have. As a woman who used this approach advises, "Almost all large firms need people with the skills you developed as a Ph.D.—writing, organizing, budgeting your spare time, and sticking to a project. Although entree is difficult, and personnel offices are not particularly helpful offices with which to deal, if you have or can find any personal contacts with anyone in upper management of the firm where you would like to work, you may be able to convince them of the usefulness of a person with experience in presenting material and taking responsibility for projects." As many of the questionnaire respondents found, either of these approaches can work, provided they are carried out with energy and conviction.

More specific advice from these Ph.D.'s in nonteaching positions centers on two problems: how best to prepare yourself for a nonacademic career, and how to apply for positions that will make such a career possible. Certain points that could be helpful to a wider group of readers will appear in later chapters. Here it is important to note the advice having a direct bearing on the career problems of Ph.D.'s.

Advice on preparation emphasizes the importance of being able to use the writing and research capabilities developed in graduate school. Approximately three-fourths of the respondents felt these abilities were crucial in their being hired. "I was hired initially as a speech writer—a talent all teachers possess, if they teach well," wrote a man now director of editorial services at a large New York public relations firm. "My samples—freelance speeches and those articles not written in academic prose—also helped." A budget analyst for an electric power cooperative tells how he was hired: "Facility with the English language did the job. In a small way, my ability to organize ideas and thoughts [also] helped." A training specialist for a nonprofit prepaid health insurance plan acknowledges, "My skills as a writer and as a teacher of writing were the most important factors in my selection for the position . . . especially my editorial and nonacademic writing experience after graduate school."

Once they have found their new positions, these Ph.D.'s report overwhelmingly that their writing and fact-finding skills are "extraordinarily useful." The evidence is that the research and analytical skills developed in graduate school *are* widely applicable in the outside world—provided that you take the time and trouble to practice adapting the style, tone, and organization of your writing to suit various audiences, and provided that you "learn that footnotes aren't the only way to make a point." If you haven't been doing any nonacademic writing, many questionnaire respondents urge you to start now; it can make more difference in your new career than you realize.

Other kinds of nonacademic work experience are also highly recommended. Ideally, these Ph.D.'s say, you should have started to broaden your work experience as soon as you decided to specialize by going to graduate school. A Midwestern university administrator wrote: "Recognizing that there was little except research practice in grad school, I attempted early to broaden my interests in many areas . . . from working with people in civic capacities to housepainting, machine shop tooling, etc., just to get a feel for what was going on outside of the college libraries."

When you are busy with your academic work, you may not especially want to take on routine jobs in college offices, on the staffs of their printing plants or newspapers, or in bookstores or computer centers, unless you urgently need the money. Many English Ph.D.'s interviewed, however, urge you to consider such jobs because they will later help give you credibility in managerial or administrative work, the media, and business. Several dozens of the questionnaire responses reveal how a Ph.D. seemingly by accident fell into a very good nonteaching job because of skills learned or contacts made by serving part-time as an administrative assistant, a bookkeeper, a proofreader, or a computer programmer. If there are any "administrative internships" available near you, or some of the many other kinds of internships and cooperative work programs (see Appendix E), these too could be very useful.

Several other Ph.D.'s point out that as you start planning your job search, you shouldn't overlook things that you know how to do well even though you may not have studied them in school or thought of them as part of your career. One Ph.D. candidate in English and German felt frustrated at not finding a job in which he could use his writing and editing skills and his knowledge of German. Finally, through a chance encounter made when he was busy with his hobby of working on old car engines, he was offered a temporary position with an automotive magazine. Soon its editors realized that they wanted him on a permanent basis; he now has a full-time position he enjoys very much, in which he writes and edits as well as reporting on the latest continental developments in engine design, doing all the magazine's translation of German articles and corresponding with German automotive experts.

Two other ways of preparing yourself for nonteaching positions are easy for the graduate student or Ph.D. to overlook because they don't seem thorough or scholarly enough to fit the kind of academic approach you have learned to make to problems. One is simply to make the time, as an English Ph.D. now working in the information/ foreign policy branch of a U.S. embassy urges, "to read outside the main field of study—history, economics, newspapers."

A second helpful kind of unacademic preparation is community activity, particularly if you are interested in an administrative career. The communications manager of an East Coast bank, who also directs a training program for community leaders, writes: "The most important thing I have done [in finding a job] is to become involved in community and nonacademic pursuits. My volunteer work with citizens' groups actually led to both my present positions." Says another Ph.D. in English, now the developmental officer at a Midwest research library, "Job-hunters should sharpen their résumés with volunteer work outside academia, and I especially recommend politics and public affairs—either partisan or issue."

Alternatively, after you have finished graduate work and left the campus, try being a local fund-raiser for your college. Several Ph.D.'s now in "development" (i.e., fund-raising) for educational institutions or nonprofit foundations got their start this way. If you haven't time to learn through volunteering, says one of them, "most fund-raising and public relations offices in nonprofit organizations have assistant-level jobs. Pay is low, but for the Ph.D. with little 'hands-on' experience, two or so years in such a slot would be the best training of all."

A different kind of suggestion, this one from a technical publications editor for the U.S. Geological Survey, involves acquiring "a dual background in English and some scientific or technical field [which] will allow English majors to move into diverse fields. The clear communication of scientific and/or technical information occurs rarely and could provide many jobs for English majors."

On the question of how to carry on your job search, these Ph.D.'s are careful to disclaim knowledge of any universal system; they agree that "job-hunting is an idiosyncratic thing." Nonetheless, most of the questionnaires do offer hints on what has worked for the respondents. If a few of their pointers should suggest too much of the "hard sell" to you, remember that they originate in the actual experience of Ph.D.'s who not long ago were in the position of many readers of this book.

First, they urge you to realize that you have more contacts than you are aware of. Begin to make legitimate use of them: let people know that you are changing your career direction, have certain abilities to offer, and would be available for interviews. Almost certainly you have a wide potential network: your family and their business associates, perhaps your spouse and his or her family; other friends;

professional acquaintances in other fields; faculty members from your school who have gone into nonteaching positions; chance encounters on a plane or at a meeting.

The usefulness of your personal network is based on the idea that you have decided on a cluster of related skills that you have to offer, that you are investigating certain areas where these skills are in demand, and that you are both confident of your abilities and open-minded about where you may apply them. As more than one Ph.D. has found, "It helps to be *convinced yourself* that you have several specific talents to offer."

A number of the questionnaire responses recommend a technique first devised by Bernard Haldane and recommended more recently by Richard Bolles in *What Color Is Your Parachute?* (see chapter 4). This process is now familiar to most job-seekers as "interviewing for information, not for a job."[21] A woman Ph.D. in English, now a financial analyst for an investment house in New York City, agrees with such advice: "If you know someone in the field you are interested in, or in business generally, write him or her, asking if you might stop by and get advice on your future. Since you are not asking for a job, you are not embarrassed (if, for instance, this is a friend of the family), and the person is likely to be flattered and to see you cordially. A great many jobs are found though someone knowing someone who has a job [vacancy], and this sort of interview can turn up these openings."

Another suggestion: "take every exam possible," says an economic specialist in a U.S. embassy, "particularly civil service and other government exams, especially 'non-schedule' exams, like the foreign service exam. We [Ph.D.'s] have practice in these things and should do well." Even if you are not sure that you want some of the positions for which the exams will qualify you, it's usually not a bad idea to take these exams and have a good rating on your record.

About the actual application process, "Make a lot of inquiries *in person*," says a technical writer. "Don't avoid this process by substituting well-written inquiries. A person at the door is harder to dismiss and easier to reply to than a letter on a desk."

When you're through with the informational interview stage, try to make appointments with people in a position to hire you, not with personnel screeners or other middlemen. If you *must* go through a personnel department, try in addition (through business directories or your own inquiries) to find the name of the person who could hire you in the department where you would like to work and send him or her an individualized letter and a résumé. (Be sure that the résumé is not an academic vita, and that it describes your skills into terms appropriate to whatever field you are now approaching. See chapter 4.) Says a successful investment analyst who was formerly a college English teacher, "Write directly to companies you would like to work for, stressing whatever your particular motivation for a change in career. But write only after *learning*, and beginning to understand, what it is that each of these companies does."

When you are interviewed, you will inevitably be asked, "Why would a person like you, with a Ph.D. and teaching experience, want a job in a different field?" Take time to think about this question and to talk it over with your friends, so that you can "have a good, clear, nonhostile, nonself-pitying answer ready."

Nearly every respondent who now has a good nonteaching job says, in one way or another, "You must be persistent and aggressive." Once you are at the stage of having actual job interviews instead of exploratory conversations, emphasize your most practical and active side. Don't put your potential employer into the role of friend, therapist, or parent substitute and confess to her or him the inadequacies of your background or your doubts about the career change you are making. Don't vacillate and try to get the interviewer to tell you what to do. Convey decisiveness and action. "Aggressiveness is more prized in the business world than in academia, so kindly harassment can get you somewhere. . . . Have the confidence, if you see, say, an editing position, to convince a businessperson or whomever that your English degree is *preferable* to that of someone with preparation in the particular subject field."

Throughout all this, says a man with a new job as writer/editor for the Army Corps of Engineers, "Your commitment to the job search must be total. One can—and ought to—have more than one job search going on—at least this was my approach. This means that virtually *all* of one's energies must be put into the job hunt in several sectors; for example, teaching jobs, academic administration, jobs in business and industry. I'd urge students to get the thesis done as early as possible so that the hunt can be given full attention—this is vital. . . . I spent weeks talking to people who are, or have been, editors before getting my own job."

Finally, as many Ph.D.'s urge, don't let yourself get discouraged. Says a program officer with a private foundation: "Be optimistic. Before, I doubted, but now I am fairly certain that graduate work in English is relevant training for other work. God knows all sorts of occupations can use people who are articulate, trained to think, intellectually honest, and can write a sentence."

3. Exploring Your Assets and Options

He who has found his work has found his life.
—Sign in a placement counselor's office

My job's simple—only 35,000 careers to follow. Which one do you
want to know about?
—Another sign in another placement counselor's office

So far, this book has dealt with various abilities that you may have
used and perfected through your college or graduate school study of
the humanities. For some of you, identifying these capabilities (such
as editing, writing, or research skills) and then finding that you can
make a simple, direct transfer of them to the nonacademic world
may be enough to send you off on a new phase of your career. Thus a
college English teacher may start her own freelance editing business
because her friends have often asked her to edit their papers (see
chapter 8), or a newly graduated English major may find that the
same writing ability that helped her earn a B.A. with honors is also
useful to the state and national headquarters of a political party (see
chapter 14). If finding an alternative job were always as simple as
this, there would be small need for vocational counselors, college
placement offices, or books such as this one.

Many of you, however, even after realizing that you have more
widely marketable skills than you used to believe, may still be uncertain of your new goals. Although you no longer always identify yourself in academic terminology as "an English major," "an American
history teacher," or "a Restoration drama specialist," it is sometimes
hard to be sure just where you do belong.

Some of you are uncertain because there are too many *apparent*
choices. "One of the hardest things about being alive in the twentieth
century," a young man in the middle of a career transition com-
plained recently, "is that there are so many hundreds of specialties
and subspecialties that anyone with a good liberal arts background

would *theoretically* be able to succeed at, and it's kind of paralyzing to try to find out about the whole spectrum of them and to see just where one might fit in."

Others of you feel stuck at dead center because, after doing "all the right things" academically throughout school and college, you have trouble standing out from the crowd enough to arouse the interest of possible employers; despite the wealth of theoretical options before you, it is hard to get job interviews.

Still others may be hesitant about what to aim for, what move to make next, because even though you may be holding positions that pay reasonably well and sound logical for someone with your background, you have found that you don't enjoy them. As one of the Ph.D.'s mentioned in chapter 2 wrote, "People should look very carefully to see what they are getting into before they accept certain bureaucratic jobs. Otherwise they may jump at something that sounds good and pays well, only to find that it's so boring that it's a kind of living death."

These situations are only three of many that might lead you to take a closer look at yourself—and not just that academic self who comes through on your résumés or *vitas*—so as to find out what combinations of circumstances makes you come alive and do your best work. Far too many people go passively through high school, college, and graduate school, jumping one educational hurdle after another yet becoming more and more out of touch with their true strengths, concerns, and talents. Influenced by family pressure, societal expectations, or the obvious rewards of certain professions, they may become teachers, nurses, computer experts, engineers, or lawyers because entering such professions seems to be expected of them. It often takes either a personal crisis or a collapse in the job market like the current one to make such people stop short and ask themselves whether the work they've been preparing for is really what they want to do with the rest of their lives.

If you have arrived at such a turning point, consider it an opportunity. Before you rush to the advertisements to see what positions are currently open, you should consider finding out more about yourself and what you have to offer.

This step is a reversal of what many people consider the normal process. "First of all, find out what work is available," they have been taught. As a result, they sometimes develop an excessive reverence for Department of Labor statistics, for all sorts of media "occupational forecasts" and projections, for headlines ballyhooing "the ten hottest career fields of the 1980s" or "the eight growth areas throughout the United States where you are most apt to find a job this year or next." This tendency to worship as sober fact what can be at best only the sum total of many people's rough estimates I would characterize as the "hard-information fallacy." Richard Bolles, whose *What Color Is Your Parachute?* should be known to most readers of these pages, has devoted most of one issue of his newsletter to "The Virtues and Defects of Occupational Forecasts." In it he says: "The source of the information is often biased. . . . Forecasts are often wrong because although the *Occupational Outlook Handbook* accurately pinpointed the vacancies that would be developing, it did not anticipate the great increase in the number being trained. . . . [And] finally, . . . there are openings for every job in the world. All that forecasts do . . . is to define 'the degree of competition.'"[1]

This is not to say that one can ignore what is going on in that abstraction often summed up as the "job market." After all, how many scriveners, or astrolabe makers, or alchemists are needed today? My point is that *before* looking around at the world of employment, you should know as much as you can about who you are and what you have to offer. And again, *after* you have looked clearly at yourself and then out at the world, you will constantly have to keep checking back and forth between what you have discovered about yourself and what you observe in the world outside.

One of the simplest means you can use to determine just what you have to offer is to find a friend, mentor, faculty member, or coworker who knows you well and will answer such questions as, "What do you see as my strong points? Is there anything you notice about the way I work that I might not see myself? What would you do if you were my age and in my position?" If there is someone with whom you can talk as frankly as this, fine. But there are two unwritten rules for benefiting from this kind of informal, unstructured counseling: first, your mentor must be objective enough not to think of his or her own profession as the only one worth going into; second, when this adviser suddenly asks you, "But what would you *really* like to do?" you must listen closely to what you hear yourself saying. (I remember answering, when an adviser asked me this at a turning point in my own career, "I'd really like to start my own freelance editorial service." Yet, like so many people who ask for clarification and then fail to heed it, I didn't listen to what I was saying; it was not until two years later that, with a friend, I actually did organize an editorial consulting service.)

Another option open to nearly everyone who has attended a college or university is the campus placement center or career planning center. Also available are job counseling centers connected with YMCA's, YWCA's, YMHA's, churches, minority group agencies, state employment services, and women's career planning centers. As nearly all these offices and agencies tell their clients, the term "placement center" is a misnomer. They do not "place" people; they have far too many clients to do so; the jobs they hear of are apt to be filled from various sources so soon that the older practices of the 1940s and 1950s—whereby counselors sometimes had time to look through their files, find and notify the two or three candidates they considered best qualified for a job opening, coach them on how to apply, and follow through on the results of their interviews—are completely outmoded. For one thing, it would be contrary to the spirit if not the letter of Equal Opportunity legislation for counselors to give what might be seen as preferential treatment to certain candidates; for another, it would be short-sighted to "hold each candidate's hand," making him or her dependent on the counselor to find a position. The current thinking of most placement center directors and their staffs is that they serve clients and employers best if they become "offices of career planning," where job-seekers can learn the *principles* behind a successful job search, can find out how best to use their assets and what the full extent of their options may be. Once they have internalized these principles, they can use them over and over as they change, in the course of their working lives, from one job to another perhaps ten or a dozen times.[2]

It follows, then, that you will benefit from the services of a placement or career planning center to the extent that you make your relationship with the office an active rather than a passive one. Take the initiative; make an appointment early, several months or longer before you will need a job. Apparently it is hard for many students to bring themselves to do this. "Students wait until there is a crisis or they need a job to do any career exploration. The idea of planning is still foreign to them," says James Krolik, the coordinator of the University of Michigan's Office of Non-Academic Career Counseling and Placement.[3]

Between making and keeping your first appointment with a counselor you should find the time to drop in at the center, scan its bulletin boards, browse in its library, and do some thinking about both what you hope to do and why. Start making an inventory of your strengths and assets rather than expecting a person who has never before seen you to divine them from your academic record or to glean them all from a first fifteen- or twenty-minute appointment.

After you see your placement counselor, you will probably have some assignments to carry out—a self-inventory blank to fill out, some reading to do, some people to see, some lists to make. Do the assignments energetically, then report back. Several placement counselors, including Rick Fite of the University of Washington, have told me recently that English majors are less likely than any other group of undergraduates to follow up a first appointment with a later one. Fite, who himself majored in English, is puzzled by this attitude on the part of undergraduates in a field which can, after a little exploration, lead to such a variety of careers. He speculates that many English majors have taken the media's job forecasts so seriously as to have become almost paralyzed.[4]

Students who visit a placement center only once often have a simplistic view of its function; they fail to realize that, in addition to one-to-one counseling, most placement centers today try to help job candidates become aware of their "interests, skills, values, and motivations" as a result of group counseling, workshops and seminars, meetings with successful persons in many fields, and testing.[5]

This word "testing," which strikes terror into some job candidates, holds for others an aura of infallibility, of scientific diagnosis, amounting to a magic guarantee of being headed for the "right career" once one has passively submitted oneself to a battery of aptitude tests. Of course neither extreme view is right. The three tests most often used in connection with job candidates and their choice of career direction—the Miller Analogy Test, the Minnesota Multiphasic Test, and the Strong-Campbell Interest Inventory—tend to reveal simply what mental characteristics you may share with a large body of people who have done well in certain occupations; they cannot predict the success of any one person in a particular field, because these tests do not take into account important factors such as motivation, work habits, or ability to interact successfully with other people. If, despite the fact that both counselors and employers rely less on such tests today than five or ten years ago, you still want to take them, almost any placement or career planning center should either be able to give them to you or tell you where you can take them.

Another way of gaining self-knowledge sometimes favored by placement centers or by psychology departments is called "values clarification." Academic courses are given in this field, and several recent texts expound it.[6] The process involves your taking self-inventory tests wherein you answer questions indirectly revealing your commitment to various values, usually arranged in paired opposites: for example altruism versus egoism, philanthropy versus the profit motive, preference for being other-directed or inner-directed, for short-term goals versus long-term ones, for working alone or in groups, for accepting or trying to change the status quo.

After a series of values clarification sessions, students tend to be enthusiastic about the peer-group discussions of their own beliefs and their bearing on career choices.

Information thus gained can certainly be important in a job search provided that you do not—as some students are tempted to do—make a prolonged clarifying of values an end in itself. If you look only at yourself—at the unique person you are, and especially at your job "requirements"—you can fall into another of the great pitfalls of job-hunting, the "narcissistic fallacy." But you must not look only at yourself; you must also take into account the world of work; you must develop what a member of the English Department at the University of Washington, Roger Sale, calls "respect for the thing out there." Otherwise you could refine the picture of your ideal values and their corresponding requirements to such an extent that you might easily persuade yourself that only a few positions in the world could meet the criteria dictated by your intellectual, physical, temperamental, and other requirements. In any case, as Richard Thain points out in *The Managers,* "Prior self-assessment has its limitations. It's sometimes only on the job that true self-perception may emerge."[7]

At the other extreme from the subjectivity to which values clarification can lead is a new and highly structured way of pinpointing career potential: attendance at an "assessment center," available to only a few categories of job-seekers at present. As Allen Kraut, who has written widely on the application of the behavioral sciences to industry, describes these "centers" (which actually are programs rather than places), "the heart of the technique is a series of situational exercises in which a dozen candidates for management take part while being observed systematically by several raters who are usually managers themselves. The exercises are simulated management tasks and include individual exercises such as an in-basket [test], and group exercises such as a leaderless group discussion."[8]

There is divergent opinion about the validity of the criteria of such programs. Since the exercises are constructed by people who think they already know what qualities are important for successful managers in a particular field, the candidates are rated on how well they measure up to standards predetermined for such positions rather than on the whole spectrum of their aptitudes.[9] Nonetheless, reports from humanities Ph.D.'s who have recently gone through the assessment center process at one of the "business orientation and placement counseling programs" sponsored by New York University, Harvard, or Pennsylvania's Wharton School of Economics indicate that many of the candidates enjoyed the testing. In particular, a number of Ph.D.'s in English enjoyed the "in-basket" exercises, which gave each candidate directions something like this:

Assume that you are the marketing manager for XYZ Widget Company. You are leaving in two hours for a regional sales conference in San Francisco. Before that time there are eight tasks in your "in" basket. They include, among others, drafting a speech to give at the conference tomorrow night, writing a letter discharging an incompetent employee whom you hired just three months ago, thinking up a new plan for marketing widgets in Japan, and responding to an irate customer whose $10,000 order was sent by slow freight instead of the speediest possible method. There is obviously not time to do a thorough job on all these projects. Which ones will you do, which can you merely outline and delegate to someone else? Can you finish the ones you undertake to do in this short time? Do as many of them as you can in the allotted time, then write a memo explaining the order in which you did them and if necessary justifying your omission of some.

Humanities Ph.D.'s, reporting in the *New York Times* and elsewhere on their experience with these tests, on the whole found them exhilarating. After the first few moments of shock and panic, they saw that they could think themselves into a totally new situation, rank conflicting claims on their time in a logical priority, make decisions more rapidly than they had expected to, and write for a variety of audiences against nearly impossible deadlines. Although they realized that they had other capabilities that these simulated situations did not challenge, they felt for the most part that they had discovered a new side of themselves, and were pleased.[10] At present the availability of such centers is somewhat limited: they are used for selection and promotion of management candidates in certain large corporations such as IBM and AT&T, as well as for career development of some librarians and members of other professions. Kraut, however, foresees the expansion of the assessment center idea to help the upgrading of women in industry, and he concludes that assessment centers may well be useful before long in entirely new areas.[11]

The various ways of finding out about one's skills and talent mentioned here—conversation with a friend or mentor, use of a placement or career planning center, taking aptitude tests, going through a "values clarification" process, or attendance at an assessment center—all involve at least one other person besides yourself. But you may wonder whether you can't simply discover your skills and talents on your own. Can you? Is there a way to be objective about yourself? If you are patient and persistent, if you don't get discouraged and give up on a project that will take several days with no immediate promise of a tangible return, if you don't mind putting down on paper for your eyes alone various memoranda about unacademic parts of your life which may have taken place years ago and which may seemingly have nothing to do with your current job crisis— if you meet these criteria, you can probably discover a good deal about yourself on your own.

You will find the authors of several books on careers ready to guide you. In *What Color Is Your Parachute?* Richard Bolles presents a "Quick Job-Hunting Map" which he recommends to "the undecided college student or the housewife going back to work, or the mid-career changer, or the man or woman whose job has been terminated, or anyone else facing obstacles in the job market."[12] For those looking for work for the first time, he offers a simpler form of the same self-inventory process in *The Three Boxes of Life: And How to Get Out of Them.*[13] Eleanor Berman in her book *Re-entering* has an excellent chapter, "What Can I Do?" which provides a discussion of the whole problem, along with self-inventory blanks whereby you can successively list and analyze your "Personal Achievements," your "Top Ten Achievements," your "Personal Characteristics," and your "Work Satisfactions."[14]

The earliest and probably the fullest exposition of the self-inventory approach to job-seeking comes from Bernard Haldane, who ever since 1957 has been writing and speaking to increasingly responsive audiences about the implications of his "system to identify motivated skills" (SIMS). Although academic people, skeptical of "how-to" books as most of us tend to be, may at first dismiss Haldane's approach as simplistic, they have been known to change their minds after working through the exercises in *Career Satisfaction and Success.*[15] By doing so, many people who thought themselves locked into one particular career path have found themselves to have more job-related strengths, and hence more options, than they had realized. Indeed an interdisciplinary seminar of graduate students and Ph.D.'s who met with Haldane for two quarters in 1980 at the University of Washington found his approach to be very helpful to them in their search for alternative careers.

To summarize some of Haldane's ideas that may be useful to readers of this book: he believes that, rather than trying to benefit from the conventional wisdom of "learning from our mistakes," we can all make better career choices if we build upon our successes. To this end he directs us to remember and to list as many of our past successes as possible, defining a successful experience as anything specific that we have accomplished, whether trivial or momentous, private or public, that has given us pleasure and satisfaction. Next, we are to analyze these accomplishments according to charts he has devised, a process designed to reveal consistent patterns in many seemingly unrelated things we have done well. It is most important, Haldane believes, to concentrate on those skills we feel satisfaction in exercising and to play down those we exercise without enjoyment. It is the skills that we enjoy using that we are eager to draw upon and develop; these Haldane calls one's "strongest motivated skills."

By discovering a pattern throughout our successes, whether in academic or nonacademic work, whether professional or play activity, we begin, according to Haldane, to see our identity as an integrated whole rather than simply the total of our academic courses, degrees, and job descriptions. (Thus the Ph.D. looking for nonacademic employment might find the process of "forging a new self," of "freezing, changing, and refreezing" referred to in chapter 2, somewhat less dramatic than Kurt Lewin and his followers paint it.)

Finally, once we have noticed certain patterns that carry through most of our accomplishments—such constellations of actions, for examples, as "calculating, counting, keeping records," "inventing, designing (an object or a system)," "directing or supervising others," "persuading, influencing, or selling," "observing, inspecting," "performing before a group: acting, music, demonstration," or any of his ten other categories of related skills—we can become more openminded about kinds of work we might consider.

As Haldane concedes, his SIMS is not a panacea. It can, however, make a helpful contribution to redefining yourself. And, since each skill you credit yourself with when filling out one of Haldane's selfinventory blanks represents not merely a vague aspiration but a capability backed up by a tangible achievement, Haldane's SIMS may help you test the realism of your goals as you investigate career alternatives. Moreover, these exercises can give you a sharpened sense of capabilities you may want to build upon if you undertake further education or training.

Once you have found out, through whatever method you choose, the strengths and skills you can count on yourself to put to use in work you enjoy, then it is time to start looking outward to see how you may find or invent a position wherein you will fill a need. The following chapter deals with ways of doing this.

4. Presenting Yourself

In every step of your analysis you must consider what you have to offer. The question is always "What can I offer to meet the needs of the employer?" It is never "How can I get a job?" No one is interested in what you want. Many people will be interested in what you can offer.
—Eli Djeddah, *Moving Up*

Today the logistics of the job search are discussed so widely in books, articles, TV programs, and talks, that they can hardly be a secret to any reader. We all know, by now, that looking for a job can itself be a full-time job, that a good résumé is important, that application letters should be carefully written and proofread, and that interviews should be thoughtfully prepared for and followed up with a short appreciative note.[1] Beyond such basics, is there anything in particular that liberal arts students looking for nonteaching careers may need to hear? On the basis of having listened to the problems of a good many such job-seekers, I would like to offer a few additional suggestions.

Probably a precept of Eli Djeddah's, "Only when you identify with other people's interest will there be any interest whatsoever in you," is the most important one for this stage of your search.[2] You will already have thought carefully about what you are like, what you can do best, and under what conditions you can do it (see chapter 3). Now is the time to change roles, to look at yourself, as far as possible, from the employer's point of view, to present yourself as someone with specific assets useful to a going concern.

Liberal arts students sometimes have trouble making this shift in point of view. You are so used to thinking of yourselves in terms of specific English, history, language, or philosophy courses and seminars taken, A's received, or classes taught, that you may forget to ask yourselves, "What am I showing an employer that I can do to help him next week or next month?" Another pitfall awaiting some students (both among the newest crop of graduates and those who have been out for some years teaching) is the tendency to think their hard work in college, their need, or their desire for a particular position must somehow carry weight with an employer. With only a few exceptions, however, employers hesitate to hire applicants who give the impression that their lives depend on getting a particular position. The employers know that if things don't work out and they have to dismiss such employees, they themselves will feel uncomfortable and guilty; that if the candidates are as desperate as they appear about getting a particular job, there may be unseen personal problems; and that when there are too many personal problems, they may become the firm's problems too.

At first, seeing yourself as having been on only one side of the job-seeking process, you may find it hard to put yourself in an employer's place. When you think about it, however, you will probably realize that you have sometimes had to pass judgment on another person seeking to come on board a project you were involved in. You may have supervised, hired, and fired assistants in connection with a summer job; you may have had to decide whether to accept one applicant or another for shared housing, a position on a campus publication, or membership in a club. Possibly you have served as a student member of a faculty search committee. Remembering these experiences, ask yourself whether you were more inclined to vote for a person who appeared to want desperately to join your group or the one who not only had specific assets to bring to your enterprise but seemed independent and resilient—appreciative of the chance to work with you, yet not without other resources if turned down.

Once you learn to see yourself from an employer's point of view, you have a focus for the various parts of your job search: your background research about the position, use of "live" sources of information, presentation of your candidacy through letters and résumés, developing a portfolio of work, and being interviewed.

DOING BACKGROUND RESEARCH IN PRINTED SOURCES

Employers will hardly think that you respect their time or your talents if you show only a vague awareness (or none at all) of what their company, office, or department does. (See chapter 14 for William Oliver's comments on job candidates with advanced degrees who applied for the position of "legislative humanist" without having found out what this new but well-publicized position involved). Whether you hear of an advertised position or simply want to explore the possibilities of a broad field, ask yourself "What do I already know about it?" and then see what information you can add rapidly to that nucleus.[3] Consult the available printed sources before you begin to question live ones. Go to your public or university library or your campus placement center and look at government reference books (beginning with the most general, such as the *Dictionary of Occupational Titles*, then reading the pamphlets about various occupations). Next consult information issued by professional societies. (For specifics of finding these, see Appendix D and the Bibliography.) If you are considering a particular firm, look it up in *Moody's Industrial Manual* or *Standard and Poor's Register*.[4] You may also find, through using the indexes of *Fortune* magazine, *Business Week* , and the *New York Times*, articles on the particular company that interests you, on its competitors, or on an industry as a whole. Moreover, you can learn a good deal by looking at a firm's annual reports—often obtainable free of charge from the company's main office, or available in the business section of a library.

If you are trying to find out what a whole field is like rather than looking up a particular firm, get in the habit of reading not only your local paper but papers with national circulation such as the *New York Times*, the *Wall Street Journal*, and the *Christian Science Monitor*, and the magazine *Publishers Weekly*. Don't focus on the job advertisement sections; read as many of the articles as you can so as to see the impact of national events, new legislation, and developing technology on the field you hope to enter. At the very least, you'll become familiar with some of the problems touching your chosen area and with the language in which they are usually discussed.

Using Live Sources of Information

The best chance to make productive personal inquiries usually comes through spontaneous conversation with people you know or meet by chance who are doing the kind of work you would like to do. Follow up every opportunity to talk to people in editing, publishing, PR work, fund-raising, consulting, or whatever your career goal is. Go to open meetings and seminars of groups such as the Society for Technical Communication, the American Society for Training and Development, the Public Relations Society of America, or Women in Communications.

Take notes; join whatever groups you can afford to; in any case, try to establish a few ongoing contacts so that you may ask more questions later. Try to conquer the feelings of shyness and the dread of sounding naïve common to nearly everyone; ask questions about what your informants spend most of their working time doing, what the satisfactions and frustrations of their jobs are, how they came to be doing such work, and what advice they have for anyone hoping to enter it now.

Another way of mining people for information is by seeking out prominent people you don't know, and doing what counselors call "interviewing for information, not for a job." This plan has been recommended by Bolles, Djeddah, and many other writers on jobs and careers.[5] The idea, as most readers already know, is to phone or write persons active in a field you wish to enter, tell them that you are beginning (or considering changing) your career, that you do not expect them to know of a job for you but that you would appreciate fifteen minutes of their time to discuss your résumé, your plan of action, or whom else you should see.

Try this kind of information gathering if the idea appeals to you and you can do it naturally. If you do so, try to get from each informant a few names of other persons you might talk with. If you are making appointments on this basis, don't let your shyness lead you to bypass the executive with an impressive downtown office in favor of the lesser known freelance writer, editor, or PR person who works at home. The former, surrounded by secretaries who can unobtrusively control the length of your visit, may be less reluctant to see you than the latter, who can be extremely vulnerable to interruptions eroding his or her most precious sources of capital—time and energy.

This kind of brain-picking may work well—as it did for several Ph.D.'s in English who mentioned it in chapter 2. Yet sometimes it may lead to frustration for either you or the person you approach. Having talked with numerous editors, PR persons, publishers, bankers, and others who are constantly besieged with requests for "a few minutes of their time, and some advice on careers," I am convinced that the key to successful "informational interviewing" lies in using empathy and judgment. If you ask for fifteen minutes of a busy person's time, start to leave after fourteen minutes. And do save yourself time and embarrassment by having done some reading and exploring on your own *before* seeing someone important in your field. You will appear lazy and passive if you have to keep saying, "Yes, I *do* know of that source, but I haven't gotten to it yet."

In all such interviews, try to be clear with yourself (and the other person) about your motives. Having let him or her off the hook by saying, "I don't expect you to know of a job for me just now, but I would certainly appreciate your advice," *mean* it. Don't keep waiting for a job offer. Try to use tact, too, in seeking such appointments to see people. If you phone someone who seems hesitant to see you, don't push. Above all, avoid sounding as if you thought that your interest in the other person's work gave you a claim on his or her time.

The person you would like to talk to may be faced with urgent dead-lines, or may have just seen so many other earnest advice-seekers as to be completely drained. An editor in a publishing firm said to me recently, "I could spend at least ten hours a week, if I had the time, just listening to and advising liberal arts graduates who want to break into publishing. But I just don't *have* that kind of time." And a placement counselor at a Midwestern university volunteered to me, "Maybe the idea of the 'informational interview' has been overdone lately. I think it works best for young job-seekers just out of college. With older people, employers sometimes get the feeling that they are only pretending to want long-range advice—that actually they are desperate for jobs right now." [6]

WRITING LETTERS OF APPLICATION

Always send a cover letter when mailing out a résumé—whether you are applying for a specific advertised job or inquiring about pos-sibilities in that "unpublished job market" that Bolles, Djeddah, and others estimate as containing about 80 percent of the jobs at any given time. [7] If you are applying for a position that has a formal job description, your letter has certain necessary parts. The first para-graph should establish a connection between you and the job adver-tised: you can explain where you saw the notice of the vacancy, or mention something you have heard that interests you about the orga-nization, or relate your own background to the aims of the company to which you are writing. [8] Next comes the main paragraph in which you give facts establishing you as a suitable candidate for the posi-tion; you can highlight or refer to your enclosed résumé without re-capitulating it. In your final paragraph you indicate your availability for an interview and (this is tremendously important) indicate how and when you can be reached by telephone. [9]

The kind of letter you should write when no job is advertised but you want to engage the interest of a potential employer is more of a challenge. This way of operating may seem especially difficult to for-mer teachers, used as you are to seeing a certain number of listed va-cancies as the total source of positions within an area. In writing, "cold," to possible employers who have not indicated a job opening, you have a chance to make resourceful use of some of the back-ground information you have unearthed. Try to capture the reader's attention with it at the beginning. You may have read an article in the *Wall Street Journal* describing new developments within a company; you can mention your interest in such plans and ask whether there will be a need for editors, PR persons, writers, or whatever your new specialty is. You may have come across an article by the person whom you are writing; you could mention how it has clarified a problem for you, or that it has led you to do further reading on the subject, or inquire whether related articles are appearing soon.[10] Or, establishing yourself as a long-time reader of a periodical on which you would like to work, you could refer to and enclose a list of eight to ten ideas for articles not covered within the past two years that you think would appeal to their readers. Then, as in the more specific kind of application letter, write a strong second paragraph outlining your capabilities and tying them in with the work of the firm or agency. In a final paragraph explain how you can be reached by phone, or else say something like, "I would very much like to talk to you about some of these ideas. I plan to phone your office next Tuesday to see whether we might get together some time in the near future."

Students and teachers of English and related subjects sometimes have difficulties writing application letters. They try too hard. Feeling that their writing ability, a cherished part of their self-image, is on exhibit, they agonize over every phrase until their desks become littered with unsent letters. Such students should take comfort from the idea that in composing application letters and résumés they are attempting something that by its nature will never completely meet their standards of good writing. As Howard Figler points out, "The résumé, application, and other standard forms are impersonal; they lack the single most potent quality in any writing—a direct connection between one human being and another."[11] Whatever you do when writing letters to employers, try to individualize them as much as possible; have someone else read them before they go into the mail; and try to speak to the employer's needs rather than your own.

Tailoring Your Résumé to a Specific Field

Many of us when writing our résumé try overly hard to get maximum mileage out of everything we have ever done. We tend to forget that the purpose of a résumé is not to claim credit from some celestial scorekeeper for all the hard work we have done during the past few years; it is simply to get an employer to ask a candidate to come for an interview. Yet, although the purpose remains the same, fashions in résumés have changed several times within the past twenty years.

Not too long ago, job-seekers for academic and other professional positions were advised to prepare a *curriculum vitae* (c.v.), which detailed, as its name implied, the course of one's life from secondary education until the current year. The c.v. is still widely used in the natural sciences. In the humanities and in business, however, an analytical format soon became more common: headings such as "Education," "Teaching Experience," "Administrative Experience," "Business Experience," or "Publications" divide the entries into appropriate groups and each group is listed in reverse chronological order. With this format, employers who want to focus on a particular portion find it easy to do so. During the 1970s a third pattern, the "functional résumé," came into wide use by men trying to make drastic mid-life career shifts, and by women returning to the job market after bringing up their families. As Marcia Fox explains in *Put Your Degree to Work*, this is the "résumé that lists a summary page or so of 'skills' completely divorced from any job context. Not only will the employer refuse to believe such a lengthy recital of skills but the lack of pertinent facts is apt to make him irate. You make be understandably dismissed as a disorganized person given to puffery." [12]

Today in the early 1980s many employers and job-seekers are most comfortable with a fourth format, one that uses the categories of the second but adds a descriptive phrase or an example for each major position held. Such an arrangement gives an employer a fuller picture of what you can do than is possible through a bare statement of where, when, and what you have studied and taught. When choosing these examples or phrases, start by asking yourself such questions as these: "What work have I been carrying on? With whom? With how many people? Over how long a time? What was the result or end product? Was it judged to be successful? Has there been a measurable change as a result of what I have been doing? In doing what I did, have I supervised other people (and how many)? Did I handle a budget (of what amount)? Did I apply for and get grant support or other outside fundings? Have I (or has anyone) written up a report on my project/course/program?" As you jot down answers to these questions, become increasingly aware of the language of your new field, whether it be PR, publishing, administration, personnel work, or something else. You can pick up much of the language and many of the concepts by reading professional journals, browsing in the job advertisements of the Sunday *New York Times*, and attending meetings and workshops.

Although you should put down on a preliminary work sheet everything you have done that you can possibly translate into the terms of the new career you wish to enter upon, when you compose your final version you will want to be selective and to be sure that the examples you choose approach the language of your new field. Consider having more than one kind of résumé if you are thinking of applying for different kinds of jobs. You might have one for editing positions, one for work in the fund-raising office of a foundation, and one for a business position. Depending on the kind of position for which you are applying, you will want to highlight in each résumé three or four of your strongest achievements by giving specific examples, quantifying any statement you can, and using active verbs.

Thus instead of describing yourself simply as having been an instructor of English, 1975-81, you might consider, where applicable, saying that you "taught basic writing skills to 80 students each quarter," or "designed and taught upper division courses in technical writing and technical editing," or "designed and coordinated an interdisciplinary writing course, involving liaison with three instructors of history, sociology, and anthropology." Under some circumstances, you might add a descriptive sentence such as, "The course, now in its fourth year, has grown from a pilot section of 15 students to eight sections annually, totaling 166 students during 1981-82." If you have written successful grant proposals, be specific about the funding source, the amount, and the purpose. Other words and phrases you could use to emphasize and clarify some of the things you did might be: "chaired faculty personnel committee for two years," "designed and made quarterly surveys of course content preferences of 240 English majors and premajors," "coordinated arrangements for intercollege writers' conference, involving ten speakers, five panel discussions, and an attendance of 480 students." "Whenever you can legitimately do so, mention projects that you have "chaired," "coordinated," "designed and executed," "directed," "managed," "obtained funding for," "planned," "supervised," or "written and tested behavioral objectives for."

Such translation of academic duties into "real-world" phraseology can, like everything else, be overdone. Don't feel that you must use any occupational jargon that truly offends you (as "input," "feedback," "prioritize," and "parameter" probably do).

The résumé, like the letter of application, can be uncomfortable to write. Probably nobody enjoys doing his or her own. So put together a first draft, then have someone whose judgment you trust read and comment on it. There is no way that it can become great writing; be satisfied if you achieve writing clear and specific enough to make an employer want to talk with you. There will always be some of your best achievements that will elude the categories and the upbeat, quantitative phrasing of your résumé. Fortunately one of the purposes of the interview is to give you and an employer a chance to explore together in person many matters to which no paper presentation can do justice.

DEVELOPING A PORTFOLIO OF YOUR WORK

Another way of presenting yourself which can make a useful supplement to your résumé is through a folder or portfolio of about half a
dozen examples of your work. Unlike majors in journalism, advertising, and the graphic arts, most liberal arts job-seekers tend not to
think of collecting or using such samples to show an employer. Yet
doing so can count heavily in your favor. A young woman with an
M.A. in French who now has an excellent job as a technical writer for
an engineering firm tells me that she was offered it largely because
her employer was impressed by seeing, at the interview, a copy of her
200-page master's thesis on Buffon's *Histoire Naturelle*. An English
teacher I know was appointed to a position as placement counselor
largely, she was told, because of reprints of several articles on community college policy regarding part-time teachers that she brought
to the interview. Presenting tangible evidence of your ability to con-
ceptualize, to start and finish a piece of writing, individualizes your
application. It helps establish you as having something extra in ideas
and energy to contribute over and above the minimum requirements
for a position.

Many recent B.A.'s and a good number of graduate students flinch
at such advice. "I haven't had time to write anything but assigned
papers," they say. Yet even if this statement should represent your
current writing output, it is not too late to change. Your folder of
work need not be ambitious or extensive. It could include reviews (of
films, plays, music, sports events, art, or books) published by a campus or local paper. Depending on the kind of job you are looking for,
it might also contain prospectuses of new courses, grant proposals
you have written, reports on committees or fund-raising drives you
have worked on, programs of conferences you have coordinated, letters to a newspaper, newsletters or press releases for an organization,
or brief accounts of other projects that you have had a hand in or
directed.

Whatever your folder includes, it should demonstrate to a nonacademic employer that you can write in crisp, understandable language for a general audience. If such writing has been published,
fine; if it has been duplicated and distributed by an organization, that
too will show that you can finish what you start to write and can get
it out into the world. The kind of sample you should ordinarily *not*
include would be either a handwritten draft or anything written for a
class assignment. In any case, keep your folder from being over-
powering because of quantity or ponderous tone. Have your pieces

professionally typed and photocopied so that they look inviting to read. Have more than one set made up, so that if you are asked to leave your portfolio at the end of the interview, you won't count too heavily on getting it back. (At the very least, have extra copies of two or three pieces that you can leave.) Don't go in for gimmicks, such as elaborate binders or fancy title pages; these can seem distracting, as well as rather suggestive of high school reports. Above all, try to vary the contents of your portfolio to suit the kind of work for which you are applying—or else say something like, "Not all of these samples of my work have a direct bearing on the kind of work I'd hope to do for you; I brought them along, however, to show that I can write in different styles to suit a wide range of audiences."

Enjoying the Interview

When your background research, your résumé, and its cover letter have worked together to win you an appointment for an interview, you are at last free from the constraints of such formal, impersonal communication as they represent. You know that you can look forward to a conversation with a living person—that no longer does your success depend in part on your gift for succinct phrasing or your proofreading skill. Even so, if you are like most people, you may be immobilized by fright. Anthony Medley, who deals with such paralysis in his book, *Sweaty Palms: The Neglected Art of Being Interviewed*, has blunt advice. "Don't think about yourself so much. Most interviewees think about themselves to the exclusion of everyone else."[13]

Yet there are ways to cut down on the self-centeredness that most applicants feel before and during an interview and actually to enjoy the experience. Here are a few that have helped some job-seekers:

1. You will probably feel less put upon if you stop to consider that the interviewer, too, may feel insecure. Except for personnel representatives, most people in the awesome position of hiring others have had no systematic training in interviewing. Personnel representatives, however, usually do preliminary screening interviews, leaving the ultimate hiring decisions to department or agency heads who are often overworked, wary of hiring the wrong person, and more aware of what qualities they don't want in a new employee than of what qualities they are looking for.[14]

2. Be ready to *listen* to the interviewer, rather than thinking so much about what points you are going to bring up next that you fail to take in what he or she is saying. Try to listen more than you talk.

3. On the other hand, when you are asked questions, don't be so

hesitant to go out on a limb that you confine your answers to monosyllables. (Note how, in chapter 14, William Oliver mentions some of the candidates interviewed as giving the search committee a lecture on government, and others as sinking into a limp, exhausted silence.) Each of these responses suggests concentration on yourself rather than on the other person. Yet if you have done your homework, you can have your mind comfortably filled with issues and ideas connected with the job rather than focusing so much on any personal threat that you feel.

4. Have your portfolio in hand; it will be something tangible to look at with the interviewer, to get him or her to ask questions about, and to use as a bridge for a wide variety of points you may want to inject into the conversation. (If you have sent your portfolio ahead with your résumé, have another copy of each with you. Employers, like everyone else, sometimes mislay papers or lend them to someone; you can't count on any document's being on hand at the interview except those that you bring with you.)

5. Realize that the interview is a two-way affair. "As [job candidates] in any field prepare themselves for interviews with companies, they should also prepare themselves to interview the company," says Alonzo Johnson, a member of the computer science faculty at Southern University currently on assignment at Bell Labs.[15] Furthermore, as Ivan Settles of the University of Washington Placement Center points out, failure to ask questions in an interview suggests to the interviewer that you aren't much interested in the company. A bulletin published by the University of Washington Placement Center suggests that you ask specifically about the job responsibilities, the table of organization, the main people you would be dealing with, their functions, and how these people interrelate. You might also ask what the interviewer considers the ideal experience for the job, about training programs, about a typical first assignment, and about some of the best results produced by people in this job. Finally, you might ask, "How often would my performance be reviewed? Are you planning more expansion? Which of your locations have the type of job I am looking for? Is relocation important to promotion? What percentage of supervisory positions are filled within the company?" and, in closing, "What is the next step? When may I expect to hear from you?"[16]

6. See any job interview as probably one of several dozen you will have during your whole working life, not as one crucial "all or nothing" event. With each successive interview you should become more comfortable and more effective.

7. Realize that in every hiring process there are many factors at

work that you can't know about—internal politics, external pressures, budget uncertainties, personal idiosyncracies, and the impression left by the person who had the job before you. Realizing all this should help you face rejection, if it comes, philosophically rather than as a judgment about your personal worth.

8. If you are genuinely interested in the kind of work you can do, don't be afraid to let your enthusiasm come through. At a meeting of placement counselors where I informally polled 66 of them on what they considered the single most important element in the job-seeking process, the largest number (38) gave belief in the value of one's work, and enthusiasm about doing it the highest ranking.[17] (If by chance you *aren't* enthusiastic about the kind of position for which you are applying, consider the fact a warning signal. Ask yourself why you don't like this work. Be prepared to take heroic measures to change either your attitude or your work before you go much further.)

Aside from the above specifics of presenting yourself in person and on paper, there are also a few general principles which it may be helpful to keep in mind:

In order to find a job or change jobs, you need to have at least one fixed point that you can count on. It may be time: be prepared to spend from 90 to 180 days, most counselors suggest. It may be money: if possible, gather together enough, whether from savings or borrowing or from a job you hold while looking for another, to support yourself for that long. It may be the very real security of knowing that you *do* have a job, even if not the one you ultimately want. It may be belief in yourself and what you have to offer.

Never forget that, despite the job shortage, people do get hired, even in fields or by firms where, according to rumor, "it is well known that no hiring is being done." In fact, as Djeddah points out, sometimes the very firm that has reorganized and made massive staff cuts will unexpectedly need to hire a few new people. They may have fired too many of the staff, or some of the wrong ones; or, at the first news of impending cuts, some of their key people may have left for other jobs and now need to be replaced.[18]

In other firms, vacancies occur because of employees' retirement, promotion, or illness; new programs develop through the unexpected funding of grants or contracts; top management sometimes has a chance to implement innovative ideas by creating positions that personnel departments have never heard of. Of those people who are hired, many take a newly created or vaguely defined opportunity and gradually, after they are on the job, see that it is redefined to fit their capabilities and talents.

You should make both a long-range plan and some contingency plans as well, so that if you find yourself in a short-term peripheral job you can turn it to good account. (You can, for example, use such a marginal job to add to your repertoire of skills, to try out new course material, or to tap as a source for articles, innovative programs, or a book). You can also use almost any alternative job experience to help qualify you for more permanent employment.

Usually you will not find your ideal alternative job to be the first one you get. Be prepared to proceed by zigzags perhaps from an hourly job in your chosen field to a salaried, full-time one only vaguely related to this field, and then finally, with luck, you might make a lateral move to a salaried job representing your first choice.

A common criticism of twentieth-century American society is that too many of us "tend to define ourselves by our jobs." Unfortunate as this tendency is, an even more self-defeating one is becoming widespread. Too many people hunting for position these days are defining themselves by their joblessness. We have all met the weary, dispirited job-seeker who, after "looking" for several months or longer, has begun to take a wry pride (it would seem) in having "written two hundred and forty-three application letters without ever having been invited for an interview," or having "been interviewed seventeen times and never offered a position." No matter how time-consuming your job search may be, you will make a much better impression on others, including potential employers, if you avoid focusing all your thought and conversation on the state of being unemployed.

One way of escaping this temptation is to shake up your mind by taking a few short courses or workshops in techniques relevant to your chosen alternative field (for examples, see chapter 5). Another is to contrive to do some sort of work, no matter how marginal, while you are job-hunting. Teach one course (if you enjoy teaching, even if it is on an hourly or perhaps a volunteer basis.) Write (and get yourself published, even if you write only minor book reviews, news items, or freelance articles, unpaid or underpaid, in your local paper). Be a freelance editor, if you are qualified (even if you have only one client every few months). Work on improving the reports and internal communications of a business concern; do tape-recorded interviews for a local oral history project; help a political candidate by working on his or her press releases and speeches. Doing any of these things will increase your sense of professional continuity and your versatility. Having such activities in your background should make you come through at job interviews as a more interesting person than you would if you were just one more worthy, well-qualified, admirable but unemployed person with a degree in the liberal arts.

When you *do* find the position you want, don't just settle in and take it for granted. See what you can write and add to your folder of examples of your work. Look ahead; keep your résumé and your placement file up to date. Ask yourself whether you have capabilities that aren't being used in your position, and try to find ways of using them. Alternatively, ask yourself what you are learning in your current position that could add to your competence in the more nearly ideal position that may still lie ahead.

If these ideas seem completely self-evident to you, fine. You may not need this book. Go ahead and hunt for jobs following your own instinct. If, however, you want examples of how some of these strategies work in practice, you will find them in the following chapters.

5. Will a Different Degree Help?

In the late throes of graduate work and in the first ones of full-time teaching, you could pick up certain repetitive sentences from me and my colleagues, particularly in late evenings: "You know, it sounds crazy, but I've been thinking of switching to law school" or "What's three years out of a lifetime?" or "Do you realize what lawyers make in New York?" . . . It wasn't actually *being* lawyers that attracted us; the *image* was invigorating.
> —Roger Rosenblatt, literary editor of the *New Republic*

One of the . . . reasons why most people go back to school is . . . to postpone decision, and create a never-never land between one's past and any future career. The "eternal student" is becoming more and more a familiar figure in our land.
> —Richard N. Bolles, *What Color Is Your Parachute?*

Perhaps, rather than looking around for alternative ways to make use of your humanities background, you are considering starting all over again in a different graduate or professional program. "I think I might as well give up on my field and get a degree in something practical this time," graduate students often tell placement counselors.

Law school is probably the most popular choice, at least in fantasy, and many readers can empathize with the early daydreams of Roger Rosenblatt and his friends. Somewhat less popular than going to law school, yet still exerting a magnetic influence on many restless or discouraged graduate students in English or other liberal arts fields, are certain other graduate or professional programs: librarianship, counseling, social work, public affairs, business administration, or one of the health sciences or health services.

Although there has lately been a good deal of talk about "career switching,"[1] there is as yet very little hard information about what happens to young people who start preparing for their second professional career before ever actively commencing their first one. Edward Noyes, director of Yale University's Office of Career Planning, who has long had serious doubts about the motivation of many students in going to graduate school right after getting a bachelor's degree, is concerned about the new trend toward seeking a second kind of graduate or professional preparation simply as a hoped-for answer to the job crisis. In fact he shares Richard Bolles's concept of the "eternal student" as someone who may well be deluding himself into postponing (or giving up too soon on) job-seeking.[2]

Neither Bolles, Noyes, nor anyone else means to say that such dual preparation is *never* a good idea; under some circumstances, as examples later on will show, it can turn out well. Yet if you are beginning now to think of "going back to school to get a different advanced degree, one in something *practical* this time," you should try to find out just how realistic your picture of your entry into another field may be.

To gather solid information, you should first explore the *Guide to American Graduate Schools*,[3] then write to the official association of your intended profession—the American Bar Association, the American Library Association, or other appropriate ones—for career literature and answers to specific questions. You should also write to or talk with a faculty adviser at each of the schools to which you hope to apply. Then talk to half a dozen students now working for the degree you want to get, to people looking for jobs in the field, and to those holding such jobs. It is remarkable how many liberal arts graduate students keep saying for years, "I'd like to chuck it all and go to law school," without having made firsthand contact with any source of data against which they can measure the practicality of the idea for them.

As you make personal contacts and write letters, be sure to test certain assumptions commonly held by graduate students and other job-seekers looking at what they consider greener fields. Without saying that these five assumptions never hold true, placement counselors and graduate admissions officers nonetheless urge you strongly to see whether you have grounds for believing them true in your particular case.

1. "Once I've added a library (law, social work, or other) degree—no matter where I get it—to my background in English [or history or modern languages], I have a passport to a whole new job market." But things do not always work out this way. Through your choice of institution you may already be limiting your job target more than you realize. First, there are differences in emphasis. Before you apply to a school of library science, for example, find out whether it concentrates on preparing its graduates to be school librarians, to work in

large public libraries, or to become scholarly research librarians.[4] Given your advanced degree in a humanities field, you might try to work toward the last of these goals. Schools of social work too— in fact all professional schools—have their different emphases, strengths, and weaknesses, a fact sometimes overlooked by those longing to get into the field and become accredited as quickly as possible in a new profession. Second, there are differences in quality of education provided. Before you apply to a particular law school, for example, find out the percentage of its recent graduates who passed their bar exams on the first try, as well as those who have been hired by law firms in the area where you hope to work.

2. "The new field I've chosen is a highly practical one. There will always be a need for social workers (or lawyers, librarians, clinical counselors)." Don't take this idea for granted. Call your local branch of the Bar Association for their latest figures on the number of newly graduated lawyers who have passed the bar exam and are still out of work. A representative of one law school said recently that such candidates "were finding the job search increasingly difficult, just as it is in any profession." The new lawyers were waiting an average of six to nine months before being placed, with those faring best who were willing to relocate in rural areas.

Clinical counselors, too, however much they may be needed, are not being hired in the numbers they were a few years back, and the files of placement centers bulge with dossiers of job candidates with doctorates in counseling, several years' clinical experience, and a string of published research articles. When college and university budgets are slashed, student counseling centers are sometimes the first programs to be eliminated. As for social workers, although their employment picture nationwide is better than that of counselors, most large cities have a backlog of unemployed caseworkers and M.S.W.'s. Note, incidentally, that social workers and librarians alike are now writing and reading books and articles on career alternatives for persons with accreditation in their professions.[5]

It is important to keep in mind that even with the most currently "marketable" of the degrees often considered desirable by disenchanted English Ph.D.'s—master's degrees in health planning and in business administration—there is no guarantee that by the time you may have received one of them and are again on the job market, the demand for them will have kept up with the supply. Currently, in the early 1980s, one sees more and more articles questioning the recent uncritical worship of the M.B.A. degree.[6] Keep in mind, too, that several successful job-hunters interviewed for this book, who could have persuaded themselves to go back to graduate school and get an

M.B.A., worked their way without it to exactly the positions they wanted in business or in government.

3. "If I could get admitted to graduate school once, I can do it again—perhaps even more easily now that I've finished one graduate program." This conviction may not be borne out by the facts. As graduate schools respond to university-wide cutbacks in funding and to charges of producing more highly educated people than there are jobs for them, admissions policies are inevitably tightened. Where once your academic record and your graduate or professional school aptitude test scores were the main criteria, admissions committees today often take into account your age, your "commitment to the profession," your previous work experience, and your chance as they perceive it of becoming an effective, practicing member of your profession. (Although admissions counselors at several schools of social work told me that the candidate's age and his long-range professional intentions after getting an M.S.W. did not affect his or her candidacy, few graduate or professional schools have such a laissez-faire policy.) Some health science programs, besieged as they are by hundreds of qualified applicants for every available place, have turned down an applicant with an excellent academic record in another professional field, insisting that he or she "already has a profession."

In particular, do not count on the hope that your having a Ph.D. in a humanities field may either cut down slightly the requirements for a degree in your new field or tip the scales in your favor. One admissions officer at a school of library science said that having a Ph.D. in English or American literature would be held as "neither a plus or minus, but simply an irrelevancy. In this field, you can go to school for twenty years or more, but it doesn't necessarily qualify you for a job." An admissions adviser in a counseling program said that having an advanced degree would count in an applicant's favor only if a teaching assistantship had been part of the program. A faculty member of a law school conceded that people with Ph.D.'s in English would probably make good lawyers, "since everything a lawyer does, he does with words"; at the same time, he said that having a graduate degree in English would count neither for nor against an applicant to his school.

4. "If I could support myself through graduate school once, I can probably do it again." Here, too, careful investigation is in order. You may be less likely to get a teaching assistantship the second time around. In particular, find out about any departmental restrictions on working part time along with your studies. Although such work is often possible, there are some programs, particularly at many law

schools, where it is forbidden. "The three-year program leading to the degree of Juris Doctor is a total commitment, a very serious, difficult study," said an admissions counselor at the law school of a large state university. "The course work should take all one's time and energy. Therefore the applicant must register for full-time study and must not take a paid part time job during the nine-month academic year."

5. "With my first graduate degree in a humanities field plus my new degree in my second field, I'll have a broad background that should make me more valuable to employers, enrich my life, and be a double insurance against disaster." It is probably true that your second professional preparation *should* do all this and more, yet in the present state of academia, compartmentalized as it is, there is some doubt that your double preparation *will* serve these purposes.

On the whole, placement counselors have been finding that candidates with advanced degrees in several subjects usually do no better in the job market than those with one M.A. or Ph.D. These counselors tend to think that there is almost no candidate harder to help than the one who took several graduate degrees in a row without getting any practical or professional experience along the way. William Bliss, director of the Yale Alumni Placement Service, goes so far as to say, "In general, the 'professional student' will never be a very good worker. The Ph.D.-lawyer will probably have trouble finding a legal job after law school." Some employers feel threatened by an applicant's double preparation; others tend to see him or her as indecisive, or cast in the role of a loser.[7]

Once you find a job in your new field, moreover, you may run into various kinds of academic territorialism. For example, Theodore Greider, a member of the library staff at New York University, writing in the *ADE Bulletin,* points out that combining a Ph.D. in English with an M.L.S. does not automatically increase your chances for a satisfying career. After making a survey of librarians at 122 institutions, Greider concludes that there are real obstacles to be overcome by the "subject-matter expert" wishing to become a scholar-librarian. Many employers told him that Ph.D.'s would probably move to other jobs as soon as they could find them. "If good librarians with relevant Ph.D.'s are available as applicants for positions in reference, book selection, cataloging, then they would certainly be seriously considered. On the other hand, I can think of four who were with us for periods of one to ten years (two in languages, two in history) who all moved out eventually to full-time teaching posts." One cynical employer even replied, "I will tell you that attaching the least marketable products of various departments of instruction to the library is something I will personally resist. Let 'em drive taxis! Many of us who hold subject Ph.D.'s also have library school degrees and have librarianship as our major commitment, not as a second-best choice; . . . it would not surprise me if MLA and other scholarly institutions were thinking that libraries would be a wonderful place to dispose of their surplus Ph.D.'s—a surplus, one might note, the academic departments themselves casually and irresponsibly produced." Another took the view that he did "not see a great need for language and literature Ph.D.'s except in those libraries where book selection in these areas is a major activity."[8]

These attitudes, and especially the territorialism, uncovered in Greider's article are paralleled in other fields. Admissions counselors at law schools, for example, warn that "nobody should go to school as a second choice"; and an advisor in a graduate school of public affairs said that while applicants with B.A.'s or M.A.'s in English would be welcome, those with Ph.D.'s would probably be looked at with some skepticism. On the whole, most academic or professional persons tend to wonder why, if a neophyte expresses extreme interest in and commitment to their field, he or she didn't start out there in the first place.

This is not to say that combining two fields of professional training is impossible. Even Greider, after outlining the many obstacles a Ph.D. in English may meet as a beginning librarian, goes on to suggest that, *depending on one's particular interests and temperament,* there may be opportunities:

> In a positive way, I can conclude by saying that librarianship can provide a most interesting professional career for the Ph.D. truly interested in books and their nature, the book trade and antiquarian trade, bibliography (national and international), the technical processes necessary to make books available to the academic community, and the activities involved in assisting users of all levels of learning with the books that are at hand. Given a lack of interest in freshman themes and term papers, perhaps even a disenchantment with the world of formal academia and its offerings, and given a willingness to pursue a profession other than that of academic instruction, I think that the Ph.D./ M.L.S. will find a very considerable satisfaction in the various pursuits of librarianship.[9]

As one gathers from reading Greider's article, the fusion of careers he is exploring is a highly individual matter.

This important idea, the realization that "in making any career change, what matters more than any degrees is your understanding of what you want to do," is the point that Donna Martyn, director of the Harvard Office of Placement Services, urges you to keep in mind as you look at law school, social work programs, schools of librarianship, and all the other options: "There's no magic, no invulnerability, in any degree or any combination of them. Another degree will work for you only if the training will help you to do a job you've set your sights on." [10]

Thus, if during your first graduate work or one of your early jobs, you envision what you most want to do, and if it involves combining fields, taking another graduate degree might be practical. Four cases will help illustrate this point. A young woman who received her first degree in music, majoring in the flute, worked for a year as public relations coordinator for a civic opera company, then went back to school for an M.B.A. to combine her musical and administrative interests. She is now happily established in her third year as business manager for the symphony orchestra of a large western state. A young lawyer who became interested in American history during his military service went back to school to get a Ph.D. in American constitutional history, which (after meeting some skepticism at job interviews as to why he made this shift) he is now teaching as an assistant professor at a university. A Ph.D. in nursing research became so concerned about the differences in various cultural attitudes toward health, hygiene, and medicine that she went to graduate school for a second Ph.D. in anthropology; she uses the materials of both disciplines in her interdisciplinary research. And Terry Wetherby, a San Francisco woman who majored in English, earned an M.A. in creative writing, became interested in the women's movement and in civil rights, and wrote a book about women "doing a man's job," decided that if she was going to work effectively for causes she believed in, she needed a power base. Seeing that she would be a more effective spokesperson for civil rights and women's rights as a lawyer than as a freelance writer, she is now in her second year of law school. [11]

These inner-directed people each had a plan; their second period of graduate study helped fill a need which their own work and thought had generated. They didn't shift fields because somebody told them to, or because an occupational forecast predicted more jobs in their new areas of interest during the coming decades. In fact, they didn't so much shift fields as enlarge their fields to be at home in two areas.

The point that Donna Martyn, Edward Noyes, William Bliss, and other counselors emphasize is that, while there are indeed many opportunities to apply to other fields some of the capabilities learned as a graduate student in the humanities, you may be able to do so more easily than you think without arming yourself with another graduate or professional degree.

Career-switching is becoming much more common today than it was even a generation ago. Indeed, job counselors have recently predicted that many people will have three or more separate, though related, careers one after another during their working lives. But such switching need not involve another complete course of professional training.

There are alternatives to such an ambitious plan. Assuming that you want to build upon and use, not abandon, your preparation in the humanities, you can sometimes manage to acquire enough work experience in a new field to test whether you enjoy it before you decide on expensive and lengthy academic preparation. This is what Richard Hart, a recent B.A. in history with an aptitude for writing, did. Upon graduation, not finding the kind of position he had expected, he took a job as a messenger with a large law firm. Within six months, through getting to know his employers and asking them for more responsibility, he was promoted to one of the several legal assistantships within the firm. In this post he wrote draft pleadings, settlement demand letters, and outlines of factual issues such as damage suits, as well as doing most of the writing involved in many of the firm's divorce cases. For the past two years Hart, who says he thoroughly enjoys his work, has been receiving a salary comparable to that earned by an assistant professor in a university; he points out that he has learned enough about what an attorney does so that now, in deciding to enter law school, he believes that he is making a realistic choice. Hart says that he is glad to have acquired his introduction to legal work on the job, rather than by taking one of the available one- or two-year courses for prospective legal assistants.

If, however, your choice of a new field is one in which you believe a certain amount of course work to be essential, consider supplementing your humanities degree(s) with a few shorter, less academic courses than the ones you took toward your degree(s).

For example, if you find that you want to combine your writing training with an interest in film-making and make documentaries for educational or environmental or medical agencies, you should ordinarily not insist on getting a degree in documentary film. You should instead, following the example of many professionals in the field, concentrate on learning about subject areas (education, environment, or whatever), and meanwhile take several good practical courses in film-making; what you will need, as the careers of two film-makers mentioned in chapter 13 show, is the basic technique, not another degree. (Excellent film-making courses are given at

M.I.T., Boston University, Indiana University, the University of Washington, U.C.L.A., at certain community colleges, and, of course, around the country at specialized schools such as the San Francisco School of Art and Photography.)

In addition to film-making, there are several other courses that English M.A.'s and Ph.D.'s report as being valuable. Some of these are noncredit courses, some are offered by continuing education programs, some are undergraduate courses, and some are given at community colleges. Graduate work quite properly makes students afraid of superficiality; but this fear can be carried too far. Your reasons for taking some of these shorter, less academic courses would be different from your reasons for having entered graduate school, for now you would be trying to acquire just enough familiarity with a subject, its vocabulary, and the best books to read about it so that you could go ahead on your own.

Among the courses that people to whom I talked had found valuable supplements to their graduate training in English were:

Accounting. Taking one basic introductory course has been recommended by people in publishing as helpful for aspirants to this field, even for editorial positions. (A counselor at one university placement center always advises liberal arts students who may be unsure of their math skills to take introductory accounting at a community college, where it will probably be given at a concrete level, rather than in a university school of business administration, where such courses tend to be abstract and theoretical.)

Advertising and layout. These would be helpful not only to those hoping to enter advertising (see chapter 11) but also to anyone who edits a newsletter or does publicity for a visiting speaker or an organization, or works as a campus information specialist.

Basic computer language. This is useful for, and increasingly understandable by, people doing editing in fields that are becoming more and more quantified, such as nursing and health services research, sociology, and history.

Editing and copy editing. This background would obviously be useful for anyone entering the fields of journalism or publishing and helpful too for those who want to stay in teaching or do academic writing.

Grant proposal writing. Short courses given in this make it much easier to draft proposals for yourself or for the organization you work for; moreover, once you have gotten this expertise, your services are often in demand to use professionally for others (see chapter 9).

Graphics courses have sometimes helped people with graduate degrees in their entry into publishing. The expertise acquired here is also immensely useful if you are in an organization, an academic department, or a learned society that issues a newsletter.

Introduction to health services. This course, along with world health, would be particularly helpful for anyone beginning to do editing in health care fields.

Photography. Having taken a basic course in black-and-white photography is an asset for those who want to work on magazines or newsletters. A course in film-making can start you toward assisting with and ultimately making documentaries in connection with whatever position you may find as writer, editor, educator, journalist, information specialist, or PR person.

Publication procedures. Such courses, though not always easily available, may be a good entry into the world of publishing (see chapter 10).

Reading development. There are various institutions such as the Warren Reading Foundation of Seattle specializing in instruction in how to improve students' reading ability at all age levels. Having taken a course at such a school or in Michigan State University's reading instruction program could be a helpful addition to your preparation for some kinds of community college teaching or for working in a college's "individual development center" or "study skills center."

Technical writing and technical editing. These would be immensely helpful for work as editor or writer in connection with business, industry, or public agencies (see chapter 12 and Appendix D).

Urban planning. Although the whole program leads to a degree, taking one or two introductory courses would be an excellent background for a position as writer or editor with some of the many public or private planning agencies. These agencies prepare feasibility studies and impact statements, as well as material addressed to the general public; they are in constant need of people who can help them write prose that is clear, logical, and interesting.

Writing for publication. Such courses, given with varying emphases in noncredit studies, in communications, and as part of technical writing and editing sequences, have obvious uses in almost any position for which you might apply. They will also help you in building up the folder of samples of your writing which nonacademic employers keep telling us that people with degrees in English should be able to show them.

Some of the content of these courses could, it is true, be learned on the job. But if you take one or two of them, you will have a springboard from which to go ahead and learn still more on any job to which they are applicable. And, perhaps more important to you just now, your having taken a few such courses will show an employer that you are interested in applying your writing and research skills to his needs. Of course, if you get into a field such as publishing and find that you would like to work in such a specialized area as law in relation to publishing, then after you have gotten a foothold in publishing and know that you want to stay there, it might be realistic to go back to school and get a law degree as "mid-career training." Such a return would represent a combination of your already well-developed interests rather than merely a search for an added credential.

Roger Rosenblatt, in his speculations on the value of a literary background, considered and then rejected the idea of going to law school. His conclusions may be worth keeping in mind. Inevitably, he points out, a person schooled in literature lacks a *complete* education, for no education can be complete. Yet the study of literature, Rosenblatt is convinced, teaches us a great deal. He urges us all, therefore, to acknowledge that a graduate degree in English is a good one, and then to see how each of us can build on it in our own way.[12]

6. Teaching New Clienteles

Half of all American adults are learning [something new] each year
—sewing and sailing; sales and surgery; swine breeding and Swahili.
Learning by adults is no longer confined to schools or colleges. Most
of it goes on outside of formal education: in work-places, churches,
libraries, the military, even prisons and old-age homes.
  —Carol Aslanian of the College Board, as quoted by Ronald Gross,
                                          Christian Science Monitor

Teachers wanting or needing to make a career change often think that
they must either leave the teaching field entirely and go into business or else retrain themselves for another profession. It is true that
many businesses and professions are heavily staffed with former
classroom teachers. A communications consultant to banks and government agencies; an education specialist for a large insurance company; the promotion manager for a publisher; the co-owner of a firm
of designer-producers of stage scenery; the director of fund-raising at
a Midwestern university; the director of school and college relations
in the personnel department of the Boeing Company; the director of
a university placement center; a training specialist for Blue Cross
in an Eastern state; an author of popular fiction and another of best-
selling nonfiction; and the first woman president of Twentieth-
Century Fox Films—all these people have one thing in common, the
fact that they started out as teachers.[1] As chapter 1 suggested, if you
have taught, you have almost certainly developed capabilities that
will be useful in other kinds of work; later chapters of this book will
deal with some of these possibilities.

Yet if you are a dissatisfied or jobless teacher, you have at least two
other options. You can develop different specialties to teach—offshoots or branches of your subject currently in demand—or you can
find different clienteles, often adult students who want intensive
work in a subject to help them reach professional or personal goals
of their own. Frequently these two options are combined.

New or Emerging Specialties

Teachers of English and foreign languages should look beyond the MLA job vacancy lists with their emphasis on traditional period and genre courses. Think about preparing yourself to teach new specialties for which demand is increasing: technical writing, technical editing, English as a second language, women's literature, and children's literature.

Scientific and technical communication, one of those specialties currently receiving increased attention, is, according to two of its practitioners and professors, "a relatively new professional field. Its basic function is to convey scientific and technical information clearly and accurately through various media to a wide spectrum of readers who range from the general public to experts in such fields as the sciences, engineering, medicine and social sciences." [2] As Paul V. Anderson of Miami University pointed out at the December 1976 meeting of the Modern Language Association, "ever since World War II, industry and government have been asking, with increasing frequency and firmness, that colleges and universities provide more instruction in writing to students in science and technology." [3] Professor Merrill Whitburn of Texas A&M University, Professors Myron White and James Souther of the University of Washington, and other faculty members in the institutions now having programs in technical writing and technical editing cite numerous examples of graduate students in English who, after adding some work in technical writing to their regular program, began to receive job offers. Many of these English Ph.D.'s are now teaching both technical writing and traditional college composition or literature courses. (For further discussion of technical writing, see chapter 12.)[4]

Children's literature, too, is an expanding field, despite the patronizing attitude with which some people, both within and without departments of English, look upon "kiddy lit." (For those of you who need to be convinced of its importance, read what Professor Carol Gay of Youngstown [Ohio] State University has to say about its functions.) [5]

If you are interested in developing the specialty called English as a second language (ESL), you should know that although there are sometimes jobs for people with B.A.'s in English, you will be in a stronger position if you have also had a minor or at least some course work in one or more of the following: anthropology, comparative foreign area studies, education, linguistics, psychology, sociology, or speech and hearing science.

There are entry-level positions in this field requiring a B.A. in En-

glish or in a modern foreign language, with special training in teaching ESL listed as desirable but not mandatory. There are some positions here in the United States, especially in community colleges or
special ESL institutes (such as the one at Seattle University, Seattle,
Washington), teaching English to recent arrivals from other countries; more positions, however, are overseas.[6] If after getting some experience teaching such classes you wish to go on and become a specialist in teaching others how to teach ESL, you will have to take at
least an M.A. in the graduate program of one of the increasing number of colleges and universities that offer teaching English as a second language. Among these institutions, to give only a few examples,
are Iowa State University, Ames; University of the Pacific, Stockton,
California; University of Minnesota, Minneapolis; Trinity University,
San Antonio, Texas; University of Northern Iowa, Cedar Falls; Southern Illinois University, Carbondale; San Francisco State University,
California; and the University of Washington, Seattle. For similar
programs be sure to look in the catalogues of colleges and universities in your area.

Other new courses are beginning to be in demand. Native American literature, for example, or popular culture, or fiction of the British Commonwealth are three such offerings, particularly apt to be
found in the branches of the state university systems of California
and of New York.[7]

But teachers need not stick even as closely as this to the usual
course offerings. Many of the skills and techniques that you may
have learned so as to meet academic emergencies—grant proposal
writing, for example, or environmental impact statement writing, or
principles of public relations—as well as topics involving publication procedures (copyediting, proofreading, indexing, graphics) are
in demand as subjects for short courses, conferences, and workshops. So, too, are many kinds of courses connected with writing:
courses in overcoming writing blocks, techniques of oral history,
writing local history, genealogy, writing autobiography and memoirs,
journal writing. And, in the business community, courses in memo,
report, and letter writing are well attended, as are such courses as
"Management Writing," or "Becoming Your Own Editor." There is
demand, too, for courses that will help people in their personal development: courses in understanding the arts (contemporary film
and drama, the films of a particular country or director, film and
videotape making) and courses in particular techniques (time management, public speaking, or stress management).

Insofar as these are not traditional academic courses, it is your performance and teaching ability that will count, rather than academic

credentials. You may, therefore, find that reading and experimenting on your own, talking to established professionals in your new field, and taking one or two intensive courses will get you off to a good start. If you have earned credibility through several years of teaching conventional subjects in an established educational institution, it is often not as hard as you might imagine to branch out and give these nonacademic workshops and short courses on your own. (See the account by Gloria Campbell, chapter 13.) If you really enjoy the process of teaching, you may find it challenging to develop a new specialty and teach it to adults anxious to apply it in their own lives.

Overseas Teaching

Whether you majored in English or another liberal arts subject, your B.A. or M.A. will often qualify you for teaching overseas students who want to learn English. Among the places that offer good opportunities for American teachers of English are Japan, Taiwan, and Hong Kong. Opportunities for teaching other liberal arts subjects— history, philosophy, art, classics, and literature—are occasionally to be found in New Zealand and Australia.[8] In East Asian countries, particularly Japan, there is a steady demand for language instruction in colleges, universities, and schools, as well as in private language institutes run somewhat on the principle of the Berlitz schools. Language departments and placement centers in the United States periodically receive requests from Japanese private schools and institutes for English teachers. Although some of these requests are for persons with special training in TEFL, others call for only a B.A. in English or another modern language plus, ideally, some teaching experience. The few Ph.D.'s who apply are made very welcome, since the doctorate is still considered a prestigious addition to a teacher's preparation. Knowledge of Japanese is definitely not required of teachers of English in Japan because teachers are encouraged to use the oral-aural method and thus to speak only English in the classroom.

Although the pay may not be high and the work is demanding, accepting a one- or two-year contract gives one a chance to live in a thoroughly different environment and to be exposed to a new language and culture, as well as to the eagerness of the Japanese people to learn English.

If you are simply looking for a way to support yourself while you enjoy the experience of living in a foreign milieu, then teaching English to adults (businessmen and women and professional people, usually in classes held in their offices or places of business) in

Tokyo, Nagoya, or other large Japanese cities has much to be said for it. There is also an active interest in English and American literature on the part of many young Japanese.

Other teaching opportunities abroad may be found in UNESCO-sponsored schools, for which you can consult the list of vacancies, updated monthly, in most placement centers. There are occasionally regular appointments available, usually for an initial year or two with further possibilities open, to teach American or British literature in a college or university. For information about the latter, you can get names and addresses of the fifty Tokyo colleges and universities at the Japanese consulate in many large cities. You can also consult placement center listings for New Zealand and Australian universities for a list of openings at any of them. For teaching job advertisements in any of the British Commonwealth countries, look in section 4 of the Sunday *New York Times*, and don't overlook the "Education" columns in the London *Times Literary Supplement*.[9]

Recruiters come to the West Coast college and university placement centers at least twice a year in search of teachers for Australian secondary schools, and although neither the Australian nor the New Zealand universities send recruiters, the school representatives can give inquirers considerable information about their country's system of higher education, where to apply, and what specialties may be in demand. The actual hiring for both Australian and New Zealand universities is largely done by correspondence. Sometimes, however, a faculty member on sabbatical leave from one of these universities will be deputized to interview candidates for positions.

On the whole, American college teachers who have gone recently to either Australia or New Zealand send back favorable reports. Schools and colleges have high standards but apparently put less pressure on faculty, both in terms of class schedules and of publication, than do American ones. In New Zealand at least, tenure may come sooner and with less personal stress than it often does here. Faculties are cosmopolitan, being a mix of persons from Canada, the United States, England, South Africa, Australia, and New Zealand, plus a scattering from continental Europe. Opportunities for research in the national libraries are good. The main disadvantage would appear to be a lower salary scale than ours and the distance of Australia and New Zealand from America and Europe.[10]

All in all, almost any kind of teaching in a foreign country is, as Victor Kolpacoff of the University of Washington's English Department points out, an excellent thing to do just after you receive your degree. You plunge directly into teaching, sink or swim, and you have a chance to see whether the classroom is where you want to spend the rest of your professional life.

ALTERNATIVE INSTITUTIONS AND PROGRAMS

Community colleges

Now that the physical expansion of community colleges has slowed down, the job crunch is as pronounced there as it is everywhere else.[11]

Accordingly, full-time positions in English at most community colleges are almost as hard to come by as positions on the regular promotion ladder in four-year institutions, and for various reasons they are much sought after.[12] It is therefore only part-time community college teaching jobs that I am considering in the category of "nontraditional teaching." These positions too are becoming scarcer, although opportunities to teach one or two sections of English composition have been known to open up during the last few days before each quarter begins. Ideally, you should have your résumé and letter of application in the hands of both the English department chairman (or in some colleges the humanities division chairman) and the college's personnel office several months in advance, but you should also be within reach of the placement office just before and after the beginning of a quarter. Changes in enrollment sometimes mean that part-time teaching vacancies can occur and be filled within a single day.[13]

When you apply to teach in a community college, do remember that here, as everywhere, the more individualized your letter is, the better. Show in it that you know something of a particular college's aims and of its clientele. Do not make the mistake of thinking that all community colleges are the same, that all humanities courses they offer are vocationally oriented or remedial. At Queensborough Community College, Bayside, New York, which has been called one of the best two-year colleges in the nation, two-thirds of the student body go on to four-year colleges and earn bachelor's degrees. Mort Young, writer of a syndicated column on education, singles out Queensborough as giving "academic courses on a par with those given in four-year colleges."[14] Other community colleges around the country, among them Bellevue, Shoreline, and Green River in the Puget Sound area, Lane in Eugene, Oregon, Foothill College in the San Francisco Bay area, and Columbia-Greene, Hudson, New York, to take only a few examples, offer many courses comparable with those given in the freshman and sophomore years of four-year colleges.

Qualifications for community college teaching are ordinarily an M.A. plus two years' teaching experience. Holders of Ph.D.'s are acceptable, though not actively sought after. Holders of master's of arts in teaching and of the new degree of doctor of arts in teaching are warmly welcomed. These official requirements are of course only the minimum. For part-time no less than full-time instructors, English and humanities departments are looking for people who have not only excellent academic backgrounds but a wide range of interests and a communicable sense of the excitement of their subjects.[15]

Those who have had experience in both four-year and two-year colleges have often found that there is less difference between the two kinds of schools than one might imagine. In many community colleges (and certainly the ones in or near a large city) you will find that classes are lively; your colleagues are enlightened; and academic standards can be exactly as high as the instructor chooses to make them.

The one serious flaw in the community college rationale in many areas of the country, according to many of those who have taught in one, is the funding structure. Because of the relationship of the individual colleges to the statewide system, a potential financial crisis always looms. As the administrators of many community colleges interpret the financial picture, the colleges' instructional budget can best be balanced by hiring half or two-thirds of each faculty on a part-time, quarter-to-quarter basis, with hourly wages, for "class contact hours" only. At one Puget Sound area community college, there are usually around 220 part-time faculty members and 80 full-time ones, including administrators. Many of the part-time faculty have considerable experience; all those who teach the college transfer courses have M.A.'s, and a number are Ph.D. candidates or hold Ph.D.'s; yet neither their professional qualifications nor their successful teaching can lift them out of the expendable part-time category when instructional funds are lacking.[16]

Despite this serious drawback, you may find part-time teaching in a community college satisfying because of your colleagues and because of the close contacts with students made possible through small group discussions and frequent individual conferences. And the community colleges' philosophy of trying first and foremost to reduce the distance between the student and the subject matter can lead to valuable insights for any instructor, experienced or inexperienced.

Continuing education courses at four-year institutions

Few if any continuing education programs, whether at a community college, a four-year college, a university, or New York's New School for Social Research, have full-time teaching opportunities. At the University of Washington, as at most state universities, appointments to teach must be approved both by the appropriate academic department and by those in charge of the noncredit studies curriculum. Qualifications for noncredit course teaching often involve having a Ph.D. or at least an M.A. (for those teaching academic subjects), plus considerable experience in teaching adults. In short, as the former director of noncredit studies at the University of Washington put it, you need to be full of "*informed* enthusiasm for your subject." [17]

While the salary for this type of teaching is, like that at the community colleges, paid at the "class contact hour" rate, there is less chance that instructors will put in what amounts to full-time work for part-time pay. With most noncredit courses, there are no department meetings to attend, no grades to give, and only a few conferences—those voluntarily arranged by the instructors of special classes such as writing workshops.

Continuing education courses in the credit divisions of most universities tend to be taught by their regular faculty members. To apply to teach in one of them, first study the catalogue and the quarterly lists of current offerings; then plan a course or several alternative ones not already given that you would like to give. Include a prospectus of such courses with a letter of application, and take or send it with your résumé to the director of continuing education of the institutions that interest you.

There are also from time to time a number of vacancies among full-time administrative positions in continuing education and elsewhere. Such positions, involving directing or coordinating all the continuing education programs of an institution, are listed in college placement centers in nearly every issue of the *Chronicle of Higher Education*, and often in section 4 of the Sunday *New York Times*. An expansion of such programs is generally predicted for the coming decade. In a similar vein, the authors of "All Education Is 'Adult Education'" point out in the *AAUP Bulletin* that even now there are all over the country "proportionally fewer college students of traditional college age [than there were thirty years ago] and more adults of twenty-five and over." [18]

Other continuing education courses

Although the typical continuing education course draws its clientele from the general public, there is a growing trend among business and professional groups to sponsor courses in writing or communications for their members. The Boeing Company has given in-service courses in expository writing and in English as a second language to groups of employees. The U.S. Office of Personnel Management in Seattle has two full-time staff persons, one of them an English M.A., who coordinate short courses and workshops in writing for government employees in the Puget Sound area. Other civil service regions have similar staffs and programs.

Numerous in-service courses are held on university campuses for classified and exempt staff. Many universities offer report writing and other classes, for which instructors, some of them graduate students or recent recipients of degrees in English, are hired on contract.

There are many other expanding possibilities. New York City, Chicago, Boston, Berkeley, and Cambridge all have a number of writing workshops and courses, some sponsored by adult education centers and others by government agencies or business. In downtown Seattle, City College offers English teachers a chance to teach college English to people already engaged in a business or profession, as do the Seattle Campus of the University of Puget Sound and several other institutions.

There are other groups, too, not often taught by college English instructors until now, because the need has only recently been recognized. Within and outside the university community, groups of professionals—physicians, health services planners, graduate nurses, psychiatrists, and others—are beginning to hire instructors to design and teach classes for them in expository writing, academic and professional article writing, and related areas. These people need no further academic credit; they are highly trained in their own fields, even though relatively inexperienced in writing. They realize that they need practice, and they are willing to pay for individualized instruction in small groups.[19]

Today the emphasis in adult writing classes has changed considerably from the former remedial tone. For example, in a university community, physicians, professors of fisheries, education, and engineering, staff members working on documents and procedures for the academic administration, others editing journals—all these and other professional people, some with Ph.D.'s—have been students recently in noncredit writing classes. Some of them are specialists in one or another of the natural sciences who have found themselves editing journals without being sure what criteria they should use for the revision of articles submitted to them. Others include physicians whose accelerated undergraduate programs allowed them no writing courses, yet whose awareness of style makes them hope to write medical articles without the jargon they see many of their colleagues using.

Such students come to class not only to hear what the instructor has to say about points of usage and organization but also to find a much-needed forum where they can share concerns and exchange comments about their problems in writing and editing. Instructors of such courses enjoy the rare privilege of seeing that what they teach matters "out there, in the real world."

Other kinds of courses for nonmatriculated students are being talked of, and in some cases implemented to meet a wide range of needs. One of the developments of the late 1970s which continues expanding in the 1980s is the Elderhostel program of noncredit residential summer courses in liberal arts subjects. These are held in two-week segments on college campuses throughout the United States, with a self-selected student body whose only requirement is being sixty years old or over. These short courses, which meet daily for an hour and a half, tend to cover a small segment of a subject—a single novel by Dostoevsky, or the ecology of a particular region, or techniques of starting to write one's autobiography. Instructors are warned that they must give the same kind of course they would offer any group of adult students, making no concessions to any stereotype of the interests of the "elderly." Instructors and students I have talked with are enthusiastic about the results.[20]

Another kind of program has been under way for some time in penal institutions: courses in liberal arts subjects given for college credit. Here as with other courses for special segments of the population, the instructor must avoid stereotyping the clientele, must resist the feeling that he or she should "water down" the subject, and must believe strongly in the value of this kind of teaching. A Ph.D. in English who taught writing in a Montana prison undertook the course with trepidation but found it satisfying to learn "to harness the energy and flow of the prose that they [the prisoners] turned in, and to help them become their own editors and critics." An anthropologist who has recently taught psychology courses to inmates of a large penitentiary reports that he found such teaching a change of pace and a challenge: "It makes you re-think what parts of your subject are really relevant to this audience. It requires clear and honest transactions and exchanges; this is one group that simply will not put up with condescension or academic gamesmanship. This kind of teaching is full of stressful and unpredictable situations that challenge the instructor to come up with original ways of motivating students and presenting material, yet still work within the structure of the correctional system." [21]

Another kind of teaching opportunity that would fit in with this growing urge to cut through academic red tape lies in a trend toward establishing drop-in centers for individualized instruction in writing. These centers, variously known as writing clinics, individual development centers, or writing workshops, are being tentatively set up at some of the community colleges in the Puget Sound area and elsewhere. They have several points in their favor: they exemplify the unstructured, problem-focused kind of writing instruction that Kurt Vonnegut, Jr., has proposed as the only really useful kind, [22] they draw students when they are struggling with a specific writing dilemma and are naturally most receptive to help; and, since these centers have the magic aura of "innovativeness" about them, they are sometimes more apt to receive funding than conventional courses would. [23]

Other new kinds of extension programs, sometimes called "universities without walls," are talked of glowingly by many community college administrators. The concept has been implemented by Whatcom County Community College, Washington, a two-year college designed to be without classroom instruction or a resident faculty. At the four-year level, Dr. William D. Rearick, vice-president of Seattle Pacific University, some time ago endorsed a similar plan. He feels, as he said on September 12, 1975, at a faculty retreat, that "there has been too much emphasis upon degree programs and upon the matriculated student. We need to recognize and cultivate programs . . . for non-degree learning. [24]

In somewhat the same spirit, Antioch University in Ohio has a fairly ambitious program of granting "external degrees" for academic work done in various circles throughout the country and supervised by persons affiliated with Antioch. Provided that you have already gained some conventional academic teaching experience and that you really believe in the value of this kind of course, there might be a chance for you to become involved in teaching some of them.

Here, of course, as with many alternative jobs, there is no neat list of vacancies to apply for. The administrator probably will not realize how useful you could be until you turn up with a sheaf of program ideas and a résumé showing good academic credentials. If your record also demonstrated some successful experience in teaching in untraditional settings, it could be very persuasive.

In themselves, part-time alternative positions can be immensely satisfying. At the same time, it is essential to look ahead and see where they may lead. According to evidence continually coming in to the various placement centers, in the world of college teaching even hard work, excellent credentials, good student ratings, and the support of your department will probably not be enough to win you advancement from part-time to full-time status *at the same institution*. Although such a promotion *can* take place, it is statistically unlikely, and the worsening state of instructional budgets makes it even less likely in the near future.[25] So, instead of pinning your hopes on gaining a full-time position at a place where there may never be sufficient funds in the budget, why not see how you can turn your part-time or peripheral experience to your advantage in other ways? Otherwise there is always the danger that your sense of hard work unrewarded may lead you into a chronic state of frustration or into becoming, as social workers put it, "an injustice collector."

If you can look upon your part-time experience as a transitional stage in your career, you will find that it can provide you with a sense of continuity with your graduate work and teaching. Even if you decide to switch to a nonteaching field for your main employment, the challenge of meeting a college-level humanities class once or twice a week can give the focus to your reading and thinking and the chance to interact with students that are important to anyone who enjoys teaching. If, on the other hand, you are trying to wait out the job crisis until more teaching openings come along, and if you are teaching a single course and enjoying it, you are automatically more employable than you would be if you were completely unemployed.

Again, through one of the ironies in which the whole employment situation abounds, while part-time or extension teaching will not often lead to a salaried, full-time position at the institution where you are, it can sometimes lead to job offers from other places. When someone from another institution is interviewing you, the mere fact that you have successfully taught certain courses can seem more important than your status while teaching them.

Many of these alternative jobs give you great latitude to experiment, to work out your own course plans and materials, to rethink old courses or try out new ones. It is easier to do this in situations where you feel that your stay is temporary than during your early years in a full-time position, where you may be concerned about departmental approbation every step of the way.[26]

Still another advantage of some of these teaching alternatives is that they may bring you a new point of view or a new interest. Teaching English as a second language, for example, whether you do it here or abroad, will probably involve you in so many questions from your students about rules that you may have taken for granted, and about exceptions to those rules, that class discussions will stimulate or renew your own interest in grammar and linguistics.

It is also possible that experience in alternative teaching may lead to writing that would be professionally helpful. If you teach English or American literature abroad, the contrast between the way you think of the authors you teach and the way students from a different cultural tradition see them could suggest a number of articles for you to write. If you teach English as a foreign language, the improvements in methods or materials that occur to you may lead you to write a new textbook or design one of the "self-paced instructional packages" currently welcomed by educational publishers. Again, wherever you teach abroad, you may be lucky enough to find materials for research involving English or American authors who have had some connection with the region, or whose manuscripts or early editions have been gathered there in a library.

If, however, you are teaching continuing education courses, the issues raised by the needs and expectations of your adult students and by your attempts to meet those needs could result in your originating a new text, or in writing articles for journals such as *College Composition and Communication* and *College English* about the issues involved. Or, conceivably, you might eventually develop your own courses and your clientele, so that such an enterprise turns into a career. In Seattle, Gordon and Mary Anne Mauermann have accomplished this during the past eleven years with their private adult school, The Writing Shop. Similar independent writing programs flourish as summer workshops at Port Townsend, Washington, at Penticton, British Columbia, at Banff, at Chautauqua, New York, and elsewhere.

Finally, some of these alternative formats for teaching may contribute, directly, or indirectly, to nonteaching careers. Several years of teaching abroad could be an asset in your attempt to become a foreign student counselor, a minority affairs counselor, or an Affirmative Action staff member on a college campus. Your overseas teaching might also be a preparatory step for a position with the central Fulbright Scholarship Office in Washington, D.C., the American Field Service Committee, the Consular Service, or indeed for almost any position involving working with people of differing backgrounds and traditions. If you are applying to business firms with overseas branches, it would interest them to know that you had lived and worked successfully for a year or two outside the continental United States.

Likewise, teaching technical writing or editing could lead to doing such writing, editing, or consulting for business or industry (see chapter 12). Teaching courses designed from the feminist point of view would help prepare you for an administrative position in one of the women's studies programs or departments. Having taught in community colleges or in continuing education programs and having become thoroughly familiar with their clientele could help qualify you as a student services counselor (working in a placement or financial aid office, for example) at a two-year or four-year college, or perhaps a member of the college relations office of a university. Again, depending upon your other experience, teaching in such programs might help you obtain a position in a publishing firm specializing in innovative textbooks and programs.

Then too, such experience might also help prepare you to direct a continuing education program. People seeking an administrative career in this field should certainly have demonstrated successful teaching in continuing education. In addition, says one university's director of noncredit studies, ideally "they should have language skills and a strong academic background, as well as experience in one or more of the following fields: publicity, media, educational research, management, market research, or counseling. They should be keenly observant of what the population is like, and willing to experiment with unconventional formats for courses without feeling that in so doing they are inevitably lowering their standards." [27]

Finally, for those interested in teaching new clienteles, it may be reassuring to see that the various nationwide adult education and continuing education movements are growing in numbers and prestige. Carol Aslanian's remarks quoted at the beginning of this chapter came from a December 1981 meeting of 200 adult educators who convened at Anaheim, California, for their 29th annual national conference. At it Robert Worthington, assistant secretary in the Department of Education, said that adult learning may hold the key to our national future, in that it can help us "rediscover the human aspect of productivity. Having emphasized capital-intensive high technology as the best route to successful economic competition in the postwar era, we've often forgotten that *people* also make a difference. That idea is now back on top of the agenda. All Americans must learn to live and work smarter." In an attempt to combine forces at the national level, the two national organizations sponsoring the Anaheim conference have agreed to consolidate and form a larger, stronger one: the American Association for Adult and Continuing Education, to be officially born at the 1982 annual conference at San Antonio. Those of you interested in exploring the possibilities of teaching adults should watch the media for news of its activities and publications.[28]

7. More than Teaching Takes Place on Campus

Even if you decide to leave teaching, this does not mean that you must leave the academic life. There are literally dozens of careers possible on nearly every campus—careers involving administration, counseling, educational research, and fund-raising among others—which offer many of the satisfactions of teaching without the strains. I find my own position as head of Graduate Admissions much more satisfying than my previous teaching one.

—A Ph.D. in English, now an administrator
at a Midwestern university

Avoid the edges of academia. This area is a maze of cul-de-sacs, over-populated with bright, frustrated, competitive people who don't want to leave academia and who vainly hope to find a way back in.

—Earl Grout, Ph.D. in English,
now eight years into an insurance career

Probably the two extremes of opinion will never meet. Some alternative job-seekers insist that if they are not going to teach in a college or university, the further away they can get from a campus, the better. Others find this stand a self-punishing one; they enjoy working with students, using the university library, feeling that they are a part of an ongoing educational effort—and often being better paid than their teaching colleagues.

Some teachers—and some students—tend to see staff members as invisible, interchangeable paper shufflers. But as a dean of a small West Coast liberal arts college points out, it is members of the staff rather than the faculty who are usually responsible for internal and external communications, explaining what the various parts of the institution are doing. It is very often staff members who help students decide what courses to take as undergraduates, how they can best finance their education, and what positions they should look for upon graduation. On university campuses it is frequently staff members who implement academic policy in specific instances, such as determining what students, under the faculty rules, can be admitted to the graduate and undergraduate schools.

Staff jobs, then, although different in methods and focus from teaching ones, need not be considered unimportant, dull, or divergent from the goals of the university. And since a number of staff positions attract people with advanced degrees and many others involve considerable knowledge of the academic world,[1] the weekly or biweekly bulletins of the staff employment office of the educational institutions in your neighborhood are certainly worth your continuous attention. Unlike teaching positions, staff positions may become vacant at any time of the year and may be filled at any time—usually from three to four weeks after the deadline for receiving applications has closed.

It must be admitted that nonacademic staff jobs are not for everyone. As Donna Martyn of the Harvard Office of Placement Services has observed, those who do best at these jobs are apt to have gotten a start as undergraduates by "picking up little bits and pieces of administrative experience,"[2] as dormitory or house tutors, class officers, or members of campus business enterprises. Then too, there is the question of how plentiful nonacademic staff positions are these days. At a small college, as Professor Neal Woodruff of Coe College warns, the number of such jobs can fluctuate widely with the ups and downs of the budget.[3] On the other hand, as William Bliss points out, "a big institution will have a lot of jobs; Yale is now the largest employer in New Haven."[4]

The following brief survey of typical college and university offices and of some of the staff positions connected with them touches on merely a few high points of several representative types of positions on public and private campuses. Although the titles differ from campus to campus, jobs like these open up at times at most universities, four-year colleges, and community colleges.

Academic adviser. To apply, you should have a bachelor's and a master's degree, one or both from the school to which you are applying, and it will of course be an advantage if you have teaching and advising or counseling experience. Currently, academic advisers sometimes hold Ph.D.'s. You must have the ability to retain, apply, and communicate a complicated set of rules and requirements as you deal on a one-to-one basis with students and their quandaries about their academic programs. Obviously it will help you get and hold such a position if you enjoy conferring with students and if you see what you accomplish thereby as being important.

Documents and procedures analyst. According to the job specifications for a "Procedures Analyst I" at a large university, this position requires one to "perform the research, analysis, and writing necessary to produce basic operating procedures" for the administration of the university. One may also "assist in writing and editing statements of administrative policy." Applicants must have at least a B.A. with emphasis in business, communications, public administration, or a related field. Obviously, English should be considered a "related field."

An "Analyst II" should in addition be able to "develop varied and complex policy statements; . . . analyze and design forms used in conjunction with procedures." According to a staff member of the Documents and Procedures Office at the University of Washington, "a successful Procedures Analyst must (1) think clearly; (2) write concisely; (3) relate well to other people; (4) have some understanding of business administration concepts; (5) be able to see both the forest and the trees."[5] The fourth criterion, incidentally, need not rule out people with backgrounds in the humanities.

Editor. Persons applying for jobs in this category may work on a college or university internal newsletter, or on public relations assignments interpreting the university to the media or directly to the community; they may work on a scholarly journal as assistant to a faculty member, or may be the project editor assisting a principal investigator who has a government grant or contract. In many states, editors under the state civil service systems have grades of I, II, III, and occasionally IV. A few others working for departments of health sciences or health services in some universities have the status of nonteaching faculty rather than staff. For individual job requirements, see the specific job advertisements in the staff employment bulletin in the college or university nearest you. For comments from representative editors, see chapter 9. In general, writing ability, an eye for detail, and an ability to organize are the main qualifications. Several campus editors who responded to the survey described in chapter 9 hold English Ph.D.'s, and a good many have M.A.'s in English or communications.

Employment representative. At many staff employment offices there are people who interview candidates for certain jobs after they have passed through the preliminary screening process for various types and levels of campus employment. Representatives for "professional and supervisory classifications" should have had some graduate work and/or professional experience. Holders of humanities M.A.'s might do well in these positions, even though no such training is required.

Financial aid counselor. In this job, one interviews students with financial problems, helps them determine their eligibility under the various university, state, and federal rules for student aid, and assists them in finding alternative sources of help. A counselor who worked in this office at the University of Washington for a year after receiving an M.A. and before moving to the Placement Center reports that it is an extremely interesting job for anyone who enjoys dealing with individual students on a short-term basis.

Grants and contracts office staff members. People in this type of office help faculty members and administrators write grant proposals and obtain and administer grants and contracts from the federal government and foundations. The abilities to write clear expository prose and to analyze statements are the main requirements for these positions. The University of Washington Grants and Contracts Office has five people on its staff, each having a quite different background, including one with a graduate degree in English. Since the whole field of grant writing and administration is a new one, and since most of what is done must be learned on the job, there are no prescribed qualifications.

Information specialist. This position in its various grades is not always clearly differentiated from that of editor. Its main duties consist of gathering and writing up material bearing on the activities of a segment of a university, such as the university hospital, or a single department, such as an educational assessment center. Those who come to such positions with a background in English tend to feel that it is far from wasted, as several information specialists point out in chapter 9.

Instructional designer. This position involves working with a teacher, a museum director, or some other expert in a subject field (usually in the sciences or the social sciences) who needs technical assistance in presenting information clearly and forcefully to a wide public. Together they plan slide or tape programs, videorecordings, displays, maps, charts, brochures, syllabi, public service announcements, or patient education handouts. The instructional designer recommends the most appropriate format for a given project, develops budgets and timelines, consults with the author(s) of the material to develop specific learning objectives, writes or extensively edits scripts, prepares storyboards, and supervises and coordinates production. Almost all writing courses (creative, expository, or technical) can be useful in preparing for this work; so too can training and experience in graphics and in the use of audio-visual material.

Minority affairs counselor. If you have had experience working with minority groups here or overseas, and particularly if you are a member of a minority group, you might look into any minority affairs vacancy that comes up. It would help in such a position to have the writing, analytical, and speaking skills you will have developed through your work in the humanities.

Placement counselor. At the placement centers of most universities and many colleges there is a staff of several counselors in addition to the director. Usually each counselor concentrates on one or two kinds of jobs: college and university teaching and alternative positions; liberal arts and public service vocations; secondary education and library positions; primary school teaching; or scientific and technical positions. Much of the counselor's work involves skills that humanities graduate students and instructors would have had a chance to develop. As a placement counselor, you would listen to the problems of job candidates who came to your office; you would direct them to resources within the placement center, the libraries, elsewhere on your campus, or elsewhere in the community. Most of all, you would try (without assuming the role of a clinical counselor) to help applicants take advantage of resources within their own experience and education that they might have overlooked. You would write statements and reports of many kinds, correspond with candidates and employers, and evaluate the written recommendations in candidates' confidential files. Finally, you would give talks to small groups of students about the placement and job-seeking process.

If you enjoy interacting with a wide range of people, and if you find satisfaction in expressing yourself in speaking and writing even though the end product never appears in published form, you may find being a placement counselor absorbing. It can call upon nearly all the qualities you have been using in teaching, and it can help develop further many of your best energies and talents.[6]

Publications office. Most large universities have editorial and printing facilities for university publications such as catalogues, time schedules, brochures, directories, and newsletters. By working in one of these offices in any capacity, including a secretarial position, you would learn a great deal about graphics, layout, typography, printing processes, and production costs that could be extremely helpful if your ultimate goal is a job with a publishing house (see chapter 10). The same point applies to various kinds of work you might secure at a university press.

School and college relations office. Since the function of this branch of a university is to act as liaison between the university and high schools and colleges, members of its staff must be able to speak easily before groups, write reports, plan public relations, and interpret a university's requirements to students as well as to high school faculty and administrators. If you feel comfortable dealing with the extensive details of course distribution requirements, entrance requirements, and the like, you might find this work extremely interesting.

Women's programs in continuing education. These offices, increasingly common on college and university campuses, not only counsel individual women students (particularly older women who have recently returned to the campus) but act as resource centers for the vocational or personal concerns of any woman student. They also sponsor several courses in which instructors help students explore literature with an emphasis on its personal impact, or study history from a feminist perspective. There are several opportunities for people with graduate work in English or history here, and more resource centers for women are opening up, under different names, in four-year and two-year colleges.

On the whole, there are several elements of your humanities undergraduate, graduate school, or teaching background that could be applicable to various staff positions. First, your information-gathering and interpreting techniques, even though originally designed for other materials, can be useful here. Second, your writing ability will be extremely helpful. You can write clearly and concisely, help others to do this, and compose reports, policy statements, and news releases.

Moreover, if you have been a teacher, you will have learned to talk easily before groups of people in class, as well as with individuals who come to your office hoping that you will solve their problems. Finally, you will have learned, through regular conferences with students, how to offer information and to explore alternatives with others, while at the same time leaving the problem-solving initiative to the students themselves. It is this tightrope that all student service counselors and many other university staff members must always walk.

To apply for such positions, you must be sure to look at the staff employment bulletin or its equivalent on your campus the day it comes out, each time it appears. After finding out where the vacancies are, you are ready for the routine of making an application, as outlined in chapter 4.

You may, it is true, sometimes find a few positions with rather fluid job descriptions and less formal rites of entry. "Temporary" positions for instance, or innovative or newly funded ones, may from time to time be filled simply because someone in authority has administrative needs that he or she finds you are qualified to help meet.

Many persons with B.A.'s or advanced degrees in English, history, modern languages, and other humanities fields have found personal satisfaction in holding a staff job.[7] It can be interesting to see from a new vantage point how a college or university works. It can be satisfying to feel that you have some hand in carrying out policy and representing an institution to the public. It is also instructive to join the eight-to-five world in which most people outside of college teaching live and work. And, once you are on the staff of a college or university, you are apt to hear easily about other openings to which you can move. Professionally, the main advantage is probably that some of this experience will help qualify you for a wider spectrum of subsequent positions in college administration, business, government agencies, or publishing.

In considering a staff position, remember that it's hard to guess from outside at the satisfactions and frustrations of any work. Your attitude will probably change after you get started. Bear in mind, too, that a position could be wrong for you at one stage of your life and right at another. The following two examples of history Ph.D.'s in administrative posts at the University of Washington illustrate these points.

"THE LAST PLACE I'D PLANNED TO WORK":
ANTOINETTE WILLS

Currently, I work in the dental school at the university, in Continuing Education. This is about the last place I'd planned to work. I have a B.A. from Vassar College, an M.A. from the University of Chicago, and a Ph.D. from the University of Washington—all in European history.

In graduate school, I planned to teach. But by the time I had been out for three years, I saw that my various jobs (freelance writing, teaching occasional courses in Women's Studies, and writing grant proposals for nonprofit organizations) were all short-term and unreliable as sources of income. I saw two choices ahead of me: to keep on with what I was doing and have my mind full of interesting thoughts as I stood in the checkout line at the supermarket, or to get a "real" job and have money to pay for the groceries when I reached the end of the line. It seemed time for a real job.

I did not find my present position; it found me. I finally got on the right list [in the University Staff Employment Office]—Conference Coordinator II—and was sent to interview for the job. The people interviewing me did not know I had a Ph.D. until the end of the interview. This was fortunate; so many employers automatically think every Ph.D. has a chip on the shoulder that I'd begun to feel that my doctorate was a drawback.

My job has two parts: logistical coordination (arranging for instructors, participants, registration, classrooms, audio-visual equipment, course handouts, and the like) and publicity (making sure that the target audience knows what is available). I put together newsletters, descriptive brochures, and news releases, plus answering queries by phone and letter. Frankly, I have so much work to do every day that I never have time to consider whether I'm bored.

Nonetheless, at first I did feel bitter. It is very painful not to be able to work at what you want to do. When I run into my former fellow graduate students, I see this pain on their faces. Sometimes we avoid each other. I ascribe this to a feeling of failure. Even though I know I didn't fail, the job market did.

[The above comment was written in March 1980; eight months later, Wills wrote a postscript.]

I have now been in my position for more than a year. I remain in the dental school, and I am beginning to feel contented. I have been given increased responsibility: now I have complete charge of planning and following through on all the information dissemination for programs. I've redesigned the brochures, devised a master printing plan and mailing schedule six months ahead of courses, and been given a great deal of discretion in shaping the marketing and the public image of the program. I also supervise the staff who do the routine things I did when I began, so my work is now responsibility-oriented rather than task-oriented. First I had to learn the job. Because I was good at it, the job grew and I was promoted with it.

I plan to continue working here, not only because I like this position but because of the university environment. I can take various classes free at the university, such as the accounting course I signed up for so as to see whether I wanted to go on for an M.B.A. Best of all is having informal access to people who share and encourage my academic interests. It is only a short walk to the Faculty Club to have lunch with people who are teaching. I have been invited to speak on women's history to public groups and to a women studies class. I chose to speak on my favorite section of the course I gave—on Renaissance women. I enjoyed the lecture. My dissertation has been published, and I have begun to think about writing a historical novel. I am making progress on the book, but do not have to worry about writing it to please a tenure committee; I can please myself. I have also been invited to teach my course on women's history again, through evening credit classes.

So gradually I have come back to being able to pursue my academic interests in an academic environment. Being on campus has made all the difference. I find that I am not really jealous of people who have full-time teaching positions because I can pursue my academic interests so purely.

There are no required classes I have to teach, no committees, not as many papers or exams to grade. I have managed a compromise that allows me to entertain myself intellectually while standing in line at the Safeway, and to pay for the groceries when I reach the cashier.[8]

"A Bureaucrat Who Is an Historian, or Vice Versa If You Prefer": MACLYN BURG

I am Administrative Assistant, Department of History. I am heavily involved in all manner of support services for the department: course scheduling, room assignments, bulletin and catalogue copy, time scheduling; faculty, staff, and student payroll matters; office management, departmental budgets; statistical analysis and compilation, not to mention the moving of offices, ordering, purchasing, and numerous other duties, some of which, in the first few months, I discovered devolved upon me only when the deadline had passed.

My previous experience includes Army service; nine years as a junior high and senior high school teacher; several years' summer school teaching at this university. Subsequently in the Eisenhower Library, Abilene, Kansas, I served for nine years as Historian and Head, Eisenhower Oral History Project. My work required research into Eisenhower's career, oral history interviews with selected people, editing of oral history transcripts, and supervising a staff, including a couple of other Ph.D.'s.

I first faced the issue of alternative employment in 1969, when it became clear to many of us that our Ph.D.'s in history were not in great demand. I refused a university teaching position so as to accept the one in the Eisenhower Library, which I think was a good choice for me then. About two years ago it became clear to my wife and me that we had to return to the Pacific Northwest to take care of our parents. Having reoriented our lives twice before, we had come to have confidence in ourselves and in our ability to meet challenges.

When the opportunity came to serve as administrative assistant in the department where I had taken my degree, it was most welcome. But this second sally of mine into the realms of alternative employment does call for some caveats, if my experience is to be of any use to other Ph.D.'s considering nonteaching jobs. My wife and I were quite free to give up our positions in Kansas, since we did not have to consider our children; they were grown up. Second, we were returning to familiar ground and to our native state. And, having sold our house in Abilene at a profit and drawn out our federal retirement, we could accept somewhat lower salaries than we otherwise would have. It also helped that my wife could return to her former staff job at the university. Since I have proved to myself that I can teach, I am not unduly frustrated not to be teaching now. Moreover, I think *that my own articles on oral history, my positions in the Oral History Association, and my being selected to chair the oral history session at the XV International Congress of Historical Sciences (Bucharest, 1980) demonstrate to others as well as to me that I have made and am continuing to make a contribution to historical scholarship.*

I would say that if someone feels a strong urge to teach and has never had a chance to prove himself, perhaps he should not apply for a campus administrative position at the beginning of his career. There are, however, several advantages to a position such as mine. Administrative assistants soon learn the inner workings of a university's administrative machinery, which could be most useful to those wishing to pursue a career in this realm. I think, too, that people like me, who have both taught and worked as public historians, have special qualifications that make us valuable to history departments. We have competency in archival science, oral history, or what have you; and we are also bureaucrats to some degree, because we have had to supervise our staffs. Our competencies permit the department to offer courses which it might not otherwise be able to offer without hiring additional staff. (Since my return, I have taught a summer school course in oral history and in the Eisenhower years, and given a guest lecture on Eisenhower in a course on the American presidency.) The department gets a full-fledged bureaucrat who is an historian, or vice versa if you prefer.[9]

Holders of advanced degrees tend to worry, sometimes with reason, about being or seeming overqualified for the kinds of work discussed in this chapter. These accounts from Wills and Burg suggest, however, that some of you with advanced degrees may find university staff positions satisfying because of rather than in spite of the resources you bring to them.

8. Freelance Editing

The good copy-editor is a rare creature: he is an intelligent reader and a tactful and sensitive critic; he cares enough about perfection of detail to spend his working hours checking small points of consistency in someone else's work, but he has the judgment not to waste . . . time or antagonize the author by making unnecessary changes.
—Judith Butcher, *Copy-editing*

"I think I'd like to get into editing—maybe freelance editing. How can I get started?"

Obviously, nearly all readers of this book will have done some editing, without even thinking of it as such, in meeting the emergencies of academic life. When you compose a résumé, a term paper, or a job application letter, you probably scrutinize your words carefully to see that they're coherent and well organized, then proofread to catch inconsistencies and typos. When a friend writes a paper, he is apt to thrust it at you with the query, "Could you just read it over and see whether it looks O.K.?" Particularly if you're an English major or graduate student or teacher, you may find yourself editing for friends and relatives who think that you are necessarily a good editor by virtue of your major subject.

But are you? If not, how much more do you have to know, how much better do you have to be, in order to serve as a freelance editor who is paid for using your skill?

Because the word "editing" is used in so many different ways, this question can have no single neat answer. In sorting out the various editorial functions it is useful to keep in mind a distinction made by the University of Chicago *Manual of Style* between two stages of the editorial process: "substantive editing" and "mechanical editing."[1] (The distinction is somewhat arbitrary, as the same person frequently does both substantive and mechanical editing while working on a manuscript.) The author who has just completed the manuscript of a book or an article is often too close to it to judge it objectively. It usually needs attention from a trained editor who considers the content—the substance—and looks closely to see whether the author has made the best possible presentation of it to a reader. Such a person, sometimes called a "manuscript editor," a "substantive editor," a "line editor," or often simply an editor, may suggest among other things that the author delete repetitious passages, clarify obscure ones, reorganize an illogically presented argument, or make transitions more explicit.

Occasionally, if the author is still too closely involved with the manuscript to perform the necessary surgery, the editor will do the actual cutting or reorganizing. But caution is essential. As the *Chicago Manual* points out: "The editor will know by instinct and learn from experience when and how much of this kind of editing to do on a particular manuscript. An experienced editor will never inflict his own way of writing on an author who has a quite different style. . . . Since every manuscript is unique in the amount and kind of substantive editing desirable, no rules can be devised for the editor to follow." [2]

If you are an experienced teacher, and one who has read widely enough to appreciate the enormous variety of effective writing styles, substantive editing may come naturally. Even so, you would do well to keep in mind the practice and precepts of one of the best-known editors in American publishing, Maxwell Perkins. Although Perkins was not, of course, a freelance editor—having served on the staff of Scribner's for all of his thirty-seven years of editing—his respectful attitude toward his authors' writing is important for all editors to consider. His letters to Ernest Hemingway, Scott Fitzgerald, Thomas Wolfe, and other authors abound in specific suggestions. [3] These were, however, always made tentatively, deferentially. Any teacher used to taking a dictatorial attitude when commenting on students' papers might well, before setting up as a manuscript editor, ponder Perkins's editorial philosophy. Writing to Ray Stannard Baker, for example, in a letter crammed with constructive queries, Perkins points out that all his suggestions are provisional ones: "I know that the author, of course, best knows his book and that suggestions can only be valuable to him as showing how a reader, if he understands the author's purpose, reacts to it." [4]

Substantive editing, then, by whatever name, is an art. Without romanticizing this kind of editing as did the nineteenth-century critic Hippolyte Taine, who called the great editor an artist whose medium is the work of other men, [5] you can nonetheless see that substantive editing—involving as it does content and basic organization—calls for tact and for considerable experience in reading, in writing, and in dealing with people.

"Mechanical editing," the Chicago *Manual's* second stage of editing, may be a somewhat misleading term, for the kinds of editing it covers—copy editing, proofreading, and production editing—involve more than mechanically applying fixed rules. But there is a certain validity in this label, in that the various kinds of mechanical editing center on preparing a manuscript for the printer.

The copy editor is basically concerned with consistency and style—style in the sense of publishing-house style (as in the Chicago *Manual of Style*) rather than in the sense of literary style (as in Strunk and White's *Elements of Style*).[6] He or she focuses on grammar, punctuation, usage, spelling, capitalization, and many other seemingly small matters. These minutiae are cumulatively important in determining whether a reader of the finished book or article will be irritated by nagging annoyances or free to concentrate on the author's ideas.

The copy editor's job calls for much more than correcting what is wrong or awkward; it often involves choosing from several equally "correct" alternatives according to the preferred "style" (of capitalization, use of headings, and punctuation, for example) of the firm or journal that will be publishing the manuscript. If the copy editor is working with an author on a manuscript not yet accepted, it is best to choose as a model either an authoritative work in the same field or the style sheet of one of that field's leading journals.

The copy editor must also be on the alert for inaccuracies in names, dates, and facts. (Here *nothing* should be taken for granted. A beginning copy editor, given a list of names to check that includes "Elizabeth Blumfiel, Elisabeth Braun, Arther Ferrill, Vickey Hansen, Cherie Martyn, and Gary McGlocklin," might hastily check the spelling of the part of each name offering two obvious alternatives and assume the other part is correct. Or a neophyte copy editor might not realize that W. Orville Mattson, M.D., whose name appears in the table of contents of a collection of medical articles is the same person as Wesley O. Mattson, M.D., Ph.D., whose name appears 300 pages later at the head of the last article in the book.)

In addition to checking such details, the copy editor's job sometimes includes preparing the corrected manuscript so that it is completely ready for the book designer and the printer. In doing so, the copy editor must identify and mark chapter headings and subheads, deciding with the author or editor how many "orders of subheads" there should be and checking to see that they are in grammatically parallel form. The copy editor must also mark quotations from other authors, tables, captions for illustrations, and charts so that the designer can choose for them type different from but harmonious with that of the main text, and the printer will see exactly where he is to use each typeface. The copy editor's job may also include seeing that a book's "front matter" and "back matter" are in order.

Those of you seriously interested in learning to edit copy will find invaluable specific information in Carol O'Neill's and Avima Ruder's *Complete Guide to Editorial Freelancing*; Howard Greenfield's *Books: From Writer to Reader*; Judith Butcher's *Copy-Editing: The Cambridge Handbook*; the Chicago *Manual of Style*; and *Words into Type*. You may also be interested in looking at and perhaps subscribing to a freelance editors' newsletter, *The Editorial Eye*, which appears fifteen times yearly in an eight-page format, containing articles on usage, jargon, editing, indexing, and markets for freelancers, as well as self-administered editorial and proofreading tests.[7] Needless to say, it won't help as much simply to pore over this material as it will to begin editing a manuscript and deciding how best to apply the precepts you have studied.

Proofreading, another component of the mechanical editing process, is called for at several stages of manuscript preparation. After the copy-edited manuscript has gone to the printer, it comes back in galleys (if it is typeset), and the author, whose labors are ideally supplemented by a professional proofreader, must proofread these galleys line by line to see that all copy-editing corrections have been incorporated and no errors introduced. After the galleys have been returned to the printer, who will next make corrections and prepare page proofs, a final proofreading is necessary.

If, instead of being typeset by a printer, a manuscript is to be typed for camera-ready reproduction, some stages of proofreading come earlier and are even more critical. The copy editor must proofread the scanner or camera-ready copy, then proofread any corrections made, and if necessary proofread once more to see that the corrections of the corrections have been made. After that, he or she must check the "bluelines" which the printer should supply on request. That is the last chance for correction before publication.[8]

Once the page proofs have been read and are in the hands of author or copy editor, an index can be made. Most nonfiction books benefit from being indexed; it is obvious that readers find them easier to use for reference; and, what is less generally realized, libraries are more apt to buy indexed books than nonindexed ones.[9] Indexing, although a specialty in its own right, is a step in book production that a freelancer often undertakes. At first it may appear deceptively simple to index a scholarly book of about three hundred pages. The equipment is minimal: page proofs from the printer, several packs of 3 by 5 file cards and alphabetical dividers, a large table on which to spread out and classify the entries as you make them, a typewriter, and a copy of Sina Spiker's pamphlet, *Indexing Your Book*, or of the section on indexing in the Chicago *Manual*.[10] But in addition you will need excellent eyesight, continuous time (your full working days for about a week), patience, and unflappable nerves.

Despite the fact that indexing involves multitudes of small decisions and that the indexer is always faced with a publisher's deadline, such work offers certain challenges and satisfactions. And enough people have taken it up as a professional specialty that there is now an American Society of Indexers, with its quarterly journal, its annual meeting, and a membership of several hundred.[11]

There is one other phase of mechanical editing that the copy editor should know as much as possible about: production editing. Typically, the production editor—who works with the book designer, compositor, printer, and binder, helping decide on the kind and weight of paper to be used, the various combinations of typefaces, and the kind and quality of illustrations—is part of the publishing firm. But as a freelancer working for an individual author or for an institution publishing a report or a newsletter, you may find yourself the liaison between your client and a printing company. Particularly in view of the increasing use of new electronic equipment that can produce camera-ready copy in fewer steps than with the traditional hot-type method, a magazine editor has recently declared that "we don't have the [former] clear distinction between editorial and production." The publishing process is "tending to [involve] a group which can do everything."[12]

Editorial freelancers, working as they do sometimes for publishers, sometimes for institutions or government agencies, and sometimes for individual authors, do all five editing-related jobs discussed above: substantive editing, copy editing, indexing, proofreading, and occasionally production editing.

Some freelance copy editors work for publishers mainly or exclusively. Although most publishing companies have staff members who do the bulk of their copy editing and proofreading, many of the larger houses also have a list of freelancers on call. In this way the publishers save money by having extra part-time staff available at peak seasons; moreover, they have a large talent pool representing various fields of special knowledge.[13]

Working with an individual author (usually before the acceptance of his or her manuscript for publication) provides a greater variety of editorial functions and more personal contacts than working for a publisher. Authors hire editors at every conceivable stage of their writing, from serving as midwife at the birth of an idea they can't quite get down on paper to making and proofreading an index. (One Los Angeles ex-English teacher, Nancy Kuriloff, appeared in a 1980 *Time* article because of her unorthodox but effective methods of helping blocked authors, inexperienced and published alike, start writing once more.)[14]

Of the many kinds of writers who frequently call upon editors, scientists are among the most challenging to work for. If you have been an English or modern language major, scientific writing may seem remote from the kind of writing you have done: you may even feel that it is alien to you. Some of the terms may seem formidable; the pattern of organization often prescribed by scientific journals may strike you as restrictive; and the way references are often cited comes as a surprise to those used to the *MLA Style Sheet*.

In short, you may feel that as a nonscientist you cannot do scientific editing. Before dismissing the possibility, however, you should realize that very few of today's successful scientific and medical editors have had a major or minor in science as undergraduates or an advanced degree in science. Most of them learned on the job, supplementing their general editing expertise in some cases with courses in technical writing and editing. Although obviously the more you know about a subject the better you can edit articles dealing with it, do not underestimate the contribution you can make by reading the work of your biologist, psychiatrist, or surgeon client as an intelligent nonspecialist. At the same time, if you do have a scientific background as well as an interest in writing and editing, you may be in particular demand as an editor.

As you get further into scientific editing and come upon criticism by scientists themselves of much current medical and scientific writing—such as critiques in *The New England Journal of Medicine* by Michael Crichton, M.D., and Saul Radovsky, M.D.[15]—you will find that these scientists tend to pounce on the same writing problems that you have met elsewhere and that Strunk and White deal with in *The Elements of Style*: wordiness, jargon, faulty reference, poor organization, overuse of passive verbs and abstract nouns, and lack of consideration for the reader. What is more, you will find that the best guides to scientific writing, such as the *Council of Biology Editors Style Manual*, Woodford's *Scientific Writing for Graduate Students*, H. J. Tichy's *Effective Writing for Engineers, Managers, Scientists*, and Robert Day's *How to Write and Publish a Scientific Paper*,[16] tend to back up the position of Strunk and White and therefore presumably your own editorial comments.

Of course, not all your clients will be scientists. Some will be urban planners, health care planners, sociologists, educators, or other professionals whose inflated use of our language has been so skillfully criticized by Edwin Newman and others. These specialists live, Newman complains, in "a world in which things that are good for society are positive externalities and things that are bad are negative externalities, in which unemployment is classified as an adverse social consequence . . . rationing becomes end-use allocation, stressful situations arise in the nuclear or matrifocal family, and people in minigroups or, if the shoe fits, maxigroups are in a state of cognitive inertia because self-actualization is lacking." [17]

Fortunately, many professional people caught up in jargon like that have begun to realize that their writing needs help. And a good editor can help—not only with an individual manuscript but also with long-term writing problems. [18] In working with scientists, educators, or members of other professions, you may attract other clients from a wide variety of backgrounds with a wide range of needs. "An editor," as Helen Taylor of the Viking Press points out, "is a plastic surgeon to books by 'unprofessional' writers. Book writing these days, unlike a century ago, isn't limited to people trained in literary matters. Let someone devise a new way of erecting chicken houses, or let him live six months in a Persian village, and the result is a book—full of facts, true—but not always too well written. That's where the editor comes in." [19]

Another group of potential clients consists of graduate students. As Barbara Reitt, an Atlanta editor, points out, graduate students have too often gravitated toward their specialized fields without much instruction in the kind of writing on which their future professional lives will depend; once in graduate school, they may receive intensive training in research methods, yet none in how to present that research effectively. [20] The editor who works with these graduate students on the organization, conciseness, and clarity of their writing can perform a much-needed service. Of course, a freelance editor working with a graduate student on a thesis or dissertation *before* it has been accepted by a graduate degree committee should make a point of clearing the fact and the scope of this assistance with the student's major professor. It is essential for editors to dissociate themselves from the infamous "thesis factories" which during the past few years have sprung up in many university towns.

There are, however, several situations in which a professor may quite legitimately say to a master's or doctoral candidate, "You've done a good job of collecting the material, and you've written a draft that shows you've done the research. But for heaven's sakes, get yourself an editor to tell you how to reorganize it, how to make it less wordy, how to make it readable." Quite often in such cases, English is not the student's native language; sometimes he or she has clogged the beginning section with a seemingly endless review of the literature; sometimes the whole draft is wordy and meandering. A freelancer can helpfully step in when the graduate student's problems are those of expository writing—difficulties which professors in a good many academic fields consider they have neither the time nor the expertise to help the student solve. On the whole, it more often seems legitimate for a graduate student in the social or natural sciences to get editorial help on a thesis or dissertation than it does for a graduate student in the humanities, fields in which learning to write well is considered part of one's professional responsibility. *After* a thesis or dissertation has been accepted for a degree, however, there is seldom an ethical problem involved in giving editorial assistance to a researcher in any field who wishes to revise a manuscript for article or book publication.

GETTING A START

Granted that there is in theory a wide range of possible clients, you may wonder just how to get started as a freelance editor actually employed by any of them. Since freelance editing is not a profession that requires examination, certification, or licensing, it is sometimes hard to know at what point you can consider yourself a "real" editor. You may be interested therefore in comparing your qualifications and expectations with those of thirty-four representative freelancers listed among 307 entries in Section 32, "Free-Lance Editorial Services," in the 1980 edition of the *Literary Market Place*.[21] This information came from a survey I made in September, 1980, of fifty-four freelance editorial firms or individual editors listed in the *LMP*. From the thirty-four usable replies to my questionnaire, some evidence emerges as to the kind of academic education and job experience successful freelancers tend to have, as well as the way they learned editing, the kinds of editing they do and the kinds of clients they do it for, the problems arising in their work, the way they set their fees, the highs and lows of freelance editing as they see them, and the advice they have for readers of this book. Before considering the results of the whole questionnaire, however, you may find it helpful to read a few profiles of individual editors derived from their questionnaire responses.

EDITOR-AUTHOR-TEACHER:
MAX KNIGHT and JOSEPH FABRY

Max Knight and his colleague Joseph Fabry have since the 1940s run an editorial service in Berkeley, California, called Pacific Features. Knight has studied political science, and they each hold Ph.D.'s in law. "We were both first freelance writers for newspapers and magazines" he says, and "later both became university staff editors. From there it was not far to do free-lance editing on the side." Their business involves substantive editing, copy editing, and indexing, mainly for academic clients. Having learned to edit on the job, Knight has taught an editing class at the University of California for some years. The two partners are, between them, authors of over twenty books, and take pride in having "three hundred edited books on the shelf." Being established in the academic-editing world, Knight and Fabry do not have to advertise: "We have a fairly steady flow of work because we are well introduced." Nonetheless, there are ups and downs in the demand: "sometimes there's no pressure, sometimes two deadlines at the same time."

Having recently retired from their university editing posts, Knight and his partner are able to work at their freelance business full time. As Knight looks back, he doesn't see that he would do anything differently if he were starting over now. "Aim high," he advises those who want to get into edit-ing. "Learn to be a craftsman and real expert in your field. Pursue the philosophy of Webster's Second Edition, scorn the Third. Decide on good style and stick with it. It is the inner security that makes a good editor."

EDITOR-WRITER-PHOTOGRAPHER, "A ONE-MAN BAND":
EDYTHE CLARK

"I always wanted to be a writer, so I went into publishing," admits Edythe Clark, who by herself runs and staffs the Brave Soul Editorial Ser-vices, Hinsdale, New Hampshire. After graduating from Beaver College in Pennsylvania with a B.A. in English and studying graphic arts for a year in Philadelphia, she became a proofreader for a book manufacturer, which, she says, "exposed me to the varying editorial styles of New York publishers." Within several years she had worked her way up to a senior editorship with a Philadelphia book publisher, where she stayed three years, "fascinated by the intricacies of the craft of writing, the business of writing." Yet, "increasingly disillusioned by the office politics," she

thought that "*freelancing seemed an attractive alternative and I'd made, or thought I'd made, enough of the all-important contacts to succeed. Naïvely enough, I embarked on a freelance career by moving out of the city to a rural area. After I'd made the move, I found [some] publishers unwilling to send manuscripts so far away.*" But, charmed by New Hampshire, and discovering that she enjoyed working with individual authors to clarify their writing even more than copy editing manuscripts sent by publishers, she has stayed in Hinsdale for the past eight years.

Now she spends about half her time as a freelancer—writing, editing, copy editing, or doing photographic assignments—and the other half taking miscellaneous jobs, whether related to her editorial skills or not (anything from picking asparagus to doing pasteup or proofreading for a large book manufacturer). "*It's a great life if you don't need lots of money,* she says, "*and if you value a flexible schedule.*"

Yet, despite low earnings, she finds satisfaction in freelancing—as when working with the author of what has turned out to be a much acclaimed work of science fiction, or when "*turning a weak manuscript around in a direction that gives it strength.*"

Clark's work week includes a wide range of activity. "*Two days of every week I spend at the office of a national magazine, editing, proofreading, and writing for their monthly issue. I rarely take weekends off, working seven days, whether at night, during the day, or very early in the morning. If I have a lengthy (600 manuscript page) book manuscript, I work with few breaks, to keep continuity. If I'm working on a story or on assignment, most of my time is devoted to that. It is a peculiar, fascinating existence. I'm a one-man band and I love it and I also hate it.*"

Freelancer for Government Agencies and Academia: Barbara Reitt

In 1965, Barbara Reitt's husband's move from North Carolina to Georgia took her away from the Duke University Press, where she had worked happily for three years as a copy editor. Hoping somehow to carry on a career connected with publishing, Reitt felt challenged to see what she could find in Atlanta that would make use of her background (an A.B. and an M.A. in English).

Fortunately, she soon decided to start a one-woman editorial firm, the Reitt Editing Service, Inc., which has grown and flourished. She now works at it "nearly full time," and makes more money than she would if she had stayed on as a university press copy editor. She also teaches a course in editing to humanities graduate students at Emory University.

Reitt's work is divided between copy editing and substantive editing; her clients are both government agencies and academics. A "typical" week, she estimates, begins with four days working in her office (a large room over her garage, with a separate business phone), where she spends seven to eight hours a day, blue pencil in hand. Then comes one day spent on "client conferences, library errands, or research, accounting and letter-writing or other chores to keep the business itself tended to."

Although she is not happy about what she sees as her "isolation from other editors and lack of formal advancement or significant rise in responsibility," in other respects she enjoys her work thoroughly. Particularly she likes helping young academics with the writing of their dissertations and their first articles, and by teaching them in her editing class. She says that she welcomes the chance to teach new scholars how to write and how to prepare [their] manuscripts professionally: "Their acceptances by scholarly journals make me feel like a million."

Reitt, who plans to take the prelims for her own Ph.D. in American studies in 1981, points out in an article, "The Editor Turns Teacher," in the journal Scholarly Publishing that "the graduate student is seldom offered the chance to practice the skills so badly needed in the production of publishable work: skill in seeking the advice of peers, in evaluating the advice received, and in putting the advice to work in arduous revision." Accordingly in 1978 Reitt asked the Institute of the Liberal Arts of the Graduate School of Arts and Sciences at Emory University for permission to develop and teach a graduate course that would prepare students for their future roles as authors. In the resulting ten-week course, which she teaches each spring, students edit and rewrite their own and one another's articles. Moreover, they learn how scholarly journals operate and they begin to develop criteria for submitting their own articles to appropriate journals.[22]

"Editing is something I learned in a publishing office, not in class as an English major. I can't emphasize that enough. Literary appreciation and editing just aren't the same." Reitt's final advice to those who want to become editors: "Love (and know) the English language, love detailed and orderly work, and be prepared to cope with pressure when deadlines stack up."

FROM TEACHER TO GRANT WRITER TO EDITOR:
ELLEN ASHDOWN

Another freelancer, a Tallahassee woman with an M.A. and a Ph.D. in English, also does both copy editing and substantive editing. Ellen Ashdown has just begun to do the former for publishers. Her individual clients are mainly academics. She founded her business in the spring of 1978, when her humanities teaching position ended. "I had had grant writing experience," she explains, and "since I was already getting unsolicited requests for editing, I decided to take the jump." She learned to edit, she says, partly through college teaching, partly by teaching herself the mechanics of copy editing; but mainly, she says, "I learned to edit by learning to write."

Currently, she reports, "approximately half of my income is from writing: magazine articles and reviews, grant proposals, brochures, advertising copy. In the last two weeks I have edited a paper for a professor of social work (four hours), copy edited a book for Prentice-Hall (about 25 hours), edited three chapters of a dissertation (six-plus hours), written a sales booklet for a real estate developer (9 hours—1½ days) and have written a few business letters for a friend who owns a foundry."

She urges those getting started in editing to approach major publishers, which she hasn't done until recently. She hopes to continue to expand her business, "to develop steady clients, and to find a way to get state and federal contracts."

Founder of a Large-Scale Comprehensive Editorial Service: Laura Horowitz

In May 1972, Editorial Experts began operations in the Washington, D.C. area. Specializing in education, government, consumer, and urban/community affairs, the firm provides writing, editing, research, indexing, proofreading, manuscript typing, and consulting services to associations, government agencies, schools and universities, publishers, researchers, and authors.

The founder, Laura Horowitz, was at the time a twenty-nine-year-old freelance writer-editor-researcher who, with a B.A. in government from the University of Chicago and an M.A. from American University, Washington, had held a variety of administrative and PR jobs in the area since 1964. Her plan was to assemble teams of experienced freelance specialists, drawing on both professional freelance journalists and "that great underused pool of talent—college-educated housewife-mothers."

For several years, while working as public information specialist at Federal City College in Washington and later as director of public relations for the mayor's Economic Development Committee, Horowitz had been talking with women colleagues about setting up a writing and consulting group. In 1971 she decided to go ahead by herself. After taking a tax course for small businesses offered through the Fairfax County Public Schools' adult education program and a one-day "prebusiness workshop" conducted by the local chapter of the Service Corps of Retired Executives (SCORE), she felt ready to do the organizational work, which took several months. For financing, she used several thousand dollars left her by her grandmother.

Now, eight years later, the firm has about thirty full-time, core staff members and some 250 freelancers organized by skill and location into project teams. EEI tries to match workers to projects according to skill and subject experience.

During its first eight years of operation, EEI has successfully completed more than three thousand projects for more than three hundred clients, including federal agencies, consulting firms, associations, and individual authors. In addition to its original seven services, it now has four others: a "temporary editorial service" (in which editors and others go out to work in clients' offices on assignments that last from a few days to a year); training in editorial skills; word processing; and publications. These last include a production typing manual, proofreading training and reference books, and the newsletter, The Editorial Eye, which has been appearing since 1978.

As for the frustrations and satisfactions of starting and running such an extensive editorial service, Horowitz mentions a few of the former: even though EEI grosses several hundred thousand dollars a year, there is sometimes a cash flow problem. And, despite stringent entrance requirements for new members, there is occasionally a quality control problem too, Horowitz says—as when "some new person doesn't follow directions, making me stay up all night to redo her work." But, to the founder of EEI, the satisfactions are greater than the problems: not only her newsletters and the books, articles, and press releases she has written herself, but "acquiring (and earning) a reputation for quality work on 'impossible' deadlines."

If she were starting her business over again now, what would she do differently? "Not much—except charge more." Advice to those hoping to start freelancing? "Plan ahead." [23]

These five editors—Knight, Clark, Ashdown, Reitt, and Horowitz —all take professional pride in what they do, and they all see freelance editing as a reasonable way to make a living, a way that they enjoy and plan to continue. When their responses are taken together with those of the twenty-nine other freelance editors who returned my recent questionnaire, it becomes possible to answer at least tentatively the questions most often asked about freelance editing.

What is the best way to learn editing?

Being a major or graduate student in English, or a teacher of it, can give you a good start toward editing competency through your interest in the use of words, the expression of ideas, and the process of writing and revising. The majority of freelance editors in my sample (twenty out of twenty-nine answering this question) were English majors, of whom six had gone on for master's degrees in English and four for Ph.D.'s.

Nonetheless, the academic study of English is hardly a prerequisite for editing—twelve editors in the survey majored in one of the social sciences, in a modern language, or in journalism, and the same number held advanced degrees in one of these other fields—nor is it a guarantee of editing skill. The questionnaire responses bring out clearly the majority opinion that although an editor benefits from exposure to good writing, he or she must also be sensitive to minute details of usage, format, and typography. "Knowledge of editorial style," as Laura Horowitz tells her class in copy editing at George Washington University, "is what distinguishes the copy editor from the English teacher."[24] Such an editor must, in short, see such works as the Chicago *Manual of Style* and *Words into Type* as sources not of rules for nitpicking but of useful conventions which, when observed, keep the reader from being distracted and irritated by small inconsistencies. As Martha Ellis, a freelancer in Sequim, Washington, says: "Editing requires a certain type of mind—one that can attend strictly to the most minute detail, yet see the overall organizational picture of a piece of work, and can restructure it if necessary. In addition, one must have some knowledge of the subjects with which one will be working, and of the myriad technicalities of scientific editing if one plans to do it. One must also keep up with the constant changes in 'correct' style."

The best way to become familiar with these matters, most freelancers believe, is as an employee of a commercial publisher, a university press, a newspaper, a printing company, or a periodical. A majority of the freelancers (twenty-three out of thirty-four) report having done this, some for as long as twenty-three years, some for only one, before starting out as freelancers. For obvious reasons they recommend such work as the best possible training in editing: as a regular staff member, you are given guidelines and supervision; you learn something of the wide variety of equally correct practices, and you see how the choice of a particular one depends on the medium, the subject, the client, and often production considerations. Since you have a constant series of deadlines, you learn to make hundreds of minor editorial decisions rapidly without too much worry. And since there are usually experienced editors around, you can consult them when you run into a seemingly insoluble problem.

Not all would-be freelancers, however, are fortunate enough to have had such experience. Therefore O'Neill and Ruder suggest: "If your work experience does not include anything even remotely connected with editing, you might get unpaid experience as a volunteer on a local newspaper or an organization newsletter."[25] Be sure, urges

Laura Horowitz, to "volunteer long enough to get some clippings and by-lines. Be picky. Choose a good publication and a good mentor." [26]

Of course there are other ways of learning editorial skills. Since almost a third of the freelancers queried are published writers as well as editors, it is hardly surprising that ten respondents concurred with the Florida editor who "learned to edit by learning to write." Although some editors take the hard line that being a writer may tempt an editor into too much idiosyncratic rewriting of a client's prose,[27] many think otherwise. A Midwestern editor, E. R. Cole of Whiting, Indiana, disagrees strongly. His advice to editors is this: "Immerse yourself in the best writing of the past and present—and then write yourself. Reading and writing are like inhaling and exhaling—no editor can survive long without them."

Other ways of learning to edit consist of taking specialized courses in editing, technical editing, and graphics. Eight freelancers mentioned these enthusiastically; of these, one had recently taken the Radcliffe College annual intensive summer course in publishing procedures (see chapter 10). Five others mentioned college journalism as helpful. Five got their start by working on college newspapers or yearbooks. Four said that they had pretty much taught themselves through reading the Chicago _Manual of Style_ and _Words into Type_, and sometimes by asking questions of a more experienced editor. One distinguished editor got her start on a long career of freelancing by serving as secretary to the editor of a scholarly journal. Of course, since hardly anyone learns editing from one source alone, many of the questionnaires credited a combination of methods. Thus Claire Connelly of Connecticut points out that "it was on-the-job training plus a degree in English plus many noncredit graphic arts courses," and Martha Ellis of Washington reports having learned through, "a few courses, a good background in English, and working for Prentice-Hall."

How does a freelancer acquire clients?

It is important to become systematic as soon as possible about seeing your editing skill as a professional activity rather than a casual favor for a friend. After you have done three or four pieces of editing for persons you know, ask whether you may use their names as references, and begin to keep copies of finished editorial work you have done. As Ashdown advises: "Begin half time. Leave no stone unturned in looking for business. When your résumé begins to look good, use it whenever you write a prospective client." Have business cards and brochures printed; distribute them to department offices of universities, to social agencies, government offices, research centers, teaching hospitals, museums—any office where research or writing goes on, or from which information is disseminated. Whenever possible, it is a good idea to write a brief note indicating your familiarity with the kind of publications the office or agency issues, and why you could be of use to them in the future.

To get copy editing sent to you by publishers, look up in the *Literary Market Place* the name of someone involved in copy editing at each publishing house to which you are applying, then write a letter of inquiry. Include a brief résumé emphasizing any special field of knowledge you have and your credentials related to editing, such as work on publications or experience teaching high school or college English. If, having also spent some time as an author's editor, you can cite several published writers for whom you have worked, you may be in a strong position to get a manuscript sent you for editing, on a trial basis. In O'Neill and Ruder's *Complete Guide* you will find a detailed yet entertaining discussion of the paths of entry, the pitfalls, and the pleasures of doing copy editing for publishers.[28]

Once you have made a start, whether in editing for publishers or for individual authors, the best sources of other editing jobs consist of personal contacts, word-of-mouth recommendations, and repeat business from satisfied customers. Such sources appeared the most important to two-thirds of the editors responding to the questionnaire. Next in order of importance came organizations with which one had some connection; last came advertising ("if discreetly and selectively used"). Geographical location, often thought of as crucial by freelancers far away from the publishing centers of New York and Boston, does not seem to be decisive in determining the volume of clients for an editing service. Several editors responding from New York City wrote of a low or intermittent supply of customers, and at the same time several editors apiece from Illinois, Wisconsin, Maine, Washington, Georgia, and Florida were keeping busy. Apparently the fact of having worked for a well-known publishing company is more important than operating from New York City.

It would seem that there are more potential clients for editors in any city or university town than one might at first realize. It is important to read daily papers and campus newspapers imaginatively, noting new research projects undertaken or public education programs funded, and then to write or call on an administrator of the project and inquire about his or her eventual need for an editor. You should try to have a portfolio of samples of your editing to leave for consideration, along with your brochure. Many agencies who would benefit from having editors simply don't realize what services are available or what editing involves. "People have funny ideas about what editors do," says Sharon Tighe of Editorial Consultants, Inc., Seattle. "We're not a monolithic computer that takes an author's prose and processes it with a steam roller so it comes out sounding as if a machine had written it. In fact it's just the opposite. People bring manuscripts that sound computerized and we help them become human and personal. A good editor senses the writer's real tone, crosses out excess verbiage, translates jargon, and helps him or her think through what audience to aim for." [29]

How do freelance editors set their fees?

This question can be difficult. Most freelancers say that they charge by the hour. This practice, however, presents problems to almost everybody—to editors who, coming from a teaching career, may feel uncomfortable at the idea of setting a cash price upon an hour of their time; to women who, editing at home, may overcompensate for occasional interruptions by charging for only ten hours when they may have spent fifteen; to very expert editors, who can work with great rapidity; and to some clients, who feel that they may be contracting in advance for untold hours of work. But somehow the hourly fee scale has become the norm. Of the twenty-one editors replying who charge this way, the rates range from a bare five dollars an hour through eight, twelve, fifteen, twenty, and twenty-five dollars an hour for editing, with fifteen to twenty the most usual. Several editors say that their charges come to a hundred dollars for a working day, and two set a hundred and twenty-five as their daily fee.

One way to clarify the question of fees with the client beforehand is to do a small sample of work, such as the first few pages or a short chapter, to tell the client how long that took to edit, and to see whether he or she is prepared to have you go ahead on that scale. Another way is to charge a flat rate per page; publishers often pay by the page when they send manuscripts to freelancers for copy editing. Still another way is to set beforehand a comprehensive fee for the entire job. Max Knight of Berkeley and his partner do it this way: "We charge strictly by the job. We even consider it unethical to charge by the hour, a system which cannot be checked and which penalizes the experienced. We look at the prospective job, then state a binding fee (not an 'estimate') to which we adhere. For an average job (so called) of, say, 300 pages, we charge from $1,000."

Probably the thing that comes hardest to the beginning editor is to hold to her or his conviction that the job of editing is a professional one, that it takes knowledge, skill, and judgment; that the editor is more than "the girl who knows where to put in the commas." Although editors know this, they may sometimes need reinforcement. As Francess Halpenny of the University of Toronto Press once remarked, "It is one of the oddities of the editorial function that it is most successful when least observed."[30] What you have to offer your clients is an invisible, intangible product. When you are dealing with clients who aren't aware of the difference editing can make in their printed material, you may have to educate them. Sometimes this can be done by showing them samples of manuscripts in three stages: first, a wordy, confusing page before it is edited; second, a photocopy of the original page, with your changes written in; and third, the final stage, after the edited version has been typed up into clean copy. (If you decide on such a demonstration, however, it's best to have a professional typist do the final copy, since you are looking for clients for your editorial rather than your typing skills.)

Should freelance editors specialize?

Some do; far more do not. Given the various possibilities of specialization—by subject matter, by type of client, or by editorial function—it is surprising that more editors don't concentrate on a single area. A few of the editors consulted do go in for subject specialization—particularly medical editing, legal material, or school science texts. Others work mainly for one or two types of client such as government agencies, academic writers, psychiatrists, or novelists. About a third of the editors responding concentrate on substantive editing, working with individual authors. Most freelance editors, however, do a wide range of editing. They like the variety, the chance to broaden their skills and contacts, and the feeling that there is hardly any kind of manuscript that they cannot somehow make better.

What are the problems and pitfalls of freelance editing?

First, there are those arising from working for publishers. Several freelancers complain that after developing a good working relationship with an author, they may lose him or her because either the author or the staff editor who sends out the copy editing may suddenly move to another publisher. Other problems in working as a freelancer for a publisher involve isolation—lack of feedback for good work done, lack of direct contact with client authors, or lack of the network of colleagues on whom most working adults depend for their social life.

Editors working directly for authors instead of publishers sometimes mention billing and payment problems. Some editors worry that editing takes more actual time (trips to pick up and deliver manuscripts, conferences with the author, and other errands) than they feel they can charge for. Others gripe about authors who "chisel lengthy free consultations over the telephone," who are slow in payment, or who claim poverty and offer, after an editor has worked for weeks on a manuscript, not the agreed-upon payment but "a percentage of the royalties if and when the book is published."

Other habits of authors, too, swell the burden of editorial complaints: overuse of jargon, excessively dull writing, or "the constant use of 'etc.' and 'and the like' to cover up their lack of knowledge." Some authors appear indecisive; others are "unaware of how long editing takes, or what a quality editing job consists of." Some seem recalcitrant; some insist on self-publishing, yet without knowing the requirements for a marketable book; others assume omniscience, arguing with the editor over each minor change. Then there are writers whose aspirations exceed their abilities, and who resist hints that they should pursue some career other than a literary one. One of the bitterest pills to swallow, a Pennsylvania freelancer reports, is when "authors erase all your good editorial work—and then the reviewers criticize that part of the book you tried to fix." In short, some freelancers feel that despite the apparent autonomy of their profession, "you are never really your own boss."

What are the satisfactions and rewards of freelance editing?

Taken as a whole, the questionnaire responses reveal more satisfactions than frustrations. Some agree with the New York City editor who says that one of her main satisfactions is "supporting myself in a style agreeable to me." In some areas of the country, editors felt underpaid, warning would-be editors, "This is a *hard* way to earn a living;" in other areas (where twenty dollars per hour is the going rate) some editors report earning from fifteen to twenty thousand dollars a year while editing only half- or two-thirds time.

Other freelancers, magnetized by anything involving publishing, write of their pleasure in playing even a small part in the making of books and the publication of articles. They like unraveling the details of indexes, footnotes, and bibliographies; they do it in the spirit in which some people do puzzles or chess problems. Another satisfaction that many editors enjoy comes from the feeling of closure they achieve in completing a long, complicated manuscript and finally seeing it emerge as a finished book. Some write of the pleasure in the recognition they have received—seeing their names in author's acknowledgments, having an index praised in a book review in the *New York Times*, or (though rarely) being favorably mentioned as a copy editor in a column in *Publishers Weekly*.

Looking at a row of volumes one has edited *is* confidence-building. Remembering the odd, messy manuscripts with which a project may have started, it is reassuring to see that one *can* make order out of chaos. As Hella Freud Bernays, a New York City freelancer, writes, "I take pleasure in doing a good job—of feeling, every time I mail a job back to a client and mark it 'First Class,' the inner satisfaction that it really *is* first class." Bernays takes pride, too, in the continuity of her clientele: one of her clients has been coming to her since 1952.

Many editors agree with Bernays that the satisfaction of building a reputation as a good editor is a very real one. Others mention how gratifying it is to see authors that they have worked hard with learn to write better and better, to the point that they have articles and books accepted, contracts offered them by good publishers, and books favorably reviewed. These editors feel something of the pleasure of the successful teacher, coach, or stage director.

Finally, even though editing itself can be a lonely job, a number of editors write of enjoying the contacts they make through it—with writers and publishers they work for, with university departments, museums, hospitals—in fact the whole gamut of public and private enterprise. As one freelancer, a former English instructor, who often goes to clients' offices to confer with authors, points out, "My life as an editor is more varied than it was as a teacher. I enjoy working for a time behind the scenes of an art museum, a biochemistry department, a state historical society, a cancer research center. It gives me an inside glimpse of many different worlds."

Obviously, whether the frustrations or the satisfactions of editing loom larger to you depends upon many factors—your temperament, your picture of yourself, your professional expectations, and whether you see editing as a stopgap job or a lifelong profession you are proud to be practicing.

But there are three current misconceptions about editing that deserve a word or two:

1. "Editing is a nice occupation if you want a moonlighting job, a first job after graduate school, a postretirement job, or if you're a housewife hoping to work at home. You can set your own schedule and keep just as busy as you want to be." One sometimes hears such a remark, but it is based on a misconception of what a freelance editor does. First, it is not true that simply because the freelance editor may work at home, on his or her own time schedule, editing is therefore done entirely at the editor's convenience and without pressure. Clients often don't realize that they need an editor until their deadline approaches; then they may try to pressure the editor into taking

on their job despite other commitments, or getting it done in less time than a thorough job takes.

Editing is not a casual time-filler. It is not something that can be taken up, put down, neglected for a while, then resumed, like stitchery or macramé. Editing goes best when you can stick with a project until it is done, keeping interruptions to a minimum to capitalize on momentum. In view of the critical ambiguity that the lack of a nonrestrictive comma can inject into an article about leukemia therapy or aircraft maintenance, for example, aspiring editors should realize that editing must be considered a serious and responsible exercise of trained judgment.

If any beginning editor needs convincing on this point, if he or she has somehow been thinking of editing as a pleasant way of being involved with books without the sweat of actually writing them, by all means read an article entitled "The Out-of-House Editor" in the journal *Scholarly Publishing*.[31] In it editors from nineteen university presses lay out the reasons why publishers are sometimes leery of sending out manuscripts to freelancers for copy editing.

"The best way to use a freelance editor is not at all," says one university press editor. Why? It is hard to find and train good ones; some freelance editors have been known to cut out the most interesting and significant parts of an author's narrative, or smooth out the author's idiomatic language until it's lost its original flavor. Some professors' wives, just because they have edited their husbands' work, consider themselves omnicompetent at editing. Some self-styled rewrite experts will typically not catch an unneeded comma before a parenthesis and then excuse themselves because "they don't fool around with nit-picking." There can be a serious waste of time and money if a press has to redo a manuscript badly edited by a freelancer. Furthermore, it is hard to estimate how much time a freelancer will take to edit a manuscript. And if a freelancer 6,000 miles away insists on holding onto a manuscript, how can a press get it back? In short, some publishers consider it such a problem to establish efficient in-house procedures for dealing with a manuscript edited by a freelancer that they wonder whether the purported saving of time and money is really worth the effort.

Such accusations are serious ones. Whether you want to do freelance editing for a university press, a commercial publisher, or for institutions or individual authors, you should realize that charges against freelance editors like the ones made in *Scholarly Publishing* are sometimes legitimate criticisms, and you should take every step possible to see that they could never justifiably be leveled at you.

2. "There's no future in learning to edit copy; pretty soon it's all going to be done by computer." Or, as one discouraged New England freelancer wrote, "Data processing and computer programming are where it's at today. Hard copy is dying out. . . . The terminal will replace the blue pencil within ten years."

Although the computer is taking over many of the purely routine aspects of copy editing, it seems that it is redirecting rather than replacing the expertise of human editors. Consider, for example, a recent article entitled "Computer Takes on Editors' Tasks," which reports on a meeting of the Washington, D.C. chapter of the Society for Technical Communications. In it John Enyart, whose company has developed the Enyart Technical Language Control System (ETLC), described part of the system as "a computer that detects and flags errors and suggests improvements in technical documents":

> With ETLC, technical writers first take an intensive training course, based on an ETLC text. The text introduces a basic 1,300-word vocabulary common to all technical fields. Each field also has a special vocabulary of 3,000 to 5,000 words.
>
> These vocabularies are programmed into the Enyart Quality Assurance Text Editor/Revisor (EQUATER). Writers must stick with the vocabulary for their fields, for the computer will flag words not in its programs. Technical writers' work is typed into EQUATER, which returns a printout complete with editorial notes.
>
> The following "errors" trigger an ETLC response: Excessive length of sentences; excessive length of prepositional phrases; improper use of relative noun clauses; present progressive participle phrase; ambiguous syntactic sequence; incomplete sentences; passive voice in verbs; first person pronouns; change of verb tense within the same paragraph; unclear reference/antecedent pronouns; nondefinition of acronyms; lead-in subordinate clauses of excessive length ("slow take-offs"); improperly placed and excessively long qualifiers/modifiers ("blivits"); common punctuation errors; compound-complex sentences; sentences ending with prepositions; compound sentences; contractions; noun clusters; and gerund phrases.[32]

It is important to notice, however, that its inventor concedes that EQUATER is not omnipotent: "A writer may override its decisions and type text that EQUATER would normally reject. . . . The final decisions are up to a human review board." Enyart admits freely, moreover, that his system can "curb a writer's individuality and produce boring copy." He defends his invention by defining its use as a strictly limited one—for "a technician confronting a problem on an unfamiliar piece of equipment." Such a person, he has decided, "needs clear, concise instructions, not entertainment."

Even with EQUATER, it becomes clear, human editorial judgment has not disappeared. First of all, an editor or a group of editors had to produce the textbook for ETLC use, to program the 1,300-word basic vocabulary and the various 3,000-to-5,000-word individual vocabularies for each of many special fields. While doing this, the same editor or group had to decide on the twenty types of "errors" to be rooted out, and program them into the computer, as well as to define and exemplify for the computer such judgments as "excessively long" and "improperly placed." Once the machine has identified each error, the correct substitutions will have to be made by live editors. And finally, as Enyart admits, human editors are also needed as a review board, going over each manuscript to see where the computer should be overridden.

EQUATER is only one example of an attempt to use electronic systems to substitute for editorial judgment in the worthy cause of clarity and consistency in writing. It would seem that all such systems can do is perform the first copy-editing steps, thus clearing the way for live editors. Computerized editing must be seen as a supplement to, not a substitute for, the brain of a living person who not only knows the subject being written about but cares about language and is aware of a writer's many options.

3. "Freelance editing jobs are becoming scarcer, because of the growing budgetary problems of many publishing houses, businesses, and academic departments and because publishers (among others) seem to care less and less about how a book is written."

Whether or not one believes this gloomy assessment depends largely on where one looks and to whom one listens. On the negative side of the picture, it is true that a number of publishing houses admit that they have laid off some of their full-time copy editors, and the editors who remain have less time than formerly to devote to the perfecting of each accepted manuscript. A 1980 article in *Time*, "The Decline of Editing," quotes Alan Williams of the Viking press as saying, "If Maxwell Perkins were around today, he wouldn't have time to be Maxwell Perkins. . . . He would be out grubbing with the rest of us, cozening agents and trying to get onto books earlier and wondering how much money to bid."[33] A 1980 series of articles in the *New Yorker* by Thomas Whiteside brings out, in passing, the same point: publishers spend less time on in-house copy editing than they formerly did.[34]

It is also true that staff writing and editing jobs with the federal

government seem to be in shorter supply than they were a few years
ago. Carolyn Lark of the Office of Personnel Management recently attributed the scarcity of government jobs to the current hiring freeze
and to dwindling requests from federal agencies for persons to fill
communications jobs. This may mean that freelancers are being called
upon to do what permanent staff editors used to do.[35]

Similarly, the decline of in-house copy editing among publishers
sometimes means that these firms are more apt to send out manuscripts to be edited by freelancers—if the freelancers are competent
and experienced. Even some editors at university presses who have
been critical of freelance work have come around to the view that
they will probably be making more rather than less use of freelancers
in the near future.[36] It is worth keeping in mind, however, that freelancers are frequently the first to go when a publishing house is faced
with a lean operating budget.

"The grass has never been greener for editorial freelancers," O'Neill
and Ruder wrote in 1979. During the five years between the first and
second editions of their book, they found that "publishers have responded to broad economic conditions by minimizing the number of
in-house employees and by expanding the role and image of paperback books in the industry. The combined effect of these two trends
has been to enlarge significantly the freelance job market."[37]

A fairly wide range of companies and industries in the private sector reports increased use of editors, both freelance and staff. At a
Washington, D.C. meeting of the Society for Technical Communication, for example, J. Dexter Nilsson, manager, General Electric Information Services Company, reported that his company is increasing
its communications staff. The qualities for which he is looking include dual competence as writer-editors, as well as "logical thought
processes; . . . ability to differentiate between the neat, careful editor
and the Nobel-prize winning writer; to know one's leanings in either
direction; and to agree with one's employer on the requirements of
the present job."[38]

It seems probable then that what Laura Horowitz advised beginning freelancers in The Editorial Eye in 1978 will be true for the
1980s: "Good performance is your best investment and advertisement. If you develop a reputation for doing a good job on time at a
reasonable price, you'll have no trouble getting work."[39]

9. Writing or Editing on the Staff of an Institution

The English writing and literature courses that I took for my B.A. and M.A. have been very helpful for editing; . . . the production details of publication I have learned wholly by working experience. Teaching English was even better preparation for editing, though I didn't realize it at the time.

—Questionnaire response from Jean McAlpine,
assistant director for communications,
Sea Grant Program, Albany, New York

Be creative, do interviewing, use resource books and other materials at public libraries, go to seminars, get out and scrounge! For certain jobs, all [your] so-called useless degrees DO have value, but usually in a different setting from the one you originally expected. Believe me, the world still needs people with your skills.

—Comment from community services coordinator
at a city public library

Assuming that one way or another you have developed expertise and you hear of a vacancy as editor or information specialist on the staff of an institution—a university, a museum, a hospital, a research project, a foundation—what might the job involve if you applied and got it? Would the duties be largely routine ones, or would you have a chance to use your own judgment? What qualifications are apt to put you in such positions? If you don't see specific vacancies advertised, how do you find out about such work? And what advice do people already holding such positions have for job-seekers?

In a questionnaire sent out to editors and information specialists working on a wide variety of institutional projects I asked such questions; the following digest of the 104 replies received may suggest possibilities to some of you.[1]

DUTIES OF EDITORS AND INFORMATION SPECIALISTS

These two job types not only include many different functions but overlap somewhat. People working in either of these positions may gather information or do background research on new developments; may write or edit an internal newsletter for one department or school of a large university; or may produce a bulletin for the alumni of a university, the patients of a hospital and their families, or for the general public.

To read the responses to my first question ("Briefly, what is your job title and what are your current duties?") is to find out that editors and information specialists, whether they work for a university, a hospital, a nonprofit agency, or elsewhere, do almost everything that could be called communication.

Among them they direct publicity campaigns for large hospitals, write news releases for daily and weekly papers, do radio and TV news scripts, edit technical manuscripts for medical journals, read proof, coordinate production arrangements with publishers, assist faculty members in running conferences, write and edit college publications relating to admissions and transfer policies, work with authors on book-length manuscripts, write brochures, edit footnotes and bibliographies for style, take photographs, get out newsletters telling either the members of one profession or the general public about recent developments within a field, and write and edit grant proposals.

Not only are their functions varied but almost every person replying reported doing several related kinds of work in his or her job. Clearly, the work week of an editor or information specialist does not consist of simply sitting at a desk and making marks with a blue pencil on a manuscript that someone else has written about discoveries that still another person has made. The tasks performed—telling the public about the latest International Arctic Ice Experiment voyage, explaining the new equipment for radiation therapy in a university hospital, or interpreting the impact of new legislation on colleges and universities—call for judgment, acquaintance with the community, writing skill, and often a familiarity with more than one of the media.

QUALIFICATIONS FOR EDITORIAL AND
INFORMATION SPECIALIST POSITIONS

In view of the nonliterary—often scientific or technical—subject matter of much of the material gathered or edited by the respondents to the questionnaire, one might assume that many of them would have a graduate or undergraduate degree in one of the sciences.

Of the 104 persons replying to my questionnaire, however, forty-two had bachelor's degrees in English, twenty-nine in journalism, eight in classics, seven in French, four each in music and psychology, three each in linguistics and sociology, two in economics, and one apiece in Biblical history and electrical engineering. Of these 104 writers and editors for various institutions, twenty-six had gone on to get M.A.'s in English; ten persons had master's degrees in journalism or communications, three in library science, three in history, and one in music. There were also fifteen Ph.D.'s represented: ten in English, five in history. Obviously, then, applicants with a humanities background are in a strong position when it comes to editing and writing posts on institutional staffs.

The consensus among both employers and employees is that most of the vocabulary of a technical subject has to be learned on the job, and that the editor or information specialist is hired mainly for his or her skill in digging out, sifting, and organizing material and writing it up clearly and effectively. Having had contact with the scientific or technical field in which one is going to work is of course an asset, but it is definitely not the main criterion. A former assistant professor of English now holding an editorial position with a university school of nursing points out: "My study and teaching of English really has prepared me well for my present job. Even though some of the problems I face in my work are unfamiliar at first, I can usually figure out how to proceed by extrapolating from the basic principles of organization and good writing I've been working with for years."

In addition to asking what degrees they had taken and what their major subjects were I asked for the amount and type of relevant experience (editing, writing, teaching, other) that each person had had before beginning his or her current job. As for the amount, answers varied widely: twenty-three had two years or less; nine had twenty or more; and each of the years between was represented by either two or three people.

In answering the question about kinds of prior experience, respondents listed their earlier jobs as shown below:

Other editorial work	35
Teaching (English, 16 persons; history, 6; journalism, 4; classics, 3; French, 3; women's studies, 2; anthropology, 1)	35
Newspaper work	14
Writing (freelance)	12
Advertising	10
Research	10
Proofreading	9
Public relations	8
Secretarial work	8
Work on staff of a magazine	5
No previous job-related experience (first job after college graduation)	4
Library	2

Needless to say, this list represents a few loosely defined jobs, a certain amount of overlapping, and many instances of persons who mentioned more than one kind of relevant position. What the answers to this question lack in precision, however, they make up in demonstrating the wide spectrum of skills valuable to an institutional editor or information specialist.

There is, obviously, no one best route to a good editing or writing position. As one example of the zigzags often taken by successful careers, Warren Downs, now writing news releases, radio environmental news scripts, articles, and booklets about marine subjects in his position as associate editor of the University of Wisconsin Sea Grant College Program, majored in cello as an Oberlin undergraduate, then earned a master's degree in music at the Eastman School of Music before getting a second master's in journalism at Wisconsin and stepping into his present job.

On the whole, it would seem that many editors and information specialists have arrived at their present positions with broad and varied backgrounds but with an emphasis on English (or other languages) rather than on technical fields. Many of them have had more scholarly and academic training then their present positions might seem to demand, yet incidental comments on the questionnaires revealed more satisfaction than frustration. In fact the respondents, who have been in their current jobs anywhere from two to eighteen years, appreciate them and want to keep them. As one editor said, "We who already have such jobs tend to cling to them with clenched teeth, because we like our work."

Despite their protectiveness of their positions, however, many people responding to my questions were articulate and expansive in telling how they heard of their positions and in passing along general advice to readers of this book.

WAYS OF FINDING OUT ABOUT EDITING AND WRITING POSITIONS

When asked, "How did you find out about your current job opening?" the responses ranged according to the following pattern. There were five main ways in which the successful job-seekers questioned had first heard about their present jobs:

1. *Through their own inquiries*
   Telephone inquiries — 12
   From sending a query letter before moving to the area — 6
   Personal visits ("banging on doors, and luck," as one respondent put it) — 6
2. *Through normal channels—advertisements and posted vacancies*
   From university staff employment office listings ("Sometimes the system *does* work!" reflected one of these job-seekers. Among these 15, 11 reported that their names had been kept on file and that they were called back six months later for jobs other than those for which they had applied.) — 15
   From newspaper ads ("contrary to the conventional wisdom," said a surprised job-finder) — 6
   From a state employment office listing — 3
3. *Through personal or organizational contacts*
   From friends, who knew of opening and told respondent to apply — 17
   From respondent's employer, who knew of an upcoming vacancy — 8
   From organizations to which respondent belonged (in four cases, it was the "Job Bank" and in three others, the "Rent a Writer" system of Women in Communications) — 7
   From respondent's faculty advisor, who knew of opening — 5
4. *Through internal promotion*
   From the fact that a new job for which the respondent was eligible opened up in the same agency or department — 7
5. *Through evolution of respondent's present job*
   From a less responsible and rather vaguely defined one — 12

   104

Some of the above ways of finding out about vacancies—such as reading ads and institutional employment listings—are so obvious that one tends to take it for granted that they won't work. Yet sometimes they do.

Two of these sources of job leads, the third and the fifth, deserve a word of comment. In learning about job openings from friends, you may expect either too much or too little. Ordinarily, such a lead doesn't (and of course shouldn't) imply that you will be given preferential treatment over other candidates in job selection; it is simply a great help to have upcoming vacancies, which one otherwise might not hear about until it is too late to apply, called to one's attention.

As for job evolution, many job-seekers don't believe in this possibility until they see it happen, but several respondents to the questionnaire *have* done so. For example, a research publications editor of AIDJEX (the Arctic Ice Dynamics Joint Experiment) writes: "The man organizing this project told me that there was a fuzzily defined half-time position in the budget for doing something that was neither secretarial nor administrative, probably for passing information among the various researchers. I wanted a half-time job, so I applied. Later the job got classified as Editor I and now it's Editor II, full time." Another editor at the same level doing writing and rewriting of medical research articles, said that his job had originally been listed at the student employment office as a part-time electronics one. After he began it, the writing part of it slowly developed. A woman who now edits the medical articles of eighty physicians in the medical research department of a large hospital started out in a secretarial position in that hospital. When the administrator for whom she was working realized that she had a good sense of language and sentence structure, he encouraged her to try for a new editing job as it was created, and he helped get the job properly defined.

Another example from the questionnaires is interesting both because of the way it shows an excellent position evolving from an unpromising source and because it points up the fact that sometimes it's not a bad idea to apply for a position for which one is "overqualified." Shirley Hudgins, for several years happily established as editor and communications coordinator of the USC Sea Grant Institutional Program, where she works with radio, television, and newspapers, came to her job via a secretarial route. She had received both a B.A. and an M.A. in English at the University of Rhode Island, where she had also taken almost enough zoology courses for an undergraduate major. After teaching freshman English at Rhode Island for two years, she moved to California; there she worked for a year in the Script Department at MGM Studios, and then for a company that made records for the automobile industry. Her editorial position evolved in the following way:

> Out of work and hungry, I saw an ad in the Los Angeles *Times* for an executive secretary working with oceanographers. I'm not a secretary by inclination or training, but the magic word "oceanographers" made me answer the ad. I was obviously not qualified for the position, but the USC Sea Grant Program, just beginning to grow, liked my background in the sciences and English. They needed at least a part-time editor for their scientific documents, so I began as part secretary/editor to the head of Advisory services. After I had held that dual position for about six months, they created the full position of editor for me.

Hudgins's luck in finding that a somewhat unpromising job evolved, after six months of hard work on her part, into a position she considers ideal inspired her to offer readers this advice: "Investigate anything that sounds interesting to you. Even if the exact position that you would be looking for is not available, check into it anyway. The ideal job usually doesn't just appear, anyway, so try to figure out where you could fit in, and perhaps do what you want without their [the employers'] knowing it."

ADVICE TO JOB-SEEKERS FROM EDITORS AND
INFORMATION SPECIALISTS

Like Shirley Hudgins, most respondents volunteered suggestions to readers of this book. Among these comments were seven recurrent themes.

1. *"Get some 'real world' staff editing or writing experience somewhere (either on your campus paper or outside), and parlay that as best as you can."* An editor from Delaware writes, "Get some hands-on practical experience—something marketable." Look for internships (summer, short-term, or any informal arrangement that you may be able to promote, yourself) to give you experience working on publications.[2] Magazines published by nonprofit corporations sometimes offer these internships, as do research centers. Established periodicals such as the *Atlantic Monthly* have had summer traineeships for college students. The University of Washington Press has offered internships for members of minority groups to give them an introduction into editing and publishing procedures.[3]

If in order to get practical experience you have to offer your services on a volunteer basis, several respondents urge you to do so to whatever extent you can afford. As a public relations director of a large hospital suggests, you should aim to "get broad, varied experience—available through volunteer work with nonprofit agencies—with progressively more advanced administrative responsibilities." "I often find work," writes Jean McAlpine, an editor in Albany, New York, "by joining an organization I am interested in anyway (e.g., the League of Women Voters) or volunteering for a local candidate I like. Some referrals and moonlighting have resulted."

2. *"Write a lot of nonfiction and get it published,"* urges a research publications editor at a state university. And, she continues,

> while you are an undergraduate or a graduate student . . . leave enough time to turn out a lot of published material and/or to work on publications (no matter how small). The market is so tight that you either must have terrific tenacity or experience. . . . When in school, . . . we lose sight somehow of the everyday work problems. Editing a newsletter does indeed pale when compared to great literature. To eat after graduation, however, it is best to spend some time working on those little, time-consuming newsletters or stories or articles that could and should be done . . . while you are taking courses. Write—get it down on paper, and sell it. Nothing better to get a job [with] than being able to lay something down on the table. Find a good editor who will tear your copy apart. Then put it back together again.

As the director of publications and information services of the University of Washington College of Engineering points out, the field which includes being an editor or information specialist "is still one in which jobs are usually awarded on the basis of performance—what you have done—rather than on academic preparation. I would suggest compilation of a portfolio. To get experience, do volunteer work. Many, many agencies, associations, churches, etc., have writing and editing tasks for volunteers." And a communications officer who manages information activities for a research advisory services program in Cambridge, Massachusetts, makes the point that the liberal arts subjects you have studied "are *not* useless . . . if the student sees them as mainsprings for thought, excellence in writing, and self-education," and suggests that you "put the latter skills to work—in journalism, public information, etc., *in any field of subject-matter.*"

3. *"Make personal contacts,"* urge many respondents. "Visit offices and departments that use writers and editors, perhaps even convincing those not advertising for editors/writers that they need them. Be sure to take or send examples of finished work everywhere." In getting in touch with people in your field, writes a manager of informa-

tion and publications for a research center, "be organized and persistent. Decide the field or fields you want to be in and find out from people there what's needed and how to go about it. *Anyone* will see you if you're looking for advice, not a job. Follow up. Be sold on yourself. Be sure to sell your *self*, not a list of qualifications."

Another kind of contact that many find helpful to morale and sometimes indirectly useful in their job search is with professional organizations—either national ones such as the American Medical Writers' Association, the National Association of Science Writers, the National Association of Press Women, the Society for Technical Communication, Women in Communications—or local ones, which will be found on most large campuses and in most cities. Some of these groups publish bulletins and journals, offer annual prizes for good writing in their fields, and sponsor speakers and workshops. Watch local papers for announcements of these workshops and of open meetings; attend and see whether they interest you, and learn what the qualifications are for membership. (Student memberships are often inexpensive and offer a good way to get in.) All these groups offer the newcomer a chance to talk with established professionals in the field. And all of them offer a demonstration of the fact that there are other *kinds* of standards of excellence than those of the world of academic and literary scholarship.

4. *"Develop a subskill,"* writes an information specialist. "For instance, the fact that I have written or cowritten (successful) funding proposals has brought me about fifteen requests from people needing to write them. I don't particularly relish that specialty, but I *could* make a career of it if I wanted to, having had the experience." Other subskills mentioned as back-ups for general editing included technical editing, indexing book-length manuscripts, graphics, photography, "professional secretarial training, which makes a better springboard than most people realize," and "exposure to computer science." As Barbara Gill, formerly of Tymshare, Inc., Cupertino, California, wrote:

> Even an introductory course in computer science, or any other opportunity to do some data entry and understand the basic concept, is valuable in technical writing and editing. Some smaller organizations train people on the job if they can show the basic aptitude and familiarity with data entry, research design, data analysis. The lingo is what's important in getting hired. Also, any demonstration that you are . . . concerned with detail, methodical about written presentation. . . . Teachers are often sought for technical writing and editing because there is a large component of training in much of the documentation.

5. *"Be willing to take a nonwriting job and try to get it turned into a writing one"* was a common piece of advice. Said a campus information specialist with an M.A. in English:

> There are always openings on campus for typists and office assistants. If you get into an office or a department that puts out printed material and you happen to have editorial skills, sooner or later they'll ask your help, and maybe you can get reclassified. I know a number of Information Specialists who got started that way. One thing to avoid: don't get in an office where you'll never have a chance to do any writing, such as Payroll or Purchasing. Look out for job openings that wind up as dead ends.

One journalist went even further: "Take anything that interests you," he urged, "even menial labor or clerical work, to establish your record as a product and reliable employee."

6. *"Don't be afraid of technical language,"* writes an editor in anesthesiology in a teaching hospital:

> From the point of view of a health sciences . . . position, it is important that one not be afraid of technical language and also be able to work with the quite structured format of technical writing. Two former editors . . . continually had problems with authors in that they tried to change technical writing into creative writing, and in this process changed the context of the material. This . . . put doubt in the authors' eyes as to the usefulness of departmental editors. I think that there is a lot of need and potential in the medical/scientific area for editors, and awareness of the field's specialized nature is necessary.

7. *"Major in English but minor in some other field of interest or expertise (environment, marine affairs, biology, music, education) as an undergraduate,"* says Warren Downs of Madison, Wisconsin. "Or, at least, if you are already a graduate student, read up on one or two such areas and take courses in them. Employers, I think, are looking for people with both writing/editorial skills *and* strong interests in *their* [the employer's] field." Similar comments stress "freelance writing after pursuing a specialty" and "freelancing with educational institutions as a source." Areas particularly recommended as needing writers currently, in addition to the ones picked out by Downs, include art, urban affairs, labor, commerce, investments, and health sciences.

Editors and writers point out that nothing you can learn is ever wasted. Says Dee Jones, Public Relations Director of Seattle's Swedish Hospital Medical Center, "Study everything you can. Someday you'll need it. I tend to eliminate subjects I find boring or unnecessary. Long ago I ruled out knowing anything about professional sports and Indian politics, among other things. In the first month that I worked as public relations director here, we signed a contract to care for all the professional players on Seattle teams (and their visiting teams), and we also admitted as a patient Jayaprakesh Narayan, successor to Gandhi. My information lacks were painfully evident."

Whatever the content you deal with, editing or writing for an institution involves many of the other skills you may have acquired through your liberal arts major. Despite the current financial crunch, a certain number of these positions remain in most such institutions. A vice-president of a state university once remarked, "Institutions such as universities need to strengthen their interpretative role if they are to survive."[4] With the widespread budget cuts of the early 1980s, this need seems more urgent than ever. Colleges and universities, museums, arts groups, health and human service writers are increasingly finding that legislators and the general public need to be educated about what these institutions do in order to have any chance at continued financial support. If you work as a writer, editor, or information specialist for such an agency, you can have the personal satisfaction of helping, even if in a small way, to ensure that agency's survival. You will also find that you have chosen a career which uses most of your talents and develops new ones. It may help qualify you, too, for related careers in editing, writing, or publishing.

10. Is Entry into Book Publishing Still Possible?

> To those of us who practice publishing it is a curious, crazy, beloved, incomparable, frustrating, maddening, demanding business or art or profession or job. Which is it? It is, at its best, a vocation.
>
> —Comment from the head of a major publishing house

> I would urge you to dissuade those people "who just love books" from seeking employment in the publishing industry. What we really need today are hard workers who can bring the books out on time and under budget.
>
> —Thomas D. Wittenberg, editor-in-chief,
> Bobbs-Merrill Publishing Company

Among the stereotypes surrounding publishing until recently was the idea that the world of book publishers, especially those on the East Coast, was peopled largely by tweedy editors who had nothing to do but concentrate on improving the quality of their authors' writing. Publishing, as Thomas Whiteside reminds his readers in his 1980 series of *New Yorker* articles ("The Blockbuster Complex"), "used to be generally thought of as a low-key, gentlemanly profession whose personal satisfactions probably outweighed its financial rewards." But during the sixties and seventies enormous changes began to take place. As Whiteside sums them up:

> This transformation involves the control of the publishing houses, which was once in the hands of private owners but is now more and more in the hands of large conglomerate corporations; it involves a changing relationship between hardcover books and paperbacks, with ever-larger sums . . . being paid for the reprint rights of a single potential best-seller; it involves changes in book promotion, particularly a reliance on television talk shows . . . ; and it involves new developments in the way books are sold in bookstores, distributed, handled by agents, and otherwise "packaged."[1]

Along with such changes in the management structure of publishing came several others: increasing costs of raw material, especially paper; escalating postal rates, making it more and more expensive to transport books from printing plants to bookstores; rising wage scales, which have forced some publishers to cut down on their staffs;[2] and advancements in information technology, leading in some fields to the point where "much information . . . is transmitted directly from computer to computer, bypassing the printed word entirely."[3]

How are such changes affecting the health of the publishing industry and with it your chances of employment in it? The answer depends on whom you listen to or read.

Whiteside quotes Morton L. Janklow, a New York lawyer who also heads his own literary agency, as believing that the conglomerate takeovers of independent publishers have been helpful to the publishing industry by making capital available so that publishers can produce "more valuable commercial works." As Janklow sees it, "the conglomerates introduced concepts that go with good corporate planning—budgeting, profit projections, and estimates. . . . Also, the conglomerates have encouraged decent compensation for good people, and that used to be rare in the business."[4] Another commentator on the publishing industry, Roberta Morgan, points out that "conglomerates provide greater employee benefits," more titles are being produced than ever before, and "there is growth in specific areas of publishing, including sales, marketing, and subsidiary rights."[5]

Whiteside, however, after quoting Janklow, concedes that the changes of the past twenty years "have inevitably created considerable turmoil among those who work in trade-book publishing . . . in the shifting of editors and authors from publishing house to publishing house in search of more secure or more advantageous arrangements; in changes in the traditional role of many trade-book editors, and also in the editorial process itself; . . . in changes in the basic quality of competition between publishers . . . ; in difficulties that certain categories of published authors are encountering in having their works kept in print and in the bookstores; . . . and in the serious problems that some authors appear to have in getting their works published at all."[6]

How will such changes, whether for better or for worse, affect those of you who hope to enter publishing? Is there still room for liberal arts B.A.'s, for recent M.A.'s or Ph.D.'s who don't plan to teach, or for experienced teachers in their thirties or forties who, seeing a dead end in their profession, realize that publishing has always attracted them? Should you give up thinking of getting a job in publishing unless you have an M.B.A., a background in information technology, or access to enough capital to start your own firm?

Publishing is a protean field, defying formal description; there are no standard educational qualifications or blueprints of routes of entry and advancement. In a 1977 pamphlet in which the Association of American Publishers attempted to explain their industry's workings, publishing was termed the "accidental profession."[7] Accidental or not, publishing keeps challenging its practitioners to try to explain what goes on in it. As change after change took place in the 1960s and 1970s, spokespersons for the industry have made several attempts to show what the various careers in publishing involve and what some of the prerequisites for success are. Despite the industry's continual permutations, there is a certain continuity in what publishers have been telling their public over the past few years. From a survey of 125 publishers (yielding 70 usable replies) that I made in 1974-75 for the first edition of this book, down to the points made by Morgan and Whiteside in 1980 and 1981,[8] there is some (though not complete) agreement on what aspirants to publishing should be warned against, what they should be able to offer an employer, and what kind of careers (given hard work, good timing, and luck) they may expect.

First, the warnings:

1. Publishing is a relatively small profession: six thousand publishing firms in America in 1980 employed probably no more than sixty thousand persons (excluding booksellers, book manufacturers, freelance editors, literary agents, and those in other related professions). It has been estimated that the number of new jobs in publishing opening up each year will be between three and four thousand. [9]

2. Starting salaries in publishing tend to be low—often even lower than those of academia. As Bert Davis of New York, a publishing placement specialist quoted by Roberta Morgan, explains, publishing usually does not pay salaries commensurate with the experience and responsibility of the people in it.[10]

3. The criteria for entry and advancement can seem elusive. Most editors and other staff members of publishing houses come to them straight after graduation from college and are trained on the job. Although recently there have been numerous courses, summer programs, and special workshops for those hoping to enter publishing, you could hold a certificate from one or more of these, plus one or more college degrees, and still have no guarantee of finding a position in publishing.[11]

4. Most publishing house staffs suffer from constant turnover.

"Cross-hiring" from one company to another is common. Probably one of the phrases most often on the lips of publishers' receptionists is, "She [or he] is no longer with us." Roberta Morgan mentions knowing "top editors in publishing who have changed jobs as often as three times in two years."[12] This mobility can represent either a threat or an opportunity, depending on your age and temperament.

5. Recognition does not often come to people on the staff of publishing firms in the way it may to those in many other careers. The acquisitions editor, the copy editor, the book designer, the production manager, the proofreader, the promotion manager, the "publisher's rep"—these and the others who are irreplaceable links in the chain between the author and the eventual reader are not widely credited with their work; they often have nothing tangible to show for months and years of idea spinning, manuscript reading, memo writing, and risk taking. They are scarcely known to any public wider than the circle of friends and colleagues they see annually at the conventions of the Association of American Publishers (AAP) and the American Booksellers Association (ABA).

6. Finally, if that overused word "dedication" still deserves any currency, it should be applied to most of the people in publishing— to those who take manuscripts home with them evenings and on weekends and tend to feel (like teachers, housewives, and parents) that there is always something more they ought to be doing.

If you have not been discouraged by these six considerations, you may want to read the following practical suggestions that people at various levels of publishing have within the past five years given to aspirants to jobs in their firms.

Before applying for any publishing job, know something about the many different kinds of positions in the field. Don't think simply of "being an editor" as the only worthwhile or interesting thing to do. Philip D. Jones, former director of the University of Texas Press, writes, "Ninety-five per cent of the people who have come to my office for advice over the years respond 'editorial' when asked what sort of work they want to do in book publishing. When asked what kind of editorial work they want, virtually none is aware that there are various kinds such as copy editing, project editing, acquisitions editing."[13]

As Chandler Grannis points out in an excellent pamphlet, *Getting into Book Publishing*, within a publishing firm there are not only different kinds of editing carried on, but there are usually several other major departments, parallel to and as important as the editorial ones. A publishing house carries on all the following activities:

Planning and developing editorial programs

Selecting and editing manuscripts and working with authors

Making and controlling budgets, estimating costs, projecting income

Designing the books, making layouts, working with artists and graphic materials, dealing with suppliers, printers, and binders

Estimating the nature and amount of a book's market, planning and producing the promotion, advertising, publicity, and sales programs to reach potential customers

Selling "subsidiary rights"—the use of the book as reprints, films, translations, book club selections, and so on.[14]

Each of these areas has many positions within it, from junior assistant to executive ones. The better informed you are in your job campaign, the more you will stand out from the crowd of hopeful humanities majors longing "to get into editing."

One of the easiest ways of becoming informed is to do some systematic background reading. For familiarity with copy editing practices, you can consult the University of Chicago *Manual of Style* or *Words into Type*[15] (see the discussion of the different kinds of editing in chapter 8). To keep up with publishing trends, get in the habit of going to the library and spending a few minutes every week with *Publishers Weekly*. You should also read some of the accounts of the publishing business written in recent years by Herbert Bailey, John Dessauer, Howard Greenfield, and Chandler Grannis, which you will find listed along with others in the bibliography of this book. In addition, Robert T. King, director of the University of South Carolina Press, suggests that job-seekers make inquiries of both the AAP and the AAUP (Association of American University Presses), "simply saying that one is interested in a career in publishing and would be grateful for information."

Next, browse. Wherever and whenever you see a book, get in the habit of looking at not only the title and author but the name of the publisher as well. Look at publishers' catalogues too; you'll find them in bookstores, and if you teach, or if you attend academic or professional conventions, it's easy to get on publishers' mailing lists. Form an idea of the different kinds of books that various firms bring out. Look at the publishers' ads for their new books in the *New York Times Book Review* and the *New York Review of Books*. Talk and listen to publishers' representatives when they visit your campus or one near you. Talk to anyone else involved in the making or selling of books. Be sure to go to the paperback expositions sponsored annually on many campuses by groups of publishers. And, of course, begin to form some specific questions in your mind—not just about job openings but about publishing trends—to ask publishers when you eventually find yourself having an interview in one of their offices.

In addition, you may be able to take one of the courses in publishing procedures offered by various colleges and universities. The best known of these courses is given each summer at Radcliffe College. There are comparable courses given annually by the University of Wisconsin, the University of Oklahoma, the University of North Dakota, New York University, the University of Denver, Hunter College, Stanford University, and Pacific Lutheran University, Tacoma, Washington, among others.[16] In addition, several other publishing houses, particularly among the university presses, occasionally sponsor internships.[17]

Although the respondents to my questionnaire were predictably divided about the value of such courses, more than half spoke well of them. A senior editor of Houghton Mifflin, for example, said that although what one learned from such a course might be picked up on the job, through hearing the twenty lectures by representatives of twenty different publishers one could at least get a good idea of the whole range of publishing jobs and know better where one might fit in. Carol Meyer of Harcourt Brace Jovanovich was also impressed by the broad survey of different publishing houses that such courses could give a student; she pointed out, too, that since many people already working in publishing enroll in such courses to advance their skills, it would be helpful to you as a newcomer to meet and talk with them.

Have something specific to offer that will be useful to a publisher. Although this point should be self-evident, too many college students apply to publishers solely on the strength of being English majors and "loving literature." It is quite true that many people in publishing have majored in English and there are many slots in publishing that draw on the aptitudes of English majors. At the same time it is to be hoped that English majors who find themselves on one of the lower rungs of the ladder in administration, editorial, production, or marketing will not act as if their chores, which may seemingly have little enough to do with great literature, were beneath them. A few publishers refuse to hire English majors, fearing just such attitudes. Although the typical English major may flinch at hearing this, Roberta Morgan puts the situation well when she says "perhaps the best thing is to have an English or journalism degree but not to take it too seriously."[18]

Other liberal arts subjects often work well to give one a good start in publishing. I know a production manager who majored in medieval history, an editor who came to publishing from teaching anthropology, three who were classics majors, an assistant to the director of a university press who majored in French and German, and a business manager who majored in history. Most publishers feel that the main thing is to have a broad liberal arts background with one or two fields of specialization. On my questionnaire, when employers in publishing were asked what degrees provided good backgrounds for applicants, they expressed these preferences:

Undergraduate major:
English	36
Communications	21
Modern languages	9
History or political science	2
Science	1
Education	1

Field of graduate study (if any):
English	16
Communications	10
Modern languages	5

A second qualification for entry into publishing, according to forty-five of the seventy editors responding, involves having some business experience. For aspirants to editorial posts, publishers stressed the value of firsthand knowledge of such business areas as marketing, advertising, bookstore sales, textbook sales, and sales management. Publishers answering my questionnaire also noted the advantage of taking introductory courses in accounting or basic computer language and of having office and general secretarial experience.

Even for editors, it was emphasized again and again, experience in bookstore sales is extremely helpful. A senior editor of Houghton Mifflin pointed out that Alfred Knopf began his career at the cash register of a Doubleday bookstore; so too did a number of Houghton Mifflin's top editors. George Ernsberger, former editor at the Berkley Publishing Corporation, explains, "The reason that bookstore selling is useful is that it forces the seller to consider the wants and interests of people unlike himself." Almost any kind of selling experience, in fact, is considered a plus and should certainly be mentioned in your résumé. Your bookstore or other selling experience need not have been extensive, as long as you have had enough to learn what selling is like.

On the subject of business courses, William Sommerfield, speaking from his experience as an editor of a New Jersey textbook firm, has this to say: "Publishing is carried out in the world of business, and any editor worth his blue pencil must be able to joust with a profit and loss statement and calculate costs with the best of the bean counters. . . . Without these skills, your creative offerings will be drowned in a sea of ledger books, financial reports, and general accounting problems. I would insist that everyone with aspirations towards the world of publishing take at least one course in accounting."

In addition to your professional qualifications, your personal ones will enter the picture. As Thomas Weyr points out in a *Publishers Weekly* article, executives in this field "are looking for things in people that are largely intangibles, such as personality, manner, a special curiosity, rather than specific skills. By and large, requirements tend to be vague." Weyr and several of the editors in the survey made the point that most people who get ahead in this field enter it young (somewhere between the ages of twenty and twenty-eight).[19] Said Norma Mikkelsen, former director of the University of Utah Press: "We each have to be versatile, efficient, interested in the books and their authors rather than individual egos. . . . We are looking for a set of personality or 'working' traits that would enhance the personality of the Press." In a somewhat similar vein, John D. Moore, director of the Columbia University Press, writes, "Much depends upon how well one communicates with others orally as well as in writing. Human relations skills count heavily in most jobs here, as in other industries."

Other personal qualities constantly called upon, people in publishing report, are flexibility (especially the gift of being able to shift easily from one task to another yet somehow get them all done), ability to meet deadlines, and great reserves of energy.

Be prepared to start at an entry-level job; in publishing almost any job can lead to anything else. As Chandler Grannis points out in *Getting into Book Publishing*, examples of beginning jobs held by men and women who later moved on to management levels include: "Mail room clerk. Secretary to an officer. Publicity assistant. Manuscript traffic clerk. Production assistant. Assistant in subsidiary rights. Assistant to science editor. College traveler (sales representative). Clerk-typist. Proofreader. Reference library assistant."[20]

Many people have found that simply to get into publishing it is practical to accept almost any job with almost any publishing house. "Learn what you can there," they urge. "Then, after six months or a year, you'll be ready to get a better job with another house. And you'll hear of it more quickly, and get it more easily, because now you're on the inside."

The two most often mentioned starting points in publishing are secretarial jobs and textbook sales. Although members of the Women's Movement have recently been insistent that women with long-range career plans should not start as secretaries ("never let them know that you can type"), apparently secretaries are more apt to be on a genuine promotion ladder in publishing than in most other fields. Helen Stewart, formerly of the Rutgers University Press, insists that she has "never known anyone with real editorial or promotion skills relegated to a secretarial job for long. No sensible publisher overlooks underpaid talent in the office."

Linda Liesem, writing from her position as placement specialist for Doubleday, goes even further: "Most of our entry level jobs are secretarial in nature and are filled by people with B.A.'s (occasionally M.A.'s) in English or a communications related field. A major prerequisite is the ability to type at least 45 wpm. While these secretarial jobs in our editorial, subsidiary rights, or publicity departments may not offer the challenge and responsibility most graduates seek, they do provide a preparation for the next step up. In the editorial department the line of progression (for which there is, however, no fixed time schedule) is as follows: editorial secretary, assistant to the editor, editorial assistant, associate editor, and editor. There are corresponding steps in other departments."

The other most frequent entry point, that of working as a "college traveler"—a sales representative who may spend half of each month visiting college campuses in a five- or six-state territory, and the other half working in the firm's regional or main office—used to be a masculine province. Recently, women have begun to hold—and do well in—such positions. These jobs are more varied than they may at first sound: each of these salespersons goes from campus to campus, dropping in on teaching faculty of one department after another, showing them new textbooks, collections of readings, and other material that they might consider adopting in their classes, telling them of other new titles to come; another important part of the job is being a scout for ideas for new books suggested by faculty members. If a college traveler is promoted to acquisitions editor, the knowledge he or she has gained of the needs in various fields will be most helpful, and the faculty members worked with may well become this editor's authors. College travelers may also move up in a publisher's marketing department.

The foregoing considerations apply to those of you hoping to enter publishing upon graduation from college or soon after. Other readers—those with graduate degrees who may have been college teachers for some time—may wonder what chance you have to transfer your writing, analytical, and editing skills to publishing. It is possible; yet it may take luck, contacts, and considerable hard work to make such a shift.

At an MLA meeting not long ago several people who had done just that talked at a panel on the book publishing industry. Anne Easton and Toni Burbank, who had gone into publishing straight from graduate school, found publishers less inaccessible than they had expected. Donald Lamm, now president of the W. W. Norton Company, who had done graduate work in seventeenth-century English literature at Oxford University before he joined Norton as a college traveler, posed the question: "Is publishing a safe harbor for the academic who is leaving the university?"[21]

He cautioned that at first you should steel yourself because, when you apply, some people *will* consider you at once over- and underqualified. You will probably have had more formal education than most people in the firm, no doubt more than the highest-paid acquisitions editors; at the same time you will not have gone through the informal apprentice year or two of secretarial work, copy editing, or sales.

For those academics who have an intense urge to get into publishing, Lamm has the following suggestions:

1. "Match your interests to a publisher's list." Look through the catalogues and the books that various publishers have issued until you find one whose range of titles comes close to your interests and special expertise. You *might* be needed as a subject-matter specialist, or some one to develop a new series of college texts. (At the same time, Lamm cautioned that although publishers "were not retreating from their commitment to English texts," his own firm had during the past year published many more texts in psychology and in business management than in literature or composition.)

2. Sound out all the college travelers you meet about their firms and the advisability of your applying for some opening there. ("Take a salesman to lunch and get him or her to tell you what the situation is really like.")

3. Introduce yourself to the head of your university press, and ask advice about where and how to apply to other publishing firms.

4. Send out letters and résumés to the heads of the college departments of publishers that interest you. (Get their names, titles, and addresses from the latest *LMP.*)

5. Suspend your hopes of a real career in publishing until you've put in an apprenticeship as a college traveler.

6. Finally—and Lamm cautioned that this is most important—do *not* abandon a teaching career if working in publishing appeals to you simply as a holding operation. The time invested in your apprenticeship with a publisher will not pay either you or your employer if you work as a college traveler, secretary, or editorial assistant for a year to eighteen months, then accept the first teaching position that you are offered.

APPLYING FOR A JOB IN PUBLISHING

Assuming that you have learned something about the range of jobs in publishing, have something useful to offer a publishing firm, and are reconciled to starting in at an entry-level job, how might you find out about, apply for, and get such a job?

Realize that the application process is a much less formal one than in academia or business, and be ready to take the initiative however you can. Publishing does not yet have very sophisticated, or even efficient, devices for screening, interviewing, or judging applicants, said Peggy Sherwood, literature editor of the Princeton University Press.[22] Publishing firms operate on financial margins too small to permit any talent searching. So you will not find them recruiting at campus placement centers, paying the way of out-of-town applicants for interviews, or keeping applicants' résumés systematically on file until vacancies occur. Although it is true that publishers are beginning to use specialized employment agencies geared strictly to positions in publishing, such placement has not yet become the norm.

Through an informal poll, an editor recently asked a dozen other people at various levels of book publishing how they got their first jobs in the industry. The replies, reported at an annual meeting of the Association of American Publishers, ran as follows: "Through a help-wanted ad." "By knocking on lots of doors." "I volunteered." "By accident." "I'm a member of the family." "Through and as a student at N.Y.U." "Eleven rejections and an acceptance." "Through my college placement service." "I was asked." "Off the street." "Through an endless chain of tenuous connections." "I bought the company."[23]

Although you will find some publishing vacancies listed in *Publishers Weekly, Editor and Publisher,* the *New York Times,* and possibly, if you live in a large city, your local newspaper, you should realize that it is mainly the higher level positions that get much advertising exposure. Display ads for "acquisitions editor with ten to twelve years' experience" are not uncommon, but steps from secretary to editorial assistant or editorial assistant to assistant editor tend to be filled in-house.

When you prepare your résumé for a publishing job application (according to a woman who counseled many people now working in the industry), put in anything that might directly or indirectly be relevant to publishing. If you have a background in science or in modern foreign languages, note the fact and be prepared to enumerate the courses. It is a good idea to classify your course work into four basic areas—science, social science, humanities, and business—and list these courses in some detail. Mention undergraduate or graduate course work in writing, translation, or foreign languages. Be prepared in an interview to discuss your undergraduate major and minors. If you have been a teaching assistant, a research assistant, or a reader for a course, include the fact, along with the name and number of the course. If you have a graduate degree, include your thesis title and your advisor's or committee chairman's name. If you have worked your way through school in a library, mention the fact; you will have learned a great deal there that could be helpful in publishing.[24]

If you have done graduate work, whether it is considered an asset or a liability may depend in part on your own attitude. Says Luther Nichols, West Coast editor for Doubleday, "If you have an M.A. or a Ph.D., don't flaunt the degree as such, but be sure to bring out in your letter of application and your résumé any expertise that you've acquired in a subject field."[25] Two editors thought that graduate degrees would be of no help to a job applicant "and might even be a detriment"; others mentioned the kinds of bibliographical and research skills learned in graduate school as useful in some areas of publishing. Thompson Webb, Jr., of the University of Wisconsin Press thought that "to qualify for editorial work at a scholarly publishing house some education at the graduate level is needed. . . . For editors the commonest (and probably the best) educational background is literature—English and languages." Another editor points out that while an advanced degree may not be necessary for most positions in publishing, it is considered increasingly important for an acquisitions editor who works for a publisher large enough to have editors who specialize in particular disciplines or areas (for example, a mathematics editor or a humanities editor).

In your cover letter as well as your résumé, said Sherwood, be as specific as possible. The letter should be a typed original, not one of two hundred duplicated and sent broadside; it should be addressed by name to a specific person and in a specific department of a publishing house (check the latest *LMP* for this). Send it in February or March, "before the tidal wave of June graduates applying." Along with mention of the courses and work experience that have a bearing on publishing, send if possible one or two pieces of your writing— for example, reviews or critiques of not more than three or four pages apiece. They should be lively and succinct. Try to give some indication in your letter that you know and care about the publishing industry, that you read pretty widely, that you have been scanning *Publishers Weekly*, that you know about *LMP*. With luck, Sherwood said, you might create in the mind of the person who reads your letter the reaction, "Maybe that's me—ten years ago." [26]

Publishers answering my questionnaire nearly all urge that applicants make the rounds of publishers' offices *in person*. As J. Kenneth Munford points out, even if aspirants don't find a job, such visitors "will pick up benefits through serendipity. They see something of how editorial offices and shipping rooms operate. They become acquainted with some of the people in the field. They can begin to judge better where their true interests lie." And Kathleen Macomber of Pantheon Books advises: "The job-seeker, carrying a well-written résumé, should go to the personnel offices of the firms he would choose to work for first, then make the rounds of all the major firms." Luther Nichols, however, dissents from part of this advice. "Don't go through the personnel department of most big publishers," he warns, "or you'll end up with a clerical job that lacks variety and a chance for promotion." He recommends writing to the editor of a specific department in a specific firm, then sending a well-written letter of application with a résumé that stresses both writing and business experience: "Better yet, visit a publisher's office, leave these and some writing samples, and shortly afterward call to ask for an appointment." [27]

If you are hoping for interviews with publishers in an area other than the one where you live, you are advised to write to those firms that interest you in a specific region, sending them your résumé and samples, and telling them that you are intending to move to the area and will be in town for a week in the near future (give specific dates). Say that on arrival you will phone them for an appointment, and when you get there be sure to do so. If your letter and résumé have done their work well, the publisher will usually see you even though he or she may have no definite opening at the moment.

For long-term career possibilities, look beyond the most obvious positions in publishing. Even if you have been lucky enough to hold an entry-level position for a year or two in a large, well-known East

Coast publishing house, you may not want or be able to stay there indefinitely. So what are your other options?

You could consider other parts of the country: as Ashbel Green, vice-president and senior editor at Alfred Knopf, writes, "One shouldn't assume that all jobs are in the East—a number of regional textbook houses have grown up in recent years, and there are trade publishers outside New York as well." A glance at the latest *LMP* will show you how much of an understatement that is.

You could also consider other kinds of publishing rather than the adult trade-book publishing that everyone thinks of first. There are, in addition, firms both large and small that specialize in children's books, academic books, religious books, mass market paperbacks, mail order publications, book club books, professional and scientific books, college textbooks, elementary and high school ("el-hi") text-bools and other learning materials, or subscription books (such as encyclopedias and professional directories). Each of these calls for special skills in writing, editing, marketing, and publishing[28]—skills you could probably develop by building on what you learned in your first publishing job.

If you are interested in some of these publishing alternatives, browse through the issues of *Scholarly Publishing*; look also at the *International Directory of Little Magazines and Small Presses*, an annual compendium listing over twenty-five hundred independent publishing firms or periodicals across the nation.[29]

One sector of the independent publishers is the feminist publishing movement. Although its small publishing houses are listed and described in the *International Directory*, if you would like to find out in depth how it operates, read *The Passionate Perils of Publishing* by Celeste West and Valerie Wheat. They are angry at the East Coast "literary-industrial complex," realistic about the capital and know-how requisite for bringing out a printing of five thousand copies, and somewhat hopeful that they—not just the feminists but all the small regional publishers across the country—may be about to have their day: "As New York publishing is taken over by a core of merchandisers who simply push 'units' from printer to shredder by the fastest route possible, a need for something else is created. It is called the small, alternative, Independent Press. Its seeds really started blowing in the 60's just as old houses began to fall in the merger swath. It is the slice of tomorrow."[30]

Working in one of the smaller, or the more scholarly, or the more widely scattered publishing houses is of course no guarantee of job security or freedom from pressure. University presses are subject to continuous financial constraints;[31] small new houses, often under-capitalized, sometimes go under. Nonetheless, it cannot be too much emphasized that if you want a "career in publishing" you should consider a wide range of jobs besides editing, a wide area of the country besides New York, and an increasingly wide spectrum of firms besides the best-known Manhattan ones.

The career of Barbara Perkins, the promotion manager of a medium-size western university press, is an example of these last points.[32] In 1970 Perkins, who had had the equivalent of an English major in college, was a former elementary school teacher married to a graduate student in English. She had been out of the job market for several years, bringing up her two children. When she suddenly found it necessary to go back to work, there were secretarial jobs to be had, but no teaching ones. When she applied for a secretarial position at a university press, the man interviewing her was impressed with her liberal arts background but warned her that the job would be strictly a dead end. Wearily, he added, "and *if* you were to take it, you'd have all sorts of miscellaneous duties, like setting up a book display booth every year at the MLA meeting. I suppose I'd have to explain all that to you."

Perkins, however, had gone to MLA meetings with her husband and knew about book display booths. She thinks that being able to tell her interviewer so was one of the lucky accidents that helped her clinch the job. Later, there were other serendipitous happenings: for example, after Barbara had been in the job a few months her immediate superior suddenly resigned, and Perkins was asked to take over the other's duties in addition to her own ("just temporarily"). Before long, the man who had interviewed her also left for another position, and Perkins was asked to see whether she could compile and produce the spring catalogue—thirty books to describe, categorize, and try to make irresistible to the reading public. She decided to try it rather than hang back, feel exploited, and protest, "But that's not in my job description."

Eventually, after several more months, her gamble in doing the extra work of the job "above" her without the extra salary or the title did in fact pay off: she was made promotion manager of the university press, responsible for all publicity on some sixty books a year. Having now held the position for six years, she considers it the "ideal job." Her own account (below) of what she does and how she feels about it is an example of the excitement that many people with liberal arts backgrounds find in noneditorial jobs in publishing houses all over the country.

From Teacher to Secretary to Promotion Manager:
BARBARA PERKINS

This promotion manager, like most people working for publishers, leads a fragmented life. I'm responsible for advertising, direct mail, catalogues, publicity, and overseeing two half-time assistants who handle review lists, news releases, and exhibits. Put briefly, when one tries to conceive of all the ways a potential buyer might hear of a particular book, it is my job to have thought of them and done something about them. Whether a customer is attracted to a book through a jacket description, a good review, a display of the book at a meeting, an interview with the author on the radio—any and all of this comes about in large part because of the Promotion Department.

The job itself never has definite, cleancut limits. Once a book is published, it becomes my baby. My actual involvement with the book, though, has begun before its publication, since twice a year I put together our seasonal catalogues, in which I describe all books that are forthcoming the next spring or fall.

The best part about working for a publisher is that the subject is always changing, often fascinating, and usually challenging. On a typical day I may write copy for a direct mail piece for teachers on a weaving book, talk with an author about the nomads of northern Afghanistan, find out how many Field and Stream subscribers there are in our state, and write jacket copy for a book on ancient Chinese agriculture.

This, even on a typical day, may be interspersed with having to decide whether our sales conference five months hence should include Salad Mimosa or cole slaw (the caterer at a far-off Hilton has called in a frenzy), how long an extension cord I must order for the after-lunch film, and what to say to an author who insists that I get him an interview on the "Today" show. The PR aspects of a job like mine cannot be underestimated in terms of the time and skill they take. Also it helps to be able to write pretty fluently. At the same time I need to be affable to authors, reviewers, my peers, booksellers, book salesmen, librarians, and our customers—even when some of the latter phone me to ask what size are the books we publish, as they want to build some appropriate book shelves.

I usually make a list toward the end of each day, jotting down the things I must do the next day or else be hanged. I am eminently interruptible, by production people with galleys to be proofread and returned to the plant immediately, authors who are frantic about having seen no reviews of their book, calls from advertising salesmen who want to make me a deal that I can't refuse, mailing bureau employees who say that the labels I sent them won't adhere to the circulars I sent, and sales reps who want to know why they don't have their order forms.

*Beyond the obvious fact that I deal with a product (ugh)—a book—
whose subject and author are always changing, I've found a very real joy
in the people I meet and work with. People in the book business, including
salesmen who drive thousands of miles a year with a car trunk filled with
books, tend to be bright and funny and interesting.*

*There are deadlines galore, and it's what I like least about this job. But if
you can't live with them, you're sunk. Living with them means learning to
tell which ones are grimmest. The promotion manager, who is given the
chore of finding each book's audience and then luring them into buying it
so that the firm can make more money so that it can publish more books so
that the promotion manager will have more deadlines, must invariably ask
herself (or himself), "Has everything been done for this book that can possibly be done?" And when, as is often the case, the answer is a baleful no,
he or she somehow has to live with that too, along with the deadlines.*[33]

Questions implicit in the beginning of this chapter (What is happening in book publishing? Are the changes of the 1970s and 1980s
creating fewer jobs? More jobs? Different jobs?) cannot be answered
definitively, even by those inside the world of book publishing. Most
of the people I have consulted, however, urge you to try to make your
way into it if (but only if) "you are so fascinated by everything connected with the making of books that you can't stay away." That is the
kind of person, they agree, who will somehow find a job as long as
book publishing exists.

How long will that be? Most people in the industry think it will
continue to exist, more or less as we know it, for the foreseeable future. They are hopeful that proposed legislation may in part reverse
the swallowing up of small companies by conglomerates. They are
not entirely daunted by the shadow of the new technology; indeed
they see that it can augment present-day publishing procedures.[34]
But they do not see it soon replacing the actual printed book that one
can hold in one's hand. After all, they point out, the much-heralded
"electronic classroom" of the sixties and seventies has fallen rather
short of its promise. Since books and the companies that produce
and distribute them may be around for some time to come,[35] they
urge qualified applicants to try for jobs: "Have the hope that you may
be able to get in, but not a *blind* hope."

11. Possibilities in the Media and Related Fields

Two trends signal heady times for communications-related industries. One is the public's growing hunger for information—to make decisions as consumers, to gain influence in their jobs, for self-improvement and entertainment. The other is technological, the emergence of new outlets for information, such as cable television and teletext, that have filled in the traditional gaps between the print and broadcast media.

—Dan Hulbert, "Communications: Signals are 'Go,'"
New York Times, October 12, 1980

The news media today, although often blamed for various national malaises from the decay of American ethics, to sensationalism, to the decline of the English language, hold enormous fascination for most of us. In particular, those of us who study or teach English language and literature sometimes tend to think, when we read a well-written news story or article, that perhaps we could have written it ourselves. At other times, on hearing how competitive the journalism field has become, we may conclude that the media form a world closed to everybody except those who began to prepare for it as undergraduates.

Obviously the communications industry today is an enormous, complex, and evolving one. It would be futile to try in this chapter to give an introduction to the whole field and its many specialties and subspecialties. For an overview of the way the media currently operate, turn to Wilbur Schramm's *Men, Messages, and Media*,[1] or a book by Peter Sandman, David Rubin, and David Sachsman, *Media: An Introductory Analysis of American Mass Communications*.[2] For a prediction of what the media may soon become, read Anthony Smith's *Goodbye Gutenberg*.[3]

This chapter, however, deals with a far more specific question than these three books do: what chance is there for readers who have majored, earned graduate degrees in, or taught in a humanities field to enter some branch of the media? In the following discussion I am using the term "media" broadly, to include both "print journalism" (newspapers, magazines, public relations, and advertising) and "broadcast journalism" (radio and TV).

NEWSPAPERS

Of all the fields involving the use of words to communicate information, newspapers are probably the most visible. There are today well over seventeen hundred daily newspapers in the United States, as well as thousands of weekly papers and trade, consumer, and other specialized publications classified as newspapers.

How can you find a position on one of them? When asked what qualifications applicants to their various papers should have, editors in various parts of the country agreed that the basic requirements were a bachelor's degree and a strong liberal arts background. Probably there will never be consensus, however, on whether a journalism major is the best preparation for a newspaper career. As Gerald Sass of the Gannet Newspaper Foundation points out, "about 80% of our editors prefer journalism school graduates over other college majors. They want graduates who can 'hit the street running'—people who can go to work competently from the day they start."[4] Professor William Johnston of the University of Washington's School of Communications tends to agree, noting that since journalism majors are not allowed to take more than 25 percent of their course work in their major field, they have a good chance to distribute the rest of their classes throughout liberal arts areas.[5] On the other hand Don Hatfield, managing editor of the Huntington, West Virginia *Advertiser*, says, "We like [our candidates] to have as much education as possible (and it doesn't matter if the major isn't journalism, as long as they've had the basics)."[6]

Next comes demonstrable writing ability. Employers will want evidence of it, such as a portfolio with clippings of your writing published in a college paper, a community newspaper, an organizational newsletter, or wherever you may have had a chance to appear in print, preferably in the last two years. Try to include a variety of samples of your writing. Do not submit academic term papers unless they are written in nontechnical language, are the only evidence of your writing skill available, and are presented in a professional looking, easy to read format.[7]

Don Carter, a former English major and now consumer affairs reporter for the *Seattle Post-Intelligencer*, advises that you should be ready to take an on-the-spot writing test. The published samples with your by-line are an *indication* of what you can do; at the same time, the person interviewing you for a job doesn't know the circumstances under which they were written, or how much they have been edited by someone else. Sometimes you may be asked to take a copy editing test, which usually involves editing one or more newspaper stories. If you do well on this, some papers will ask for a "try out" (several days or a week of actually working for the paper). Advice from one who passed this test recently is to "bone up by studying any standard journalism text on copy editing. If the newspaper has its own style sheet, try to get hold of a copy; if not, the Associated Press and the *New York Times* style books are classics. Accuracy, consistency, and concision are more important than the fine points of newspaper practice in any case."[8]

In journalism as nearly everywhere, personal qualifications enter in. Paul McKalip, senior editor of the Tucson, Arizona *Citizen*, says that he looks for "intelligence, wide range of interests, ambition to advance, skills, thoroughness, accuracy, ability to meet deadlines, excellence in spelling and grammar"; Dr. Harvey Jacobs, the editor of the *Indianapolis News*, wants on his staff "a person who is well-founded in liberal arts, insatiably curious, well-mannered in person and on the telephone, a skilled researcher on the street and in the library."[9]

The most important criterion of all, however, according to many editors, is having had some prior newspaper staff experience. It is generally assumed that you will have demonstrated your serious interest in newspapers by working as an undergraduate on your college paper. Getting on the staff is usually not too difficult and the experience pays off later, showing employers that you are interested in and committed to a newspaper career.

But experience on a college paper is only a beginning. If you intend to apply to a large metropolitan daily, you should have at least two years' experience on a smaller paper—a suburban weekly or bi-weekly, a special-interest paper, or a small-town daily. Far less departmentalized than the big city dailies, the smaller paper can offer a new reporter a wide variety of experience, plus time to learn from veteran staff members. On the larger metropolitan papers, as one assistant city editor pointed out, "the pace is so fast that nobody can afford the time to train beginners, no matter how good their background."[10] Don't assume, though, that the only value of working on a small paper is as a stepping stone to a larger one. Smaller papers— ranging from tiny weeklies to larger "nonmetropolitan" dailies—are often the communications hub of their communities. Because there is less media competition in their areas, they are read more carefully by their subscribers. These papers, too, usually are well staffed, with more persons (in proportion to the size of their circulation) digging up information than on a large city daily. "It's these papers," says Johnston, "that really have the clout in community affairs." You may find that you like such a paper and want to stay there.

On all kinds of papers large and small, competition is getting stiffer every year, Johnston warns. Rising production costs make newspapers even more risky financial enterprises than formerly; hence fewer positions are being filled, and the editors are trying to get the best possible value from each reporter. Newspaper income is precarious, too, because each paper is in competition for advertising dollars with other papers and other kinds of media. More people are trying to get into journalism than ever before: former teachers; many socially conscious persons who see journalism as a forum; and more women than ever before, many of them seeing journalism as a constructive way to serve feminist causes.

Even with increased competition, opportunities are still there, newspaper people have told me recently. Applicants simply have to be better prepared, more resourceful, and more energetic than they were a few years ago. For example, one professor of journalism told me that members of his news reporting class all go out one day a week and work as reporters for small-town papers. Many of them have arranged to work all next summer on these papers, free, for the experience.

Liberal arts majors without this "hands-on" experience must take special steps to qualify themselves. Any recent substantial work you may have done on professional newsletters or business house organs will help. If as publicity chairperson of an organization you cover events for your local paper in a professional rather than an amateur way, or if you write guest columns in a paper or magazine, or get on an "Op-Ed" page with your rebuttal to a national columnist (going beyond a mere "letter to the editor") you will help qualify yourself. Or, says Johnston, if you volunteer your services to a neighborhood paper this too can help—provided you stick at it long enough to learn how to report and to collect a string of printed stories, preferably with by-lines.[11]

Another entering wedge, if you don't have an undergraduate major or minor in communications, would be to enroll in a few courses at your nearest school of communications. You could help greatly in preparing yourself if you took from nine to fifteen credit hours of classes in reporting and advertising. Such course work might open doors to you that would otherwise be closed to an English major or graduate student who had not demonstrated such an active interest in newspapers. Johnston urges you to take newswriting and reporting: "These two courses alone will give you a basis for deciding whether you want to go on in newspaper work."

Of course there may still be a question in your mind whether your academic work in the humanities has qualified or disqualified you to be a journalist. Would there be a lot for you to unlearn? Could you make the transition?

"One of the basic attitudes that must be corrected," writes a Ph.D. in English now working in the media field, "is the fear that having been in school for twenty years studying one field disqualifies one from doing anything else. This simply is not true. However, the job candidates *must* convince himself of this . . . because he will then have to convince prospective employers of the same thing." [12]

Students of English language and literature are well suited to working on newspapers, according to Craig Sanders, who first headed the English department and now heads the communications department at Bellevue Community College (Washington): "Through their college courses they've become interested in everything—history, biography, events, people, ideas, opinions—and they've developed ability to analyze and organize." [13]

In addition, John Schacht points out from his vantage point as Ph.D. in English and former newspaper editor and journalism professor: "A newspaper person has to develop curiosity about a lot of things which he or she probably didn't follow too closely as a teacher. . . . What sort of things? In highfalutin terms, societal institutions and their interrelationships; in plain English, how things work—the city council, the school district, the numbers game setup in the ghetto, the local basketball team." [14]

English majors, Schacht wrote recently, would do well to develop the skill of writing "analytical stories." These, he specifies, are "not opinion pieces—readers aren't especially interested in what you think about something, but they are interested in what you've found out about something—and this last can mean adding up and sifting out and generalizing intelligently (which English majors certainly should have had experience in doing)." [15]

In addition to learning to collect and to analyze information, humanities majors have a few academic habits to unlearn. Obviously you will have to get used to a different time span: from starting out on a story, getting the information, writing and rewriting, the cycle is usually one of hours or days rather than weeks or months. (The relentless year-long pursuit by Woodward and Bernstein of their quarry in *All the President's Men* is certainly an exception to the typical newspaper assignment.) Those who have gone into journalism from academia, however, as Schacht did, find the change of pace less threatening than they had expected. Says Schacht: "You just learn to do it by practice. The pressure—within limits, I suppose—should be an enjoyable part of the job. I think most newspaper people enjoy the verbal legerdemain of turning out finished (if generally very minor) bits of writing in nothing flat: really nothing to it, they say, blushing modestly."[16] One other mental adjustment humanities majors do have to make is in their sense of their audience: obviously journalists haven't the luxury of scholars, who can assume that readers will on the whole share their preconceptions.

Obviously the switch from the classroom to a newspaper office isn't for everyone. On the whole, if you are going to make such a transition, the earlier in your career the better. "It's a young person's business," William Johnston says of journalism. Nonetheless, I have talked with half a dozen men and women who have made such a change after finishing Ph.D.'s in English, and another four who have done it after getting M.A.'s. Each person's story is a bit different. Some edge gradually into print journalism, like Ann Strosnider, a high school English teacher whose story of her late change to journalism may encourage some readers.

"I Didn't Think I Could Do Anything Else but Teach":
ANN STROSNIDER

I had been a high school English teacher for five years, and I was liking it less and less. What I really wanted to do was to write, not to teach students who didn't want to learn. But everything in my recent background seemed to point to my staying in teaching. I had majored in English and received an M.A. in it, and had turned into your standard Ph.D. candidate type, to the point where I really didn't think I could do anything but teach. Finally, one summer after reading Richard Bolles' Parachute and also the first edition of Aside from Teaching English, I decided that there had to be a way whereby I could do what I really wanted to do. So I went to the University of Washington, took a course in newswriting with Fendall Xerxa—a wonderful discipline in learning to write fast and accurately—and while I was there worked on the Daily. The latter was very helpful in my later job applications, since I had clips to show people when I was interviewed.

The next fall I was back in my classroom, but by then I had started freelancing. Weaving and Fibre News had an ad in a Seattle paper for a writer: I sent them copies of my clips and to my surprise they phoned me, interviewed me by phone, and started giving me assignments. They paid well—by the column inch—around $150 for each article. Although not a weaver myself, I found that I could translate the technical language of weaving into nontechnical articles which were well received. I also wrote a good deal about the marketing side of weaving, about arts and crafts fairs, about the "one per cent for the arts" program, and I did profiles of individual weavers and other craftspersons.

Through friends I made doing these articles, I got assignments from other crafts magazines—Fibre Arts, Ceramics Monthly, and By Hand. I also began to do restaurant reviews for Seattle area papers. If you're a good writer, you can write about anything. Ask questions, keep learning, and try to put yourself in your reader's place.

Once I had quite a good collection of clips from these magazines, I started calling on editors in their offices. I went to every newspaper office, large and small, within driving range of our house. I was surprised at how encouraging nearly all of the editors were, once they found that I did have a portfolio of published articles to show them. Only one paper refused to see me at all. Nobody put me down because I was older, or hadn't already worked on a paper.

Eventually I took a leave of absence from my teaching job in order to devote full time to freelance writing and jobhunting. Finally I heard about the free listing service of the Washington State Newspaper Publishers' Association, sent in my capsule résumé, and got a call from my present employer, the Federal Way News, as a result. Although three interviews with them didn't get me the job I'd applied for, a month later they called me about another job, and they hired me as copy editor and "Living" writer; after they saw that I could cover all sorts of meetings well, they made me a reporter. I've been a full-time journalist for ten months now, and I like it much better than teaching.

Even though I took a pay cut by leaving teaching, and even though I put in a forty-eight hour work week (plus sometimes working on a story at home over the weekends), it's well worth it. The three deadline days each week (our paper comes out on Sundays, Wednesdays, and Fridays, so the deadlines are Mondays, Wednesdays, and Fridays) are gruelling yet somehow very satisfying. I feel a much greater sense of accomplishment than when I was grading papers and preparing lessons.

I'd like to urge people who are thinking about changing from teaching English to using their writing skills to take steps and do it. Get started by freelancing for small specialized magazines. They often do need writers, and many of them do pay. Lots of them aren't listed in Writer's Market; you have to keep alert for advertisements, as I did; or pick a field in which you'd like to become an expert; send in a query letter about an article you'd like to write, and keep going from there.[17]

Strosnider's narrative highlights one of the big differences between applying for journalism jobs and for academic ones. Among newspapers the whole process is apt to be much less formal. Some vacancies are widely advertised, some are not. Watch for listings in campus placement centers, in the classified ads of the newspapers themselves, as well as the lists of "jobs, internships, and scholarships" posted on the bulletin boards of the school or department of communications on any large campus. Get in touch with your state newspaper publishers' association, which may publish free monthly listings of job candidates such as the one that brought Strosnider her present job. Get acquainted with the dozen or so journalism periodicals, among them *The Quill, Columbia Journalism Review, Editor and Publisher, Journalism Quarterly*, and *Pro/comm* [The Professional Communicator], published by Women in Communications, Inc. You'll find some of these in your public or university library. Though they don't all carry regular job listings, browsing in them will help you get acquainted with the whole field.

If you are sending résumés or letters of application for newspaper positions, you should list any courses taken in communications, political science, economics, history, or English. Give job descriptions and time span covered for any work in communications. Try to individualize your letter; show that you've read the paper to which you are applying. Study the community itself. And finally, keep in touch with your college placement office to register for interviews with media groups and large corporations that may not seem to be involved directly with media but "own and publish newspapers, house organs, or general-interest magazines, or who own broadcast stations." [18]

Most people in journalism agree with Ann Strosnider that it's crucial to visit and get to know editors in the region where you want to work. Says William Johnston: "An editor often finds a young person *from his locality* (the *local* part here is very important) rather persuasive. A person who already knows the town where the paper is can cut down his training time by half." [19]

Aside from these detailed questions about the job search and about employers' expectations, many readers may be wondering whether the whole area of print journalism may be in such a state of flux that a career in it is unpredictable. Within the past year or two, a spate of newspaper and magazine articles and at least one widely heralded book have appeared suggesting that the "electronic revolution" may be about to revolutionize completely not only our reading and viewing habits but the professional lives of anyone who works for the media.

Anthony Smith is one such writer. In his *Goodbye Gutenberg: The*

Newspaper Revolution of the 1980's, he develops at great length the idea that "electronics has been summoned to resolve the internal tensions and crises which face the [newspaper] medium today." He believes that "the social function of the newspaper is changing, as is the whole culture of journalism," and as a result the journalist will become, rather than the writer-reporter of today, someone Smith calls an "information technician." [20]

All this may be true in the long run. But what effect is such an impending change having today, in the early 1980s? In an attempt to explore this question, I asked half a dozen journalists and three professors of journalism what they thought of this thesis. Their answers were couched in less global terms than Smith's predictions. From my admittedly informal and limited survey, the following points emerged:

1. Most reporters like the video display terminal (VDT) now beginning to be in common use in newsrooms. They can learn to use it in two or three days, and it enables them to set their own type. At the same time it reduces delays and cuts down on the cost of production.

2. Working on the VDT does not mean any great change in reporters' qualifications or training. They do, however, have to be more precise in copy editing their own work, or they'll waste the time of the desk editor, who still goes over the final copy. According to William Johnston they "must have a good vocabulary, must use it wisely; the basics of spelling, punctuation, sentence structure, and, in short, of good, clear writing must have become pretty automatic for them."

3. Electronic information storage and retrieval systems are very helpful, and more and more newspapers are now able to plug into such systems. Says one journalist, "You can turn up a lot more information, now, because you know that after you've come up with it, computers can deal with it. You can investigate certain problems in seconds that not long ago would have taken days, weeks, or even months." [21]

4. In a slightly different area of writing, the fortunate few freelance writers who have access to, or who can afford to rent or buy, word processing machines report somewhat increased productivity and a much greater willingness to make continuous revisions of their own work or to accept the suggestions of their publisher's copy editors. [22]

It would seem, then, that what will be called for is not a whole new breed of print journalists, but people who, in proportion as they come to the profession well trained, may have access to tools that help them do more quickly and efficiently what the profession has always been trying to do—relay information to waiting readers.

OPPORTUNITIES IN RADIO AND TELEVISION

The idea of working for the broadcast media suggests to most people either appearing as commentator on news broadcasts or else writing material for network comedies or documentaries. Most readers have already heard many times that none of these specialized careers is particularly easy to enter. But there are many other, related jobs.

Dean Woolley, personnel director for radio and TV at Seattle's KING Broadcasting Company (NBC affiliate), says that even though nearly everyone applying for a job at KING does hope eventually to go on the air, the company employs over 220 people who are never seen or heard by the public, along with about a tenth of that number who are well known to the public. In the newsroom some of these invisible but important staff members serve as reporters, writers, editors, researchers, camerapersons, producers, and graphics specialists. In the programming department there are film editors, set designers, graphics experts, and the production director.[23]

Jean Enerson of KING, though herself an anchorperson on the evening news, says that such jobs as hers are much harder to get now than they were when she started in the field in the early 1970s with an M.A. in communications and another in political science. Enerson, who had originally planned to be a teacher, says that she "somewhat takes care of that urge now through television." At present, she says, people hoping to enter television "should consider jobs that may be less highly visible." In the early 1980s, the most productive and lucrative TV jobs, those that offer the most rapid advancement, are in technology—dealing with engineering, miniaturization, and satellite transmission. If, however, as a liberal arts major you don't have and don't want to acquire the scientific background necessary for these areas, then Enerson urges that you develop as much expertise as possible in one or more fields of interest to TV viewers—the theater, the arts, entertainment, sports—and see where you can fit in on the program planning, research, or writing side. There are opportunities to be found if you can do thorough research (yet still meet deadlines) for TV news and specials.[24]

Enerson points out, as does Carol Hale Harm of Indianapolis's Station WIAN, that there are many possibilities in the growing field of community and educational television. Although the pay is low, the field is open to new people with good ideas. You should write directly to stations in your own area and then visit the producers of programs for which you would like to write. If you have an interesting idea for a community television program, you may find yourself acting as the host as well as the writer.

Many people have found that they can get a foot in the door by volunteering to arrange for and announce programs of classical music for small FM stations. The pay is at first nonexistent, then minimal, but there is great variety of experience. Others have found William Johnston's advice useful. "Go to a small town," he urges, "and get yourself a job on a small three- or four-person station. There you'll learn to do everything." [25]

Several people now writing for the broadcast media say that cracking the market for radio scripts is far easier than selling TV scripts. You can deduce the requirements for most radio programs by listening to several of them, but TV programs come and go more rapidly; by the time a newcomer has written and submitted scripts for a series, it could have been canceled or had its direction changed completely. Most TV producers, moreover, are wary of scripts not submitted through established literary agents. Anyone who is convinced that he wants to write for TV should try to meet with a production staff; scripts for most TV programs are done by writers who live near the studios and work closely with the producers.

Currently there is room in the broadcast media for many different kinds of people. Dean Woolley says that KING has few preconceptions about what the backgrounds of new staff members should be. Their present staff "represents a wide spectrum in education, experience, and life style, including people from 19 to 84 years old." Ideally, however, says Woolley, if she were asked to pick out the single best preparation for a radio or TV career, it would include a broad liberal arts background, followed either by an internship in a university's school of public affairs or by experience in practical politics. [26]

Any basic courses you may have taken in these fields can help serve as an entering wedge, even though you will have to learn a lot on the job. An entry-level position mentioned by Woolley as a good one was selling FM advertising time. For anyone combining a knowledge of classical music with sales experience, such a position would be a chance to get on a radio staff and begin to learn the ropes while in a relatively pressure-free job.

Whatever job you start with in this field, Woolley and others agree, you need versatility. "Everyone may have to pitch in at any time and do whatever needs to be done," she explained. This is one reason why in her interviewing of candidates for any position she gives them a typing test. "In radio and TV," she contends, "typing ability need *not* relegate you to clerical jobs; it is simply your life-preserver many times a day; no matter whether you're a new reporter or the vice-president in charge of production, you will often want to type up, revising as you type, your own ideas or your version of new material that is being discussed. Anyone who stood on his or her dignity and refused to type his own stuff because it was a 'clerical' job wouldn't last long."

The qualifications for success in radio and TV would seem to involve qualities of personality and temperament as much as they do experience and education. "The prerequisite that comes to mind is great energy," says Woolley. "Be able to cope with yourself. We need self-motivated people, who don't pay too much attention to the idea of an eight-hour day." [27]

Woolley's ideas are graphically illustrated by the narratives of two young women of quite different educational backgrounds, each of whom has worked her way up from a position remote from broadcasting into a place in the broadcast media which she finds totally absorbing.

FROM THE SATURDAY MARKET TO NATIONAL PUBLIC RADIO: M'LOU ZAHNER-OLLSWANG

I never went to college, although I have an "A level" certificate in English literature from an English girls' high school. I got into radio accidentally. After I moved to Eugene, Oregon, I did a great variety of things. I worked first in ceramics; then I managed a sort of flea market, where university students and townspeople sell arts, crafts, and baked goods; and next I did the baking for a tavern, finally becoming the manager of a small neighborhood grocery store specializing in health foods and alternative foods. Eventually I started writing a pastry column for the local paper; then the column widened to cover foods generally, and I got to be known locally as a connoisseur of food (which is totally untrue).

Being a disciple of S. J. Perelman, I gradually began to shift the emphasis of my column from food to humor. Somebody suggested that I do a version of my column over the radio. I soon found an FM classical station that was receptive to my suggestion for a series. If you come up with an idea and the station hasn't already had one like it, they'll usually put it on the air.

When I began I had no broadcasting experience whatever. Processes like sound mixing were totally strange to me. The only technical thing I knew how to do was to splice tape; therefore all my early shows had lots of "sound collages." Fortunately the station I worked with, KLCC in Eugene, was very open to people coming in with just nothing, and learning about radio by helping them. Before long I got together six programs (each one a five-minute segment) and submitted them to the NPR program, "All Things Considered." Several of them were accepted, and since then I've been a fairly regular contributor to this program. This past year I won a grant

from the Corporation for Public Broadcasting which was an internship in
Washington, D.C. to learn more about broadcasting techniques. I was also
sent to Washington in November 1980, to do a half-hour retrospective show
on the anniversary of the capture of the hostages in Iran, as well as going
back in April 1981, to do a program for the tenth anniversary of "All
Things Considered."

To those who would like to get into public radio, I'd urge you to get to
know the people at a local noncommercial station that carries NPR radio.
Volunteer your time and get the hang of things. Then work up a few ideas,
submit them, be willing to do the work to make them into scripts, and keep
at it. There are informal internships that you could get if you made your
own spot. As you become more and more experienced, you have to blow
your own horn a little. You have to push. You sometimes have to call up
your station and say "Hey—that program I did on memory—where is it?
When do you plan to use it?"

Of course, in view of recent much-publicized budget cuts for National
Public Radio along with other public arts programs, I can't urge people to
explore this medium to the exclusion of all others. I think that public radio
will survive. Yet I myself am trying to broaden my base a bit by doing more
magazine writing and listening to job offers from commercial radio and TV.
I'd say that those interested should find out all they can about public
broadcasting but not put all their eggs into one basket.

I love my work. I'm independent. I get to choose what I do. If I had a
degree I might be tempted to teach audio production classes, which
wouldn't be good for me in the end.[28]

FROM DICKENS' NOVELS TO "GOOD MORNING AMERICA":
ALMA KADRAGIC

A few years ago I entered the doctoral program in English at the City
University of New York, ready to follow in the footsteps of my favorite
professor as a Victorian scholar. While writing my dissertation on nature
in Dickens' novels, I spent a good deal of time thinking about what to do
next. Since I hadn't gotten a certificate of tenure for my five years of teaching at a municipal college, and since other college jobs were so hard to
come by, I realized that my career as a college teacher was over.

I applied for all sorts of alternative jobs. The thought of getting into
broadcasting had occurred to me, but a friend who worked as a news producer for an ABC affiliate insisted that it was impossible to get a job in TV
news. However, the establishment of a new TV station to provide local
commercial programming in our area seemed a golden opportunity. Knowing that hundreds of applicants would be writing for jobs, I set out to discover someone who knew the station manager. Eventually, my father, who

taught economics at a nearby college, learned that the station manager taught a media course there. The dean of the faculty who had hired both of them became the contact who arranged an interview for me—which was inconclusive but proved fruitful. Although the station manager would not hire me for a permanent job because I had no TV experience, he told me to call the news director with suggestions for local news stories.

Although my first story suggestion was used only in an extremely abbreviated form, I got the chance to provide more and more of them, becoming increasingly familiar with what was entailed—the style rules of television news. Eventually I began to look seriously for a full-time well-paying job in broadcasting. Always leery of writing letters to people I don't know, I put my efforts into finding someone who might know someone who could tell me something useful. Through a friend's husband who worked for one of the networks, I talked with several people there, and then almost as an afterthought with someone at ABC. There the timing was right; I arrived in mid-April, exactly the moment, it turned out, to secure a job as a summer replacement. The man who interviewed me happened to be impressed with my Ph.D. and teaching background. He asked me to come back for a writing test.

My test assignment was to write a five-minute newscast. The problem: from reams of wire copy—more of which was being brought every few minutes—to determine the key news stories, while the television blared a presidential news conference. Thanks to my training on my college newspaper, and the graduate student's ability to concentrate, I met the two-hour deadline and was told I would be hired.

To underline the essential point: I got the interview through a contact, but I was hired because I did well on the writing test and because I had television production experience.

In news, every day is a fresh start. Yesterday's triumph is annihilated by today's mistake. Things do not drag on. A successful writer or producer makes few mistakes. One too many, and she's fired. I have had little difficulty in adjusting to working a day at a time. I have found it a relief to have no homework, no papers to mark, no rereading of works to be discussed in class the next day. Sometimes I reread Dickens' novels—for fun.

In the summer of 1977 there was an opening for an associate producer at "Good Morning, America" (GMA). As always in this business, I learned of the job through a friend. I applied and was hired within two weeks. The job offers much responsibility, more money than almost any academic with an endowed chair earns from teaching, and terrible working hours. I came in at midnight and seldon left before ten or eleven in the morning. For the first five hours, I was the on-duty producer responsible for all decisions relating to our show. I worked with a staff of five, supervising them in cutting film and tape news stories. Since I was the only one around at crucial times, I decided if we needed to order a satellite to get a foreign story on the show.

In October 1979, with more than two years on the midnight shift on my record, I was transferred to the Washington, D.C., staff of GMA. Just a year later, a position as full producer became available in New York. Once again the movers packed furniture and books, and once again I spent two months in a hotel already working at the new job and looking for a place to live.

These days I coordinate news coverage for GMA between three in the afternoon and midnight. The basic problem is to determine which news stories covered by the evening news program can be omitted from the morning news and which need to be told again. Then I have to make sure that anticipated events occurring the next day will be covered that morning by so-called advancer stories. Finally, with a breaking story, I help determine the extent and degree of coverage we might want. Before leaving, I prepare a three or four page report that the show producer uses in putting together the lineup for the morning broadcast.

In seven years at ABC I have been promoted three times and I have changed bureaus twice: what may be the normal work pattern of satisfaction followed by boredom, griping, trouble with superiors, followed by resolution, satisfaction, and so on is much accelerated in broadcasting. Neither good nor bad lasts forever. Turnover in personnel helps employees avoid burnout and at best generates creative tension.

Since broadcasting is my second career, I am always trying to find out how other people entered the field. My conclusion is that there is no straight path into broadcasting. While some get their start at small out-of-town stations, others do it in New York or Washington or Los Angeles. Some have degrees in broadcasting or communications. More do not. There is no reason why other Ph.D.'s in literature cannot make the transition to television news. It isn't easy, and it may require sacrifice of time and income in the beginning. But I find my present job more satisfying than college teaching.

To anyone who wants to make the switch, I'd suggest the following: (1) Cross-examine your friends to see if there isn't anyone who knows someone useful. (2) Look into the broadcasting or communications department at your school or another in the area. Meet faculty there to get further ideas. (3) Take a course in broadcasting to learn the terminology and focus your interests. (4) Read books about broadcasting. (5) Become familiar with your local stations, the smaller the better, and try to become involved with a project on a volunteer basis. (6) Consider cable, videodisc, or satellite television—many opportunities will exist in these new areas. (7) Ex-

cept at an educational television station, don't flaunt your advanced degrees. No one cares about them, and some may resent them tremendously.[29]

Working for a Magazine

Reputedly hard to enter and perhaps (according to a few pessimists) too precarious to worry about entering is another branch of the communications industry, magazines. With the recent death or transformation of so many national magazines (*Life*, *Collier's*, the *Saturday Evening Post*, to mention only a few), and with mounting outcries from publishers about the havoc caused by rising postage rates, you should not be surprised to hear some knowledgeable people advising you to stay away from magazines altogether. Yet nationwide, new magazines, both those of general interest and those aimed at special groups, have emerged fairly regularly in the past six years.

"How do you get a position on a magazine staff?" job-seekers ask. "Do you have to be an established writer? Or is there any other recommended route?" Here, even more than for most positions, there is no single best way. Occasionally, if you're a college student, you can win a contest and become a summer "guest editor." You can be a graduate student in political science who happens to send some poems to the *Atlantic Monthly* and their acceptance in turn leads to an entry-level position and ultimately to an associate editorship—as happened in the case of one of the *Atlantic*'s editors. You can read an ad in a newspaper, apply when you're fresh out of college, and get the job—as several members of the staffs of *Mademoiselle* and *Ms.* have done. You can use your experience on one magazine to get yourself a job on another or to serve as your backlog of knowledge if later you decide to start your own magazine.[30]

Members of the magazine staffs I talked to agree on two things: the requirements of magazine work differ from those of the other media, and you should start by getting any periodical experience you can, if necessary on a small one as a volunteer or an intern. A good background in writing could lead easily into copy editing and, with any luck, ultimately into manuscript evaluation, editing, and rewriting. Aside from that, whatever you can learn about page makeup and printing processes is a plus, even for work on the editorial side. As a writer-researcher for a general publication, you have to know how to get information from people's lips as well as from libraries. If you want to work for a scholarly journal, your graduate school training—even if in a different field—can be immensely helpful.

One suggestion for working your way onto the staff of a scholarly or professional journal is to convince an overworked and understaffed editor that he needs your kind of general assistance—even on an hourly basis—for proofing, evaluating manuscript overload, copy marking, or rewriting.

If you hope to get into the editorial rather than the production part of a magazine staff, it certainly doesn't hurt to have published articles of your own. The best way, says John Schacht, is to concentrate at first on the smaller magazines. Of the students in his course at the University of Illinois in freelance writing for magazines, he estimates that at least half get something published in a magazine while they are still in the course. Having studied *Writer's Market* to know where to send their work, they get it accepted by a variety of lesser known but widely read weeklies or monthlies, among them *Focus/Midwest, Chicago Tribune Magazine, Illinois Schools Journal, Graphic Arts Monthly, Bicycling, Quill and Scroll, Air Progress, Chicagoland, Illinois Issues, Illinois Times, Christian Century, Jewish Frontier,* and the *Journal of Popular Culture*. As Schacht says, "The main point in freelancing, and almost the only point, is to figure out what readers of a particular magazine are interested in—then write it. Any magazine editor I've ever heard talk about freelancing has said this, or something like it: 'If you want to write for my magazine, *read my magazine.*'"

David Brewster, former English teacher and now editor of Seattle's *Weekly,* believes: "The successful magazine writer has to find out what people are potentially interested in, to collect facts, opinions, hypotheses, to be aware of nuances on all sides, and then ultimately to take his own stand." Although Brewster was not actively looking for more staff members, he had the following advice for those hoping to get into the magazine field: "First, have a good broad Liberal Arts background. But don't *lean* on your degree or degrees. You have to have done *and published* some writing that you can show when you apply. It doesn't matter as much where you've published as *that* you've published, that you've developed some expertise in writing for an audience. So sit down and write. Then get your pieces placed (and don't overlook 'little magazines,' university magazines, and periodicals put out by foundations and special interest groups that can't pay anything. They're a good place to get started)." [31]

PUBLIC RELATIONS

Liberal arts majors should also consider another field, that of public relations, which according to the *Occupational Outlook Handbook* employs more persons than any other branch of the media. The rapidly expanding field of public relations is currently rather loosely defined, both in its scope and its methods. Some people lump it together with advertising, and others consider the public relations consultant a person who whitewashes, in some secret and probably disreputable way, the activities of his or her clients. But Jerry della Femina, head of the influential Madison Avenue PR firm of Della Femina, Travisano and Partners, told a seminar of the Public Relations Society of America, "There's nothing mysterious about what a PR person does; it's all based on a lot of research and a lot of hard work." [32]

The PR field lacks a single formalized kind of training or means of entry. To be sure, there are excellent courses with labels like "Theory and Practice of Public Relations" which you can take in almost any university's school of communications; yet only one of the ten practicing public relations people I talked to had taken one. Usually people come into the world of public relations after being newspaper reporters, teachers, editors, or writers in other fields.

Occasionally if you have a job or close contacts with a business whose workings you come to know extremely well, you may start doing small pieces of newspaper publicity about it and in time be able to turn yourself into a full-time PR person for this specialized area. A young woman who writes press releases, brochures, newsletters, and trade journal articles for heavy industry (logging, concrete, fiberglass, and general construction) got into public relations in such a way. As she says, since nearly everyone in her family worked in heavy industry, she became so saturated with information that it was easy to start writing. Now, with her own one-woman agency, she has branched out into other business areas. [33]

Other people go from reporting or teaching into public relations simply by taking on a few people or organizations as clients, setting up their own one- or two-person consulting firms, then acquiring more clients. At a 1976 conference on careers in the media, several of these PR persons told aspirants to their field what they saw as the requisites. According to Fern Olsen, who five years ago founded the three-person firm of Harmony Graphics, Inc., in Seattle, the requirements for a PR career are curiosity, enthusiasm, and a background in journalism. "There's no such thing as a forty-hour week in this business," she reported. "You have to be flexible in everything, and willing to stick with an assignment until you get it done, whether it's daytime, evening, or a weekend." A woman doing freelance public relations pointed out that "you always have to keep combating the negative image of PR. In each job you do, you may have to establish your credibility all over again. In publicizing a project for a social service agency, for instance—*you* know you're a professional reporter and PR person, but to the social workers you may seem an outsider, an amateur, because you haven't a degree in social work or public administration." [34]

A former English teacher who became a freelance consultant after twenty-five years of newspaper reporting told a group at a workshop on jobs in communications: "there is a big field in PR; people *do* need you; many businesses and nonprofit organizations are looking for freelance PR people, among them public information agencies, school districts, small theaters, and organizers of special events." She feels that a background combining teaching and journalism gives one most of the necessary skills to be a public relations consultant, and that the rest are best learned on the job.

While some people set up on their own as consultants and are hired by new or small businesses, most public relations today is carried on by large firms specializing in public relations for their client business firms, though sometimes also working with advertising firms. (Fewer and fewer firms today do *both* advertising and PR.) The Public Relations Society of America performs an important function by trying to educate the public, teaching that public relations isn't all a matter of press releases, press parties, and hoopla, designed by apologists to atone for the sins of their clients. Instead, says an account executive for a large PR firm with offices both in New York and on the West Coast, public relations firms increasingly perform an educational role in campaigns for ecology, improved health care, or peaceful social change. [35]

A woman who recently joined a large PR firm with offices in New York City and on the West Coast is typical of those who realize the positive potential of public relations. As account executive for a new firm manufacturing water treatment systems that eliminate industrial wastes, she sees her firm as "actually *doing* something about waste treatment," and thinks of herself as helping bridge the gap between the industrialist and the public. She writes press releases and articles for trade journals, helps with sales presentations, decides which exhibits and trade fairs her client should be represented in, and in general "finds out where her client wants to be and then helps him to get there."

When I asked her if she had had a background of courses in communications, marketing, or technology, she explained that she had no course work beyond her B.A. at Wellesley College, where fourteen years ago she had majored in Biblical history and taken more than enough English courses to have had a second major in English. It was mainly her previous position as editor-in-chief for a research organization that had gotten her the new PR job; she felt that "even in today's highly specialized world, experience counts more than academic credits."

To enter the field of PR, she prescribed involvement "in doing PR for political campaigns, or as a volunteer for some organization or cause that excites you. PR is one field in which nobody cares where you get your experience. If you're a woman just thinking about returning to the job market, you can start getting experience wherever you are. Publicizing events for your P.T.A. is PR; so is writing newsletters for the A.A.U.W., the A.C.L.U., your church, or any other group you believe in. Jump in and get some practice and build up a bunch of published work that next year you can show employers. Meanwhile, if you want to do some reading, there's the *Public Relations Quarterly* and the book that's considered the bible of PR, Cutlip and Center's *Effective Public Relations*." [36]

This method of breaking into PR was one that Jerry della Femina agreed with. He thought that anyone interested both in people and in ideas could get into PR if he had enough determination. (He himself came into it from advertising, and got into advertising—with no college credentials—by sheer persistence. Having worked at every manual job he could find for seven years while he wrote ads and other copy, he got a few ads placed now and then on a freelance basis and showed them to employers as he made the rounds of New York offices.) When I asked him whether academic people, former teachers and graduate students, would be passed by as "overqualified" in PR, he said: "No—not if they're really interested in the kind of thing that PR does, and see its possibilities. Nobody is overqualified for anything—unless he thinks he is. You can put all you've done and all you know into almost any job—if you see the possibilities. But tell your English types that they've got to be 'street wise,' not just 'book wise.' Tell them that they've got to read all sorts of people writing today, not just the great ones. Tell them to read Jimmy Breslin and Hunter Thompson. Tell them to keep their eyes and ears open for everything that's happening." [37]

ADVERTISING

Distinct from public relations yet drawing on many of the same kinds of skill is the advertising business. L. Roy Blumenthal defines the two to point up the difference: "Advertising is the use of paid

space or time for the presentation of a sales message. . . . Public relations is the use of all communications media for the promotion and
furtherance, subtly or overtly, for a commercial property or a cause
without the use of paid space." [38]

Among several advertising people interviewed, Steve Seiter of
McCann-Erickson had fairly specific advice for job-seekers. First he
warned that employers are turned off by vague expressions of "interest in advertising." The more you know about what subspecialties
exist within this huge field (writing, art direction, account management, media, and others), the better your chance of getting a job.
Copywriting is probably the closest to the background of applicants
with degrees in English, although account management is a possibility for those who, in addition to having writing ability, can deal
with clients and their business problems.

To work with one of the larger advertising agencies you need previous experience. Ideally, urged Seiter, you should take an introductory course in advertising in a university communications department, then get as much and as varied writing experience as you can.
Before you apply for a job in advertising, try to get involved in editing a newsletter, getting out house organs for business, pamphlets,
brochures for organizations, or press releases for a political campaign. Next, if you are geographically mobile and are definitely interested in advertising, you might consider trying to get into one of the
training programs given by some of the New York City firms such as
J. Walter Thompson or Ogilvy and Mather.

Meanwhile, if you are applying to an advertising agency in person,
approach your interviewer with a résumé and samples of your writing. In this field (unlike many of those discussed in this book), employers look for creative writers who demonstrate their enjoyment
in working with words not only in straight exposition but in poetry
and fiction. [39] One young woman who was recently hired as copy-
writer for a group of women's clothing stores got the job, improbably
enough, on the basis of a fanciful semiautobiographical novel she
submitted along with her application. If the agency considers that an
applicant shows writing talent, it is sometimes willing to give the
rest of the training on the job.

Here, as everywhere, it is essential to get firsthand information
from people now in the field or those who have recently worked in it.
Talk with former ad agency people on the faculty of the school of
communications nearest you. Look for notices of lectures and sym-
posia sponsored by Alpha Delta Sigma, the advertising fraternity:
many of its events that are open to the public are highly informative.
Go to any open lectures or discussions sponsored by the American

Advertising Federation. Read some of the recent analyses of the impact of advertising, and make up your own mind about the charges leveled against it by Vance Packard and Ralph Nader. Plan hypothetical ads for new and existing products. Outline some of them and get criticisms of them by people in the field to whom you talk. When you have steeped yourself in the background of the field, have decided what part of it that most interests you, and have thought about what contribution you could make, you will have learned how to present yourself to a potential employer, and he or she may appreciate your knowledge and energy.

Most of these fields just discussed—print journalism, radio, TV, magazines, PR, and advertising—are changing rapidly as a result of "cold type" techniques, increased computerization, paper shortages, postal rate increases, the takeover of many publishers by conglomerates, and shifts from traditional to new marketing methods. Generalizations made today, in the early 1980s, may have to be completely recast within five or ten years. Meanwhile, any investigating that you are able to do on your own will be likely to turn up more information.

On one of his visits to the University of Washington campus, the British poet and biographer Robert Gittings commented on the apparently fixed boundaries in the United States between the academic world and that of the media: "It seems unfortunate that here in America one finds such stratification, such sharp boundary lines, between people in different sectors of the literary and intellectual world. Over here you tend to get your feet firmly placed on the rungs of one particular ladder—whether teaching or reporting or publishing or whatever—and you hardly ever seem to look back or across, or consider any other possibilities. In Britain, on the other hand, it is easier to go in and out of academia, sometimes writing for the BBC or for a magazine of general interest, sometimes teaching or writing a scholarly biography."[40]

It is just possible that the present widespread uncertainty about careers may have one beneficial side effect: more open-mindedness among both the academic and the communications professions about one another. Whether or not such open-mindedness eventually becomes common in America, your cultivating it should help you in your own search.

12. Writing, Research, and Other Opportunities in Business

> **The types of courses normally found in liberal arts assist in one's development in that they teach a person to think. If we can think clearly, arrange information in a logical sequence, present it in an organized manner and have the ability to accept change, then the only other ingredients necessary for success would be the intelligence to accept new information and the motivation to be successful.**
>
> **—IBM recruiter**

Business people sometimes have doubts when they think of hiring academics. Academics thinking about job-hunting in the business world tend to have uneasy questions in the back of their minds: "If I take a job with a firm, will I be selling out? And to whom and to what?" During the past five or six years, however, some academic institutions and some corporations have deliberately tried to face and examine such stereotypes. Their doing so has been part of a joint effort on the part of both graduate schools and corporations to bring humanities-trained people into the world of business.

In a 1979 article in *Across the Board*, Joanne Landesman lists and explores misconceptions common to one group or the other. She considers first "stereotypes many business people *think* academics have about them, their activities, and the world in general":

> 1. "Filthy lucre"—money is dirty. It is essentially bad. It is to be mistrusted no matter how . . . obtained or . . . used. Those who don't have it are superior beings, especially if they work very hard.
>
> 2. Business is essentially unethical. . . . If it doesn't produce products in themselves unethical, then it markets them dishonestly or makes too much profit from them.
>
> 3. Profit—translated into dollars and cents—is the sole motive of all business. There is no other motive. Any apparent concern for the public good is a mask. . . .

167

4. Business exploits labor. All businesses are unfair to their employees. There are no exceptions.

5. Business people are narrow-minded and have no outside interests. They breathe, eat, and sleep business. . . .

6. Business people are not interested in the arts. They are barbarians. The only reason they give money to museums is to get tax write-offs.

7. Business people are not so intelligent as academics.

8. Business people think they are more intelligent than academics.[1]

Of course, a few academics do hold some of these beliefs. But there is also "a set of stereotypes that seems to be held by business people about academics," and often held firmly, argues Landesman. For example, many people in business would say:

1. Academics are intellectual snobs who practice cultural elitism.

2. Academics have an aversion to money.

3. Humanities academics choose to devote their careers to the humanities because they are fuzzy thinkers and have an innate incapacity to deal with numbers or "hard" facts.

4. Academics are averse to competition. They choose the academic life because it protects them from the competition of the "real" world. . . .

5. Academics are attracted to teaching because it offers job security. They are . . . averse to risk-taking.

6. Academics are radicals, trying to do in the free enterprise system.

7. What professors do all day is so different from what business people do all day that it defies description. It also defies description because they really aren't doing anything.

8. When professors aren't actually in the classroom "teaching," they aren't "working," i.e., any time out of the classroom is "free time." Professors have long vacations, summers "off."

9. "Scholars" don't have to work with people, and have weak interpersonal and communication skills.

10. Teaching isn't work. It is a refuge for the mediocre. "Those who can, do. Those who can't, teach."

11. The knowledge gained by a study of the humanities is of no use outside the book club or the concert hall, and certainly of no use in the daily practice of business.[2]

Landesman succeeds pretty well in showing the unreasonableness of such stereotypes. If you are a liberal arts academic who is considering a foray into the business world, you may want to search your own thinking for traces of the first set of prejudices. And if you are approaching interviews with business employers, you may want to read Landesman's article to see how she counters these all too common views of humanities students and professors.

Landesman's article is one of several resulting from the Careers in Business program, first conceived between 1974 and 1977 by Dr. Dorothy Harrison of the New York State Department of Education and Dr. Ernest May of Harvard University. The pilot session was held for seven weeks in the summer of 1978 at the New York University Graduate School of Business Administration. Its aim "was to take a selected group of Ph.D.'s in the humanities and related social sciences, familiarize them, in an intensive period of exposure, with the concepts and practice of business, and open up career paths for them in corporate life." [3]

The first program attempted, through concentrated courses in accounting, economics, marketing, management, quantitative analysis, and the legal and social framework of business, to offer the equivalent of a semester's work for an M.B.A. Fifty students, chosen out of five hundred applicants, completed the course. Since 1978 somewhat similar programs have been presented, with local modifications, at the University of Pennsylvania's Wharton School of Economics, at the Harvard School of Business Administration, at the University of Texas at Austin, and elsewhere. [4]

Although these seminars are too new for a definitive evaluation, it is noteworthy that they are held at all, that they appear to be spreading, that corporations are willing to invest substantially in helping fund them, and that graduate schools in humanities fields are eager to cooperate with graduate schools of business administration. Because these seminars and institutes offer new models for interaction between business people and academic humanists, it is to be hoped that new mutual understanding and respect will eventually result. Since these programs have been publicized fairly widely in the *New York Times* and other papers, they may have an indirect exemplary effect out of proportion to the numbers of their graduates and the companies who have hired them.

But many readers of this book thinking about looking into business careers will not have a graduate degree; others who have completed M.A.'s or Ph.D.'s may not have the time or the chance to participate in one of these programs. Bearing in mind that such attempts at increased mutual understanding between business and the humanities *are* going on in some places, your role may be to work slowly, pragmatically, on your own, to see whether and where you can fit into a business enterprise. What then are the business areas in which a person specializing in English or another one of the humanities can be most useful and most welcome?

Currently there are six broad categories of such fields: sales and marketing; personnel; training; consulting; management (and with it research and development); and, most important in many ways, writing and editing.

SALES AND MARKETING

First, one must tackle the stereotypes many of us have about selling. If we have learned to read with enough sensitivity to avoid making sweeping generalizations about racial, national, or cultural groups, we can certainly realize that not every salesman we meet is a Willy Loman. We can even go further and realize that not every sales transaction of a large corporation is one of infant formula or military equipment for developing countries. Selling also goes on that involves things that most of us cherish—books, cameras, camping equipment, paintings, pianos, subscriptions to plays and operas, tickets to Tokyo—as well as things we deplore.

A Ph.D. in English now serving as a life insurance, pension plan, and equities salesman in the Middle West developed this point further in his reply to the recent Modern Language Association questionnaire: "Be as open-minded as possible. . . . Be especially open-minded about sales. There are always openings for salespeople. This [work] should be a natural for anyone who can form ideas clearly and articulate them." [5]

Another English Ph.D. who responded to the MLA survey, now a salesperson and satisfied with the change, is a real estate broker on the West Coast. As she writes, she is "an independent contractor, able to choose my own clients, determine my own hours, and select how much or how little I choose to do. I enjoy this total control over all aspects of my work."

Aside from the negative stereotypes that some of us hold about salespersons and their values, there is another theoretical objection that some career changers with M.A.'s or Ph.D.'s have to sales: seen from the outside, sales can seem too simple a career. Since selling positions usually require no previous acquaintance with the field, we tend to think, "If I could have gone into a career like this straight out of college, wouldn't I be throwing away the years I spent in graduate school and teaching if I made a complete break with my past and went into selling now?" Such reasoning, however, is based on two fallacies: first, that college and graduate work have no value other than their vocational one; second, that if one goes into sales work, one has to remain in it indefinitely.

This quality of sales work, that one can usually enter into it and make a fresh start (on-the-job or special courses for trainees are often provided at company expense), is one that many career changers find refreshing. Humanities-oriented people going into sales have discovered a number of other advantages. Such work usually doesn't claim your whole life; you can (sometimes though not always) leave it behind you and write or study or do whatever you wish evenings and weekends. Sales work (and its theoretical framework, marketing) offers excellent ways to learn about the world of business, or about particular businesses such as publishing, advertising, interior design, fashion, public relations, investments, and real estate. People who have spent some time selling in one of these fields know firsthand the market's needs, whims, and changing currents. They can often move on a sounder basis into other branches of business—personnel, training and consulting, management, or writing and editing—than if they had spent the same amount of time in business seminars without having had direct selling experience. And if they want eventually to break away from their original choice and work themselves into a different career, their experience in understanding the minds of people both like and unlike themselves can stand them in good stead in advertising, public relations, arts management, or fund-raising for colleges, museums, and nonprofit foundations.

PERSONNEL

After one gets beyond entry-level positions in this field, personnel work contains "strong elements of both teaching and counselling," says Richard Thain in *The Managers*.[6] Predictably, the lower positions tend to call less on one's judgment and more on ability to follow and interpret rules than many liberal arts majors would like.

The wording of job descriptions and the writing and interpreting of personnel evaluations has come in large firms to be a specialty in itself. There are also manuals and programmed learning guides to be written and edited, questionnaires, tests, and application forms to be designed and updated, and a great deal of correspondence to be dealt with. Although many people doing this kind of writing in personnel departments have come up from entry-level personnel jobs, occasionally a "communications expert" is taken on for that purpose. If you are interested, watch the job descriptions for personnel vacancies in large companies.

As one advances in the personnel field, one may find positions involving affirmative action, and others involving government compliance with other regulations, which can be challenging, not only exercising one's judgment but giving one a chance to work for causes in which one may believe deeply. Similarly the position of ombudsman, increasingly a personnel function in some corporations and institutions, can call upon nearly everything one knows—not only about one's business or professional field but about human nature.

At a seminar for humanities majors seeking alternatives to teaching, Eric M. Leithe, assistant vice-president for personnel at a Seattle bank and himself a former English major, told his audience that among the many career tracks in banking, one of the best, he thought, was the one that started out with personnel, then led into research, and subsequently could lead into international banking. [7]

To find out more about personnel work and its role in business, read issues of *Personnel* and also the *Personnel Journal*; talk to people involved in personnel at any and all levels; browse in your placement center library; and scan the newspapers for short courses and seminars in this increasingly important field.

TRAINING AND DEVELOPMENT

One Ph.D. in English who taught Shakespeare, Renaissance literature, and technical writing in colleges and universities for twelve years before resigning to enter the training field, has this to say: "North America supports—to the tune of $20 billion a year—a *fourth* level of education which goes under the general name of Training and Development (and which might more formally be called 'non-institutional adult education'). T&D—which is supported directly by business and government and consists primarily of various kinds of courses designed by internal training staffs or purchased from outside suppliers—would be the most likely refuge for unemployed Ph.D.'s." [8]

This Ph.D., president of a consulting firm that conducts letter and report writing workshops for corporations and government agencies, feels that T&D has given him "opportunities to grow—both as a teacher and as a researcher—to levels of instructional competence and professional accountability undreamed of in the universities."

Positions for teaching writing to business executives and staff members are sometimes part of in-service training programs that teach entrants to a company job-related skills or update the knowledge of long-time employees. Boeing, Safeco, IBM, AT&T, and many other companies offer such programs; Pacific Northwest Bell often takes experienced teachers and trains them to teach other employees.

One woman who has made this kind of application of the techniques of investigation, planning, and organization that she developed in graduate school is Ellen Messer-Davidow, a Ph.D. candidate in English at the University of Cincinnati. Working on a committee set up by the Office of University Commitment for Human Resources, she helped design and establish an "administrative/management training program" for women and minority faculty members already hired by the university. The curriculum dealt with such topics as "Collective Bargaining," "Organizational Planning, Motivation, and Evaluation," "Techniques of Management as Viewed by Major Decision-Makers," "Affirmative Action Impact on Higher Education," and a dozen others. Such seminars suggest various potential offshoots, both in educational and business settings, as well as offering, in themselves, interesting examples to other institutions.[9]

In-service courses in various kinds of writing are the ones most often requested by employers. As Fred Pneuman of Weyerhaeuser says, such courses can often help upgrade the writing of company executives, most of whom had no writing courses in college and who over the years have followed more and more closely a set format in their business writing. Other companies, ranging from small ones such as the Human Resources Development Corporation to giants such as Boeing, have established or are establishing courses for their staffs.

What actually goes on in these courses? Does an English Ph.D. who teaches them simply preach adherence to the principles of what used to be called "business English?" According to Blanche Adams, who teaches the executives of an accounting firm, her job is broader in scope than that. One of her typical assignments when I talked to her had just been to help a department head recast letters so that they would have a conciliatory rather than an adversary tone toward a client who was causing problems. Another was to rewrite the firm's reports in terms that stockholders and officers of client companies not specializing in accounting could understand. Still another was to redo several kinds of internal communications so that the staff members to whom they were sent would be interested enough to read them before having them filed. Somewhat to her surprise at first, Adams's clients have respected her expertise. Meanwhile she is trying not only to deal with their writing piece by piece but to establish guidelines for the future.[10]

On the West Coast, the account firm that hired Blanche Adams is, along with another accounting firm, making somewhat of a pioneering effort. On the East Coast, however, it was over twenty years ago that Dr. Henrietta J. Tichy began to help accountants, engineers, and other business executives to write better. A Ph.D. and an associate professor of English at Hunter College, Tichy also enjoys a career as consultant and lecturer for firms in management, science, and technology. She has been invited to advise and teach specialists in advertising and promotion, financial analysis, library science, manufacturing, marketing, medical writing, personnel and training, production, public relations, research and development, and other branches of business and industry. If after reading the comments on technical writing in this and earlier chapters you still wonder what it is, what it does, to what extent it differs from the kind of writing you have been trying to achieve or to teach as a humanities major or instructor, Tichy's text, *Effective Writing*, will give you an excellent survey of the field and its problems, and one that reveals how familiar many of them are.[11]

According to speakers at a 1980 workshop on the topic of business in the 1980s, there will be increasing demand in the next few years for training programs administered within business firms. Technology is becoming more complex; the requirements and standards laid down by management are becoming harder and harder for employees to meet; and, since the public system of education appears to be performing less well than it used to, it must be supplemented by private industry. Hence the growth of "the corporate university—vast and expanding programs designed for and given within corporations like IBM, AT&T, and General Motors."[12]

Although programs in various kinds of writing are among those most frequently given, humanities Ph.D.'s should not think that the training field consists of nothing else. According to one Ph.D. in medieval English, now program development coordinator of an insurance company: "With a teaching background you can train [in] practically ANYTHING, given a little time to prepare, so capitalize on your ability to *plan* and *teach* courses when you're looking for a job."[13]

Persons like the ones quoted who have made a switch from teaching to training suggest ways to find out about jobs such as theirs: first, "join the American Society for Training and Development (ASTD) and get into the training grapevine as soon as possible."[14] Next, go to your university library and look at two periodicals: the *Training and Development Journal* and *Training: The Magazine of Human Resource Development*. When looking for jobs in the training field, advises a person who has found many good ones, "capitalize on *skills* (e.g., writing, research) rather than just your degree. But don't apologize for it either. After all, you spent four years of your life on it, so it is worth something. . . . There's a *lot* of opportunity in the field.

[You] must remember, however, that to succeed in the training profession it takes about 1 percent subject matter expertise and 99 percent showmanship or at least technique. This probably runs contrary to your own ideals, but if you view the whole thing as 'rhetoric' it's not all that remote from what your literary studies have taught you." [15]

CONSULTING

If you design and teach courses for business and industry, you could work either as a member of a firm or as an outside consultant, hired on contract, course by course. If you work independently, you may enjoy the unfettered feeling of having no college department chairperson to cope with, no academic red tape of grades and credit hours. On the other hand, you will have to market your services yourself, which can be time consuming and risky. If you are a member of a firm, you will have a ready-made clientele, although often a smaller percentage of the income from the courses and possibly less freedom for innovation in teaching.

Either arrangement can be challenging and profitable, provided you really enjoy teaching, you believe in what you are doing, and, as one successful consultant (a former associate professor of English) says, you "disabuse [yourself] of the notion that, having been deprived of [your] 'higher calling' by economic circumstances, [you] are being forced into a 'lower' line of work." [16]

The essential thing is to take time to prepare individualized courses, tailored to the needs of your students. It is also a good idea to enlist the cooperation of your students' supervisors so that they understand and support what you are trying to accomplish.

There are three ways you can enhance your credibility with most business firms that may need your services: first, by respecting your time and expertise enough when negotiating for the course to ask a good round sum for a fee, not some minimal hourly wage such as adjunct instructors often receive (incidentally, be sure to figure in your preparation time when setting your fee); second, by having had previous teaching experience, preferably in a college or university;[17] and, finally, by making sure that your courses appear to be professionally "packaged"—by which most firms mean that you should have the course materials crisply printed up in an attractive format, ready to distribute to the students at the beginning of the first session. Your business employer is apt (no matter how unfairly) to consider faintly purple dittoed sheets, spontaneously scrawled assignments on the blackboard, and changes of syllabus in midstream as signs of amateurism (rather than responsiveness to the needs of the class.) [18]

Once you have decided that you want to be a consultant, for example in technical writing, work out on paper a tentative syllabus to fit the needs of a business or professional group with which you have had some contact. Make an appointment for an interview with the person in authority to set up such a course; show him or her your syllabus; explain that it is as yet only a skeleton, to be fleshed out with additions from written material actually done in the field in which your clients work, and ask to see samples of such writing. If you sound confident and logical, you should have no trouble in getting your first contract—and later a repeat one.

At a 1980 seminar on the topic "Consulting to Industry," Robert Bowman of the Pacific Northwest Bell Training Center talked about "consulting styles." He sees two basically different ones: the "doctor-patient style" ("Here is what is wrong with what you have been doing, and this is my prescription"), and the "process-offering style" ("I have some ways of doing things that I'd like to demonstrate to you, and you can decide whether or not they'll help you in what you're doing"). Find which style suits you better, urges Bowman, and use it. In any case, he says, "When you walk into an organization as a consultant, you're like an anthropologist walking into a remote village with a culture of its own." Each industry, and each firm within an industry, has a lot of traditions. The consultant is often apt to hear, "We do it this way." He or she had best not come in with too much of a missionary spirit, even though many people in the organization know that they urgently need what the consultant has to teach them. [19]

If you become a consultant, you will have to keep updating what you know and finding different ways to present it. Since your students will be adults, attending your sessions voluntarily because they realize (or their bosses realize) that they need to know what you can teach them, you will probably find the level of attention an exciting one. If you find that you enjoy and do well at consulting, consider it as a career, not just a stop-gap. The feeling is often expressed these days that "in business, you can expect to see a greater dependence upon consultants in the 1980's than ever before" (see Appendix C). [20]

MANAGEMENT AND RESEARCH AND DEVELOPMENT

These terms can of course cover vastly different positions in different firms, and usually the best way into management is through learning the business at various levels on the way up. Fred Pneuman of

Weyerhaeuser suggests that a good way for a person with writing competence to get started is to "assist with or produce top management productions," including reports, speeches, and audiovisual aids. Eventually, perhaps, "with supplemental business training, an English major could work his/her way into company management by making use of communications skills to further company objectives."[21] In a similar vein, a personnel manager of one of the four hundred blue-chip companies surveyed by Linwood Orange told Professor Orange that "if these [English majors] have the imagination and are willing to accept the challenge, there is no job in management . . . which could not be theirs and in which they could not be of definite service."[22]

As a member of management, you might also become involved in planning or performing some of the activities covered by that all-purpose magical phrase of our time, "research and development." The more experience you have had in writing reports, helping design and interpret marketing surveys, and making long-range plans and projections of any kind, the more likely you are to move into this area. To find such positions in a company where you have not already had experience, probably your best move is to present yourself as someone already involved in the "problem-solving" approach. Obviously you will have to have something in your experience to back up your claim—courses in business theory, or, better, examples of successful problem solving in another business or in a nonprofit organization.

If you are interested in management, consider taking one or two courses in management theory—either as electives while you are still an undergraduate or as noncredit courses for your own enlightenment while you are in graduate school or teaching. Look around for positions as management trainee in any industry that interests you. If you obtain one of these, you will be assigned to several different departments in rotation, where you will work under supervision, learn how experienced workers do their jobs in your field, see the difference between line and staff duties, and get an excellent overview of the industry. In the 1979 edition of Linwood Orange's pamphlet, *English: The Pre-Professional Major,* the listing of positions successfully held by former English majors includes several managerial ones, including managerships of communication services, process systems, production center, systems center, and sales administration.[23]

However much you want to get into management, try not to let the current media emphasis on the M.B.A. degree lead you inexorably back to graduate school to get one, at least until you have been in business long enough to know that you are fascinated by the *theory* of business and that your goal is a specific kind of position that is difficult to obtain without such a degree. If you are tempted at all by the M.B.A. degree, read some of the recent articles playing down its value (such as "The Money Chase" in *Time*, May 4, 1981).[24]

WRITING AND EDITING

Seemingly the most logical slot for an English major in business, this area has many subdivisions: internal and external communications (both general and technical editing and writing), public relations, advertising, and the upgrading of writing for company executives and employees.

Editors and writers of internal communications for businesses may have such assignments as putting together a company newsletter or writing reports to keep the various departments abreast of what the others are doing. Or such editors may have more specialized assignments, involving the ability to do technical writing. One woman who has worked for the past year for an optical instrument company does some of both kinds. In addition to supervising and copy editing all the firm's publications, she writes for the monthly in-house newsletter. "Once you get over your surprise at not being in a job connected with the humanities," she says, "you find a certain excitement in solving the problems of how to organize the technical material you work with. Sometimes you have the challenge of interpreting material from specialists in one part of the company to specialists in other parts of it. And there's a pleasure that comes from learning more and more in order to make new ideas and information clear to other people."

Her preparation included a B.A. in English, a quarter in the graphics program at a community college, an internship in public relations at a city visitors' and convention bureau, an editing internship at Battelle Research Center, a position at Honeywell, Inc., plus freelance editing as a member of an editorial consulting firm. She had had no academic work leading directly into her present field. "But just because you start out not knowing a great deal about the area in which you find yourself working," she says, "don't think you're doomed to stay uninformed. Get books from the public library, beginning with the most general ones. Then work up to the more technical ones in the university library. Don't be afraid to ask questions, and don't begrudge using some of your own free time to fill in your background."[25]

Other "internal communications" positions involve working on or producing not only employees' newsletters but magazines, annual and quarterly reports, house organs (there are fifty thousand of these currently issued), interdepartmental memoranda, program evaluations, handbooks, instruction manuals, and policy manuals. Stephanie Campbell, personnel officer of the Rainier National Bank of Seattle, said that they had three or four full-time people in such writing jobs. This bank also has "staff coordinators" who write speeches for senior officers, do research for these and other speeches, and travel around to branches, gathering news for the bank newspaper.[26] Two other large Seattle banks have hired women with backgrounds in English—Angela Hollis and Blanche Adams—full time for several months to work with them on complete revisions of their manuals of policies and procedures. A Wall Street investment firm not long ago hired a Ph.D. in English on the strength of her writing ability even though she had no previous background in finance. She writes analyses of various investments and edits the work of other securities analysts.[27]

To uncover other positions writing or editing in-house publications, look up large companies in your area and find out, through someone you may know who works at one of them, through their personnel offices, or through the business department of a public or university library, what newsletters, handbooks, or other material these firms publish for their employees. Look at as many issues as you can, to get a feeling of what is being done. Then, whether you apply for an advertised position or talk with a company officer "cold," you'll have a chance to develop some ideas of your own about what you might contribute to such projects.

Still other internal communications, aimed at a less general audience within an industry, often come under the heading of technical writing. "Scientific and technical communication, or technical writing," according to Professors Myron L. White and James Souther of the University of Washington's Technical Communications Program, "serves the need for getting technical information to nontechnical people."[28] STC has grown enormously since World War II for several reasons. First, engineers and scientists are so busy with their work that they need qualified people to write up their results for laymen to read. Second, because of the proliferation of new products, many more product owners' and users' manuals are needed. Third, the increasing demand for environmental impact statements in construction and industry calls for specialists able to write them.

Although more and more employers are looking for technical writers, "they aren't always sure what they're looking for," says White. Businesses that do need a technical writer may not know just how one could help them. Available jobs are "apt to be where you least expect them," says Souther. Banks, consulting firms, ports, hospitals, and even educational institutions now hire technical writers.

"The use of computers and video printing systems will affect technical communication most profoundly," predicts White. "Computers can help manage the huge amount of specialized information that technical writers have to handle, and thus improve communication between scientists and their audiences."

According to Souther, "people often speak of technical writing when they really mean technical editing." For technical writing, much of which is equipment oriented, you are substantially better off if you have had, if not a college minor in science or math, at least some courses in and some working familiarity with these fields.

Professor John Walter of the University of Texas says that technical writing is a species differing from other types of exposition in four ways. First, the writer-reader relationship is a close one. The technical writer "usually knows who will be reading this document, and why." Second, there is a clear function and purpose for most technical writing, in that "it must inform the reader and provide a basis for immediate action." Third, the style and form must be "clear, simple, and unambiguous." Finally, in the organization of technical writing, Walter believes that "a logical pattern must often give way to a psychological pattern," that is, the writer recognizes "the importance of giving the reader (often a boss or potential customer) *what* he wants *when* he wants it." In case any readers with literary backgrounds dismiss technical writing as unchallenging, Walter reminds them of a comment by the Shakespearean scholar, G. B. Harrison: "It is far easier to discuss Hamlet's complexes than to write orders which ensure that five working parties from five different units arrive at the right place at the right time equipped with proper tools for the job. One soon learns that the most seemingly simple statement can bear two meanings and that when the instructions are misunderstood the fault usually lies with the wording of the original order." [29]

Many technical writing jobs involve both writing and editing. Technical editors often take draft material from others and prepare it for publication; jet propulsion laboratories have hired editors to do this, as have applied physics laboratories at large universities. Writer/editors are also being hired by industrial and institutional libraries to abstract works to put in their newsletters to update the knowledge of their staffs, says Souther.

There are also many chances to do freelance technical writing, on contract, by the job, for which you can set your own hours and, within limits, your hourly fees. The Society for Technical Communication offers information on how to start a freelance technical writing service.[30]

Whether you are applying for an advertised position or looking for work as a freelancer, Souther suggests five steps to reach your goal: (1) Your humanities B.A. or advanced degree should have given you the interest and competency in writing that you need (Souther himself was an English and drama major and graduate student, and his colleague Myron White wrote a dissertation on D. H. Lawrence). (2) Employers will have more confidence in you if you have taken one or more courses in a technical communications program such as the ones at Boston University, the Montana College of Mineral Science and Technology, or one of the several dozen others around the country.[31] (3) If through taking one of these courses you can arrange for an internship in which you actually work for two or three months doing editing or writing for a company, a research institute, or a periodical, this experience will be extremely helpful both in what it teaches you and in what it conveys to an employer.[32] (4) Before you look for a job you should browse in the business section of a public or university library, or any company library to which you can get access, to find out what kinds of articles and reports are being published, looking at not only the ones issued by the various companies but also the articles in the journal *Technical Communication.* (5) Souther urges you to "develop a portfolio to show what you have done and can do. Get together a few articles you have edited, articles that you have written, brochures that you may have designed—perhaps half a dozen examples, showing both variety and quality."

There are also positions as writers, editors, and researchers for consumer publications of the less specialized kind. In these fields, business firms and nonprofit organizations alike make use of information specialists and writers in many ways. One of the commonest is putting together catalogues and handbooks for the general public. Another is in issuing brochures or articles designed to increase public good will. Most utility companies and investment houses, as well as nonprofit foundations from art museums to zoos, regularly send out newsletters or magazines. In addition they use fliers, bulletins, letters, and brochures to raise funds or publicize special events.

In every metropolitan area there are several hundred business firms and nonprofit agencies that make use of writers for their consumer publications. Typical among them are local and state arts groups, the American Cancer Society, the American Red Cross, the United Way and other community social agencies, fund drives, major cultural institutions (theaters, musical foundations, art schools, opera companies, and museums). Other institutions employing writers and information specialists include four-year and community colleges, all major hospitals and health plans, all large banks and insurance companies, and industry oriented magazines.

In the banking world you can either move into writing and PR jobs through management training (as did probably three-fourths of the people now holding them) or be hired directly for the writing job. When you apply, take with you not only your résumé but samples of your writing and any speeches you have prepared. Most banks try to match an applicant's educational level with the appropriate job. Personnel departments often take résumés and keep them on file for a year. Since there are frequent job changes in this field, even if your inquiry meets with the reply, "I'm sorry, but we have no vacancies at this time, and we do not anticipate any," you need not feel that the door will never open.

You will find still more potential positions editing or writing for consumer publications and house organs if you are free to relocate geographically. Look in *Writer's Market* under the headings "Company Publications," "Consumer Publications," and "Trade, Technical, and Professional Journals." You will find there are over six hundred pages of companies issuing such magazines, among the best known of which are those published by the airlines and automobile manufacturers. Every major airline has a magazine for its customers similar to United's *Mainliner*, and each of the main auto manufacturers has a magazine, such as *Ford Times*, sent to new owners of its cars. Editing one of these is usually a full-time position, for which you could eventually be qualified after working on smaller local publications.

Among other kinds of consumer publications, you should not overlook those in health care. For example, Vicki Hill moved from a PR position at Group Health Cooperative in Seattle to a post as information specialist for the Satellite Project at the University of Washington School of Nursing. At Group Health, part of her job was to prepare a pamphlet, *Group Health Cooperative: Using Its Services*, which was sent to over one hundred thousand subscribers to the organization.[33]

For those of you hoping to find or develop writing, editing, or training positions in business, several people I have interviewed have a few suggestions. Their comments on how they got their jobs may offer a few clues. Ellen Messer-Davidow says that she got her assignment as special assistant to the president on the basis of having done a lot of writing (both journalism and fiction), having experience with various organizations that were working for social change, and having made personal contact with the university administration.[34]

Even though you realize that there are many ways in which business firms might be able to make use of your skills—as a writer or editor, in personnel, in training, management, or possibly in research and development—you may think you have a problem in bridging the *apparent* gap between your humanities background and the segment of the "real world" you are trying to enter. In view of the fact that not all business executives are initially enthusiastic about people with liberal arts degrees, you must demonstrate that you have brought with you from the campus not only information but mental elasticity and an ability to solve problems.

There are various ways of making these qualities visible to a business employer. To John T. Harwood of the College of William and Mary the problem is "ultimately a matter of rhetoric; it is a matter of translating academic experience . . . into the categories by which businessmen perceive themselves and their work." Accordingly, he steeped himself in job advertisements and their business terminology, repeated a good deal of the language of the advertisement in the cover letter with which he answered each ad, and found himself receiving offers from various businesses.[35]

One must, however, not think of a business career as a panacea for every unemployed humanist's problems. A few people *are* genuinely unfitted by temperament for the business world. A career search must finally be an individual matter. Nonetheless, one cannot always know how adaptable one is until one has explored careers that may not initially be appealing. When Earl Grout first came to my office in the University of Washington Placement Center, he and I thought that some sort of teaching position, whether in a university or in a nontraditional setting, was a "must" for him. For several months he would consider nothing else. The following narrative by Grout shows how he has modified his ideas, yet has finally, in a setting where he would not have expected it, found essentially what he wants to do.[36]

"BY GOING AWAY I GOT BACK TO WHAT I WANTED TO DO":
EARL GROUT

Near the end of 1974, after I had turned in my dissertation on James Boswell and had received my Ph.D. in English, I decided to leave the academic world because I found no opportunities there.

The want ads eventually led me to the insurance industry. I needed a job and they had one—selling. The advantage of insurance was that they didn't expect me to know anything about their business when I started. For once the usual roadblock of "prior experience" was gone, and the way was open. I found a good company, New York Life, and went to work—selling.

I did fairly well, qualifying for a production club my first two years and then for a management program. I became an assistant agency manager and had the job of recruiting new agents. After four years at New York Life, I took my current position with Safeco. My duties are designing and writing training courses, writing scripts for audiovisual productions, and doing any number of special projects that involve writing and editing. I also teach various insurance subjects to agents and employees. I am now doing things I like.

Looking back, I can say that I did not enjoy selling life insurance or recruiting agents. What I was doing without knowing it was serving an apprenticeship, learning a business. When I was ready to leave New York Life, I had some solid credentials. I was in the mainstream and could find what I wanted. The fundamental lesson in this is: look for entry-level jobs, especially sales jobs, in which you can learn a business quickly. Don't worry about liking the job. It is a means to advancement at this point, not an end in itself. The only question is: can you learn the business through it? Also, give yourself time. It took me five years to get to a place I really wanted to be.

Which business, then, should you learn? Whatever it is, make a clean break with your graduate school state of mind. Avoid the edges of academia. This area is a maze of cul-de-sacs, overpopulated with bright, frustrated, competitive people who don't want to leave academia and who vainly hope to find a way back in. I would also avoid the natural havens of writers—advertising and public relations. They too are overcrowded and competitive fields, and thus can afford little opportunity for growth.

Don't agonize over which business to enter. If you wish to get back to writing and teaching, you'll most likely have the opportunity eventually. These skills combined with professional credentials are rare. If you know your business and can write well about it and teach others, you will be given the chance to do so. If you go where there are fewer people like yourself, the going may be hard at first, but in the long run, you'll be better able to base your talents in the way you want to use them.

For those who are thinking of starting a business venture of their own, the following chapter will have suggestions to offer. Meanwhile, those of you wondering how to make your own way into an existing business might ponder the threefold import of Grout's narrative: learn in depth about the business world in order to have a chance to use your writing skills where they will count most; combine short-range realism with long-range optimism about your usefulness; and, above all, give yourself enough time for the successive steps of a career change which for some people holds the possibility of excitement, financial rewards, and personal satisfaction.

13. On Your Own: The Humanist as Entrepreneur

Why do people do it [start their own businesses]? For many who take the plunge, the making of money is, like breathing, merely a necessity, not a motivating force. What really makes eyes sparkle is rooted in a traditional American dream—the chance for independence and self-expression: the dream of being your own boss.
> —Kathy Sawyer, in the *Washington Post*

Every year there are some 300,000 Americans who, as Sawyer goes on to say, "rush with lemming-like eagerness into the sea of free enterprise—against great odds and seemingly undaunted by cosmic economic fluctuations."[1]

Who are these venturers? Albert Shapero, an Ohio State University faculty member who writes widely on entrepreneurship, finds that "people starting their own enterprises follow a common pattern: This pattern can be described in terms of four major factors: (1) displacement [from one's previous occupation], (2) a strong propensity to take control of one's own life, (3) . . . the perception that it is feasible to start and run a business, and (4) resources. All four factors are necessary and interact with one another."[2]

To those of us who have worked for schools, colleges, business corporations, or government agencies, the longing to set up on our own is sometimes a powerful one. We fantasize about opening our own small perfect shop or perhaps running a consulting service with high profits, stimulating clients, and practically no overhead.

But are these fantasies translatable into reality? You can hardly have escaped hearing that out of every new business venture begun 90 percent will have failed by the end of the first year and 90 percent of these by the end of the second. Should you, as a person with a background in the liberal arts rather than business, even consider starting your own enterprise in these days of rising costs of rent, production, and distribution?

Many people do abandon their dreams of starting out on their own. Alternatively, you could shop around for an existing small

186

business to buy and run—*if* you have the capital or credit to make the purchase, and good legal advice to help with the negotiations. Or, if you decide that you want to start your own business from scratch but feel insecure without a background in current business theory and practice, you might decide to take courses in a university department of business administration before venturing out on your own. (Watch out, however, for the temptation to invest a year and a half or two years in an M.B.A. program unless—which seems unlikely— you will demonstrably need the degree itself. Academics tend too often to reach for additional degrees without realizing that what they may need is specific information rather than more credentials (see chapter 5).

On the other hand, without enrolling in extended academic courses, would-be business venturers can obtain the advice of experts through the Small Business Administration (and especially their free advisory service, SCORE, staffed by retired executives), or through the short courses and workshops offered by university extension, community colleges, and local business groups. There is also an enormous body of printed material on starting your own business, of which two books, *The Woman's Guide to Starting a Business* by Claudia Jessup and Genie Chipps and *The Career Alternative: A Guide to Business Venturing* by Peter Channing are good starting points.[3]

From a combination of reading, listening, and attending short courses and seminars, you are likely to glean certain major recommendations such as the following:

1. Have a definite idea to which you are enthusiastically committed—an idea for a product you can make or distribute or a service you can perform, in a way that seems better than it's now being done.

2. Get experience by working for another business or an institution in a field related to your intended venture before starting out on your own.

3. Try to have enough capital or credit not only to start the business but to keep it going for the first year if necessary.

4. After allocating plenty of time and funds for your start-up, add 20 percent more money and 20 percent more time than you think you will need.

5. Get professional advice from the very beginning on legal and accounting matters.

6. Make a thorough market survey, finding out who in your area now uses a product or service like the one you plan to offer; how much these customers or clients pay; what advantage yours would

have; how much possible room for expansion in your area there is. Know very well indeed what your competition has to offer.

7. At the beginning, keep down overhead in every possible way; start with an office in your home unless having a shop or office in a business district is a real necessity.

8. If you do need an office, take a long enough time to find the right one so that you won't have to move for at least five years.

9. Start out with a definite business or professional image that you want your firm to convey, and carry it out through a professionally designed logo, letterhead, and brochures.

10. Consider specializing, if you are in a large city with many competitors in your general type of business. (A bookstore in New York City called Murder, Ink has succeeded in drawing customers from all over the city because by concentrating on murder and detective stories it can carry every title in print.[4])

11. Know your financial break-even point and set yourself a quota of business you must do every day, week, and month simply to stay in operation. (But do not count on making any significant profit for the first two years.)

12. Consider attracting customers by offering extra services: sending your clients or customers a newsletter, sponsoring workshops and classes, or developing personalized services for clients with special needs.

13. Don't risk more than you can afford to lose.[5]

These points represent in rudimentary form the theoretically right way to start a business. In the literature on the subject you will find many refinements on each of them. But can anyone observe them all? Probably there are few businesses, even successful ones, whose founders have been able to do everything according to the rules: even the best preliminary estimates of prices and demand may be only extrapolations, impossible to verify until the owner has actually opened his or her doors.

Some people, therefore, tend simply to "take their idea and fly with it," starting small, obeying as many of the above principles as they can, and acquiring more capital, more and better equipment, and more expertise as they go along. Obviously this eclectic, pragmatic approach works better in certain kinds of businesses—small consulting firms for example, where one or two owners are in complete control of the volume of clients and the quality of the services performed—than in capital-intensive businesses involving an office, a plant, a product, a network of suppliers and distributors, and a tight production schedule.

Through a combination of circumstances—often the four that Shapero mentions plus luck and timing—entrepreneurial success *can* come even to "unworldly" English Ph.D.'s and other liberal arts types. In the 1978 MLA survey, for example, seventeen Ph.D.'s in English reported success in starting and running their own businesses.[6]

From my own survey of thirty small businesses recently founded by persons with an English or other liberal arts background, I have chosen six owner-founders to contribute first-person accounts. My criteria for choosing them were, first, that the businesses had proven successful—that is, that they had been in operation with annually increasing volume for over two years (in most cases, over five); second, that the owners enjoyed running them and believed in what they were doing; and, third, that they were businesses developed from scratch by teachers or others in professions involving English or the arts—people who differ from the typical entrepreneur with a lot of capital "just looking around for a good little investment," whether it is a health food store or a boutique. It follows that the businesses discussed below have a fairly close connection with the liberal arts background or life experience of their owner-proprietors.

These particular half-dozen occupations may not be for you. Not everyone has the capital to start a bookstore or the special knowledge to found a publishing business, a communications consultantship, a documentary film company, a freelance editorial service, or an archival management company. But many readers may learn something from the way these owner-founders set about starting their businesses and the roadblocks they met and dealt with along the way.

1. BOOKSTORE OWNER

Most people who like to read fantasize at times about opening a bookstore. Two young women, a junior high reading teacher and a school mental health worker, have opened such a store and have run it successfully for the past seven years, even though it's only half a block away from one of the largest university bookstores in the United States. Of course, as Sally Argo and Cindy Burdell admit, they don't have much time to read now.

CINDY BURDELL and SALLY ARGO

We are co-owners of Arbur Books in Seattle. We sell new, general books to a frugal university public. Most of our stock is quality paperbacks, although we also carry mass market paperbacks and hard-cover editions of fiction, biography, and current history. We carry magazines and out-of-town newspapers too. Currently we employ one part-time person. Several incredibly bright and helpful volunteers each donate an evening a week so that they can begin to learn the book business.

We opened for business on December 1, 1975, after having spent about three months looking for an existing bookstore to buy, and realizing that there was generally a reason that the stores were for sale. We soon realized that, little though we knew, we could probably do better starting from scratch than with a failing business. We were best friends, we both had small inheritances, and we were both tired of what we'd been doing. At Mills College we had studied philosophy and drama respectively, and neither of us had any business experience.

We obtained a bank loan with no difficulty—probably because we had quite a lot of collateral. We had advice (and much encouragement) from a family member, a lawyer, and from one of his partners who was instrumental in our lease negotiations. Two men in a local book distributor's office were extremely helpful in teaching us about the book business. We went to a free one-day general seminar put on by the SBA, then later took a course at the Seattle–First National Bank called "Financing a Small Business," and attended a three-day "Bookseller's School" put on at Berkeley by the American Booksellers Association.

The first year, we each spent about sixty hours a week in the store; now it's only forty to forty-five hours for each of us. We work some nights and weekends, but have mornings off occasionally and some weekdays off. These hours can be trying, but on the whole we feel that our schedule is quite "liberated." We both order books from publishers' reps, special-order books for customers, run the cash register, answer questions, shelve new titles, send back to the publishers old titles that haven't sold, straighten up the stock, bring up backstock from the storage room, and so on. We each do every job. For a while one of us had to pay the bills, which was very trying. Now we have a regular bookkeeper.

We were lucky in many ways. First, since one of us had grown up in the area, we had access to many people who were of great help, and they took us fairly seriously. Second, and most importantly, we had money. When we applied for the space we now occupy, we were essentially ignored until the store owners saw our financial statements. Money talked, even though we had no business or book experience at all. We were not hampered by our sex, either, as probably most independent bookstores are woman-owned.

We do have a few frustrations: the constant battle for cash flow, the shortage of space in our present store, and the minimal vacation time. The main thing we'd like to do within the next few years is to find a larger space for less money. We've been undercapitalized since day one, and it continues to haunt us. We still don't completely earn our living from the store, and unless we enlarge, the prospects of ever getting to the point where it will really support us look bleak.

The best part of all is when a customer tells us what a great store this is. Suddenly all the frustrations and heartache and poverty disappear. Some days we think those kinds of things are all that keep us going. We'd never been in debt before, and owing incredible amounts of money to hundreds of different publishers (and to a bank) is an appalling burden. When we opened, we had an inventory of eight thousand dollars worth of books. Now we have eighty thousand. So we have lots of assets, and lots of bills.

Advice to others? Think carefully before you go into books. It's a very difficult business to succeed in as owners of an independent store. It's perfect unless you really need to make a lot of money: it's hard, but fun, and you meet the best people in the world.

2. BOOK PUBLISHER

New publishing ventures abound in most regions of the country (see chapter 10, and also the *International Directory of Little Magazines and Small Presses* by Fulton and Ferber). Some of them are quite small, and are dedicated to one particular kind of book, like the Seal Press, Seattle, founded by Barbara Wilson and Rachel Da Silva, which publishes feminist fiction and poetry. It has an average press run of 500 to 1,000 copies, publishing three or four titles a year. "It's very satisfying to run such a small operation that you can print the books exactly the way you want to," says Barbara Wilson.

Another publishing company, Madrona Publishers, Inc., Seattle, began in 1975 with Dan Levant, who carried on operations from his home for the first three years; he contracted for copy editing and other services as needed. By 1982 his catalogue listed eighty-five titles. A typical press run is 5,000 to 10,000, although a recent book, *Volcano: The Eruption of Mount St. Helens*, had a first printing of 120,000 and a second of 50,000. Many of the titles are regional, although increasingly the books published have nationwide appeal. As a by-product of his greatly increased volume of business, Levant has acquired a staff numbering one part-time and five full-time employees; he still hires freelancers for additional jobs as needed. His wife Sara, a former English major at Wellesley who had worked for another publishing company before officially joining her husband's firm, now has the title of managing editor and promotion manager. Madrona's building on the Seattle waterfront houses editorial and production offices.

DAN LEVANT

I am the owner-editor-in-chief of the Madrona Publishers, Inc., a book publishing firm in Seattle which I founded in 1975. The reason I started Madrona was that I had reached a dead end in the job I had (promotion manager for a university press); I was not willing to relocate; so I had to start my business to create my own job. Also, I felt that the opportunity was there and that the time was ripe.

My background included a bachelor's degree in business administration and a master of fine arts degree. I had had a considerable amount of marketing experience in my field, and enough high-powered experience in New York City to have a feel for the national book publishing industry, plus the experience (in my previous job) of distributing books worldwide from Seattle.

As I started to plan my own firm, I got very little useful advice from anybody. There was some help from an accountant, a little from our bank—but this is a very common problem for small businesses, not being able to get good advice. At one point I hired a consultant on financial management for small businesses. At fifty dollars an hour, I used him carefully. I also took a course myself in the same subject. Financial management is generally the largest gap in the skills of the small entrepreneur, who usually comes to the business with specific product-related experience and skills, but very little in the way of general management skills. By way of capital, I used my own savings plus bank loans; the latter were short-term, unfortunately.

The satisfactions, so far, have been the obvious ones: knowing that what you're building is your own; being the boss; being often exhausted but never bored; being absolutely unable to predict what will happen tomorrow. The greatest frustration is difficulty in financing growth without access to adequate capital.

For any small business, be sure you have the temperament for the kind of pressures and anxieties you'll face. Can you stand owing a lot of money? Not being able to pass on the serious problems to a boss? Insecurity about future income? Work that has to be done without enough time to do it?

Having an adequate and at least partially realistic financial plan is essential. How much money will you need, and how will you get it? For anyone interested in book publishing, it is essential to understand the difference between publishing a book and building a book publishing industry. One has to be prepared to deal with all the functions of publishing carried out by large companies, yet without adequate time or staff. It's a very, very difficult business to operate on a small scale, and I wouldn't recommend it to anyone who hasn't some grasp of the industry nationally, a high tolerance for insecurity, and an incredible amount of patience.

3. COMMUNICATIONS CONSULTANT

A demand for special courses in writing, custom-tailored to the needs of executives and staffs of government agencies, hospitals, social agencies, nonprofit foundations, and businesses has increased during the past decade (see also chapters 6 and 12). Gloria Campbell of Kirkland, Washington, has responded to this demand by creating her own one-woman business in which she designs, markets, and teaches such courses throughout Washington, Oregon, and Alaska.

Her story may strike responsive chords in some readers for three reasons. She is a "returning woman" who left college to marry during her freshman year, spent twenty years in secretarial and other business positions, then went back to school in her forties after two of her three children were grown up. (She received her B.A. with a Phi Beta Kappa key after two more years at the University of Washington, and her M.A.T. a year later, just after she had begun to teach English in a community college.) She has made the trip from business to academia and back to business without too much difficulty. Finally, convinced that writing teachers must themselves write in order to teach effectively, she contributes occasional articles on education and on women's careers to the *Christian Science Monitor* and other periodicals, conducts a weekly column in a local paper, and is working on a book.

GLORIA CAMPBELL

Trying to decide what I do used to frustrate me. When I finally settled on "I teach people how to improve their writing," this usually tended to lead to my questioner's volunteering that he or she had "never been very good at grammar." Because so many people seem not to understand that writing involves considerably more than grammar, I decided to sidestep the grammar issue by referring to myself as a Communications Consultant.

So what do I do? Here are the main things: training and teaching (this covers a lot of territory, from one-day seminars to nine- or ten-week courses or open-ended arrangements); working with individual clients on a writing project; teaching them how to write résumés; preparing and writing up my own teaching materials for courses; keeping my own hand in as a writer; studying constantly to expand my own knowledge and keeping abreast of

the fields involved (writing, teaching, and training); assessing local training needs and writing proposals; coping with all the details of running a
small business; and giving talks to various groups.

My background was ideal for this work. I had about twenty years of
various business positions behind me, so that by the time I added my B.A.
in English and M.A.T. (Master of Arts in Teaching), I had enough credentials to make me acceptable to almost any clientele. My community college and continuing education teaching years were invaluable springboards
to the kind of teaching I now do.

When I first started in this field, I really had no one to turn to. Essentially, I learned by doing. Certainly I had gained much from working with
others, but I knew no one in the adult training field. Consequently I sat in
on as many sessions watching other instructors as I could. Various professional organizations have also been useful in providing information that it
would have been hard for me to come by on my own. The American Society for Training and Development and the Society for Technical Communication have been the best sources of ideas.

To date, most of my clients have come by word of mouth. This is of
course a very desirable (and very inexpensive) method of getting clients.
Early in my consulting career I decided to build slowly and solidly, which
meant I had to do my very best work on every job. Now that I have taught
workshops and short courses for the U.S. Civil Service Commission, employees of the City of Seattle, for managerial groups, engineers, anthropologists in the field, secretarial groups, Indian tribal council employees, and
the academic and professional persons in my continuing education classes
at the University, I plan to do more marketing to increase the range of
needs I am able to serve.

This work has both great satisfactions and great frustrations. I truly love
the contact with students, and I find most of the people I work with well
motivated, interested, and interesting. I derive a great deal of satisfaction
from seeing them overcome their fears and limitations, make progress on
their jobs, feel better about themselves, and rekindle or develop a love for
ideas, literature, and people. On the negative side, I often feel baseless. I
don't really belong anywhere to anyone. This feeling has subsided a good
deal of late, but was a big problem at the beginning. Work like mine can be
lonely—although I sometimes find the aloneness rewarding. Some of the
people I work with are resistant, at least initially, to what I am teaching
them, especially those in certain professional fields, such as engineers,
technical writers, public school teachers, accountants—people who feel
that writing is a nuisance, or who are embarrassed or angry about their
lack of skill.

Now I need to decide whether to expand my business. There are several
options: encompassing other parts of the communications field, expanding

the writing and editing part of my services, moving more and more into management training, or doing more professional writing and publishing myself.

My best advice to young would-be consultants is to get a wide background. Have a lot to offer your clients. Be flexible, articulate, people-conscious, well organized, patient, energetic, capable of marketing and of doing the whole show. Consulting is not for the faint-hearted. It is rather for those who like to do everything themselves, to keep abreast of and even ahead of developments in education, business, and economics. The best consultants have a finger in many pies, know quite a bit about a lot of things, and bring what they know to a wide variety of clients.

There is no place for the person who wants everything provided by the company (university, agency, government). You really have to find your own place in the business-governmental community when you are a consultant. But if you do, you can fill a space that no one within the company or agency can. You can be extremely valuable to your clients and have a sense of high self-worth.

When I started out on my own, many people used to ask me whether I wouldn't really like to have a real job (i.e., a forty-hour, five day week). Nobody asks me that any more. This proves, I hope, that a few people actually see my profession as almost legitimate.

4. DOCUMENTARY FILM-MAKER

Although people advised them against starting a film company, Charles Meyer and Bestor Cram are glad now that they formed their own documentary firm, Chester-Barley Films, Inc., in 1975. During the past seven years they have completed some twenty-five documentaries, ranging from *Closer to Home*, a fifteen-minute documentary portrait of four people living in half-way houses, to *Massachusetts Story*, a fifty-eight-minute film showing the impact of offshore oil drilling on the whole Cape Cod region. They have also been closely involved in the making of fifty other documentaries. Their clients have included M.I.T., the Metropolitan Boston Transit Authority, the National Science Foundation, the Harvard Graduate School of Education, the Metropolitan Area Planning Council, and many others.

BESTOR CRAM and CHARLES MEYER

Chester-Barley Films produces independently, for the private and public sector, educational and documentary films about social issues. We also work as freelance cameramen, soundmen, and editors for other producers. In addition, we act as film consultants to the academic community. During the seven years of CBF we have come to see ourselves as film documentarians.

The product we produce is a completed film that we develop from its original concept into a script, then shoot and edit. Some of the services required in the making of a film, such as the processing and printing, we subcontract out. These services are highly technical, requiring very specialized equipment and skills. Our clientele consists of institutions, companies, and groups of people who want to present a point of view or teach something.

We began our partnership in 1975. We had met one another in the M.I.T. film department, where we both continued teaching full-time. We completed a film together, Lenny and Ike, a portrait of a young man starting a new business and his relationship with his business mentor. With this film completed and entered in various film festivals, we set off to make other films. Twenty dollars—the cost of business cards—was all we needed to get started, because we had a contract for work to do immediately. So each partner put ten dollars into a joint checking account and signed a contract with the Harvard Law School for a series of films dramatizing the procedures of evidence.

At first we worked from our homes, with rented camera equipment. The films, based on actual court cases, showed the techniques and points of law that contributed to the manner in which the evidence was introduced in court. The films were distributed to law schools throughout the country. Like many of the contracts we've worked on since, this one came from a man who had received a grant to produce a film, but didn't know how to make one. We did. Although starting out on our first contract was unbelievably easy, there were subsequent lean months when there was no contract in hand, just good cheer in the office, dreams of films to be made, and the ability to weather the uneven productive periods.

Our backgrounds complemented one another. We shared a concern for social issues and a desire to make some sort of statement about them; we also had each had several years' training in photography, and experience teaching it. Charles Meyer, a still photographer, taught at the M.I.T. film section for four years and learned the fundamentals of film production as a member of the staff, doing some freelance work but also putting in a lot of volunteer time. Having started out as an American studies major, he earned a B.A. in photography at Goddard College, and he also worked briefly for one other film company, and ran a small arts movie house in Yellow Springs, Ohio.

Bestor Cram graduated from Denison University with a B.A. in economics. After returning from four years as a marine in South Viet Nam he studied film and television for a year at the West Surrey College of Art and

Design at Guildford, England. Both partners had also held lots of unrelated jobs, including picking apples in Vermont and selling the New York Times on the streets of Paris.

Very little formal planning went into the setting up of our business. We learned on a need-to-know basis. Each partner had a full-time teaching job when we began. From asking around among professional people we knew, we gradually found the persons in each field (insurance, accounting, legal) who would be able to help us best. Both partners, however, still do the principal amount of the accounting as well as all secretarial chores. We do have a CPA who reviews the books yearly and is consulted on specific matters such as the depreciation of capital investments. We were surprised to find that not very many professional people locally knew a whole lot about the film business. So while we were getting professional assistance, we were also educating these specialists about the nature of our work.

Advice has been sought from other people in the business and it was, and always is, "Don't do it." It's very expensive to make movies, and people and companies in the business are notoriously bad about keeping contracts, paying bills, and meeting deadlines. A great many film projects never get completed. Some people were reluctant to tell us many specifics about their business because they saw us as new competition and, ultimately, as a possible threat.

Since we both still teach film, though part-time now, our work weeks usually are spent doing some or all of the following: research, freelance production, teaching, in-house production, accounting, answering the telephone, secretarial chores, sales, budgeting, reading, proposal writing, script writing, correspondence, equipment maintenance, and staying in touch with the rest of the film-making community. We now have about $35,000 worth of production and office equipment. Each job has helped pay for something, so capitalization has come about through the reinvestment of profits. Investing in a work/office space was our first major financial decision: it meant taking on a constant overhead. It represented a significant commitment to the business, especially since film-making is not the kind of business that depends on people having access to your office.

Our current projects include the following: making a film to present to prospective investors in new housing developments for the elderly; documentary projects for commercial and public television; public service announcements; work for state and federal agencies and for various non-profit organizations. In addition to producing films ourselves, we hire out as a production crew for other producers. This is common in most cities where independent producers and film-makers fill in some of their slack time with production work on other projects.

One of our greatest satisfactions has been a recently completed film for a private corporation. We did the whole thing—wrote the script, produced and directed it, shot and edited it. We are in the unique position of being hired to become experts about something we know nothing about. Each project is different. The greatest frustrations, Charles thinks, are the films that have never been made. The greatest frustration, Bestor thinks, is the difficulty of combining artistic and creative pursuits with commercial needs and expectations. Another one: Sometimes there isn't enough time to accomplish everything you have set out to do, and then all of a sudden, no one has hired you for anything at all.

Our overall direction is to continue concerning ourselves with current social issues and to discover cinematic ways to present the discussion of these issues. Our advice to anyone who would like to start a documentary film company: live lots of lives; explore; have varied experiences; travel; live abroad; develop as many of your interests as you can, as far as you can; identify your commitments and ideals; then get the technical background and make a movie. But be prepared to struggle.

5. EDITORIAL CONSULTANT

There are over 250 firms across the country offering editorial services in *Literary Market Place*, and probably as many more as yet unlisted (see also chapter 8). They are set up in several different ways: one-person firms, or cooperative groups with six to twenty equal members, or large organizations managed by one or a few people with many editors hired as employees. What follows will give you a glimpse into the operations of an editorial cooperative.

DOROTHY BESTOR

Editorial Consultants, Inc., is a firm of twelve freelance editors. Some of us edit full time; others combine editing with teaching, administration, or writing. We come to the rescue of writers, project managers, museum directors, doctors, dentists, nurses, and psychiatrists when vagueness, dangling participles, unintelligible sentences, poor organization, or bureaucratic language threaten to bog down the clear message they are trying to commit to paper. Our current listing in Literary Market Place reads: "Copy editing, design, indexing, manuscript analysis, picture research, production, consultation, research, and rewriting."

E.C.I. began in the spring of 1975. As two women who were often asked to do editing in their spare time, we started with an idea and a list of friends who might like to join us. The idea was the late Emily Johnson's, director of the Office of Scholarly Journals, University of Washington, and mine: that since requests to do freelance editing came unevenly— sometimes several at once, and then none for some time—it would be helpful to us and to our clients to form a small group of freelancers who could share the jobs and exchange ideas about the questions and quandaries that editing involves.

Our members have represented different age groups (from late twenties to the sixties) and different educational backgrounds (three of us have Ph.D.'s, seven M.A.'s, and two B.A.'s—from twelve colleges and universities). What we have in common is that we all had considerable professional experience with the writen word before joining E.C.I. For example, one member is a former acquisitions editor of a New York publishing company, one a graphic designer for a Seattle publisher, one a former senior editor of World Book encyclopedia. Seven of us are also teachers of college English. We realize, however, that we all have a great deal more to learn. And so we have guest speakers on aspects of editing and publishing at our monthly meetings; we take as many courses as we can in graphics, layout, and publication procedures; and we are in touch with other groups of editors and writers.

At the beginning, we obtained most of our advice from Emily Johnson. Legal advice came from an attorney, the husband of one of our members, who helped us incorporate by the simplest and least expensive method. During the past two years we have also sought the advice of a marketing specialist and of the SBA.

We started with a minimum of capital: twenty-five dollars from each member went into a joint account; during the first year or so, our only expenses were for brochures, business cards, a telephone listing, and postage. We each did our editing in our own home. Since then we've expanded to the point of having a listing in both the white and the yellow pages, a modest amount of advertising, a tape phone-answering device, and more recently a twenty-four hour answering service. We have just now after five years rented our first office, a very inexpensive one out of the high-rent area, part of a suite that we share with four other professional women. The way our financial affairs work is that each editor settles the fee in advance with her client; it's usually twenty dollars an hour, but may vary or may be on a flat contract basis. After an editor is paid by the client, she sends our treasurer a check for 15 per cent of the fee. Most decisions affecting the corporation are canvassed first by a five-member board and then voted on at our monthly meetings.

We all really enjoy editing. We work in the hope that we can take almost any manuscript and, through applying the principles of Strunk and White's Elements of Style, Sheridan Baker's Practical Stylist, and the University of

Chicago Manual of Style, make that piece of writing briefer, clearer, more internally consistent, and easier to read. In so doing we try to respect the author's intention above all, refraining from making changes just because "we would have written it that way." Those of us who write ourselves find no conflict between our shifting roles. In fact, I think that each activity is a helpful stimulant to the other.

When we began, we had no idea how many organizational problems we would run into. We have solved some of them, but not all by any means. For those freelance editors who may be thinking of joining together in a group, the following check list may offer a few starting points:

Structure of the organization: Will every member have an equal vote in decision-making, or will there be a president or central board who will in effect employ the others? If you have a central coordinator to distribute assignments to the others, is he or she full-time or part-time? One of the editors, or a hired business manager?

Legal considerations: If you incorporate, will you be a nonprofit or for-profit corporation? (Check carefully; each form has some surprises.)

Membership: What are the criteria for selecting new members? How can you tell the quality of their work? What kind of training ought you to give them? If a client should have a complaint, how is it adjudicated? Should you keep adding new members in the hope of having someone available for nearly every kind of project that might turn up, or should you keep to a small workable group who know each others' strengths, limitations, and work habits well? If you decide to stay small, should you subcontract assignments to nonmembers when you are too busy to do them, or should you simply refuse them?

Distribution of editing jobs: Is everyone supposed, as far as possible, to find his or her own jobs, or are assignments to come through a central coordinator? If the latter, on what basis are they to be distributed? If not everybody has a continuous flow of jobs, is this the responsibilty of the group?

Fee structure: Should there be a uniform fee that all members charge, or does it work to have each member set his or her own, depending on the kind of job? Should members pay the group a commission on only the editing assignments obtained from the group, or should they pay it on all editing and related work, even for long-time clients worked with before joining the group, or for persons met through personal contacts rather than through the group's advertising?

Amount of time to be committed: Do you all want to work at editing full-time if possible, or will some be doing it in spare time? How will the time of editors who take on nonediting responsibilities for the group (marketing, phone referral, and such) be compensated?

Business expenses: *If you work in your own homes, under what conditions will the telephone company charge you as requiring business phones at business rates? How does your city's business and occupation tax affect you? Will your gross or your net income be taxed? At what point, if ever, will you be justified in the expense of renting an office?*

Telephone availability to clients: *What is the cheapest and most effective way of being sure that clients can reach you—having a member answer the phone at home or in your office; using a tape-recorded answering device; or subscribing to a professional answering service during business hours?*

Marketing and advertising: *How much of the group's time, energy, and money should be spent on marketing activities? How can one establish whether advertising is a better source of jobs than referrals from past clients and from each member's circle of personal and professional contacts?*

It is fortunate that we all enjoy editing and believe in it as a professional activity. Otherwise we might sometimes feel overwhelmed by the many unforeseen organizational problems that inevitably develop as a business grows.

6. MANAGEMENT CONSULTANT

Sally Maddocks never thought when she was in college that she would run, and enjoy running, her own business. An English major and a poetry student of Theodore Roethke's at the University of Washington, she had as her main outside interest playing the violin. After graduation she took an M.L.S. and got married. Then in 1975, after a divorce, she worked for a year for the university manuscript collections, then had a job for a year as a secretary for a university department. During that time, a phone call asking her to do some part-time archival work led to her great idea. Now president of Archival Management Consultants, Inc., she heads a corporation with four assistants.

SALLY MADDOCKS

AMC designs systems for (1) active filing and information systems, (2) inactive records storage, and (3) archival and historical research and storage systems. We collect materials, store them, and keep track of the contents on a word processor. We also design data input systems for prepackaged sort systems. We are part owners of a storage warehouse for in-

active business records, and we store archives of great monetary value.

I founded the business as a sole proprietorship in 1974. In those days I worked as a secretary during the week and did all the archival work myself on the weekends.

The only things in my typical English-major background that prepared me at all for this was some work in records managements which I had taken in library school, plus a part-time job in the University Archives during one year of graduate school, and later another year's part-time work there on a special project. I had no background in any sort of business venture.

How did I get started? I didn't seek advice from anyone; I just plunged in and started. I had a phone call from my former boss, the university archivist, asking whether I would like to create a little archival collection for one of the largest and oldest lumber companies. I arranged to begin doing the job on weekends. I commuted to the company on the ferry every Saturday; the company paid me six dollars an hour, mileage, and ferry tolls. I hired one assistant (they paid her the same amount), and we spent a year on the project. After the year ended I noticed that I'd been making twice on the weekends what I was making during the week in my office. When the dawn broke, I asked my current boss for a raise. When he only mumbled about "soft money—budget crunch—maybe next year," I phoned the lumber company to ask if I could finish their archival job full-time over the next six months. Since they said "Yes," I scooped my things out of my desk, left, and haven't been back since. I walked over to the retirement office and arranged to get my $900 retirement money sent me, whereupon I called IBM and ordered a new IBM Selectric typewriter (to be paid for out of said retirement money). Then I went downtown and plunked down two dollars for a business license. That was my first day of being officially in business.

During the next three years I acquired archival jobs for two large churches, an insurance company, an order of Catholic sisters, several manufacturing firms, and a local history society. One client led to another. Everyone knew everyone else. Most of our clients also hire us on retainer to manage the collections and to provide reference service as needed after the collections have been finished and policies and procedures developed.

About three years ago, our clients began to ask us to do other jobs related to records management; so we broadened our work to include management consulting. Active records flow into inactive records, and some of those eventually become historical.

At the same time, I met a man who had laid all the groundwork for a commercial records center to store business records and keep track of them on a computer; what he needed was an investor and partner. I agreed to do it, since I'd been thinking of doing the same thing a year or so hence. Our two business ventures are now interrelated in that we share clients and we offer each other's services in sales promotions.

I work usually about six (sometimes six and a half) days a week. My work day is about ten hours long—or short, depending upon my general state of fatigue or spriteliness. I interview lumber barons and tape record their stories for a company history I've been hired to do the research for; I do all my firm's bookkeeping and write the checks; I do research at the Washington State Historical Society; I meet with publishers and with my staff. I return what seems like one hundred phone calls a week. I interview women who want to go to work for me and I check with each of my staff to see how things have gone during the week.

I have four women working part-time for me. They are all highly intelligent, and remarkable workers. One is a former teacher of college English; one was in English education; one taught accounting; one was in journalism.

It was my decision to design a corporation around the philosophy of Mitsubishi (i.e., treating the employees very well—profit sharing—flexible wages, going up and down depending on the income of the company). The four women started at $12.50 an hour. One is now making $35.00 an hour. We have a profit sharing program: after three years of service, they can have (together) 10 percent of the issued shares of stock of the corporation. I am now setting up a benefit program for retirement and health and dental insurances. They get no paid vacations. We can't afford it. "No work, no money." The same goes for me. Everybody gets a subscription to the New Yorker magazine for a gift during Christmas/Chanukah.

Plans for the future? We have a five-year plan developed that will take us into a national marketplace. Some of our clients are now multinational corporations anyway. We have begun developing a marketing plan to implement our growth policies. We do not intend to become a large company, just a broader one. Our one big plan is to cut into the consulting business of our nearest rival by 10 percent. The warehousing business will ooze down the West Coast to Portland, Oakland, and San Diego.

If I were starting over, I'd do absolutely nothing differently.

It will sound awfully Pollyanna-ish to say "work hard and don't spend money when you start a business," but it is true. In this order, my advice would be:

1. Work out of your home and eliminate overhead.

2. Package everything beautifully and make sure that everything that leaves your office is perfect.

3. Do all the work for clients, leaving no stone unturned. Work extra time if needed. Be dependable. Always report what you do.

4. *Be helpful and cheerful. Remember that you are hired to solve problems, not create them. When confronted with a problem, think up three options for solution and allow the client to choose the way he or she wishes to solve the problem. Never get involved with your client's office politics.*

5. *Buy equipment only when you have the money to do so.*

6. *Go to your bank and borrow money only when you have capital assets or accounts receivable to cover the debt. Your banker will appreciate it and lend you anything that isn't nailed down.*

7. *Never let a lead go cold.*

My satisfactions to date have been the hiring of a superb staff, completing jobs that will somehow leave behind a trace of history, saving a whole lot of money for my clients and making their businesses run more smoothly, and making a lot of money. I have also been interested in watching my own sense of "business knowledge" flower. I was apparently a "natural," though I wasn't aware of it until I started AMC. The area of finance now seems obvious to me, and I've wondered why people spend so much effort studying it in graduate school. Accounting ledgers seem especially obvious, and can be read like novels. You see what people are trying to do, and how they try to solve their problems.

What, if any, clues can the liberal-arts-oriented would-be entrepreneur gather from these accounts? These businesses certainly differ in clientele, scale, kind of services or products, and volume. But there are a few common denominators.

1. All these entrepreneurs had at least one, and usually two, indisputably solid bases to start from: with some it was capital; with others it was several years' experience in the field; in addition, all of them had or soon found contacts who helped considerably.

2. Most of them sought and got paid professional advice as needed.

3. Even though most of these entrepreneurs lacked business expertise to start with, they had escaped two attitudes common to some liberal arts majors: either that financial matters were somehow beneath them, or that finance was so complicated that they could never understand it.

4. Everyone who started a business had a great deal of time and energy to put into it.

5. The amount of advice available from business persons already established in their fields varied greatly from the self-protective wariness of the film-makers to the openness of the booksellers.

6. All but one kept down overhead by starting out initially with an at-home office, and kept putting earnings back into equipment or in-

ventory. The initial expenditures that everyone felt necessary were a phone answering service and a distinctive logo, carried out in stationery, business cards, and brochures.

7. Most reported that word-of-mouth advertising provided the bulk of their new clientele.

8. Each was still enthusiastic about being in his or her business and full of future plans. Probably they would all agree that "you should know a *lot* about financing" and at the same time that running your own business, as Sally Argo says, "is hard, but fun."

14. Even Government Needs to Be Literate: Opportunities in Local, State, and Federal Agencies

The bloom is off the boom in state and local government employment. Nevertheless, cities, counties, townships and state agencies are expected to hire millions of new employees in the 1980s to fill jobs in expanding fields and to replace workers who quit, retire or die.
— "Government: Local Action," Edward Cowan,
New York Times, October 12, 1980

As this book goes to press, the outlook for government employment is undeniably a mixed one. Early in 1981, Wayne D. Rasmussen, chief historian, Agricultural History Branch, U.S. Department of Agriculture, predicted, "Probably 10,000 recent college graduates, mostly with B.A. and M.A. degrees, will be hired as a result of the federal entrance examinations in 1981. Generally, historians do well on these examinations, mainly because of the breadth of their education."[1] (Other humanities majors, of course, presumably benefit on such exams from the breadth of *their* education.)

Yet since Rasmussen wrote, sweeping new cuts have been made at municipal, state, and federal levels. Each week brings more news of social and health service jobs dropped because of the budget. At least 300,000 jobs under the Comprehensive Employment and Training Act have been swept away. And proposed budget cuts for the near future threaten still more jobs.

It would be foolhardy to pin great hopes on a government career just now. At the same time, Edward Cowan's point is a valid one. Some replacements are always being made, some few expansions being provided for, even in times of drastic retrenchment.[2] Then too, administration policies have been known to change from month to month in unexpected ways. It would seem that you should not entirely write off the possibility of working for the government.

If either interest or desperation leads you to investigate government work along with other options, you may find that your search calls upon even more of your initiative, patience, and persistence than you have needed for the other positions mentioned in this book. Yet I have interviewed a number of people with liberal arts backgrounds who, at the end of several months' search, have found government positions in which they feel very satisfied indeed. Some of these career changers tell you about their work in the case histories at the end of this chapter.

Before beginning to look for any government job it is of course a good idea ot define your goals and resources. As Charles Ruemelin suggests in his *Guide to Government and Public Service Employment,* you should think through carefully such questions as the region where you want to work, at what level (federal, state, or local), in what branch (legislative, executive, or judicial), how closely directed you like to be, how research-oriented you are, how directly you hope to make use of your academic background, how willing you are to travel in your job, and whether you hope to start upward on a career ladder or are merely looking for an interim position.[3]

Ruemelin advises that you assess your resources realistically in terms of five types of capabilities: (1) specific skills, "which may include computer programming, interviewing, polling, statistics, questionnaire design, writing and editing abilities, typing (which can serve as entrée to an excellent opportunity but can also stigmatize you as a clerical assistant), and coordination of volunteer programs"; (2) "generalist skills," including "analytical abilities, problem-solving capabilities, the capacity to express yourself, and the ability to work with others [toward] a common objective"; (3) any campaign or other political experience you have had; (4) any "working knowledge of a particular field (transportation, economics, welfare policy, energy planning, etc.)"; and (5) the possible residual value of other experience you have had. "Remember," Ruemelin adds, "that almost any paid or volunteer work experience or avocational pursuit can at least indirectly enhance your employability. If you have participated fully in any job, you have learned a great deal more about the organization and its concerns than the actual performance of that job may have demanded."[4]

Having decided what you want (and you should give this careful consideration) and what you have to offer, you are ready to identify the particular job or range of jobs you want and to begin the process of submitting forms, taking tests, and waiting to hear the results. With unusual luck, you may find that your job hunt takes under three months, as did Ana Zambrano, a Ph.D. in English and specialist in Victorian literature who taught English at the University of Southern California. She took an M.A. in public administration in night school, set her sights on an administrative job in the Long Beach and

Los Angeles area, sent out a large number of applications, and after three months was offered and accepted a position that seemed to meet all her requirements, that of an administrative analyst working for the City of Long Beach.[5]

Lacking such clear ideas of what they want at the beginning of their search, other job-seekers have conducted a longer hunt with results that were equally satisfying to them in the end. Sometimes you can make your own way, if you are determined enough, to the post you want by starting at an entry-level job and gradually getting yourself reclassified upward, shaping your responsibilities and your job titles yourself as you get farther and farther into the work of a government agency. The experience of one woman with a nearly completed Ph.D. in German and English literature who started back to work after her children were in high school is a case in point.[6]

She recommends that you look through the range of municipal jobs, talk unofficially with anyone you know or can make contact with to find out what the job really involves, then set your sights on a particular area and prepare yourself, in as much of your spare time as you can manage, to work in it—whether in budgets, social services, community development, minority affairs, or whatever subdivision of the municipal structure most interests you.

WORKING FOR YOUR MUNICIPAL GOVERNMENT

Despite occasional local differences, the process of hunting for a governmental position is similar in most cities. From time to time, positions with city offices are advertised in newspaper classified sections and at campus placement centers, but certainly not all of them will be publicized this way. To find out what other municipal jobs exist, it is probably best to go down to your city hall or municipal building to scan the bulletin boards and make inquiries. Usually a receptionist will be helpful about answering your questions and will, if asked, direct you to sets of loose-leaf notebooks containing descriptions of hundreds of jobs and their requirements. Be sure to remember, however, that only a few of these jobs are open at any one time and that you must find the tentative calendars of exams that will be given in the near future for specific jobs. Often there will be a list in the daily newspapers of upcoming examinations and the filing period (sometimes only ten days) within which applications will be accepted.

As you look through the job descriptions, do not be put off because few of the government jobs involving writing or research are classified under the headings "Writers" or "Researchers." In one western city, for example, at least twenty departments employ writers as public relations people, but hardly a dozen are so labeled. A few of these positions are titled "Information Officers," but most carry some such label as "Administrative Assistant," "Administrative Trainee," or "Urban Affairs Intern." Nevertheless, the writing or research expertise you have may be called upon in even the least impressive-sounding of these jobs, and you may be on your way to a position in which writing becomes one of your main responsibilities.[7]

The municipal departments in most large cities where writers are employed in one way or another include the department of human resources, the office of community relations, the office of government relations, the planning services, the arts commission, the board of public works, the human rights commission, the department of community development, the communications division of the general services department, the environmental management program, the office of urban conservation, the office of women's rights, the human resources' division of aging, and various cultural and historical commissions.[8]

Before being called for your tests, you should find out all you can about the activities, programs, and problems of the kind of agency you would like to work for. Consult your campus placement center for sources also; collect and read critically any bulletins the agency distributes to the public; and don't forget that the business and government departments of most public libraries, as well as most colleges and universities, have clipping files on various government departments.

An example of one city department using writers is the Department of Human Resources of Seattle, a widely diversified department. A personnel officer suggested the following information about kinds of positions of possible interest to readers of this book.

Positions:
>   Administrative Assistant: Would make use of research, writing, and editing skills.
>   Planner: Does report writing, monitoring of programs, systems development, and research.
>   Administrator: Writes reports and proposals, reviews those of others, prepares grant proposals and other written material.
>   *Qualifications:* A liberal arts background which includes research and writing expertise would be extremely useful. To be competitive, the applicant should also have some experience, paid or volunteer, in committee organization or in interviewing people. Although a degree in public administration or public affairs would be an ideal addition to a writing background, the Department now

gives on-the-job training; there are also city-sponsored in-service courses in management training.

How to apply: The department sends job descriptions to college and university placement centers, requesting résumés and applications. After these are screened, interviews are held, and the job is awarded directly. For someone with research and writing skills, the chances seem reasonably good.

Still other positions listed that call on writing and research abilities include such titles as human relations representative, community relations specialist, community relations coordinator, community service specialist, and program coordinator. Most of them included in the job description a phrase such as these: "Duties: writes, reviews, edits, and submits press and other related releases pertinent to department planning, projects, programs, and policy"; "Must have ability to prepare analytic reports"; "Should have the ability to write clearly, concisely, and accurately, and to evaluate, approve, and prepare materials for news, radio, television, and other media release."

It is true, however, that most of the positions call for something in addition, such as "from one to three years' experience, paid or volunteer," working with community relations, minority groups, recreational activities, or something else. You have two ways of meeting this test: some of these positions allow substitution of additional education, such as graduate work, for some of the years of experience;[9] for other positions, you may have a chance to present volunteer work, or jobs you may have held while working your way through college or graduate school, as evidence that you meet the qualifications.

Municipal officials at nearly all levels agree emphatically that their agencies need people who can find and organize material, write reports and speeches, draft summaries, plans, and proposals, as well as evaluate the proposals of others. In particular, every office and agency needs people who can transmit ideas clearly and concisely. Here then is an opportunity for some of you, if you have the drive to get past the apparent hurdles looming up during the first part of your search for such positions.

APPLYING TO COUNTY GOVERNMENTS

Most county departments are separate from those of the city and state which, to a great extent, they parallel. To apply for jobs, the procedure is similar to that of applying for municipal positions: you must familiarize yourself with the range of job descriptions, find out which jobs will soon have open filing periods, then apply, and fi-

nally, if found to be eligible, take an exam. If you pass with a suffi-
ciently high rating, you are put on a register, and then as a vacancy
needs to be filled, you may be interviewed.

Because many counties, like many cities, have suffered recent budget cuts, they have had to stop accepting applicants' "interest cards"
and notifying job-seekers of upcoming application filing periods or
exams. But in most areas such filing periods are listed in the newspapers and on bulletin boards in the county courthouse; complete
information is usually available in the various county personnel
offices.

Among the typical county departments and commissions in which
readers of these guidelines might find congenial positions are the
arts commissions, community and environmental development departments, community relations, housing, community development
planning, human services, long-range planning, personnel, public
employment programs, and youth affairs bureaus.

Here, as with municipal positions, you will find that other experience or capabilities in addition to your writing, editing, and research
skills will be called for in the job description. It is up to you either to
make the most of experience you have had or else to make your entry
as a secretary and ultimately get your position reclassified as an information specialist, special writer, public relations specialist, or
whatever it is that you and your employer find will not only describe
what you are doing but give you a chance for advancement.

WORKING FOR YOUR STATE GOVERNMENT

Probably the state government offers an even greater number and variety of possibilities to readers of this book than does city or county
government.

One Ph.D. in English who had taught successfully in a university
for six years found, upon deciding to make a job change, that she
could do very well in a public relations position at the museum of a
southwestern state. She is now in charge of its publicity for all media
and enjoys making budgetary decisions as well as supervising every
detail of the releases about the museum in newspapers and posters,
on radio, and on TV.

Her experience in getting the position was typical of the way many
state jobs at the higher levels are filled: "First you have to get to know
the institution where you want to work, so as to find out definitely
that there will be a job. Then you have to present your qualifications
to the person who can hire you in such a way that he or she does
decide to hire you. Then you have to find out what the job will be

called, what state department of personnel exam to take and when to take it so that you can get on the register and be interviewed for that job. With me, the whole process took about six months, from when I first heard that there might be such a position created until I started work."[10]

Other state positions cover a wide spectrum. For the current listing—not of actual jobs but of the various state and interstate agencies, offices, and commissions across the country and in your own state—consult the latest edition of *The Book of the States*, issued biennially; *Selected State Officials and the Legislatures*; and *State Administrative Officials Classified by Functions*. All three are published by the Council of State Governments, Lexington, Kentucky.

A survey of actual jobs, offices, and commissions—not spelled out in these three reference works but discernible through information provided by each state personnel department—yields many positions or agencies that might interest people with backgrounds in research and writing:

Editor: Writes and edits newsletters, as for instance for the state education association.

Education specialist: Plans programs at all levels for institutionalized students and sometimes teaches these courses, for example at prisons and other state institutions.

Human rights commission: At times there are positions involving public relations, writing, and research here.

Staff development center: Teaching and evaluation goes on here. Some background in education courses as well as in research techniques is required of job applicants.

Office of community development: Involves research, writing, public relations.

Office of citizen participation: Involves research, writing, speaking, public relations skills, along with experience in working with groups of all kinds of people.

Personnel department: Positions here require the ability to write clearly and to evaluate material written by others.

Publicist and editor of newsletter (note also other PR positions for other commissions): Experienced and versatile writers are needed to work with individual legislators in their communications caucuses and to write press releases.

Research analyst: Such positions, which may occur in connection with almost any state commission or department, are well worth looking into. One advertised through a university placement center recently was with marine land management. The requirement was a B.A. with "one year's experience in research helpful, not mandatory."

Research positions in the legislature: These are sometimes available and involve serving on a back-up committee to provide information to a legislator. Although it helps to have a specialty such as education or environmental studies, you may soon find that you have branched out into other fields.

Research and writing positions on state board for community colleges.

Research and writing positions on your state's council for higher education.

Secretary to a legislator: Acts as researcher, as speech writer, and may help get out periodic report to constituents.

Although most of these jobs are carried on in the state capital, some jobs for which you might be qualified (i.e., community affairs analyst, community affairs consultant or planner, community service specialist, or information officer) are performed in other areas throughout most states.

The qualifications listed usually include a B.A. plus relevant experience; only in some specialized technical fields is a graduate degree specified. Nonetheless, having advanced degrees in any of the humanities will not brand you as "overqualified" if you can show the connection between research abilities you have developed and the kind of work you are seeking. When applying you should, however, stress any unacademic work, paid or volunteer, that you have done, and present graduate degrees as merely an added qualification. In the eyes of many legislators, moreover, these degrees will seem desirable. David Strohnmeyer, a member of the Oregon legislature, says, "Government is a good field for people with writing and researching abilities."

It is important to remember that there are two kinds of state jobs. Some are under state personnel department rules and others, including many legislative jobs, are exempt from them. To obtain one of the latter posts, in which you might do back-up research and eventually writing for a legislator, the best plan according to Strohnmeyer and others is to get started before a campaign begins, so that you can "pick a winner and latch on to him or her." Demonstrate your usefulness in information gathering to a candidate; help write his campaign material, on a volunteer basis if necessary, until the time comes when he may be in a position to add you to his paid staff. Says Representative Jeff Douthwaite of Washington: "Patronage jobs follow people who show willingness to work at the grass roots level."

If you are looking for a personnel department job, it will be necessary, as Strohnmeyer puts it, "to work both ends of the system at once." That is, you have to line up a particular kind of opening with a particular agency or commission, but you cannot actually be appointed to that job unless you are on the state's central register.

To get on the personnel register in your state, you should go to the nearest office of state personnel and look at all the job descriptions and the dates of upcoming tests. You cannot take a test until one for a specific job category comes up, and this does not happen until a vacancy has been announced. Having taken the tests, and passed with a high score, you are listed in the register, and any state office or agency that has a vacancy in that job category may then request your services.

Should you succeed in getting on the register before you have lined up an agency that wants your services, it helps to visit your state capital about once every three weeks with your portfolio of recent work and copies of your résumé. Make the rounds of department heads, chairmen of commissions, and offices of any group that could conceivably need someone with research, interviewing, or writing ability.

Despite the long time it takes to get hired, most people employed by a state government find the work interesting in itself and valuable in what it can lead to. If you are hoping eventually to get into journalism, your work for a legislator or a committee will have given you a background in state politics, and probably in one or two special areas such as education, the environment, transportation, labor, or civil rights. If on the other hand you would like to stay in government work, there are career positions for writers in most state capitals. Successful experience in working for a state government can also help you if you hope eventually to work for the federal government.

WORKING FOR THE FEDERAL GOVERNMENT

The national capital is a place where, according to several people interviewed, advanced degrees do carry a certain prestige. "So many people working there have law degrees or Ph.D.'s in economics or in planning that it has come to be expected that people involved in the higher levels of the various government agencies will have impressive academic qualifications," says Diane Bolay of Health and Human Services. You can get lists of open federal positions at your nearest Office of Personnel Management (the new name for the civil service commission job information center.) This list is fuller and more recent than the information likely to be available at your campus placement center. There are also some federal positions available from time to time at local branches of federal agencies, such as the ten regional offices of the U.S. Department of Education.

Application procedures for federal and state positions are, in general, parallel: in most of them, you have to obtain a "rating" before you can be hired for a specific job. In seeking a federal job, you should know that the lower ratings, GS-2, -3, and -4, are for clerical or semi-skilled positions. Sometimes, as the case history of Marjorie Skotheim, below, shows, the only apparent way for even a very well-qualified college graduate to get into the federal system is to take one of these positions and then gradually get promoted and transferred from within. The PACE exam, often taken by college graduates and graduate students, leads to grades GS-5 and GS-7. This exam, formerly considered the sole rating place for most applicants with a bachelor's degree, is being de-emphasized. It is now (December 1981) being given only once a year, and candidates for it must preregister from three to four months in advance. Check with the nearest Office of Personnel Management on dates, places, and the newest regulations if you plan to take this test. If you have an M.A., a Ph.D., and/or several years' professional experience, you are qualified to apply for a rating of GS-9 or above without examination; instead you must file a Mid-Level Qualifications Brief.

In any case, receiving your rating, as the authors of the MLA's *Guide for Job Candidates* point out, is only the beginning: "Do not wait to be contacted about a job. Since your GS rating is little more than a 'hunting license,' you must actively seek employment by contacting as many agencies as you can."[11] If you are interested in the specific details of tracking down and applying for federal jobs, read the concise summary in the MLA *Guide* and the fuller treatment in the handbook by Susan Lukowski and Margaret Piton, *Strategy and Tactics for Getting a Government Job.*[12] Bear in mind, of course, that anything you read about government jobs may be in the process of becoming outdated, so supplement all reading with personal investigation.

Joanne Burns, a counselor at the University of Washington Placement Center, sums up the situation this way. "What people in the federal government really tell us is that the best way to get in is to find out which agency you want to work in, then take any job you can get there, and work for promotion or transfer. One key to doing this successfully is not to sit passively at your low-level job, if that's what you have to start with, but to speak up, ask for additional responsibilities, and be willing to take some personal risks or inconveniences on your way to the position you want."

Another point that Burns makes is that there are certain classes of federal positions not filled through examination procedures. Among these are positions with the CIA, the Foreign Service and one of its branches (the International Communications Agency), the Agency for International Development, the National Security Agency, and the Postal Service. Some of these agencies advertise for and recruit independently at university and college placement centers. As one example which may be heartening to those of you who have demonstrable language ability, Burns tells of a recruiter from the NSA with a Ph.D. in Japanese area studies who found that his assignment left him more time for his own scholarly pursuits than he had expected. His work for the NSA is on flextime, so that he can do his own research, attend professional meetings, and teach his own course in Japanese culture at a nearby university, Burns also tells of the NSA's recent recruitment of a young woman with graduate work in French, whose language skill so impressed the agency that they had begun to train her in the Japanese language. According to Burns, "You don't have to have advanced fluency in a particular language; what you have to show is an 'unusual language aptitude' or a strong academic background in linguistics. The NSA trains such people to do linguistics research or cryptology, though not many people realize the extent to which the agency does that sort of thing." [13] If you are interested in such possibilities, go to the nearest placement center or OPM office and obtain their booklet.

In view of the "job security and generous fringe benefits" of federal employment, it is an area worth looking into. If you are interested, you should be sure to consult the latest issues of the following four volumes: the *Congressional Directory*, the *Congressional Staff Directory*, the *Federal Career Directory*, and the *Guide to Federal Career Literature*. [14]

There is also to be found, particularly around universities and research institutes, another kind of federally funded position exempt from civil service procedures. Such positions, advertised through campus placement centers and by word of mouth, involve writing and editing for the Department of Health and Human Services or other projects operating through federal grants or contracts. In most cases, the monthly salaries are paid through the university system. The fact that such positions, operating on "soft money," may end after ten months or a year or two is balanced, in the minds of a number of persons with M.A.'s and Ph.D.'s in the humanities who have held them, by several considerations. The work is interesting; moreover, those who do it think, in their more optimistic moments, that it could have an impact on public policy on such matters as nursing homes, health maintenance organizations, ways of keeping hospital patients' records, and other urgent problems. If you obtain such work, the writing and editing you do will involve practical application of much that you have learned as a graduate student or instructor. The salaries in such positions, moreover, tend to be higher than those for comparable editing and writing jobs in education or industry.

You might also want to look at the expanding field of quasi-governmental jobs involving the arts. If you have communication skills, some background in the arts, and some administrative experience, you might investigate positions opening up at all four levels—city, county, state, and federal—involving editing newsletters, doing public relations, or administering grants for the visual and performing arts. People filling this kind of position are more apt to have a writing background than to be themselves practicing artists.

"Arts Management can involve practically anything—public relations, museum administration, fund-raising, personnel, grant proposals, working with city, state, and national commissions, liaison with artists, with academia, and with business," according to Jan Furey, who is in charge of the Arts Management Program at Seattle's Cornish School of Allied Arts. "If you think you want to get into this field, you should first decide what branch of it most interests you, and next you should test your idea by getting practical experience in such an area. Try to get an internship in a museum, a gallery, or any well-run arts organization. Volunteer if necessary." [15]

"After such participation," Furey continues, "you'll know what part of the field you want to enter; this is the time to take courses such as we give in our program at Cornish (i.e., Introduction to Arts Management, Graphic Design and Production for the Arts Manager, Marketing and Public Relations, Bookkeeping for Small Non-Profit Organizations, Grantsmanship, Performing Arts Production Management Basics, and How to Apply for Public Arts Commissions). You can find similar programs in the New York, Chicago, and San Francisco areas, and increasingly in many other large cities." [16]

Two other kinds of work increasingly sponsored by the government and often congenial to persons with research training in history or English are archival management and oral history. The former, sponsored by agencies ranging from county historical societies to the federal government, tends to draw upon persons with M.A.'s or doctorates in history for its full-time professional positions; others interested should investigate programs in archival management offered by library schools; the one-year master's program, "The Public Historian," given by the University of California at Riverside; and such courses offered by university departments of history as one begun at the University of Washington in 1980.[17]

Oral history—that is to say the process of interviewing (usually with tape recorder) persons who have participated in or witnessed historical events or periods of social and economic change, and subsequently preparing such testimony to be available to historians or other writers—began to be pioneered by the Oral History Research Office of Columbia University in 1948. It has since become more and more firmly established as an adjunct of historical, anthropological, literary, and sociological research. Although a good deal of the current gathering of oral history is carried on under university, business, or private auspices, it is sometimes done as part of county, state, or federal archives programs. Those interested should write to Columbia University's Oral History Research Office for its list of publications; there is an excellent introduction to the method and its aims in their report *Oral History: Looking to the 1980's* and in the most comprehensive of their publications, *Oral History: From Tape to Type*.[18]

All in all, there are so many different ways to work for the government and so many different routes to these positions that any summary runs the risk of giving an unduly schematic or confusing picture. Readers may therefore find more encouragement as well as some concrete suggestions in the following case histories, in which four persons with liberal arts backgrounds tell how they obtained their government positions, what duties they actually perform and what they think of them, and what suggestions they have for readers of this book.

From German Baroque to Budget Analysis:
BETTY BLAIR

Except for my experiences as a member of political action groups, I had no formal background that would normally qualify me for a management position in government. My educational credentials consisted of an undergraduate English major, an M.A. in German, plus having finished everything for a Ph.D. in German baroque literature at the University of Illinois except my dissertation. My work experience was mostly part-time and occasional (substitute teacher, freelance writer). Nevertheless, I decided government management was where my interests and abilities should lead me on my re-entry into the job market.

The decision was easier than the doing. My credentials, in fact, seemed to most employers either inappropriate for entry-level management or, when I turned to clerical possibilities, a clear case of overqualification. I felt very fortunate when I finally got a job as a secretary in a city depart-

ment *where the duties included writing and editing a departmental news-letter. I was luckier than I knew. The articles I wrote for the newsletter sometimes required some basic research and analysis and led naturally to assignments to prepare reports on the department's management and operating problems. When the work I was doing was clearly no longer secretarial, my supportive boss recommended a reclassification of my position. My title became "research and evaluation assistant" and I began to work with a planning group in the department that did systems and management analysis. That was a giant step.*

I learned a great deal from the more experienced analysts in the group I worked with, but I also took courses at the University of Washington at night (accounting, computer applications, mathematics). I joined a professional society of industrial engineers and stocked my personal library with accounting and systems analysis texts.

But the most useful kind of preparation was probably the one I already had—the ability to analyze a problem into its parts, do research, and write about what I found out. All of these I had acquired long ago as an English major.

My next move was to the Office of Management and Budget in the position of program budget analyst. A small tightly knit group at the heart of city government, analysts represent the mayor's management position; their responsibilities and impact on departments exceed civil service definitions of their place in the hierarchy. In my three years in that office (under three department heads and two mayors), I was responsible for monitoring and analyzing programs and budgets that ranged from the tiny Energy Office to the huge Engineering Department.[19]

Now two years later, I work as assistant to the director of the Customer Service Division, City Light Department. The division's 377 employees provide direct financial and technical services to the utility's residential, commercial, and industrial customers. I do every kind of administrative work from coordinating special projects to assigning daily tasks. I am still in what is described as a staff position. The variety is enormous and the work is fascinating, but I would eventually like to move into a line position where I would have more direct responsibility for the success of operating programs.

The whole process of getting a job and moving up takes effort, persistence, and as much self-confidence as you can muster. There were 260 applicants for the position I now hold. Some of those applicants were also well qualified. It is important to remember that rejection is not a judgment of your adequacy, especially when the numbers of applicants for government jobs are often so large. Professional personnel people can accidentally knock you out at the initial screening by making some strict interpretation of the application you have submitted. And the pile of sev-

eral hundred résumés somehow has to be winnowed to a manageable
dozen or so for the boss to look at. Don't get discouraged. And if you don't
get the kind of job you want at first, maybe the toehold approach will work
for you too.[20]

LEGISLATIVE ASSISTANT TO A UNITED STATES CONGRESSMAN:
LISA KENNEDY

Before recently resigning to take my chances as a freelance writer, I
worked for two and a half years on Capitol Hill as a legislative assistant to
a U.S. congressman. I came to my job straight out of graduate school—
fresh from lots of research and writing done while getting my M.A. in International Studies at Johns Hopkins, but without any professional experience other than having been a professor's research assistant in college and,
later, a part-time "programme assistant" with the American Council on
Education in Washington. I found out about my position through "chain
contacting": I started my search with a list of Hopkins alumni working on
the Hill, called every one of them, set up appointments with each, and
never left their offices without obtaining the names of at least three other
people to see. Within six weeks I had a job of the kind I'd been warned I
could never get without "influence" or prior experience.

As I applied for various positions, I think my total background (which
included a B.A. in political science from Mount Holyoke, where I had history and Romance languages as minor subjects), was seen as an asset, but I
imagine that the main things that helped were having attended the "right
institutions," having achieved significant academic success, and making a
good initial impression. My M.A. was a decided advantage, even though it
was hardly a prerequisite for the job I obtained.

I found that a legislative assistant's job is very demanding, requiring
multiple skills. Given the small size of congressional staffs (relative to the
number of issues a representative must be familiar with), any one L.A.
will have many issue areas. My job was to be the congressman's international affairs expert as well as his "fountain of knowledge" for such wide-
ranging issues as nuclear power, consumer protection, and the outer continental shelf. My duties included preparing a daily "floor memo," which
briefed the congressman on all bills coming up for votes that day; writing
speeches relating to any of my specialty areas; attending legislative committee meetings (as well as preparing the congressman for attendance at
them); serving as his representative at conferences, receptions, and meetings inside and outside the office; drafting legislation and amendments to
upcoming legislation at either the committee or the House floor level;
placating constituents and supplicants; working on several immigration
cases; answering constituent mail, and God only knows what else. The job

was extremely varied and involved a great deal of writing and interpretation; I'd say, however, that oral skills were as important as any others, since political business is more apt to be carried on orally than in writing.

The single most important skill in a L.A.'s job may be that of "creative collaboration" with others in a vast framework of political wheeling and dealing. One must also be able to communicate with ease and understanding—in a conciliatory fashion—with persons of radically different persuasions. I did feel that I was using all of my skills and gaining new knowledge all the time.

To others who would like to find the kind of job I had, I'd say that the needs of a congressman are eclectic. On the whole, general analytical training coupled with communications skills (both written and oral) seems to me the only indispensable requirement for most nontechnical jobs. A background in liberal arts thus remains just as satisfactory as any other for a great many jobs. What is necessary is to present that background in its best light—not apologetically, but with the conviction that it has indeed provided you with the best training for a diversified job, and with those skills that will enable you to adapt to new demands.[21]

EXECUTIVE DIRECTOR OF A STATE COMMISSION FOR THE HUMANITIES: WILLIAM H. OLIVER

For the past seven years I've been executive director of the Washington Commission for the Humanities. Ten years ago I left graduate school (where I'd gotten an M.A. in English, and was a Ph.D. candidate with everything done except my dissertation), to take a job as counselor at a state-run treatment center for delinquents; this post led to one as volunteer service coordinator in the office of Governor Dan Evans, where I wrote grant proposals, reports on volunteers in social service, news releases, newsletters, reports, and testimony for legislative hearings. This led in turn to my present position, which, since it was a newly established one, I got without much competition. (I had first written around to about fifty potential employers, all of whom I'd known through prior work.) Each of the employers I've had wanted a person who could do independent and careful research, think quickly, comprehend situations requiring discretion or innovative approaches, and write and speak persuasively. In each case the job that I had to do was brand new. We started with a blank piece of paper and a sharpened pencil and began new enterprises. Careful, prompt research for precedents was needed, along with creative, imaginative approaches to problem-solving.

When I left graduate school in 1969 it was because of the Viet Nam War; I was a conscientious objector, and my first job represented my alternative service. Now that I've had these three jobs with the state and a "quasi-governmental" job with state wide responsibilities, I don't plan to go back and finish my dissertation. My graduate school experience has been a help, though. My ability to do competent research and to write persuasively has been most useful in my last two jobs, and graduate seminars were helpful training for discussing and promoting ideas in any setting. What I've been doing in Olympia for the past seven years as director of the Washington Commission for the Humanities has been quite varied. I solicit and help to shape applications from arts groups throughout the state for grant support; I help negotiate grant awards; I supervise the production of news releases and other copy for WCH and general publications; I am responsible for grant requests to the National Endowment for the Humanities and other financial supporters; I analyze and help to shape national trends in legislation and new programs that involve the humanities. The pluses of my work are its constant change, the fact that there is a minimum of hierarchy to deal with, as well as good colleagues and bosses, good pay, and lots of opportunity to follow my own inclinations regarding the work to be done. There are of course a few minuses: among them the problems of existing on "soft" money (grant funds), and the ambiguity of an unpredictable future with no clear career ladder to give one a sense of a life purpose.

People who want to work for state government or in a quasi-governmental job like mine should get as much experience as possible outside academic circles—even as a volunteer or unpaid intern. Grant writing, nonprofit organization management, working with boards of trustees, would be good areas to read about, investigate personally, and perhaps find careers in. One should also explore information about the private sector. When I was job-hunting, my ability to do competent research and to write persuasively was most useful. Now that I'm on the other side of the desk and conducting job interviews, I've observed several things that you should tell your readers. Job applicants with academic backgrounds tend to be incredibly naïve, sometimes quite arrogant, almost always unrealistic when they go outside their campuses for interviews.

For example, in the spring of 1980 our commission, in cooperation from the State Legislative Leaders' Foundation, announced a new position, that of legislative humanist. The job description, posted widely on bulletin boards of university English, history, anthropology, and other departments throughout the state, began by explaining that the legislative humanist's "responsibilities will be to assist the Washington Legislature in conducting reviews and evaluations of executive agencies, departments and programs as mandated by the Washington Sunset Law." Qualifications were listed as including (1) strong scholastic credentials in one or more fields of the humanities (candidates must possess a master's or doctoral degree in a humanities discipline); (2) demonstrated ability to write and speak effectively; (3) sound research skills; and (4) proven ability to work effectively with diverse groups.²²

We screened résumés from over eighty men and women; there were twelve finalists, eleven of them with Ph.D.'s. We (the three other search committee members and I) were shocked in several ways by the behavior and assumptions of the candidates:

1. They for the most part had not done their homework. Only four of the twelve finalists had even gone to the newspaper files in the library and looked up and read the new, fairly well publicized, Washington "Sunset Law." Of these four, only two had gone on and read more than was in the daily papers. Only six of the twelve appeared to know much of anything about the state legislature and its workings, and, worse, very few of them seemed to realize how much there was to learn.

2. Most of the candidates we interviewed showed little sense of the need to modify their conversational style to fit their audience. Some were pedantic; they wanted to give us a lecture on politics or the shortcomings of the legislature. Others were tremendously diffident—as if they were absorbing energy during the interview rather than giving it off. We'd strain to hear them; they'd suddenly stop talking and just sit.

3. Most of the candidates seemed to have great political naïveté: they couldn't accept the fact that politics is not a rational process, that a bill that finally gets to the legislature usually doesn't look like the one on which committee members and legislative aids worked so hard.

In short, aspirants to positions, whether they have any college degrees or whether they have Ph.D's, need to become familiar with the literature, problems, assumptions, and preconceptions of the field. Too many applicants seem to believe that they can get a job on the strength of a degree alone, and that all the details of the new working environment will be acquired without any deliberate effort on their part.²³

ASSISTANT TO STATE FIELD DIRECTOR, CARTER/MONDALE RE-ELECTION COMMITTEE: MARJORIE SKOTHEIM

I never planned to get into political work—I just did. I'd been an English literature major at Grinnell College, Iowa, and had spent all my college summer vacations as well as two college semesters abroad, living and working and studying in Russia, France, and Germany, working on my three foreign languages. My plan, if I had one, was ultimately to do something in New York City or Washington which would capitalize on my fluency in these languages.

I went with a few introductions from friends of my parents, who are located at Whitman College. I had two unofficial "clubs" to call upon if I needed to—Whitman and Grinnell. I strongly recommend contacting people you may not know personally but who are affiliated with the same institution you are (alums, former faculty, etc.). It was at the suggestion of a Whitman graduate that I called the Personnel Office of the National Endowment for the Humanities and went in for an interview. I was hired as a grants information assistant. One of the things that helped me get hired was my typing scores. I was amused, but also distressed, that nowhere in Washington was there apparently any use for my Russian, French, and German—which I'd worked so hard at. People in offices invariably said, "We have hundreds of native speakers of those languages right here, so why would we need you?" So typing, which I'd happened to learn in eighth grade to do very fast and very accurately, was actually my best entering wedge. Although I'd hesitate to say to someone "type your way up," for me it was the way in. You have to discern when your typing position has exhausted its usefulness, though, and to be ready to jump at something else when the time comes.

Since starting full-time work for the government in 1978 I've had five positions, the first a temporary, four-month one as grants information assistant at the National Endowment for the Humanities. When that was over, although I could have stayed on in a clerical capacity, I thought I'd investigate any political opportunities that were open. I tried the civil service route, but since I never do well on standardized tests, I didn't get a very high rating on the PACE exam. As a last resort I went to the Congressional Placement Office; they'll see anyone who walks in, accept your résumé, and give you a typing test. My typing test, unlike my PACE exam, turned out very well—so well that the woman in charge said, "We can certainly find you a position." And she did: as secretarial/administrative aide in the office of Vice President Mondale. I don't mean to say that a typing score alone got me into Mondale's office, but without the typing, I would not have been hired.

Thirteen months later, just as I was deciding that I'd been at the White House long enough, organizing the office and the daily schedule of my boss, researching and drafting answers to constituent correspondence, and coordinating social functions at the vice-presidential residence, I heard that one of the men in the office was leaving for Chicago to set up an office there for the Carter-Mondale Presidential Committee. I asked to go with him, even though it would mean a cut in salary. I knew that the duties there in Chicago would have to be more varied, because the staff would be smaller and versatility would be essential.

During the first three months in Chicago I was office manager. My boss started making political contacts and left it to me to get all the practical details organized. After we got things set up, I was in charge of the administrative affairs of twenty-four district offices throughout the state as well

as of State Headquarters; I supervised the activity of the volunteer workers, wrote press releases and organized press conferences, managed the
payroll paperwork for sixty staff members statewide; and helped the campaign director in determining budget allocations and policies and in
scheduling visits of substitutes for President Carter.

This job led, by October 1979, to a related one as assistant to the Illinois
coordinator of the Democratic National Committee. Here I took care of inquiries of volunteers, delegates, and political figures about the forthcoming
Democratic National Convention and the fall 1980 campaign. I also conducted statistical research and took care of travel and housing arrangements for delegates to the national convention. After the convention, I
became assistant to the state field director of the Carter-Mondale Re-
election Committee. By then there was a field operation of forty-five paid
staff members to oversee, with thirty district offices and a budget of
$350,000 statewide. One of my main jobs was to be the contact in state
headquarters for all the field personnel; another was to oversee distribution of campaign materials; and another was to help set up and serve as
liaison for phone banks involving over 250 lines statewide; and still another was helping organize presidential and surrogate events in Chicago.

During a typical week there, I'd have to do: (1) Something to organize
an event (a voter registration rally, a turnout when the President or Mrs.
Carter came to Chicago, or something on that scale). I'd go to all the
organizers and say, "I want this many hundreds of people to be at Civic
Center Plaza by eight tomorrow night," or "I need twenty busloads arriving
from the South Side," and I'd make arrangements with the transit authorities. (2) Some liaison work, peppered throughout every day. At first
my boss, the Illinois field director, would have me make phone calls that
ordinarily he would have made, so as to give me credibility. (3) Call thirty
to forty political leaders and invite them to an event. This was network
building—just being on the phone to a large category of people, and asking them all to do the same thing. (4) Scheduling—as when an administration official would come to town and the scheduling office hadn't taken
care of planning his or her day; so my boss would throw the problem at
me, with a few guidelines. (5) Handle problems for the field staff (i.e.,
about fifty people throughout Illinois, all responsible to my boss). I'd handle it when they needed more campaign material or more money, or
wanted my boss's office to get a senator to come and speak at Northern
Illinois University, or needed to have President Carter call someone on the
phone. (6) Writing—this was laced in and out of doing these things every
day: memos explaining why a phone call was needed, or whatever. I wrote
more substantive memos in the Chicago office than in Mondale's office. All
the writing I did in Mondale's office I'd consider "fluff writing"—it had to
be smooth and grammatical, but writing birthday greetings, or even con-

stituent correspondence, is not as challenging as composing, say, political briefings based on notes taken while listening to a political strategist.

Now that the campaign is over, I've accepted a new position in Chicago with one of the three members of the Illinois House of Representatives from my district.

Political work such as I've been doing the past three years takes a lot of energy and commitment. For the time being it becomes your whole life. You may get to the office around seven or eight in the morning, and stay till 9 P.M., or till midnight—seven days a week. One man in the Chicago office thought that at thirty-eight he was getting too old for that kind of life.

One thing that surprises me is the way I've enjoyed throwing myself into it all. In college I wasn't politically minded. I often didn't read the daily newspaper for weeks on end. But it personalizes politics to be actually in the middle of them. Besides, certain functions have to be carried out in any organization—and to do so, you don't really have to be interested in politics as a whole. But for me, even politics as a whole has become intensely interesting. It has a lot more to do with people and their idiosyncrasies, and what people do to one another, than I'd realized as an English major interested mainly in poetry and in the eighteenth century.

One of my professors at Grinnell used to talk about literature altering sensibilities. I would add that literature changes people from the inside, legislation from the outside. Some changes can be legislated, some cannot. I am probably still most interested in those changes which cannot be legislated. And yet, I do think that much the same curiosity about people, and about ways of changing people, which impelled me to study literature as an undergraduate has also sustained me in the much more public sphere of politics and government.

The thing I've found most difficult about the transition from what I'd call the "contemplative" to the "active" world is that one's standards are allowed to be so much higher in the former than in the latter. You simply have no time, in an active world, to maintain the very high standards you have developed as an academician. What you come to understand, finally, is that, for "activists," other values have come into play. Doing something fast may not have been highly valued when you were an undergraduate English major, but all of a sudden, being fast and adequately literate (instead of exquisitely literate) makes you a rare commodity. I'll admit that I still have problems with this (i.e., esteeming my work) but on the other hand, I'm glad that what I value is no longer as narrowly defined as it once was.

I'd advise anyone wanting to get jobs like mine to do some of the things I wish I'd done in college, but felt at the time that I was too busy to do:

writing for the college paper, for example, and working with some campus or community organization, and having regular summer jobs. Also, I'd advise you to be prepared to make some drastic changes in the way you interact with others. I had to go through a process that I think of as a sort of exercise in "toughening up." Since I'd been brought up to be polite, considerate, and empathetic, it was hard for me at first to say things over the phone like, "But we must have those telephone lines in by tomorrow" or "Get me five busloads of people, no matter what." I learned that when you put your foot down, people do what you say.[24]

As these four accounts suggest, working for the government can be full of challenges and surprises. Work in any one sector gives you a chance for mobility: once you have been hired in your first government position, it is usually not too difficult to transfer to other regions or other government agencies.[25] Furthermore, the variety of government positions is enormous. You can be a researcher or writer in a "working with people" program such as Health and Human Services, personnel, or consumer affairs, or an environmental program such as conservation, or an administrative field such as management analysis. In the words of Dr. Ruth Von Behren, who made a long leap from her graduate work in German medieval history to her current GS-11 position as management analyst for the State of California, "When you decide to work for the Government, take your intellectual curiosity with you; working in an unfamiliar area can be intellectually stimulating."[26]

15. For and About Women

"What are you majoring in? English? Well, that's always a nice major for a girl."
                                                    —Senior man to freshman woman

"Our new communications training program that the lady from the University has been running this year has had such good results and taken in so much money that I think next time we could afford to hire a man."   —Alleged remark by the administrator (male)
                                                    of a state agency

The problem of job shortages and the waste of training and talent dealt with in this book are certainly not confined to a particular age group, race, nationality, or sex. They are human problems. Because these problems are no respecters of sex, up to now this book has addressed men and women as a single audience. Is there a need before closing to talk to women readers as a group, as if some of our career problems were unique?

I think there is—for two reasons.

First, if you have majored in a liberal arts subject you are in a "traditionally feminine" field. It is still true, as Sande Friedman and Lois Schwartz pointed out a decade ago in *No Experience Necessary: A Guide to Employment for the Female Liberal Arts Graduate*:

> Traditionally, the female liberal arts graduate is cursed with a double disability; she is both a woman and a liberal arts graduate. Little girls generally have not been raised to have career ambitions and the liberal arts curriculum doesn't help. While commencement speakers at women's colleges have always made a big issue about the importance of educated women in society, it has always been taken for granted that the society of which they spoke was home and family. And, when they told you the intellectual tools you developed, your ability to deal with new problems in an ever-changing world, and your constant drive to broaden your horizons would make you a better, more fully rounded

human being, they usually expected you to use your intellectual tools in the supermarket, your ability to deal with new problems to combat sibling rivalry, and your constant drive to broaden your horizons to plan your family's summer vacations.[1]

As a language or literature major and a woman, it's sometimes hard to be taken seriously. There are so many of us—*some* of whom may have gone into one of the humanities fields because doing so seemed expected of us. But others chose our majors for more positive reasons. In the minds of many employers and advisers, however, women liberal arts majors are often lumped together as representing "feminine" qualities and roles: appreciating the roles of others rather than initiating creativity; interpreting, rather than asserting; being in a field that is soft, full of ambiguities, and entirely lacking in definition, rigor, or accountability.[2] As Jessie Bernard shows in *Academic Women*, "the roles assigned to women in our society are emotional-expressive," and society considers that there are certain "masculine subjects" (notably physical sciences and technical disciplines) and "feminine subjects" (notably languages and literature).[3]

Since there are so many women humanities majors, many of whom are not taken seriously as having something to contribute "out in the real world," and since of these the female English (or French or classics or history) major connotes to many people the stereotype of the conventional, compliant young woman, someone headed for a low-key, low-paid position in the bottom ranks of education, publishing, or librarianship, we would do well to take an objective look at ourselves and see how we can somehow stand out from the crowd.

Another important reason why women have special career problems lies in our tendency, because of the way we were brought up, to work around obstacles rather than to take the initiative and confront them. As girls we were apt to be offered advice of the "Least said, soonest mended" or the "You must cut your garment to fit your cloth" variety—advice meant to play up the idea that it is wise to develop and depend on adaptive skills rather than come out and ask for what we need and want. So, too, do anecdotes about women writers (Jane Austen writing her novels in the family parlor and hiding her manuscript under a blotter when callers came; Harriet Beecher Stowe stealing time for her writing from days spent coping with housekeeping and bringing up seven children; Tillie Olsen snatching a moment here and ten minutes there to get down a few sentences of the story shaping itself in her mind while she nursed her daughter through scarlet fever.)[4]

But our adaptiveness can be either an asset or a liability. If it leads us to look at alternatives, to try to see what all our options are before we make a career choice, to think imaginatively rather than in a conventional, linear manner about what we may do with our talents, then of course it is an asset. If, however, it leads us to stay in an unpromising position for years, hoping for a promotion that will never come yet finding ways to fool ourselves into thinking that we are satisfied, then obviously our adaptiveness is doing us no service at all. It is up to us to take a second look at what we are doing.

This adaptiveness is connected, in the eyes of some women analysts of women's career patterns, with another characteristic that the circumstances of our lives have encouraged. Professor Margaret Fenn, author of *Making It in Management: A Behavioral Approach for Women Executives*, believes that "women react rather than plan; they don't set goals." Fenn explains:

> Women respond on demand, and measure their worth in the eyes of others. . . . This lack of goal-setting and planning is a reflection of a different time perspective. Women live in short, discrete time cycles. Women usually don't project beyond each discrete interval until they literally are faced with the end of that interval. For example, women seldom plan beyond "until." A woman says, "I'm going to school until. . . . I'm going to work until. . . . I'm going to stay home with my kids until. . . . I'm going to return to work until. . . ."
>
> Because women are other-directed, they seldom have experience in personal goal-setting. . . . Because they aren't prepared and don't have plans and don't have goals, they don't achieve; and because they're not high achievers, women feel inferior. . . . As a result, women fall right back in the old dependent, passive, ambivalent trap.[5]

In her effort to help women take charge of their lives, Fenn makes a sweeping generalization that may have the effect of a putdown. She overlooks the increasing number of women who do try to plan their careers carefully, as well as the occasional woman who, though successful, admits to not planning ahead at all. In any case, if one accepts even a part of Fenn's diagnosis, one can easily become discouraged. The usual next step is to blame "society." There is, of course, a great deal that must be done on a large scale to improve the working conditions, pay, and legal status of women. According to a document presented in July 1980 at the United Nations Conference on Women at Copenhagen, "stagnation and deterioration describe women's condition. . . . In most countries since 1975, . . . females account for half of the world's population, but put in two thirds of the world's working hours; they receive only one tenth of world income, and own only one per cent of its property."[6] Here in America, as Gloria Steinem has lately been reminding her audiences, "U.S.

Labor Department statistics show that the average secretary has approximately two years more education than the average boss." And "women of color with a college degree still earn less than white males with an eighth grade education."[7] There is, then, enormous improvement to be made overall.

In this chapter, however, you will not be reading about overall efforts to improve the external framework of women's work; the emphasis here is on attitudes that you as a woman may hold individually, choices that you make as you try to decide what your life's work is going to be and how you can best carry it on.

What can you do to escape the trap of dependency, passivity, and ambivalence Fenn so forcefully describes? I would like to gather together and underscore for women some of the points made in earlier chapters, and there are additional ideas that women I have interviewed have urged me to call to your attention.

Identify your real strengths. It's especially important for you as a woman to find out as early as possible what your "strongest motivated skills" are—what work you can do, or can learn to do, both with real competence and with enjoyment (see chapter 3). As women we need to have tangible proof of our strengths, first because of our tendency to play down achievements ("I'm just a housewife and mother," or "I'm just a high school English teacher"), and second because we are too apt to be compliant to others we hope to please. So you as a woman job-seeker will need, even more than a man would, to make an objective self-assessment and to revise it every few years, in order to give yourself proper credit for skills and talents that went unnoticed as you worked for your family, volunteered on community projects, or took college courses not having an obvious bearing on a career. You'll need your self-inventory, too, as ammunition against the well-meaning advice of parents and friends who may try to nudge you into certain professional areas, particularly managerial ones, currently in the spotlight as "Ten Coming Career Fields to Watch in the 1980s." Try to resist, too, the spate of articles and books that tell you, as a supposedly upwardly mobile career woman, exactly whom to associate with (successful coworkers in line, not staff, jobs), what to wear (an expensive-looking skirted suit), what to carry (a briefcase rather than a purse), and how to justify ever-increasing expenditures on clothes and personal services ("you owe it to yourself").

Find out about the jobs "out there" and what women are actually doing in them. While you are taking stock of what your talents, skills, and preferences really are (as opposed to what you are told they ought to be), you must keep looking everywhere for specifics of what other women do in their jobs. Women must be especially careful to avoid the "narcissistic fallacy" (see chapter 3). It's no use doing such a thorough job defining your values and your psychic and material needs that you end up seeing yourself qualified only for an ideal one-of-a-kind job that may neither exist nor be possible for you to create.

If possible, find a role model and a mentor. It will certainly help you if you can find a woman doing what you hope to do, whether she is someone whose achievements you merely read about or a relative, friend, teacher, or colleague whose career you can watch closely and who will talk with you and try to answer your questions. Don't be afraid to ask specific ones, such as these: "What do you do in your job? What do you like about it? What do you dislike? Please tell me what you did yesterday. Was this a typical day? If not, how did it differ from a typical day in your job? Of all your duties, which ones take the largest share of your time? What advice would you give anyone who wants to do what you are doing? What are the salary ranges for jobs in your field? What was your preparation for this job? Would you suggest the same preparation today, or are there additional requirements now? What are the advantages and disadvantages of your occupation? Are there any questions I should have asked that I did not ask you?"[8]

It may also be helpful to you if you are lucky enough to acquire a "mentor," someone of either sex who know you well, takes an interest in your developing career, and helps you feel continuous moral support. In Terry Wetherby's collection of interviews with successful women (*Conversations: Working Women Talk about Doing "A Man's Job"*), one finds again and again such statements as, "It just never occurred to me that I wasn't equal to anybody else, because my father [or brother or sister or friend] got me started at this kind of work, and believed in me so much that I didn't waste any time doubting myself; I just went ahead and did what I wanted to do."[9] Similarly Cindy Burdell and Gloria Campbell (in chapter 13), Suzanna Juhasz in *Careers and Couples*,[10] and several women in the MLA survey of Ph.D.'s who found career alternatives to teaching reported receiving active encouragement at every stage of the way from a person who believed that they could reach their goal.

Explore available campus and community career planning agencies. Whether you are an undergraduate, a graduating senior, or an alumna, don't lightly dismiss the potential help that your college or university placement center, office of career planning, office of women's programs, or office of cooperative education can give you. It's easy to be turned off by a friend's remark, "Oh, I went there, and they didn't have any jobs for me to apply for." It is important to realize, however, that the main function of such offices, and similar ones sponsored by the YWCA, local women's groups, and certain government agencies, is not just to give you names and phone numbers of two or three potential employers—although this *can* happen.[11] What they do have to offer is help in assessing your career assets and liabilities, counseling about whether to go back to school or to begin to look for jobs at once, guidance in writing résumés and letters of application, a library of material on job-seeking and on specific careers and companies, and sometimes entry into support groups of women at the same stage of their career search as you (see chapter 3).

The agencies discussed above are nonprofit. There are also other kinds: one includes professional, independent career counselors, often on the staffs of "individual development centers" or "career counseling services." Usually these are thoroughly professional enterprises, staffed by counselors with good academic preparation who, for reasonable fees, will give you aptitude tests and in other ways explore your options with you. Still another kind of service is the private employment agency. There are many entirely reputable ones; but there are more factors to be aware of than meet the eye. For example, you may be asked to pay them your entire first month's salary if you get a job through them; you may be switched from a job they mentioned in an advertisement to something quite different from what you had in mind; and, as most clients fail to realize, these agencies are basically working for the employer, not for you. In using any career services, whether they have academic credentials or are frankly commercial employment offices, the key word is "selectivity." Use them when you need them; see what each agency has to offer; if you have any doubts about their programs, inquire of others who have used them and of some impartial business or professional resource persons. In any case, know what you want from these counselors; do your homework; do not sit down like a dutiful passive child in one of their offices with the attitude, "Just tell me exactly what to do, and I'll do it."[12]

Get firsthand experience through internships. Fortunately, during the past decade, solutions have been developed for those job-seekers who used to be discouraged because they "couldn't get a job without experience, and couldn't get experience without a job." Increasingly, colleges and universities are helping their students to get placed as interns (or sometimes as "externs" or "co-op education" students) in short-term positions in which they can learn something about their possible career fields and be useful to an employer at the same time. (See Appendix E, "A Note on Internships and Cooperative Education.") The campus and community career planning offices discussed about are often useful in setting up internships or helping students make the arrangements for them. Increasingly, colleges and universities have full-time counselors attached to their placement centers who arrange internships for liberal arts students in the offices of city departments, private businesses, museums, social agencies, and hospitals, where you may learn public relations skills, write and edit newsletters, help prepare instructional films or videotapes, or develop your abilities at technical writing and editing.[13] Other colleges and communities have set up agencies to bring returning women into contact with internship opportunities; there are, to cite just a few of over a hundred possible examples, "Continuum" in Newton, Massachusetts, "Project Re-Entry" at Boston's "Civic Center and Clearing House," another agency with the same name at Drake University, Des Moines, Iowa, and the Office of Career and Life Planning at the University of Washington.[14]

Sometimes it is possible to invent your own very informal internship. A graduating senior at the University of Michigan who wanted to become a freelance writer, but didn't know how to get started, did this. Having worked for six months as a waitress and saved enough to live on for the next six months, she approached a successful writer whose magazine articles she admired with an offer to do his typing and correspondence, check on facts at the library for him, return library books, answer phone calls, listen to him read aloud his first drafts, do practically any writing-related job that he needed done, in exchange for being able to see how he went about his profession and exactly what the stages were between the first germ of an idea and the finished article. After six months, she felt that she had learned a great deal, and subsequently she began to send out articles of her own—which have begun to be published.[15] Although some women will find it discouraging that this woman voluntarily put herself in the position of "handmaiden" to a successful male writer, it is important to realize that she set up the internship for a fixed time, knew what she wanted to learn, learned it, and went on her way.

Think in terms of a long-range plan. Try to be an exception to Margaret Fenn's statements about women. It may be argued that it is impossible to make long-range plans in the unsettled world of the 1980s, with new technologies on the one hand and economic dislocation on the other leading to constant radical changes in the work that many people do. But planning *is* feasible at several stages of your life. As an undergraduate majoring in one of the liberal arts, you can plan to take minor subjects or elective courses to be in one of the natural or social sciences so that if you want to be hired as a writer "you will have something to write *about*" (see chapters 5 and 9). This does not mean that you can't take any courses simply for the joy of taking them, that you must test every single elective according to a vocational yardstick; it does mean that you will benefit from having some sort of professional or business goal in mind rather than simply drifting from quarter to quarter.

As a recent B.A. applying for your first full-time job, you again have a chance to plan. Instead of being chagrined if you have to take an entry-level job, concentrate your search for one in a department or field where you can learn something that will help you in later jobs and advance you toward a long-range goal.

The importance of planning and goal-setting also applies if you are returning to the job market after years out of it bringing up your family. For example, Phyllis Needy of the University of Washington tells how horrified her friends were to find that, with her B.A. from Stanford and both paid and volunteer job experience before her marriage, when she decided to go back to work in her forties she started as one of the extra Christmas sales help in a department store's luggage section. But Needy had planned to make this kind of start. "I felt I needed to do that," she explains. "It had been twenty-one years since I had earned a paycheck. I needed to start at something where I could learn what it meant to work, and more importantly, some place where I could succeed. A paid job is not the same as being a volunteer. As a volunteer you are welcomed and praised. As an employee, it is taken for granted that you will do your job. I needed the discipline of reporting on time, staying all day, and following orders. . . . Before I was through, I had learned a lot about management as well as about luggage, because when I was alone on the floor, that department was my responsibility." And when Needy was ready to move on, her experience of taking responsibility stood her in good stead. After several upward moves, she has become a program coordinator at the University of Washington's Placement Center, where she counsels women, as well as graduates of both sexes from the School of Business Administration, in how to look for jobs.

Needy is a good example of someone who has herself taken the advice she gives to students: "Negotiate with yourself. Be clear what the possible tradeoffs are when you are considering entry-level jobs. And don't worry, as so many women do, about 'What people will think if I accept this?' It's O.K. to take a seemingly routine job at the beginning if you know why you are taking it and what you expect to learn from it. . . . You need not stay where the opportunity is limited, but you can learn from every experience."[16]

After you become established in a mid-level job and hope to move upward, you again have a chance for long-range planning. Lolita Burnett, manager in charge of Human Resource Planning at a Pacific Northwest Bell office, tells of her own self-evaluation. After graduation from college she started with Bell in the Directory Assistance department; after working there for two years and receiving some raises and commendations, she realized that she wanted eventually to move into management. So she asked for a conference with her supervisor, who had been very supportive; together they analyzed Burnett's assets and what she still lacked in order to be considered supervisory material. Her pluses were that she had a college degree, was already with the company, represented a minority race, and had good performance ratings. Her sole minus was "low visibility," which she began to remedy by volunteering for all sorts of extra assignments that brought her to the attention of her superiors. Within another year, she was on her way to her present position, which she holds at the age of thirty-two. She does not consider it her final move by any means.[17]

Learn about the new technologies. When asked "What is the biggest difference between the job market today and that of five years ago?" several placement counselors came out with the same phrase: "the new technologies." Whether you are going to be or to supervise a secretary, you should know firsthand something about the various kinds of word processing machines and should be able to make up your mind whether they live up to claims made for their indispensability in the editing and revising process. Whether you hope to be a teacher, a textbook writer, a PR person, a marketing specialist, or a specialist in training and development for a business firm, you will want to know about the latest audiovisual techniques.

Whether you are in business, a government agency, or academia, you will want to know as much as you can about the new field of information storage and retrieval. If you are connected with the mass media or with any branch of publishing, you may want to look at Anthony Smith's *Goodbye Gutenberg* for an analysis of changes taking shape in print journalism, and you will probably want to consider enrolling in at least an introductory course in computers so that you can begin to see for yourself what some of these changes involve.[18] Today in the 1980s, there is hardly a field that computers do not touch, from academic research to graphic design to marketing, and it is not accidental that Harvard University and Bryn Mawr College have made the taking of at least one course in basic computer language a prerequisite for graduation.

Don't, however, let the fact that you should learn as much as possible about these fields lure you back to a full-time academic program unless you have very good evidence that you need another degree. It is often possible to make a start toward learning about these and other technologies through part-time courses and seminars, as a reading of the continuing education advertisements of section 4 of any Sunday *New York Times* will demonstrate. Increasingly, too, companies and institutions are setting up in-service training courses in these fields.

Consider looking for positions in fields, or with firms, usually dominated by men. Insofar as you have learned about one or more of the technologies just mentioned, you will have started to break out of the typical "female liberal arts graduate" mold. Many successful women advise that you go further and, even if you are looking for a position as a writer, researcher, editor, information specialist, program coordinator, or publications director, learn enough about a usually male-dominated field so that you can apply your skill at working with words and ideas in a field such as transportation, environmentalism, marketing, manufacturing, health care, or hospital administration. By so doing you will have a chance to learn a valuable specialty and you should stand out from the other applicants.

Some women tend to shy away from these technical fields initially on the ground that the subjects involved aren't congenial to them. But some who do obtain jobs in these fields, such as the former English major working as a writer for an optical equipment manufacturing company (see chapter 12), find that once they have gotten over the shock of not finding themselves involved with the humanities, they discover that their work is challenging. You might also consider the example of Suzanne Ricard, a recent M.A. in French literature with a long-range goal of being a writer. After getting her master's degree she was quite happy to take for her first job one as technical writer for an engineering firm. For the present, she says, she's glad to be writing about boilers and compression systems, believing that she has a better chance of learning to be a good writer by working on material with which she has no emotional involvement than she would if she were dealing with literature and the arts.[19]

Other women are hesitant for other reasons about trying to break into traditionally masculine areas. In *Academic Women* Jessie Bernard reports that women in these areas are "in a particularly vulnerable position," because "when the informal group structure in any work setting is institutionalized on a one-sex—in this case male—basis the introduction of women upsets established patterns and creates difficulties."[20] As the experience of many women shows, it is not only in academia that these difficulties arise. Women who have overcome them report that the best means of doing so involve knowing one's job very well indeed and dealing with colleagues objectively rather than defensively.[21]

Don't, however, automatically rule out all "typically female" jobs involving teaching, nurturing, counseling, and the other "helping professions." If you have one of these positions that offers scope for your talents and training, in an institution or a firm that appeals to you, and if you enjoy and believe in your work, don't think (like Kate Brown in Doris Lessing's *The Summer Before the Dark*) that you *must* abandon it or risk being exploited.[22] The important question is not whether your choice looks like a "liberated" one, but whether it makes use of your strongest motivated skills in a way that will help you flourish and grow.

In thinking about your career future, avoid boxing yourself in by negative definitions. Phrases like "I'm too old," "I have no skills," "I have no contacts," "I'm overqualified," "I've been out of the job market too long"—such ideas should be deleted from your mind immediately. Don't use them even to your friends or let them linger in your own thoughts. Often this kind of thinking surfaces when suddenly displaced homemakers come in to a campus placement office and bewail the fact that they "have no business skills," and besides, they ask, "Who would hire a forty-eight-year-old woman?" In the immediate literal sense they have a point: no employer is going to say "If I can just manage to get a forty-eight-year-old woman on my staff, I'll have exactly what I need." Yet in the long run, when women of forty-eight, or thirty-eight, or fifty-eight are hired, it is not as women of those ages but as people who know better than any other available candidate how to plan a conference, get out a newsletter, or do something else that needs to be done.

Expect to enjoy your job, but to have something less than the most thrilling experience in the world. So advises Kathrine Gambill, cooperative education coordinator in the College of Arts and Sciences at the University of Washington. She feels, as do a number of other job counselors today, that the media and some women workers themselves may have oversold the "back to work" concept and the picture of the upwardly mobile managerial woman. That is, too many women who are just beginning to look for jobs tend to see in them solutions for everything wrong with their marriages, their children, their social life, their financial state, and their self-image. It takes from three to six months to settle into a job, Gambill believes, and to evaluate it objectively. By that time you will probably learn that every position, even the most glamorous one, has both its joys and its doldrums. If you are the kind of person for whom the bloom of things—relationships, possessions, places—tends to wear off quickly, don't expect to find your ideal job immediately. If you tend to find fault constantly with your neighbors, your husband, your children, don't expect to find a perfect set of coworkers who will appreciate you and your talents. If you are chronically behind every month in paying your bills, don't think that having more money (and probably along with it a higher standard of living) will automatically bring solvency.[23] It all depends on avoiding unrealistic expectations when you start out, and on taking an objective, long-range view of the problems that inevitably crop up.

Depersonalize. If she could give one single piece of advice to women starting their careers, says Phyllis Needy, this would be it. Inevitably you will be turned down some of the time as you look for jobs; and after you are hired, some of the time you will see your best ideas vetoed, your hard work unappreciated, and perhaps someone else given a promotion that you thought you deserved. It is natural and human for both men and women to feel unhappy at such times, but probably men get used to a series of such roadblocks earlier in their lives and are by and large less apt than women to take such rejections personally. If your first reaction over a professional setback is, "But I tried so *hard*," or "I needed that raise so *much*," or "Being passed over for the promotion just isn't *fair*," say it out loud once, right away, to a good friend or counselor; then try to get beyond the feeling of being personally betrayed. Easier said than done? Yes. But it can be done if you focus on the long-range goals of your career ("What can I learn from this rejection?") or on an overview of the agency you're working for ("What do they think they need that they don't realize that I have? How can I show them that I do have this quality?") Such a shift in emphasis can lead to seeing your setbacks more as intellectual challenges than as deliberate personal slights.[24]

Learn to practice assertive behavior—a kind of response to others increasingly seen today as helpful in business, professional, and personal life. As Leise Robbins of the U.S. Office of Personnel Management points out, women in particular need to learn assertiveness because, feeling powerless as we often do, we sometimes without realizing it try to manipulate others or work on their sympathies rather than rationally and calmly setting out to achieve our goals.[25]

A good introduction to the basic principles of assertiveness appears in *Taking Charge on the Job: Techniques for Assertive Management* by Lyn Taetzsch and Eileen Benson. Many women—and men as well—benefit from taking a class in assertive behavior rather than simply reading about it. If you succeed in internalizing the main tenet of assertiveness, that your ideas and feelings are just as important as those of anyone else—not *more* important, but equally important—you may experience unforeseen but helpful changes in the way you interact with others. When you want or need to have something done, you will no longer expect people to read your mind; instead, you will make an objective request, offering a plan instead of an emotional plea. You will stop trying to manipulate people. When you feel thwarted, instead of letting negative feelings build up, you will speak up promptly to the person directly responsible for whatever is bothering you. When people voice criticism of you, you will deflect its impact by agreeing with whatever element of truth it contains, and you will admit any mistakes you have made simply and quickly, without extravagant apologies. You will keep trying to remember that it's your behavior that is being criticized rather than you as a person.[26]

Don't assume that you are going to be rejected. An unfortunate result of the current job crisis is that it tends to feed the sense of incipient martyrdom that probably everyone has to some degree. Too many of you think that it's a foregone conclusion that you can't possibly get a job you want; that of course you'll never get promoted; that of course you'll be left out of the men's staff meeting or not put on the program of the national organization. There is a paradox here. On the one hand, your fears may be justified. Women *do* often still find themselves discriminated against in unbelievable ways; for hair-raising examples concerning some very well qualified women college teachers you have only to look at *Careers and Couples*.[27] On the other hand, continual focusing on the chance of rejection makes one self-conscious, hampers one's work, and detracts from the image of calm, competent objectivity that successful and assertive women convey; in fact, dwelling on possible rejection can easily become a self-fulfilling prophecy. Although we do not all have either the luck or the temperament of Marcia Carsey, an English major from the

University of New Hampshire who became at thirty-four the vice-president in charge of comedy development at the ABC network, what she says is worth keeping in mind: "You just jump with both feet into whatever seems exciting to you. If you're bright and eager to do whatever's to be done, you just do it, that's all. It [has] just seemed always kind of *easy*. Just work and *do*. I think the worst thing you can possibly do is program yourself into thinking it's difficult. . . . I've encountered *no* discrimination whatever."[28]

As your career progresses, consider the uses of "women's networks." Within the last few years, groups of business and professional women have increasingly been joining together in loosely knit but sometimes fairly powerful groups. Each group has a certain theme or common denominator, even though its membership may cut across occupational lines. For a complete listing, topic by topic and state by state, see chapter 10 of *Women's Networks* by Carol Kleiman, a definitive survey of the activities and the rationale of these and many other networks through 1980.

The amount of structured activity varies enormously from network to network. Many groups meet at monthly intervals with the objective of giving women a chance to meet one another over a meal to exchange business cards and news of jobs opening up in their offices, grants to be applied for, and other developments in their particular fields. Their motives, according to Kleiman, are partly to further women's advancement in business and the professions and partly "unabashed self-interest." As Kleiman explains: "It wasn't until I began reading about women forming networks in art, health, sports, business, and politics that I understood more of what I had been trying to do, what we were all striving for: We needed more than simply to know each other. We needed a support group, a personal network, even for our own self-interest. We needed to exchange helpful information."[29]

You may perhaps ask, "Why do these groups have to be *women's* networks?" Kleiman points out that men have had informal "old boy" networks for years; they don't think twice about it: "They just do it. . . . men play the leadership game better than women. Because of their socialization, men grow up knowing all about how to network. They play team sports. They are taught how to collaborate and work with each other. They learn not to hold grudges. They learn to share. Along with reading, writing, and arithmetic, they absorb the fact that *they need each other*."[30]

Before you decide that you haven't time for one of these networks, or that you aren't a "joiner," or that they "are just excuses for a lot of chit-chat," you might give a thought to what Dr. Pauline B. Bart, a sociologist, has to say: "Every woman needs a network, a circle of women friends, for her survival. Without networks, women don't know there are other competent women around. You think you're the only one. It's important to know you are not unique, that more than just one woman at a time can rise to the top." [31]

Finally, prepare to take responsibility for yourself. Networks can be truly helpful, as can counseling, being tested, reading about jobs, consulting role models, and working at internships. But after all the comparing and weighing and listening, after all the supportive strokes from husbands, brothers, teachers, friends, or colleagues, do be prepared to become your own final arbiter, self-starting and responsible. Some women never reach this stage; they are continually asking the world for advice and standing—like somewhat overgrown college seniors—on the brink of their careers, still wondering in middle age, as some of Jane Howard's interviewees confessed in *A Different Woman,* "what they are going to be when they grow up." [32]

What you and every other woman worker must realize is that you and only you can make the series of decisions large and small that will determine how the twenty, thirty, or forty years of your working life still ahead of you will add up. "Career decisions" are often thought of as the big questions: What will be your major subject, your degrees? Where will you look for a job? If you have a choice, which one will you take? Will you get promoted, and how soon? Will your salary equal that of a man doing comparable work? But after these matters have been decided, there are dozens of small decisions-within-decisions that will beset you every day and every week. Will you go to the library on weekends, on your own time, to read about new developments in your field? Will you keep up with business or professional journals, or would you rather read something not connected with work, just for your own enjoyment? Will you go to professional conventions even if they come on holidays when you might prefer to spend time with your friends or family? Will you automatically accept every chance to chair meetings and give talks around the country that may come as you get established in your field, or will you sometimes refuse such opportunities because you would rather work for a community project or a political candidate? Will you accept a promotion simply because it sounds honorific, or will you consider turning it down if your new post will take you away from the part of your work that you truly love doing?

Obviously, there is no "right" set of answers for every woman. The decisions that are right even for you will vary from one time to another in your life. Since the kinds of work with which this book deals usually do not have the clearly marked promotion ladders that college teaching and some other professions have, and since the careers that you carve for yourselves may not have the steady progression in salary that many business careers offer, it is especially important for you to set goals of your own. Avoid, if you can, being seduced by the current media image of the upwardly mobile managerial woman, working for your M.B.A. in the evenings, dressed for success in your good skirted suit, and evaluating every move in terms of increased salary and prestige.[33] You need not be taken in by this widely held but shallow image if you have your own inner picture of who you are and where you want to go, and if you consider the various precepts for success you read and hear of as possiblities to explore rather than as rules to take literally.

16. In Conclusion

"I've enjoyed your book [or article or lecture] on alternative careers for humanities majors. Now could you please spend a few minutes with me and tell me how to go about getting a job?"
—Student (anywhere) to visiting speaker on careers

The above reaction to what an "expert" says in a book, an article, or a talk about jobs and careers is standard. Many of you, it seems, who read or listen to writers or speakers about careers and job-seeking tend quite naturally to think, "What they say is all very well, but I need something more, some person I can talk with, some phone number I can call, something that can help me escape right now from the whole irrational, unfair job situation."

Those of you who come to "authorities" with such questions, spoken or unspoken, are at once right and wrong in doing so. You are right in that there is indeed something more than you can absorb from reading a book or hearing a talk. But you are wrong in insisting that this important extra is something that anyone can package and deliver to you.

This something extra is of course what you, the job-seeker, have to contribute to the process. Taking the ideas and the examples of this and other books, you will have to turn them over and twist them this way and that, looking at them from different angles in the light of your own experience, your temperament, and your chosen field so that you can discard some ideas that may not fit your situation and extrapolate from others that appear workable.

What main ideas do the preceding fifteen chapters offer that you can reexamine and adapt for your own needs? As you meet them again in the following summary, you will find it helpful to promise yourself not to say, "Yes, but. . . ," or "Of course I agree with that, but I don't have time to do it right now." Instead, try to make yourself follow up each chapter that is at all relevant to your interests by taking at least one deliberate action—whether going to the library to look up a specific point, or making an appointment to talk with someone about the requirements, frustrations, and satisfactions of his or her job. As you do so you will need time and a certain detachment from your own immediate crisis.

Learn to avoid the apologetic, defeatist stance that so many people like you have developed. Look objectively at what you've been learning to do while majoring in a humanities field. Look at the *process* involved rather than the content. Once you have seen just what capabilities you have developed, you will need to take an active, inventive role in finding out where they are needed (chapter 1).

If you are a graduate student or hold a graduate degree, try to extricate yourself from the ambivalent state of mind of many graduate students in the humanities, a state at once rather too humble and too arrogant. You are too humble if you accept the world's stereotype of the vague, dreamy, impractical graduate student; you are too arrogant if you value your work and your special knowledge so much that you look down upon the uninitiated and scorn them for not giving you a job simply because you have worked so hard.

Next you must analyze why it was that you were drawn to the idea of graduate work and an academic career and where else besides the classroom you might find such experiences. Your biggest job is to convince yourself that there is intellectual challenge outside the university classroom, and that you can learn, teach, plan, organize, and communicate in many other roles than that of a college or university faculty member. You must learn to stop thinking of nonacademic positions as "second rate or second best" (chapter 2).

In order to find these alternative positions—or to invent your own job—you must look closely at yourself and pinpoint not only what you know how to do well but what you enjoy doing. In this self-inventory try to avoid endlessly contemplating your psyche and its needs, values, and idiosyncrasies or swallowing uncritically the various predictions as to "the ten hottest career fields of the next decade" (chapter 3).

Coping with the logistics of the job search is not so much a matter of outguessing a potential employer or choosing the most ingenious approach as is sometimes thought. Examining the employer's requirements comes closer to the heart of the matter. Find out everything you can about the project, department, publication, or business you are hoping to work for—not just the specifics about your chosen firm, but the context in which it operates. Doing this can make you realize that the details of your academic distinctions and the urgency of your need for the job are far less significant in the hiring process than the employer's question, "What can this applicant do for me now, next week, next month, and next year?" Gear your application letters, your résumé, and your interview behavior accordingly.

Remember that although the various careers explored throughout this volume have a common denominator (the ability to organize and analyze material and use language well), the way you approach and hold a position in each of these occupations or professions may be radically different. Talk to people who are doing what you want to do; ask them how they heard about and got their jobs, as well as what they would advise someone just starting out to do. It is important to notice what is possible, what is usual, and what is simply unthinkable as a way to enter or advance in each field. For example, try to find where you can and cannot expect—given hard work and luck—to receive a promotion from volunteer work to paid work, from part-time to full-time, from hourly to salaried, or from clerical to professional status. In book publishing, for example, as you saw in chapter 10, there is often a gradual progression from entry-level secretarial or traveling sales positions up, finally, to editorships; in radio, public relations, or writing for local or state government officials it is not unusual for a volunteer position to turn into a paid one. If you don't observe or deduce where the entrances and exits lie for the kind of position you want, you can waste years of your life in chronic frustration. If you do pay attention to the rites of entry and advancement peculiar to different fields, you can use your varied experience to increase your employability (chapter 4).

Should you become tired and frustrated in the job-seeking process, you may be tempted to start all over again in a different field, one you imagine is a "practical one where there are always good jobs." Many successful practitioners of alternative careers and many placement counselors recommend that, bearing in mind that currently there are no safe bets, you should try to make the most resourceful use of the assets you already have or could acquire through short-term courses before pinning too much hope on the gains that might accrue from making a second long-term commitment (chapter 5).

If you are one of those who want to go on teaching at all costs, you should realize that the shortage of traditional teaching posts in colleges, schools, and universities does not mean that no teachers of liberal-arts subjects are being hired at all. Such teachers are being employed more and more frequently in nontraditional programs or settings. Teaching, even though part-time, in such programs can offer you a sense of continuity with the full-time teaching you may have done; it can also give you great latitude in designing and testing new courses. If you do well in teaching courses for a varied clientele, you will find it very rewarding. You will encounter highly motivated students, and you will meet a considerable challenge in adapting academic material to a different format without either talking down to your audience or feeling that you have bent academic standards (chapter 6).

If you are interested in remaining in a campus atmosphere, why not investigate some of the openings for nonacademic positions advertised on most campuses? In departments of student services, in work on university publications, in fund-raising and alumni relations, and in several other areas you may find chances to use your abilities to a far greater degree than you now imagine. But you must decide on the basis of personal investigation whether or not such positions are for you (chapter 7).

Some former teachers find freelance editing a challenging and profitable career. In order to succeed at it you must train yourself very thoroughly (or, ideally, have received training on the staff of a publication), you must really enjoy the editing process, you must exercise considerable tact in your relations with your clients, and you must be confident enough about the services you offer that you can be businesslike in seeking out new clients and in charging for your editorial time and skill (chapter 8).

Serving as a staff editor for one of the many institutions with ongoing editorial needs represents still another kind of editing and writing career. The institutional editor, who may perform a wide range of tasks, builds up a great deal of knowledge about one field. Yet there is enough variety within most such jobs that the institutional editors interviewed for this book reported finding them interesting and demanding. Such work can make use of nearly all your talents, spur you on to develop new ones, and sometimes help you become qualified for related careers in writing or publishing (chapter 9).

Book publishing, once considered an elegant profession for graduates of Eastern colleges who cared deeply about books, liked to work closely with authors, and didn't need to be paid very much, has recently come to be a branch of big business. And getting a foot in the door of this extremely competitive profession isn't easy. The consensus of the advice to entrants to this field from established publishers is: first, be willing to start with a low-paying entry-level job; second, know something of the many different possible careers in the industry (so you don't think that being an editor is the only desirable position); and finally, if you have a hard time getting advanced, try to "make your presence and your work contribution felt, but not your desperation" (chapter 10).

If you have a bachelor's degree in English or communications, possibly you think that the writing you have done gives you an automatic edge when applying for a job in print or broadcast journalism. If you have or are approaching a Ph.D., you may think that the aims and audiences of the media are so different from those you are used to that there is an unbridgeable chasm between the two worlds. Actually neither supposition is true. Having taken such a major does not necessarily qualify you for a job in the highly competitive media world, nor will having an M.A. or a Ph.D. automatically disqualify you. Of the media's various branches—daily metropolitan newspapers, smaller suburban and neighborhood weeklies, general and special-interest periodicals, commercial radio and TV, the public broadcast system, as well as public relations and advertising—each has its particular path of entry, which you should explore thoroughly (chapter 11).

Job-seekers with B.A.'s or graduate degrees in the humanities are beginning to find some areas of the business world less inhospitable than they expected; similarly, some banks, insurance companies, manufacturers, and other large corporations are beginning to realize that persons educated in the humanities, particularly those with graduate degrees, may represent untapped sources of talent. When looking for such positions, you should be explicit about your abilities and what you can offer a company; you should have samples of written material you have produced; and you should know as much as possible about the terminology of the business you are hoping to work for (chapter 12).

If you wish to start your own business enterprise, you may have found either encouragement or warning from the sampling of case histories here presented. If you produce or distribute a product, you will be plunging into a capital-intensive business where cash flow is a constant problem and where it takes a particular kind of temperament to cope with the pressures of owing money to many different people at once and of "not being able to pass along the serious problems to a boss." If you are setting up as a consultant, you face different problems—the early days of your business when the phone doesn't ring, the question of how to price your services and how to market them, and the knowledge that you don't belong to any sheltering firm, school, or other institution.

Whichever kind of small business you start and develop, there may be certain common denominators: the sense of never-ending "work that has to be done without enough time to do it," and yet at the same time—if you triumph over the statistics of early failure for four out of five small businesses—the revivifying sense of personal achievement (chapter 13).

There is hardly any occupation or profession discussed in this book that cannot be carried on for your local, state, or federal government. Although the process of applying and being hired for certain government positions is a bit involved, once you are on the payroll of a government office or agency, both lateral and upward mobility are often fairly easy to achieve. Often, too, you will find relative job security and generous fringe benefits. Writing, coordinating, and information-gathering jobs can be found in a great variety of branches of the government. Many who have made the transition from academic to government employment find that "working in an unfamiliar area can be intellectually stimulating" (chapter 14).

Women readers of this book share with men the career problems discussed throughout. Those of us educated in the humanities do, however, appear to have an additional set of career problems in the way we have perceived ourselves and the ways in which until recently we have let others perceive us. We need therefore to make a special effort to identify our real strengths, find out the full range of job options, and if possible seek out role models and mentors to help us get started. No matter how much constructive use we may make of courses, advisers, support groups, and the resources of placement centers, libraries, and women's networks, we must realize that it is up to each of us to set our own goals, preferably in terms of a long-range plan that suits our talents and circumstances; it is up to each of us and no one else to revise those goals from time to time, and to determine how to reach them (chapter 15).

Many of the foregoing points from chapter 15 apply no less to men than to women. I hope that both sexes may find it challenging to follow the lead of a Ph.D. in English now writing for a public utility company, whose advice to readers of this book is to "find out where your strengths and talents truly lie, and then learn how best to sell them."

If, without giving in to feelings of rancor or desperation, you can follow or adapt some of the suggestions in this book, you will have done two important things. Even though you will not have changed an educational system that badly needs rethinking, you will have regained your own feeling of autonomy and personal worth. And if you and others like you refuse to see yourselves as victims of a narrow and rigid system, if more of you begin to realize that you can take the methods and insights of the humanities into new territories, even the system itself may in time grow more flexible and more humane.

The Ph.D. Job Crisis: A Summary

Since 1971, when a ground-breaking article, "The Future Market for Ph.D.'s," by Dael Wolfle and Charles V. Kidd, appeared in *Science*, and 1972, when it was reprinted in the *AAUP Bulletin*, the academic world has been exposed to data showing how many doctorates have recently been granted, as well as to projections and forecasts of the extent to which Ph.D.'s can reasonably expect to find academic teaching posts in the near future. Following up the line of inquiry begun by Wolfle and Kidd, several other scholars have made further inquiries. If you would like to know the precise numbers of humanities Ph.D.'s granted in recent years, discipline by discipline, and follow the reasoning of those who assert that only one or two out of ten new holders of doctorates can rationally look forward to a life of college and university teaching in tenure-track positions, consult Allan Cartter's *Ph.D.'s and the Academic Labor Market* (New York: McGraw-Hill, 1976), Dorothy Harrison's article, "The Nonacademic Job Market," *Bulletin of the Associated Departments of English and Foreign Languages* (September 1976), and Betty Maxfield's and Susan Henn's *Employment of Humanities Ph.D.'s* (Washington, D.C.: National Academy of Sciences, 1980). As Maxwell and Henn show, "The number of Ph.D.'s awarded in the humanities has increased steadily from an average of about 250 per year during the 1920's to approximately 4,500 per year during the 1970's. More than 25 percent of the total number were awarded in the 1960's and over 44 percent in the 1970's" (p. 7). As they go on to point out, "English/ American literature and history, the two largest humanities fields (27.8 percent and 25.9 percent, respectively, of all 1920–78 humanities Ph.D.'s) . . . [increased] from an average of approximately 50–65 Ph.D.'s awarded per year in the 1920's to what will be over 1,000 Ph.D.'s per year in the 1970's. The third largest field, modern languages, grew at an even more rapid rate, increasing from just over 30

Ph.D.'s awarded per year in the 1920's to more than 800 per year in the 1970's" (p. 7).

Figures, charts, and tables dealing with these matters abound. The best and most comprehensive summary appeared in *Rackham Reports* (Spring 1980, p. 1) published by the Horace H. Rackham School of Graduate Studies, University of Michigan, Ann Arbor Michigan. Its authors and the editor have given me permission to reprint it here.

OF IVORY TOWERS, FADING DREAMS, AND THE 9-TO-5 WORLD
by DALE MATHEWS and MARY EASTHOPE

> Nine out of ten Ph.D. students in the humanities and social sciences in American universities expect to find university teaching jobs. Only one out of ten succeeds. A Carnegie Council report released in January 1980 predicts no improvement in the academic job market before the end of the century.
>
> Predictions of a decline in employment opportunities in all fields in four-year colleges and universities were probably first made public by the late Allan Cartter, professor of education and economics at the University of California, Los Angeles. In 1965 he forecast that "the seller's market for college faculty will quickly disappear in the early 1970's." By 1976 he was writing, "The academic sector is likely to absorb only about 12,000 new doctorates annually for the next several years, and average only about 7,500 during the 1980–1995 period. Therefore, academic demand will probably require not more than 35 percent of graduate school capacity output for the next few years, declining to about 20 percent in the 1980's."
>
> The outlook for graduate students in the humanities and social sciences is particularly disquieting. Dorothy Harrison, coordinator of doctoral programs for the New York State Department of Education, reported in 1976 that by 1990 some 60,000 nationwide will not find the teaching jobs they seek. Currently, U.S. universities produce some 11,000 doctorates annually in the humanities and social sciences, eight times the number of available faculty jobs. To compound the problem, a sizable portion of available jobs are not considered "satisfactory" because they may be temporary, non-tenure-track appointments.

APPENDIX B

Procedures Developed by One Editing Firm for Working with Clients

1. Be sure that your client has his/her own copy of the manuscript; otherwise, Xerox a copy and keep it, for safety, in a different place from the one you're working on.

2. If there is to be extensive reorganization of the kind that involves cutting, pasting, and reordering of paragraphs, it will help you to have another copy that you feel free to carve up. (Cutting it up without having an original to compare it with can lead to confusion and despair.)

3. Make sure that the client tells you what his chosen format is to be and, if it's not immediately self-evident, who the probable audience for his piece is to be. Get him to give you a journal style sheet or model if possible.

4. If you are editing a graduate school thesis or dissertation, be sure that you have a letter in your files from the student's director in which he spells it out that for a particular reason (usually because English is not the student's native language) an editor is permissible and advisable.

5. Find out what the client expects to get back from you: a lightly copy-edited manuscript? Heavily copy-edited material, perhaps with considerable tightening and some stylistic changes? Camera-ready copy? Thorough reorganization of sections? Suggestions for future writing which he can apply on his own in later portions of the work? Checking of facts, footnotes, or bibliographical form? (If the last-mentioned, or if the client wants you to index the manuscript, be sure that you know what you may be getting into as far as time goes, and that he knows what may be involved in terms of fees.)

6. Decide on a manual of usage appropriate to the client's field; show it to him and see that he agrees with you that this is to be the arbiter, in case of doubt.

7. If possible, resist the temptation to make editorial comments page by page until you have skimmed through the whole manuscript.

8. Make a list of the revision symbols or abbreviations you use and give it to the client so that he can easily interpret your comments. (Ideally, of course, you will go over many of your comments with him.)

9. Make a list, for your own reference, after skimming the whole manuscript, of recurring points on which consistency is important throughout the whole work—spelling of proper names, use of acronyms and abbreviations, questions of punctuation after initials such as HEW and HSA's, etc.). Then add to, and refer to, this list as you edit. A copy of this list should accompany the edited manuscript, as it will be most helpful to the person who reads proof.

10. If possible, no matter how many comments you put on the pages, take the time to type up a one-page summary, for your author, of your overall comments and suggestions. (Put it on your business letterhead, and date and sign it; this sheet, a copy of which you will keep in your files, will protect you in case the author later claims that you told him the book was a masterpiece and should be published immediately, or on the other hand grumbles that you destroyed his creative product, or made no constructive suggestions one way or the other.)

11. Obviously, keep an exact log of time spent; check with the author if you think things are going more slowly than he will pay for; and keep checking on his deadlines, while letting him know your own time schedule.

12. No matter how amusing, bizarre, or interesting the subject-matter of your clients' writing may be, and no matter how good a story the clients' problems would make, do not yield to the temptation to discuss them with your friends. Professional confidentiality should be the rule at all times.

13. Despite everything, remember to enjoy what you are doing. As the editor, you may think you have problems; but be thankful that you did not have to write the manuscript yourself.

Are You Meant to Be a Consultant? A Questionnaire

This questionnaire was developed by Don Swartz, director, International Institute for the Study of Systems Renewal, a division of Organization Renewal, Inc., and is adapted here by permission.

Can You:

yes no

____ ____ Accept rejection and not take it personally?

____ ____ Stay off-stage and let someone else take the bow?

____ ____ Make things happen even though you don't have positional clout?

____ ____ Accept success without external applause?

____ ____ Handle unfounded blame for another's failures?

____ ____ Deal with demands of cost/value justification?

____ ____ Accept being taken for granted?

____ ____ Avoid the seduction of giving your service away?

____ ____ Confront your client and risk losing your job or assignment?

____ ____ Maintain confidentiality even when sharing information might "give you power"?

____ ____ Tolerate aloneness—even in a crowd?

____ ____ Say "No" when you need time for yourself?

____ ____ Avoid the trap of "pleasing" when the data or gut says otherwise?

____ ____ Give help to people you don't like?

____ ____ Give help without giving advice?

____ ____ Move in and out of emotional situations without debilitating involvement?

____ ____ Reveal your strengths, openly and without apology?

____ ____ Put a fair price on your services—and ask for it?

____ ____ Sell yourself as a unique product in the market place?

____ ____ Say, "I'm not the right person for the assignment"?

____ ____ Readily give credit to other professionals for materials and ideas you use?

APPENDIX D

Technical Writing Programs and Other Resource Organizations

Because of the proliferation of business and professional associations and because of their frequent changes of address, it is no longer practical to provide an appendix of "resource organizations" as in the 1977 edition of this book. I want to point out, however, that nearly every kind of profession or occupation discussed in this book—advertisers, broadcasters, editors, indexers, publishers, women returning to the job market, writers, and many more—has one or more national associations devoted to its interests. Many of these groups publish career information and sponsor conferences, workshops, or journals. To find the names and addresses of such groups, see *A Career Guide to Professional Associations* (Cranston, R.I.: The Carroll Press, 1980) or the *Encyclopedia of Associations*, 15th ed., 3 vols. (Detroit: Gale Research Co., 1980).

There is one group of useful addresses that I am including here because it is not often met with elsewhere—the list of colleges and universities offering programs in technical writing and technical editing. For admission requirements and a description of course content, write the director of each program.

Division of Technology
College of Engineering and Applied
  Science
Arizona State University
Tempe, AZ 85281
Prof. John Brockmann

Technical Illustration
Los Angeles Trade-Technical
  College
400 West Washington Boulevard
Los Angeles, CA 90015
Prof. Laura Ann Gilchrist

School of Liberal Arts
Metropolitan State College

1006 11th Street
Denver, CO 80204
Prof. Joy Junker

Department of Technical Journalism
Colorado State University
Fort Collins, CO 80523

Department of Journalism and Mass
  Communication
Iowa State University
Ames, IA 50010
Dr. J. W. Schwartz, head

Science Information Program
Illinois Institute of Technology
Chicago, IL 60616

255

William Rainey Harper College
Palatine, IL 60067

Communications Division
Rock Valley Community College
Rockford, IL 61101
Prof. David Bloomstrand

Science Communication Program
School of Public Communication
Boston University
112 Cummington Street
Boston, MA 02215
Prof. Harold G. Buchbinder, director

Writing Program
Department of Humanities
Massachusetts Institute of
    Technology
Cambridge, MA 02139
Prof. James Paradis

Scientific and Technical
    Communication
Michigan Technological University
Houghton, MI 49931

Technical Industrial
    Communication
Kalamazoo Valley Community
    College
Kalamazoo, MI 49006
Prof. Russell Briggs

Department of Rhetoric
University of Minnesota
St. Paul, MN 55108
Prof. Victoria M. Winkler

School of Journalism
University of Missouri
Columbia, MO 65201
Prof. Joye Patterson, coordinator,
    science writing

Department of Humanities
University of Missouri-Rolla
Rolla, MO 65401
Prof. Sam Geonetta

Biomedical Communications
    Training Program
University of Nebraska Medical
    Center
42nd and Dewey Avenue
Omaha, Nebraska 68105
Prof. Reba A. Benschoter, director

Department of English
Box 5308
North Carolina State University
Raleigh, NC 27650
Prof. Carolyn R. Miller

Technical Communications
Department of Humanities
Clarkson College
Potsdam, NY 13676

Department of English
Syracuse University
Syracuse, NY 13210
Prof. Carol Lipson

Master's Program, Technical
    Communication
Department of Language, Literature,
    and Communication
Rensselaer Polytechnic Institute
Troy, NY 12181
Prof. David L. Carson, director

Technical Writing Programs
Department of English
Bowling Green State University
Bowling Green, OH 43403
Prof. William Coggin, coordinator

Department of English
Case Western Reserve University
Cleveland, OH 44106
Prof. Marilyn S. Samuels

Department of English
Miami University
Oxford, OH 45056
Prof. Paul Anderson

Department of English
205 Morrill
Oklahoma State University
Stillwater, OK 74078
Prof. Thomas Warren

Department of English
Carnegie-Mellon University
Pittsburgh, PA 15213
Prof. Beekman Cottrell

Department of Humanities
The University of South Dakota
  at Springfield
Springfield, SD 57062
Prof. Zane Dickinson

Department of English
Box 4530
Texas Tech University
Lubbock, TX 79409
Prof. Gary C. Poffenbarger

Department of English
Eastern Washington University
Cheney, WA 99004
Prof. Judith Kaufman

Program in Scientific and Tech-
  nical Communication
356 Loew Hall, FH-40
University of Washington
Seattle, WA 98195
Prof. James W. Souther

Department of English
University of Wisconsin-Stout
Menomonie, WI 54751
Prof. Morrell Solem

Department of Humanities
Alderson-Broaddus College
Philippi, WV 26416
Prof. Barbara A. Smith

A Note on Internships and Cooperative Education

The idea of supplementing liberal arts education with some sort of applied experience or field work has been gradually increasing in popularity during the half-century since Antioch College began its program of alternating periods of classroom study and off-campus paid work in a student's chosen field. Within the past ten years, several institutions in various parts of the country have developed "internships," among them some for English majors and other aspirants to careers in writing or communications.

At Fiorello LaGuardia Community College, New York, freshmen spend three of their four quarters in classroom study, and then in either their third or fourth quarter they work on off-campus internships sponsored by the college's Cooperative Education Division. Sophomores alternate two quarters of classroom study with two of internships (some of them abroad). Some of these students have been secretary-translators in Madrid, teachers in Puerto Rico, teacher's aides on a Navaho reservation; others have worked with publications at a Planned Parenthood affiliate or learned editing in the publications office of FLCC. (See "Work Opportunities for the English Major: A New Look at Career Possibilities," *ADE Bulletin* 36 [March 1973]: 22–24.)

At the University of Puget Sound and Pacific Lutheran University, both in Tacoma, Washington, students who complete their newly developed professional programs (the Writing Institute at UPS and the publications procedures course at PLU) can look forward to gaining experience for two to three months in the offices of local businesses, publishers, or private agencies where writing and editing is carried on. At North Carolina State University the English Department has set up a whole writing-editing curriculum involving many options for course work and for writing experience gained from employment in local offices, agencies, and printing and publishing firms. A similar but more elaborate curriculum has been in force for the past several years at the University of Redlands in California. At Lane

Community College, Eugene, Oregon, there is a full-time person (formerly an English teacher) coordinating placement of interns who are Language Arts majors. Reports from students in all these programs are enthusiastic.

A somewhat different kind of internship, designed not for undergraduates but for women who have been out of college and out of the job market for some time, is a part of the "Career Explorations" noncredit course given at the University of Washington through the Office of Women's Programs. Here women take a quarter-long course during which they try to clarify their career goals as they listen to representatives of various fields and do intensive reading in areas of their own special interests. Following completion of one quarter, they often receive placement for a quarter in a job where, under supervision, they gain firsthand experience. Although these internships are not limited to the fields of writing, editing, and publishing, I know of several women who have gotten very good starts in these fields through one of the "Career Explorations" internships.

Other internships have been developed recently at research centers such as the Pacific Northwest Science Center, where interns help edit the magazine *Pacific Northwest,* and at Battelle Seattle Research Center, where interns who have taken the technical writing/editing sequence at the University of Washington have been given considerable responsibility for editing monographs in the natural and social sciences.

Probably among the best known and most flourishing internships are those sponsored annually by newspapers that select promising college students (whether majors in communications, English, or other subjects) for summer work. Interested students should ordinarily apply in November and December of their junior year for work the following summer. Several editors I talked to suggested that students might also "try to make their own internships—ask in February or March for work the following summer, when vacation replacements for reporters and desk people are needed."

A few university presses here and there are beginning to develop traineeships or internships. One such arrangement, sponsored by the University of Washington Press since 1970, has been designed as "a student training program aimed at bringing members of minority groups into scholarly publishing." In the ten weeks the first student took part in the program, she apparently received a very good introduction to the process of editing books.

Among one group of people not ordinarily recipients of writing/editing internships (graduate students in English), there is an increasing number who wish that some such arrangement were available, particularly something whereby they could learn the theory and practice of editing. At the 1976 meeting of the MLA there were reports on several programs newly designed to broaden the competence of the Ph.D. and to include practical experience through some form of internship. Among them were an optional "professional skills minor" at Pennsylvania State University and combined programs involving other departments at the University. Some graduate students, moreover, are able to get internships of a different kind: one or two quarters of supervised teaching in a community college are part of the English M.A. program at Western Washington University, at Bellingham. Probably other state universities have similar arrangements with nearby community colleges. That well-known institution, the university teaching assistantship, could be said to have some of the characteristics of an internship.

"Internship" is a general term for the supervised practical training increasingly offered to students or recent graduates. There is also a "Cooperative Work Experience Program" growing throughout the country, which offers a specific kind of internship. Member colleges and universities receive some federal funding and belong to the National Association for Cooperative Education, an organization which also admits as members students, administrators, and employers. Work done under its sponsorship usually receives academic credit (this is not mandatory, but is recommended). The program works toward two goals for the students involved in it: not only practical experience but learning. The internships held involve work which must be related to either the student's academic major or to the career for which he or she is preparing. Each student must have two separate work experiences (usually of a quarter, a semester, or a summer vacation's length) separated by a period of academic study. Most cooperative education work is supposed to be paid for, although there are a few exceptions. Kathrine Gambill, work experience coordinator for liberal arts at the University of Washington, places between one hundred and one hundred and fifty students per quarter in such internships.

One apparent drawback of internships or cooperative work experience is that they keep students from taking one or two more courses while they are still undergraduates. Professors and students closely connected with these programs, however, are quick to point out that most students involved in them learn to use their time better, become more focused, begin to acquire more realistic ideas about the world of work outside the campus, and often appreciate their liberal arts courses even more than they had before.

Notes

CHAPTER 1. LIBERAL ARTS GRADUATES IN THE 1980s

1. Quoted by Christopher Fitzgerald, "Executive Opportunities Show Decline," in "National Recruitment Survey: Careers," *New York Times*, October 11, 1981 (sec. 12, p. 22).

2. Terry Wetherby, ed., *Conversations: Working Women Talk about Doing "A Man's Job"* (Millbrae, Calif.: Les Femmes Press, 1977), p. 37. Since Carsey's current position is that of vice-president for comedy development at ABC, one wonders whether she still seriously believes that her major in English literature has absolutely no bearing on her work—which involves reading and evaluating scripts and ideas for new series, and working with authors, directors, and others.

3. These and many similar headlines abound in the *New York Times* special section, "National Recruitment Survey: Careers," October 11, 1981 (sec. 12, pp. 32, 64). They can be paralleled in almost any recent newspaper treatment of job forecasts and opportunities.

4. Christopher Wellisz, "Darker Days for College Grads," *New York Times*, "National Recruitment Survey," October 11, 1981 (sec. 12, p. 44).

5. Ibid., p. 50.

6. See the disciplines included, with slight variations, in studies such as Rita Jacobs, *The Useful Humanists: Alternative Careers for Ph.D.'s in the Humanities* (New York: Rockefeller Foundation, 1977); Betty D. Maxfield and Susan M. Henn, *Employment of Humanities Ph.D.'s* (Washington, D.C.: Commission on Human Resources, National Research Council, 1980); and Carol Rigolot, ed., *Alternate Careers for Ph.D.'s in the Humanities* (Princeton, N.J.: Princeton University Press, 1978).

7. Alternatively, consider working by yourself with such guides as Peter Elbow's *Writing without Teachers* (New York, Oxford University Press, 1973) or his *Writing with Power* (New York, Oxford University Press, 1981).

8. Quoted by Dan Hulbert, "Communications: Signals Are 'Go'," *New York Times*, "National Recruitment Survey," October 12, 1980 (sec. 12, p. 27).

9. William N. Yeomans, "Making the Liberal Arts a Plus," *New York Times*, "National Recruitment Survey," October 11, 1981 (sec. 12, p. 63).

10. Frank Harper, "English: The Key to Effective Communication," *The CEA Forum: English, Liberal Arts, and Communication: Their Value Beyond Academe*," College English Association, 11, no. 4 (April 1981): 4–5. Harper is Legal Counsel, ZEP National Chemical Corporation, Atlanta, Georgia.

11. Martin VandenAkker, Jr., "The Relevance of English Writing and Literature in Practicing Medicine," unpublished senior paper submitted at Albion College, Albion, Michigan, April 1979. VandenAkker was, when he wrote this paper, an undergraduate English major preparing to go to medical school. Questioning one hundred informants, fifty of them physicians and fifty college professors of English, he asked them their opinion as to the value of a liberal arts, and particularly a humanities, background for premedical students. Interestingly, a higher percentage of physicians than English professors responded, and the replies of the physicians were the more specific of the two sets.

12. Ernestine Hambrick, M.D., "Success: The Necessity of English," CEA Forum, 11, no. 4: 3–4.

13. Linwood E. Orange, *English: The Pre-Professional Major*, 3rd edition, revised (New York: Modern Language Association, 1979).

14. Joseph Mitchell, *Less Than Words Can Say* (Boston: Little, Brown, 1979); Edwin Newman, *Strictly Speaking: Will America Be the Death of English?* (Indianapolis and New York: Bobbs-Merrill, 1974) and *A Civil Tongue* (Indianapolis and New York: Bobbs-Merrill, 1976); on Baldrige see "None's the Word on Hazy Verbiage," *Seattle Post-Intelligencer*, July 23, 1981, p. 7; for Safire's comments, see his column "On Language" in sec. 6 in the *New York Times* (for example, in 1981 see April 14, p. 9; May 10, p. 9; May 17, p. 9; June 7, p. 10; etc.).

15. William Bliss, telephone interview, Jan. 26, 1977.

16. Donna Martyn, interview, January 3, 1977.

17. Eric Berne, "Why Don't You?—'Yes, But. . .'," *Games People Play* (New York: Grove Press, 1967), pp. 115–22.

18. James L. Adams, *Conceptual Blockbusting: A Guide to Better Ideas* (San Francisco: W. H. Freeman, 1974), p. 23.

19. Dael Wolfle and Charles V. Kidd, "The Future Market for Ph.D.'s," *AAUP Bulletin* 58 (March 1972): 5. The article first appeared in *Science* 173 (August 27, 1971): 784–93.

Chapter 2. "The Rules Have Changed": Considerations for Ph.D.'s

1. Calvin Trillin, "Thoughts on Changes in the Rules," *New Yorker*, March 7, 1977, pp. 84–90.

2. Dael Wolfle and Charles V. Kidd, "The Future Market for Ph.D.'s," *AAUP Bulletin* 58 (March 1972): 5. The article first appeared in *Science* 173 (August 27, 1971): 784–93.

3. Carol Rigolot, ed., *Alternate Careers for Ph.D.'s in the Humanities* (Princeton, N.J.: Princeton University Press, 1978), p. 9.

4. Ibid., p. 11.

5. Rita Jacobs, *The Useful Humanists: Alternative Careers for Ph.D.'s in the Humanities* (New York: Rockefeller Foundation, 1977), p. 4.

6. See, for example, John Gerber, "A Glimpse of English as a Profession," *Profession 77: Selected Articles from the ADE and the ADFL Bulletins* (September 1977), pp. 26–33; Alan H. Hollingsworth, "Beyond Survival," *Profession 77* (September 1977), pp. 7–11; Edward Sharpless, "Graduate Programs and the Eighties," *Profession 78* (September 1978), pp. 13–79.

7. Dean Victor Lindquist, director of the Office of Placement and Career Planning, Northwestern University, interview, August 21, 1980.

8. Margaret Atwood, *The Edible Woman* (New York: Popular Library, 1976), p. 100.

9. The investigation under way is the ongoing National Recipients of Doctorates' Survey; when definitive results will be published is not known.

10. "Scholarly Editing," *Research News*, Arizona State University, February 1981, pp. 3, 8.

11. Frank Freidel, "American Historians: A Bicentennial Appraisal," Presidential Address to the Organization of American Historians, April 9, 1976, in *Journal of American History* 63, no. 1 (June 1976): 5–20.

12. Ellen K. Coughlin, "Where Are the Jobs? Outside Academe, More and More Historians Find," *Chronicle of Higher Education*, January 8, 1979, pp. 1, 11.

13. *Career Opportunities for Historians* (Pullman, Wash.: Gamma Psi Chapter of Phi Alpha Theta, Department of History, Washington State University, 1981), p. 3.

14. Ibid., throughout.

15. Robert Burke, Department of History, University of Washington, speaking of his university's program.

16. In the spring of 1978 the Advisory Committee on the Job Market, a standing committee of the Modern Language Association, identified and sent questionnaires to over 1,100 Ph.D.'s in English and foreign languages holding positions other than teaching ones. Questions asked were designed to elicit information about the kinds of jobs the respondents had found, how they had found them, whether their skills as writers or researchers were useful in obtaining the job, whether any further special training was necessary, whether the respondents were satisfied with their present jobs, what advice they had about attitudinal adjustments needed for seeking nonacademic jobs, and what advice they could give others with backgrounds like their own who wanted positions similar to theirs. In response, 160 usable returns came in from persons with Ph.D.'s in English and 166 from those with Ph.D.'s in foreign languages. Statistical results were tabulated and appeared in an article by Jasper Neel in *PMLA* for December 1978. The MLA committee, however, did not have time to analyze the wealth of opinion, information, comment, and advice these questionnaires conveyed. When finally in the spring of 1980 I was given permission to see and use 160 questionnaires of the English Ph.D. group, it was with the understanding that I would not identify any of the respondents by name, exact position, or recognizable institution. In quoting from these particular questionnaires in this and subsequent chapters, therefore, I cannot document them. Readers are to under-

stand that any otherwise unattributed comments quoted in this chapter are from these questionnaires, which I am very grateful to the MLA for permission to use. One reason I was eager to use the MLA material was that I had already begun to send out my own questionnaire to Ph.D.'s and Ph.D. candidates in English and humanities fields; by coincidence I asked the same questions, though worded a bit differently and in a different order.

17. Daniel J. Levinson et al., *The Seasons of a Man's Life* (New York: Ballantine Books, 1979). For an example of Erik Erikson's "life-cycle" studies, see *Dimensions of a New Identity* (New York: W. W. Norton Co., 1979).

18. For example, see Kurt Lewin, *Dynamic Theory of Personality* (New York: McGraw-Hill, 1955); Abraham Maslow, *Toward a Psychology of Being*, 2d ed. (New York: Van Nostrand Reinhold, 1968).

19. Ward Hellstrom, "Academic Responsibility and the Job Market," *Profession 80* (Autumn 1980), pp. 24–28.

20. June Millet and Janice Lewis, counselors at the placement centers of U.C.L.A. and the University of Arizona, respectively, made these points at a workshop in Detroit, October 16, 1981, held by the Association for School, College, and University Staffing (ASCUS).

21. See Bernard Haldane, *Career Satisfaction and Success* (New York: AMACOM, 1974), and Richard Nelson Bolles, *What Color Is Your Parachute?* rev. and enl. ed. (Berkeley, Calif.: Ten Speed Press, 1981), chapters 6 and 7.

Chapter 3. Exploring Your Assets and Options

1. Richard Nelson Bolles, *Newsletter about Life/Work Planning*, January 1977, pp. 1–3.

2. See *The Placement Manual* (Seattle: University of Washington, Placement Center, 1980), in which Ivan L. Settles, the director, says, "The Placement Center Staff does not get jobs for anyone. People get their own jobs."

3. Dale Mathews and Mary Easthope, "Of Ivory Towers, Fading Dreams, and the 9-to-5 World," *Rackham Reports* 6, no. 1 (Spring 1980): 1.

4. Rick Fite, interview, March 7, 1981.

5. See, for example, the pamphlets *As the Wheel Turns* and *Career Services* issued (n.d.) by the College of St. Catherine, St. Paul, Minnesota.

6. Among others, Sidney B. Simon, *Values Clarification* (New York: Hart Publishing Co., 1978), and Howard Figler, *Path: A Career Exploration Workbook for Liberal Arts Students—Revised* (Cranston, R.I.: Carroll Press, 1978).

7. Richard J. Thain, *The Managers: Career Alternatives for the College Educated* (Bethlehem, Pa.: College Placement Council, 1978), p. 113.

8. Allen I. Kraut, "A Hard Look at Management Assessment Centers and Their Future," *Personnel Journal*, May 1972, pp. 317–26. See also Edgar H. Schein, *Career Dynamics: Matching Individual and Organizational Needs* (Reading, Mass.: Addison-Wesley Publishing Co., 1978).

9. Gary L. Hart and Paul H. Thompson, "Assessment Centers: For Selection or Development?" *Organizational Dynamics*, Spring 1979, pp. 63–77.

10. *New York Times*, Sunday, November 4, 1979, sec. 3.

11. Kraut, "A Hard Look," pp. 325–26.

12. Bolles, *Parachute*, pp. 182–217.

13. Richard Nelson Bolles, *The Three Boxes of Life: And How to Get Out of Them* (Berkeley, Calif.: Ten Speed Press, 1978).

14. Eleanor Berman, *Re-entering: Successful Back-to-Work Strategies for Women Seeking a Fresh Start* (New York: Crown Publishers, 1980), chapter 3.

15. Bernard Haldane, *Career Satisfaction and Success: A Guide to Job Freedom* (New York: AMACOM, 1974).

CHAPTER 4. PRESENTING YOURSELF

1. Those who want to refresh their minds on these matters will find a full treatment in the following: Eli Djeddah, *Moving Up* (Berkeley, Calif.: Ten Speed Press, 1978); Marcia Fox, *Put Your Degree to Work* (New York: W. W. Norton, 1979); H. Anthony Medley, *Sweaty Palms* (Belmont, Calif.: Lifetime Learning Publications, 1978); *MLA Guide for Job Candidates and Department Chairmen in English and Foreign Languages*, rev. ed. (New York: Modern Language Association, 1978).

2. Djeddah, *Moving Up*, p. 11.

3. Jason Robertson, *How to Win in a Job Interview* (Englewood Cliffs, N.J.: Prentice-Hall, 1978), p. 9.

4. *Dictionary of Occupational Titles*, 4th ed. (Washington, D.C.: U.S. Government Printing Office, 1977); *Moody's Industrial Manual*, 2 vols. (New York: Moody's Investor's Service, 1981); *Standard and Poor's Register of Corporations, Directories, and Executives* (New York: Standard and Poor's, 1981).

5. Bolles, *Parachute*, pp. 98, 104–5, 129–30, 135; and note especially his cautions about this type of interviewing, pp. 152–54. Djeddah, *Moving Up*, pp. 71–85.

6. Deborah Orr May, assistant director of the Career Planning and Placement Center, University of Michigan, interview, October 17, 1980.

7. Bolles, *Parachute*, chapter 6; Djeddah, *Moving Up*, p. 71.

8. Fox, *Put Your Degree to Work*, chapter 4.

9. Says Dee Jones, public relations director of the Swedish Hospital Medical Center in Seattle, "the need to be available can't be overestimated. Since you can't sit home all day waiting for the phone to ring, ask your godmother for a graduation present of a recorded answering device. Or hire an answering service. As job placement counselor for a women's organization I have chased more young people through sorority house and dorm phones, sent more postcards to vacant apartments, and often just given up because the young graduate was just too hard to reach."

10. Fox, *Put Your Degree to Work*, chapter 4.

11. Howard Figler, *The Complete Job Search Handbook* (New York: Holt, Rinehart and Winston, 1979), p. 208.

12. Fox, *Put Your Degree to Work*, p. 109; see also p. 115.

13. Medley, *Sweaty Palms*, p. 11.

14. Djeddah, *Moving Up*, chapter 9.

15. Alonzo Johnson, quoted in sidebar to James Borders, "Computer Science Career Outlook," *Black Collegian* 12, no. 2 (October/November 1981): 51.

16. Ivan Settles, interview, May 20, 1981; also "Check List for Interview Behavior," *Job Line*, Placement Center, University of Washington, 7, no. 4 (June 1981): 4.

17. Meeting of the Association for School, College, and University Staffing, Detroit, October 15–16, 1981.

18. Djeddah, *Moving Up*, pp. 83–84.

CHAPTER 5. WILL A DIFFERENT DEGREE HELP?

1. Richard Nelson Bolles, *What Color Is Your Parachute?* rev. and enl. ed. (Berkeley, Calif.: Ten Speed Press, 1981), pp. 68–71. See also the growing body of writing about career changes: John R. Coleman, *Blue-Collar Journal: A College President's Sabbatical* (Philadelphia: Lippincott, 1974); Peter Weaver, *Strategies for the Second Half of Life* (New York: Franklin Watts, 1980); Allan A. Swenson, *Starting Over: How to Recharge Your Lifestyle and Career* (New York: A & W Publishers, 1978).

2. Edward Noyes, telephone interview, March 3, 1977.

3. Herbert B. Livesey and Harold Doughty, *A Guide to American Graduate Schools*, 3d ed., rev. (New York: Viking, 1975).

4. You can find this out by studying the catalogues of various library schools, talking with librarians you know about the schools they attended, and consulting both the *Journal of Education for Librarianship* and its annual special directory edition, published by the Association of American Library Schools, 471 Park Lane, State College, Pennsylvania 16801.

5. Adrienne Richmond, *New Careers for Social Workers* (Chicago: Henry Regnery, 1974). See also Betty-Carol Sellen, ed., *What Else You Can Do with a Library Degree* (New York: Gaylord Professional Publications, in association with Neal-Schuman Publishers, 1980).

6. Otto Friedrich et al., "The Money Chase: What Business Schools Are Doing to Us," *Time*, May 4, 1981, pp. 58–69; Patricia O'Toole, "The Truth about the Value of an M.B.A.," *Savvy*, July 1981, pp. 14–15.

7. Bliss to author, January 26, 1977.

8. Theodore Greider, "Professional Librarianship as a Career for the Ph.D.," *Associated Departments of English Bulletin* 40 (March 1974): 45–50.

9. Ibid., p. 50.

10. Donna Martyn, interview, January 4, 1977. One might, however, make an exception to the warning expressed in this chapter. If one wants to acquire academic credentials in a second field in preparation for a career change, taking a second master's degree is usually more practical than taking a second doctoral or professional program. Some community college teachers of English have found that taking a second M.A. in a related field such as communications, comparative literature, drama, or speech was helpful; a

few college teachers have found that an M.B.A. or a master's in public administration gave them more credibility as applicants for managerial jobs than they would otherwise have had.

11. Terry Wetherby, interview, July 26, 1981.

12. Roger Rosenblatt, "The Uses of a Literary Education," paper presented December 28, 1976, at the MLA meeting, New York City, at a forum, "The Uses of the Humanities."

CHAPTER 6. TEACHING NEW CLIENTELES

1. See Dorothy Bestor, "Career Alternatives for Educators," *The ASCUS Annual: A Job Search Handbook for Educators*, Association for School, College, and University Staffing, 1981, pp. 28–34; also Sandy Pollock, *Alternative Careers for Teachers* (The Common, Harvard, Mass. 01451: The Harvard Common Press, 1979), throughout.

2. Myron White and James Souther, *Scientific and Technical Communication* (Seattle: University of Washington College of Engineering, n.d.). Interested students should write for a copy of this leaflet to the Department of Humanistic–Social Studies, 356 Loew Hall, FH-40, University of Washington, Seattle, Washington 98195; you should also read the *Journal of Technical Writing and Communication*, and you may want to write to the Society for Technical Communication, 815 Fifteenth Street N.W., Suite 506, Washington, D.C. 20005, for their brochures on career opportunities (e.g., *Facts* and *Is Technical Writing Your Career?*).

3. Paul V. Anderson, "Background and Resources for New Teachers of Technical Writing," remarks at a session, "Teaching Technical Writing; a Unique Challenge," December 28, 1976, annual MLA meeting, New York City.

4. See Merrill Whitburn, "Technical Communication: An Unexplored Area for English," *ADE Bulletin* 45 (May 1975): 11–14.

5. Carol Gay, "The Onus of Teaching Children's Literature," *ADE Bulletin* 47 (November 1975): 15–20.

6. For places to write for information, see Pat Kern McIntyre, *American Students and Teachers Abroad: Sources of Information about Overseas Study, Teaching, Work, and Travel* (Washington, D.C.: GPO, 1975).

7. For courses in popular culture, see the catalogues of Hofstra, Bowling Green, and Long Island universities among others.

8. For information on teaching abroad, see section 3 of the bibliography; also inquire for the latest information at any campus where ESL is taught (the ESL offices tend to receive frequent notices of vacancies in Africa, Asia, the Islands of the South Pacific, and elsewhere).

9. If you are interested, most campus placement centers can give you further information. Bear in mind that the Australian and New Zealand academic calendars are almost the reverse of ours, and that the Japanese school year begins in March. Don't forget the need for visas and work permits for overseas teaching. Note too that in Australia and New Zealand you may find

few, if any, writing courses in university catalogues; students there, like those in British universities, are supposed to have learned in secondary school how to write well. No matter how strong your background in teaching writing, you will need other specialties for university-level instruction wherever the British educational tradition dominates.

10. If you send a letter of application for some of these positions, don't be discouraged by a negative reply. I know of several candidates who, having been told that an overseas job was filled, were invited three months later to apply for positions that had just opened up in the same institutions. Apparently overseas employers tend to keep applications on file and go back to them more often than most employers do in this country.

11. See Selden Menefee, "Community Colleges: Finding New Directions," *Change*, Summer 1974, pp. 54–63.

12. As one example of the role of the community college, see Elizabeth Cowan, "Turnabout in the Job Market: The University Goes to the Community College," *ADE/ADFL Bulletin*, Special Joint Issue, "English and Foreign Languages: Employment and the Profession," September 1976, pp. 53–56.

13. Although most appointments to community college English departments represent a careful sifting process of more than a hundred applications per job, often last-minute changes in registration necessitate the hiring of one or two extra part-time instructors.

14. Mort Young, "When One Can't Read or Write," *Seattle Post-Intelligencer*, December 7, 1976.

15. Write for the bulletin, "Seeking a Job in a Two-Year College," available from the American Association of Junior Colleges, One Dupont Circle, N.W., Washington, D.C. 20036; see also *A Guide for Job Candidates and Department Chairmen in English and Foreign Languages* (New York: MLA, 1978), pp. 23–26.

16. Although improvements have been made here and there in the status of part-time community college teachers in the past few years, wages and morale still tend to be low.

17. Contance Wells, interview, May 20, 1975.

18. Gary K. Wolfe and Carol Traynor Williams, "All Education Is 'Adult Education,'" *AAUP Bulletin*, September 1974, pp. 291–95.

19. Such opportunities to design and teach writing courses to meet the specialized needs of the professional people are seldom advertised, because there is usually no specific vacancy; involvement in such teaching tends to be a spin-off from teaching regularly scheduled continuing education courses through an established institution.

20. For information about the Elderhostel program, write its director, William Berkeley, 100 Boylston Street, Suite 200, Boston, Massachusetts, 02116.

21. Richard Adler, "Writing Behind Walls," *English Education* 6 (April/May 1975): 234–42; William Bestor, conversation, December 29, 1981.

22. Kurt Vonnegut, Jr., "A New Scheme for Real Writers," *New York Times Book Review*, July 14, 1974.

23. See William W. Bernhardt, "Working in a College Skills Center," *ADE Bulletin* 44 (February 1975): 10–13.

24. *Seattle Times*, September 14, 1975.

25. As this book goes to press, slashes in educational budgets in general, and community college budgets in particular, have made the situation even more grim.

26. See Daniel Fedo, "The Promise of Academic Exile," *Chronicle of Higher Education*, October 21, 1975.

27. Constance Wells, interviews of April 30, 1975, and January 15, 1976; also interviews with Louise Hirasawa of Noncredit Studies, University of Washington, March 15 and October 21, 1980.

28. Ronald Gross, "Adult Learners Keep Growing, Knowing, and Growing," *Christian Science Monitor*, December 14, 1981, p. 16.

CHAPTER 7. MORE THAN TEACHING TAKES PLACE ON CAMPUS

1. For example, such positions as head of the placement center, head of the university press, and director of the office of scholarly journals are among the staff positions on many university campuses.

2. Interview, January 4, 1977.

3. Neal Woodruff, conversation at MLA meeting, December 29, 1976.

4. William Bliss, letter of January 26, 1977.

5. Mary Lou Baker, interview, May 5, 1975.

6. Recently there have been at least five members of the counseling staff of the University of Washington Placement Center with a background in English, ranging from a B.A. English major through M.A.'s, doctoral candidates, and a Ph.D.

7. Messer-Davidow to author, conversation at MLA meeting, December 30, 1978.

8. Antoinette Wills, questionnaire response of March 15, 1980, and November 10, 1980, expanded at my request.

9. Maclyn Burg, questionnaire response of October 5, 1981, expanded at my request.

CHAPTER 8. FREELANCE EDITING

1. *A Manual of Style*, 12th ed., rev. (Chicago: University of Chicago Press, 1969), p. 40.

2. Ibid.

3. *Editor to Author: The Letters of Maxwell E. Perkins*, ed. John Hall Wheelock (New York: Charles Scribner's Sons, 1950), pp. 39–40, 91.

4. Ibid., p. 172.

5. Ibid., Introduction, p. 8.

6. William Strunk, Jr., and E. B. White, *The Elements of Style*, 3d ed. (New York: Macmillan, 1979); see especially chapter 5, "An Approach to Style."

7. Carol L. O'Neill and Avima Ruder, *The Complete Guide to Editorial*

Freelancing (New York: Barnes and Noble, 1979); Howard Greenfield, *Books: From Writer to Reader* (New York: Crown Publishers, 1976); Judith Butcher, *Copy-Editing: The Cambridge Handbook* (London and New York: Cambridge University Press, 1975); Marjorie E. Skillin, Robert M. Gay, et al., eds., *Words into Type*, 3d ed., rev. (Englewood Cliffs, N.J.: Prentice-Hall, 1974); *The Editorial Eye*, published approximately 15 times a year by Editorial Experts, Inc., 5905 Pratt Street, Alexandria, Virginia 22310.

8. On proofreading, see Peggy Smith, *Simplified Proofreading* (Arlington, Va.: National Composition Association, 1980).

9. Judith Appelbaum and Nancy Evans, *How to Get Happily Published* (New York: Harper and Row, 1978), p. 129.

10. Sina Spiker, *Indexing Your Book* (Madison: University of Wisconsin Press, 1964).

11. For information, write American Society of Indexers, 235 Park Avenue South, Eighth floor, New York 10003, New York. Phone (215) 482-8566.

12. John Peter, "Editorial vs. Production: How Goes the Battle?" *Folio*, June 1977, pp. 22–26.

13. O'Neill and Ruder, *Complete Guide*, pp. 2–3.

14. "In California: Confronting the Empty Page," *Time*, July 14, 1980, p. 8.

15. Michael Crichton, M.D., "Medical Obfuscation: Structure and Function," *New England Journal of Medicine* 293 (December 11, 1975): 1257–59; Saul S. Radovsky, M.D., "Medical Writing: Another Look," *New England Journal of Medicine* 301 (July 19, 1979): 131–34; note Radovsky's bibliography.

16. *Council of Biology Editors Style Manual*, 4th ed. (Arlington, Va.: Council of Biology Editors, Inc., 1978). Available from American Institute of Biological Sciences, 1401 Wilson Boulevard, Arlington, Virginia 22209; Henrietta J. Tichy, *Effective Writing for Engineers, Managers, Scientists* (New York: John Wiley and Sons, 1966): F. Peter Woodford, *Scientific Writing for Graduate Students* (New York: Rockefeller University Press, 1968), Robert Day, *How to Write and Publish a Scientific Paper* (Philadelphia: ISI Press, 1979).

17. Edwin Newman, *Strictly Speaking: Will America Be the Death of English?* (Indianapolis and New York: Bobbs-Merrill, 1974), p. 145.

18. If as an editor you point out one or two broad underlying principles at a time to such an author, you may find that he or she seizes upon the idea and puts it rapidly into practice. Physicians, nurses, social workers, geologists, and other professional people with whom I have worked as an editor have been quick to apply such ideas as using more simple concrete words and fewer abstractions, varying their formerly monotonous sentences, and clarifying ambiguous antecedents. Probably the ideal editor, like the ideal psychiatrist, should work himself or herself out of a job as far as each client is concerned. (The editor should, however, be in no real danger of working himself or herself out of a livelihood as well, because there will always be other writers who need editorial services.)

19. Helen K. Taylor, "What Is an Editor?" in *Editors on Editing*, ed. Gerald Gross (New York: Grosset and Dunlap, 1962), p. 4. It is true that Taylor is re-

ferring here primarily to the editor in a publishing house, yet the process she describes is one often asked of an experienced editor working for an inexperienced author.

20. Barbara Reitt, "The Editor Turns Teacher," *Scholarly Publishing*, April 1980, pp. 256–57.

21. I chose fifty-four freelance editors or editorial firms arbitrarily from the "Free-Lance Editorial Services" section of *Literary Market Place*, my only criterion being that I was trying to get as representative a sample, with as wide a geographical distribution, as possible. From this point on throughout the rest of this chapter, any quotations from editors not otherwise identified will be from the thirty-four responses returned in September and early October 1980.

22. Reitt, "Editor Turns Teacher," p. 265.

23. These five accounts derive from responses to my questionnaire.

24. Horowitz, *The Editorial Eye*, October 1980, p. 1.

25. O'Neill and Ruder, *Complete Guide*, p. 24.

26. Horowitz, *The Editorial Eye*, December 15, 1978, p. 1.

27. The late Emily Johnson, who through her years as director of scholarly journals at the University of Washington served as unofficial liaison between writers and copy editors, on occasion warned her fellow members of Editorial Consultants, Inc., that their job was "not to get the author's ideas expressed in the most beautiful words possible; it [was] to see that he says what he has to say with the fewest obstacles between him and the reader. The hardest thing about training editors is to get them to respect someone else's by-line. They've got to learn that they aren't supposed to function as creative writers; they should just get their satisfaction in being paid for their work—and, if they're lucky, in finding that the author has given them a kind word in the Acknowledgments" (from a talk given to E.C.I., June 4, 1975).

28. O'Neill and Ruder, *Complete Guide*, chapter 2.

29. Barbara Huston, "Hope for Those Dangling Participles," *Seattle Post-Intelligencer*, April 1, 1980.

30. Francess Halpenny, "The Editorial Function," in *Editors on Editing*, ed. Gerald Gross (New York, Grosset and Dunlap, 1962), p. 97.

31. Mary E. Stith, Naomi Pascal, et al., "The Out-of-House Editor," *Scholarly Publishing*, April 1972, pp. 259–72.

32. "Computer Takes on Editors' Tasks," *The Editorial Eye*, May 14, 1979, p. 1.

33. R. Z. Sheppard et al., "The Decline of Editing," *Time*, September 1, 1980, pp. 70–72.

34. Thomas Whiteside, "The Blockbuster Complex," *New Yorker*, September 29, 1980, pp. 48–101; October 6, 1980, pp. 63–146; October 13, 1980, pp. 52–143.

35. Joan Holleman, "Writing-Editing Job Outlook Mixed," *The Editorial Eye*, February 5, 1979, p. 1.

36. Stith, Pascal, et al., "The Out-of-House Editor," pp. 270–72.

37. O'Neill and Ruder, "Foreword to the Paperback Edition," p. ix.

38. Holleman, "Writing-Editing Job Outlook," p. 1.

39. Horowitz, "Tips on Freelancing," *The Editorial Eye*, December 15, 1979, pp. 1–6.

CHAPTER 9. WRITING OR EDITING ON THE STAFF OF AN INSTITUTION

1. Quoted material in this chapter, except where otherwise identified, is from replies to a questionnaire I have sent to fellow editors at the University of Washington and elsewhere, fellow members of Women in Communications across the country, and to editors on the staffs of the University of Michigan; Miami University, Oxford, Ohio; the College of St. Olaf; the College of St. Benedict; Lane Community College, Eugene, Oregon; Linfield College, McMinnville, Oregon; Albion College; Virginia Mason and Swedish hospitals, Seattle; the National Council of Teachers of English; and elsewhere. Out of approximately two hundred such questionnaires distributed—one hundred for the 1977 edition and one hundred for this edition—I have received 104 usable replies. Contrary to the practice of social scientists in making public opinion surveys, wherein the size of the sample and the number of resondents falling into each category is often considered more significant than the actual statements they make, I have sent these questions out to a relatively small "intentional sample." Nonetheless, I think that these replies should be helpful to readers.

2. For a discussion of internships, see Appendix E.

3. See Naomi Pascal, "To Open Publishing Doors," *Scholarly Publishing* 2, no. 2 (January 1971): 195–201.

4. Talk by [then] Vice-president Margaret Chisholm of the University of Washington at a meeting of the Association of Professional Writers and Editors, University of Washington, December 21, 1975.

CHAPTER 10. IS ENTRY INTO BOOK PUBLISHING STILL POSSIBLE?

1. Thomas Whiteside, "The Blockbuster Complex," *New Yorker*, October 6, 1980, part 2, p. 63.

2. See Roberta Morgan, *How to Break into Publishing* (New York: Barnes and Noble, 1980), pp. 158–65.

3. Steven V. Roberts, "At Johns Hopkins," *New York Times Book Review*, May 10, 1981, p. 22.

4. Whiteside, "Blockbuster Complex," *New Yorker*, October 6, 1980, part 2, p. 65.

5. Morgan, *Publishing*, p. 159. For another point of view, however, see Celeste West and Valerie Wheat, *The Passionate Perils of Publishing* (San Francisco: Booklegger Press, 1978), pp. 1–13.

6. Whiteside, "Blockbuster Complex," *New Yorker*, October 6, 1980, part 2, pp. 111–12.

7. Association of American Publishers, *The Accidental Profession: Education, Training and the People of Publishing* (New York, 1977).

8. For the 1977 edition of this book I sent questionnaires to 125 publishers throughout the United States, asking for advice on entry into publishing that I could pass along to job candidates who came to my office in the University of Washington Placement Center. Of the 125 usable replies received, I have retained in this edition some that still seem valid; I have also supplemented my earlier survey by informal conversations and correspondence with ten people in publishing in 1981. They agree on the whole with the results of my earlier survey, adding only that the points made by Whiteside and others about the effects of conglomerates are important for everyone in the publishing industry to take into account.

9. Morgan, *Publishing*, p. 3.

10. Ibid., p. 37.

11. Ibid., p. xiii.

12. Ibid., p. 151.

13. Jones's remarks are from his questionnaire response to my earlier survey. Throughout the rest of this chapter, direct quotations, whether or not attributed by name, are from these 125 responses unless otherwise indicated.

14. Chandler B. Grannis, *Getting into Book Publishing* (New York: R. R. Bowker Co., 1979), p. 3.

15. *A Manual of Style*, 12th ed., rev. (Chicago: University of Chicago Press, 1969); Marjorie Skillin et al., eds., *Words into Type*, 3d ed., rev. (Englewood Cliffs, N.J.: Prentice-Hall, 1974).

16. For a complete list of courses in publishing procedures, see each year's *Literary Market Place*; also Susan E. Shaffer, *Guide to Book Publishing Courses* (Princeton, N.J.: Peterson's Guides, 1979).

17. For an account of how one such internship has operated, see Naomi B. Pascal, "To Open Publishing Doors," *Scholarly Publishing* 2, no. 2 (January 1971): 195–201. See also Morgan, *Publishing*, pp. 27, 42.

18. Morgan, *Publishing*, p. 26.

19. Thomas Weyr, "Getting into Publishing," *Publishers Weekly*, March 10, 1975, pp. 22–25.

20. Grannis, *Getting into Book Publishing*, p. 6.

21. Easton, Burbank, Lamm, Sherwood, and other representatives of Eastern publishing companies spoke at a December 29 session on the publishing industry sponsored by the Women's Book Association and the Modern Language Association at the 1978 MLA meeting in New York.

22. Peggy Sherwood represented a hopeful model to many of the listeners at the MLA meeting because she had made the transition from teaching to publishing. She told us that after getting a B.A. and a graduate degree at Bryn Mawr, she taught English "at all levels" for several years, and then in 1970 joined Princeton University Press.

23. Grannis, *Getting into Book Publishing*, p. 4.

24. Conversation with Emily Johnson, January 10, 1979.

25. Conversation with Luther Nichols, July 25, 1975.

26. Peggy Sherwood, talk at MLA meeting.

27. Luther Nichols, talk at Pacific Northwest Writers' Conference, July 25, 1975.

28. Grannis, *Getting into Book Publishing*, pp. 9–10.

29. Len Fulton and Ellen Ferber, *The International Directory of Little Magazines and Small Presses*, 15th ed. (Paradise, Calif.: Dustbooks, 1979).

30. West and Wheat, *Passionate Perils of Publishing*, p. 7.

31. See Steven V. Roberts, "At Johns Hopkins," *New York Times Book Review*, May 10, 1981, pp. 13, 20.

32. Her name has been changed here.

33. At my request, Perkins expanded her questionnaire response into this statement.

34. See Gay Courter, "Word Machines for Word People," *Publishers Weekly*, February 13, 1981, p. 11.

35. See Roberts, "At Johns Hopkins," p. 20.

CHAPTER 11. POSSIBILITIES IN THE MEDIA AND RELATED FIELDS

1. Wilbur Schramm, *Men, Messages, and Media: A Look at Human Communication* (New York: Harper and Row, 1973).

2. Peter M. Sandman, David M. Rubin, and David B. Sachsman, *Media: An Introductory Analysis of American Mass Communications*, 2d ed. (Englewood Cliffs, N.J.: Prentice-Hall, 1976).

3. Anthony Smith, *Goodbye Gutenberg: The Newspaper Revolution of the 1980's* (New York: Oxford University Press, 1980).

4. The Newspaper Fund, *Journalism Career and Scholarship Guide 1981* (Princeton, N.J.: The Newspaper Fund, Box 300), p. 6.

5. William Johnston, interview, May 15, 1981.

6. Quoted in *Journalism Career and Scholarship Guide*, p. 8.

7. Kenneth Jackson, "Applying for Journalism Jobs," a talk to communications students at the University of Washington, May 15, 1981.

8. Don Carter, interview, February 12, 1979.

9. Quoted in *Journalism Career and Scholarship Guide*, p. 9.

10. Linda Daniel, assistant city editor, *Seattle Times*, interview, May 10, 1975.

11. William Johnston, May 15, 1981.

12. Comment from one of the 160 responses (discussed in chap. 2) from the Modern Language Association survey of Ph.D.'s in English now employed in alternative careers.

13. Craig Sanders, interview, January 20, 1976.

14. Letter of August 9, 1976, from John Schacht, Emeritus Professor of Journalism, University of Illinois.

15. Schacht, letter of January 9, 1981.

16. Schacht, letter of August 9, 1976.

17. Ann Strosnider, interviews, June 5 and 30, 1981.

18. Advice synthesized from various journalists interviewed, plus Burt Bostrom and Ron McIntyre, "How to Apply for a Job in Media," *The Quill*, November, 1974, pp. 40–42.

19. Johnston, interview, July 16, 1976.

20. Smith, *Goodbye Gutenberg*, p. xi.

21. Comments from Johnston, Schacht, Barbara Huston of the *Seattle Post-Intelligencer*, and others. See, however, Dominique Wolton, "Do You Love Your VDT?" *Columbia Journalism Review*, July/August 1979, pp. 36–39.

22. See Gay Courter, "Word Machines for Word People," *Publishers Weekly*, February 13, 1981, p. 11.

23. Dean Woolley, talk given at a program on careers in media, sponsored by Women in Communications and FOCUS, Seattle, May 24, 1976.

24. Jean Enerson, interview, November 10, 1980.

25. William Johnston, interview, July 16, 1976.

26. Woolley, May 24, 1976.

27. Woolley, May 24, 1976.

28. Interview with M'Lou Zahner-Ollswang, February 11, 1980, plus her subsequent questionnaire response, updated by phone interview, July 1, 1980.

29. Remarks at a New York meeting of the Modern Language Association, December 29, 1980, plus a manuscript from a book in progress, *Translate Yourself: Alternates to Academic Careers*, ed. Ruth K. Angress and Bernice Kliman for the MLA Commission on the Status of Women in the Profession; updated by phone conversation with Kadragic, June 15, 1981.

30. See an extraordinarily specific and helpful book about writing magazine articles: William L. Rivers, *Free-lancer and Staff Writer*, 2d ed. (Belmont Calif.: Wadsworth Publishing Co., Inc., 1976).

31. Brewster, interview, June 8, 1976.

32. Keynote speech at Public Relations Society Seminar, Seattle, September 23, 1976.

33. Joanne Beamer, talk at Pacific Northwest Writers' Conference, July 25, 1975.

34. Talks by Fern Olsen, Norma Russell, and others at a Women in Communications meeting, May 24, 1976.

35. Public Relations Society, September 23, 1976.

36. Interview with a woman public relations account executive.

37. Jerry della Femina, interview, September 23, 1976.

38. L. Roy Blumenthal, *The Practice of Public Relations* (New York: Macmillan, 1972), p. 7.

39. Steve Seiter of the McCann-Erickson Company, Seattle, interview, July 15, 1974.

40. Gittings, conversation, August 10, 1974.

Chapter 12. Writing, Research, and Other Opportunities in Business

1. Joanne Landesman, "Can Humanities Academics Find Happiness with Businessmen (and Vice Versa)?" *Across the Board*, May 1979, pp. 55–63.

2. Ibid., p. 59.

3. Ibid., p. 56.

4. Ibid., pp. 57–58.

5. Comment in one of the 160 responses (discussed in chap. 2) from the Modern Language Association 1978 survey of Ph.D.'s in English now employed in alternative careers.

6. Richard V. Thain, *The Managers: Career Alternatives for the College Educated* (Bethlehem, Pa.: College Placement Council, 1978), p. 30. See also the rest of chapter 8 and chapter 9 of Thain's excellent book.

7. Eric M. Leithe, talk at a meeting on alternative jobs for English Ph.D.'s, University of Washington, February 10, 1979.

8. Response to MLA Ph.D. survey.

9. Ellen Messer-Davidow, letter of October 20, 1976.

10. Blanche Adams, interviews, May 10, 1975, and February 15, 1976. Adams told me that she does not use a "business English" text, depending largely instead on Strunk and White's *Elements of Style*, which her company now provides for each executive.

11. Henrietta J. Tichy, *Effective Writing for Engineers, Managers, Scientists* (New York: John Wiley and Sons, 1966).

12. Seminar sponsored by the American Society for Training and Development on business in the 1980s, November 8, 1979.

13. Response to MLA Ph.D. survey.

14. Ibid.

15. Ibid. (If you think this respondent's emphasis on technique rather than subject matter somewhat extreme, be advised that this view does apparently reflect the thinking of the "real world." For example, Linwood Orange points out that an English major looking for work in the Biloxi, Mississippi, area finally, "after exhausting all other possibilities, applied for a position on the military base, hoping feebly that there might be an opening at the post library. The result was a surprise indeed. She was offered the position of Training Instructor in Electronics. It was no mistake. The official letter . . . stated, 'We know you have no background in electronics, but your record indicates that you are highly trainable.' After receiving instruction, she began as a GS 7 and has . . . been promoted to a GS-9." See Linwood E. Orange, *English: The Pre-Professional Major*, 3d ed., rev. (New York: MLA, 1979), p. 19.

16. Response to MLA Ph.D. survey.

17. These two points are based on my own experience and that of friends and colleagues in designing and teaching courses for hospital personnel and business groups.

18. Response to MLA Ph.D. survey.

19. Seminar (ASTD) on business in the 1980s, November 8, 1979.

20. Seminar (ASTD) on business in the 1980s, November 8, 1979.

21. Fred Pneuman, letter of October 20, 1976.

22. Orange, *English*, p. 6.

23. Ibid., p. 7.

24. Otto Friedrich et al., "The Money Chase," *Time*, May 4, 1981, pp. 58–69. Glanville's comment is on p. 69.

25. Meg Wingard, interview, October 10, 1976.

26. Stephanie Campbell, interview, July 20, 1974.

27. Talk by a recent Ph.D. in English at a conference on careers for English majors, Miami University, Oxford, Ohio, November 8, 1977.

28. Myron White and James Souther, interviews, February 10 and 12, 1981; also Jason Spence, "ENGR + CMU = STC = Technical Writing," *University of Washington Daily*, May 19, 1981, p. 10.

29. John A. Walter, "Technical Writing: Species or Genus?" (paper delivered at the MLA meeting, December 28, 1976, in New York City).

30. For information, along with a list of available pamphlets, write to the Society for Technical Communication, 815 Fifteenth Street N.W., Suite 506, Washington, D.C. 20005. See also William R. Palmer, *The Freelance Business Writing Business: How to Make a Living at It* (Monmouth Junction, N.J.: Heathcote Publisher, 1979).

31. For a directory of such programs, see Appendix D.

32. See Appendix E.

33. Vicki Hill, interview, May 4, 1976.

34. Messer-Davidow, letter of October 20, 1976.

35. John Harwood, "Nonacademic Job Hunting," *AAUP Bulletin* 60 (1974): 313–16.

36. Earl Grout, expansion of questionnaire response at my request, February 10, 1981.

Chapter 13. On Your Own: The Humanist as Entrepreneur

1. Kathy Sawyer, "Being Your Own Boss: Working Harder, Risking Money, Losing Sleep," *Washington Post*, August 28, 1975.

2. Albert Shapero, "Have You Got What It Takes to Start Your Own Business?" *Savvy*, April 1980, pp. 33–37. This list is on p. 33.

3. Claudia Jessup and Genie Chipps, *The Woman's Guide to Starting a Business*, rev. ed. (New York: Holt, Rinehart and Winston, 1980); Peter C. Channing, *The Career Alternative: A Guide to Business Venturing* (New York: Hawthorn Books, 1977).

4. See Jessup and Chipps, *Woman's Guide*, pp. 159–64. Especially noteworthy is a point made by the founder-owner of Murder, Ink that "the biggest deterrent when you start a business is getting advice from too many people. An idea is so fragile that it's easy to get talked out of it."

5. These thirteen points derive from reading Sawyer, Shapero, Jessup and Chipps, Channing, and the other titles listed in the business section of this book's bibliography, plus attendance at Small Business Administration seminars and workshops in connection with membership in Editorial Consultants, Inc.

6. For an analysis of the replies to the MLA questionnaire, see chapter 2.

CHAPTER 14. EVEN GOVERNMENT NEEDS TO BE LITERATE

1. Wayne D. Rasmussen, "Employment in the Federal Government," *Career Opportunities for Historians* (Pullman, Wash.: Washington State University, Gamma Psi Chapter, Phi Alpha Theta, 1981), p. 18.

2. Edward Cowan, "Government: Local Action," National Recruitment Survey, *New York Times*, Section 12, pp. 29–30, October 12, 1980; Richard D. Irish, *Go Hire Yourself an Employer*, rev. and expanded ed. (Garden City, N.Y.: Anchor Press, 1978). See also William Serrin, "After 34 Years, Jobs Declining in Government," *New York Times*, Dec. 27, 1981, pp. 1, 14. As Serrin's opening paragraphs indicate, "For the first time since the end of World War II, government employment is declining. . . . In the 12 months ending Nov. 1, government employment declined by 316,000 workers: 40,000 at the Federal level, 30,000 at the state level, and 246,000 at the local level." Yet Serrin goes on in the body of the article to point out that some experts do not consider this decline to be a permanent one. If current plans to restore the economy work, there will be "increased tax revenues at the state and local levels . . . enabling governments to provide increased services and employment. Or . . . state and local governments may be forced to raise taxes and thus increase employment as they seek to take on some duties passed on to them by the Federal Government." In some states, such as Massachusetts, there is "pressure now to introduce all sorts of loopholes" to allow state and local governments to continue hiring and to get around tax limitations mandated by voters.

3. Charles Ruemelin, *A Guide to Government and Public Service Employment* (Cambridge, Mass.: Harvard University, 1975), pp. 3–5.

4. Ibid., pp. 5–7.

5. Ana L. Zambrano and Alan D. Entine, *A Guide to Career Alternatives for Academics* (New Rochelle, N.Y.: Change Magazine Press, 1976), p. 35.

6. Betty Blair, interviews, February 10, 1976, and December 15, 1980. Blair started out by looking for work more obviously connected with her nearly completed Ph.D. in literature. Not finding what she wanted, she decided arbitrarily to pick something different, yet with possibilities of eventually using her analytical and writing abilities.

7. Lou Ann Kirby of the City of Seattle's Department of Parks and Recreation, interview, November 15, 1975.

8. Material obtained from loose-leaf notebooks containing job descriptions in the City of Seattle's Personnel Office. Most other cities keep similar loose-leaf listings; be sure to check on how recently any file has been updated.

9. Job notebooks in the City of Seattle's Personnel Office.

10. Susan De Witt, interview, August 15, 1974.

11. *MLA Guide for Job Candidates and Department Chairmen in English and Foreign Languages* (New York: MLA, 1978), pp. 34–36.

12. Susan Lukowski and Margaret Piton, *Strategy and Tactics for Getting a Government Job*, 2d ed. (Washington, D.C.: Potomac Books, in press).

13. Joanne Burns, interview, December 30, 1981.

14. The *Congressional Directory* is compiled by the U.S. Government Printing Office for each session of Congress; the *Congressional Staff Directory*, ed. Charles B. Brownson, is published annually by the Congressional Staff Directory, Mount Vernon, Virginia; the *Federal Career Directory* was last published by the U.S. Civil Service Commission, Washington, D.C., in 1966; and the *Guide to Federal Career Literature* is published by the GPO.

15. Jan Furey, interview, December 12, 1980.

16. See any Sunday *New York Times*, section 4, for advertisements of other such programs.

17. The new course at the University of Washington, for example, is designed to acquaint advanced undergraduate students and graduate students with historical preservation work, an introduction to archival work, federal archives management, historical photography, historical museum work, opportunities for historians in public administration, oral history (techniques and uses), and work in state and local historical societies. For further information write Professors Carl Solberg, Robert Burke, or Thomas Pressly at the Department of History, University of Washington, Seattle 98195.

18. Write to the Oral History Research Office, Columbia University, Box 20, Butler Library, New York, N.Y. 10027.

19. Betty Blair, interview, February 10, 1976.

20. Betty Blair, interview, December 15, 1980.

21. Lisa Kennedy, interview, April 11, 1980, and material from questionnaire response.

22. Job description issued from Olympia, Washington, January 1980.

23. William H. Oliver, telephone interview, February 10, 1980, and material from questionnaire response, updated October 15, 1981.

24. Marjorie Skotheim, interview, December 9, 1980.

25. Diane Bolay, interview, June 10, 1975.

26. "Clio's Children: Out of the Ivory Tower and into the Marketplace: Alternative Employment," paper presented at Pacific Coast Branch, American Historical Association, August 27, 1974, University of Washington.

Chapter 15. For and About Women

1. Sande Friedman and Lois C. Schwartz, *No Experience Necessary: A Guide to Employment for the Female Liberal Arts Graduate* (New York: Dell Publishing Co., 1971), p. xxiv.

2. For a discussion of stereotypes of women as being passive, formless, and compliant, see Mary Ellman, *Thinking about Women* (New York: Harcourt Brace Jovanovich, 1968), pp. 55–145.

3. Jessie Bernard, *Academic Women* (New York: New American Library, Meridian Book, 1974), pp. 30, 42, and passim.

4. Ellen Moers, *Literary Women: The Great Writers* (New York: Doubleday, 1976), pp. 3–4; also Tillie Olsen, *Silences* (New York: Delacorte Press,

Seymour Lawrence Books, 1978), pp. 19–20, 33, also radio interview, Public Broadcasting Laboratory, July 12, 1980.

5. Margaret Fenn, *Making It in Management: A Behavioral Approach for Women Executives* (Englewood Cliff, N.J.: Prentice-Hall, 1978), pp. 14–15.

6. *Report of the United Nations Conference on Women*, Copenhagen, Denmark, quoted in the *Seattle Post-Intelligencer*, July 13, 1980.

7. Gloria Steinem, two talks in Seattle, January 21, 1980.

8. Questions recommended by the Hunter College Career Counseling and Placement Office, listed in Eleanor Berman, *Re-entering: Successful Back-to-Work Strategies for Women Seeking a Fresh Start* (New York: Crown Publishers, 1980), pp. 63–64.

9. Terry Wetherby, ed., *Conversations: Working Women Talk about Doing "A Man's Job"* (Millbrae, Calif.: Les Femmes Press, 1977), pp. 233–34, 248.

10. Leonore Hoffman and Gloria DeSole, eds., for the MLA Commission on the Status of Women in the Profession, *Careers and Couples: An Academic Question* (New York: MLA, 1976), pp. 17–21.

11. Increasingly, placement centers tell students something like this: "The term 'Placement Center' is a misnomer. We do not 'place' you; you place yourself. What we do is help you become aware of your options, and we try to provide resource materials so that you can wage your own job-seeking campaign and then make an informed choice."

12. "Doing your homework" includes doing some personal inquiring and some background reading about fields and organizations where you might like to work; following up some of the titles listed in the bibliography of this book; and getting your own first draft of a résumé down on paper *before* you ask a counselor to help you.

13. To cite examples of different kinds of schools: Lane Community College, Eugene, Oregon, has a full-time counselor (a former high school English teacher with an M.A. in English) whose entire time is spent arranging internships for language arts majors. The English Department at the University of Michigan has a full-time staff member who serves as liaison with its majors, the Office of Career Planning and Placement, and firms offering internships. The Writing Institute at the University of Puget Sound usually arranges internships for its students as part of its year-long sequence.

14. For clues to other internships, see Berman, *Re-entering*, Appendix E, "Career Information"; also Carol Kleiman, *Women's Networks* (New York: Lippincott and Crowell, 1980), "Listings," pp. 137–210.

15. Conversation with Professor Tom Lenaghan at the University of Michigan, March 18, 1980.

16. Based on many conversations with Phyllis Needy, my former colleague at the University of Washington Placement Center, plus the sketch of her career in Berman's *Re-entering*, pp. 50–53.

17. Talk given by Lolita Burnett at a "Women in Business" breakfast, Seattle, April 10, 1980, plus subsequent interview with her.

18. Anthony Smith, *Goodbye Gutenberg: The Newspaper Revolution of the 1980's* (New York: Oxford University Press, 1980).

19. From response to one of my questionnaires, plus information offered while Ricard was a student in an article writing course of mine.

20. Bernard, *Academic Women*, p. 50.

21. An interesting conversation I had recently with a Catholic sister in charge of the placement center at a Midwest women's college offered a different point of view, as far as women's careers are concerned, from the one I set forth in chapter 5. She cited many examples to back up her contention that at this time, when women are trying so hard to gain advancement and salaries equal to those of men, it is better to have earned all the degrees and credentials possible to make it unmistakably clear that one is extremely well prepared.

22. Doris Lessing, *The Summer Before the Dark* (New York: Alfred A. Knopf, 1973). Says Lessing, through her heroine's stream of consciousness: "This [being] the supplier of some kind of invisible fluid, or emanation, like a queen termite, whose spirit . . . filled the nest. . . . This is what women did in families. . . . And she had performed this function [for an organization called Global Foods]. . . . She was going to fill the role again in Turkey. It was a habit she had got into. She was beginning to see that she could accept a job in this organization . . . for no other reason than that she was unable to switch herself out of the role of provider of invisible manna, consolation, warmth, 'sympathy'" (p. 52). I think that throughout the novel Lessing fails to make her case.

23. Kathrine Gambill, interview, February 15, 1980.

24. See especially Betty Lehan Harragan, *Games Mother Never Taught You: Corporate Gamesmanship for Women* (New York: Warner Books, 1978), for consciousness raising about taking criticism impersonally.

25. Leise Robbins, "Positive Business Attitudes," talk at the "Forum for Women Entrepreneurs," Seattle, December 7, 1976.

26. Lyn Taetzsch and Eileen Benson, *Taking Charge on the Job: Techniques for Assertive Management* (New York: Executive Enterprises Publications, 1978).

27. Hoffman and DeSole, eds., *Careers and Couples* (see note 10 above).

28. Wetherby, ed., *Conversations*, p. 64.

29. Kleiman, *Women's Networks*, pp. xiii–xiv.

30. Ibid., p. 3.

31. Ibid., p. 9.

32. Jane Howard, *A Different Woman* (New York: E. P. Dutton, 1973), pp. 130–43, "When I Grow Up."

33. For an example of the scrambled priorities of a woman who must have taken the current media hype about the upwardly mobile woman rather uncritically, see Thomas J. Cottle, "'Goodbye, Kids, Mother's Leaving Home': A Family Separates," *Atlantic Monthly*, May 1980, pp. 43–48. The mother chronicled here seems a particularly bizarre example of confused motives, not simply because she left her husband and children for her career but because, as the case history shows, she did it in such an ambivalent, secretive, and ultimately damaging way.

Bibliography

Books and articles about jobs and careers proliferate with such speed and profusion that any bibliography, to be useful, must be highly selective. Should you want to explore the printed sources further, the bibliographies contained in many of these books will help you to do so, as will your campus placement center library.

Some of the titles below deal with the specifics of making a career choice. Others have little or nothing to do with the question of how to find jobs in a particular field, but provide a great deal of background information about how an industry or profession operates. (A very few, such as Roberta Morgan's *How to Break into Publishing*, do both.) Still others, such as Anthony Smith's *Goodbye Gutenberg*, or Antony Jay's *Management and Machiavelli*, attempt sweeping theoretical—and sometimes highly controversial—analyses of their fields.

Within the topically arranged list below, asterisks indicate titles I consider especially informative and useful; daggers signify titles of a few books which, though no longer listed in *Books in Print*, seem to me valuable enough to be worth tracking down in a library or secondhand store.

1. BACKGROUND OF THE PROBLEM

American Historical Association, *Careers for Students of History*. Washington, D.C.: AHA, 1977.
> Discusses a range of nonacademic careers, with particular emphasis on government work and historical administration, editing, and preservation. Many students of English would not find it hard to qualify themselves for some of these careers.

Benderly, Beryl Lieff. "Thinking the Unthinkable: Learned Societies React to the Job Shortage." *Change: The Magazine of Higher Learning* 9 (June 1977): 13–15.
> Shows what efforts the professional societies representing humanities and social sciences disciplines are beginning to make to help graduate students in their fields find nonacademic careers.

*Cartter, Allan M. *Ph.D.'s and the Academic Labor Market: A Report Prepared for the Carnegie Commission on Higher Education. New York: McGraw-Hill Book Co., 1976.

Data and projections on possible future academic employment of Ph.D.'s.

The CEA Forum: English, Liberal Arts, and Communication: Their Value Beyond Academe. Vol. 11, no. 4 (April 1981). College Station, Texas: Texas A & M University, 1981.

Pamphlet containing short but persuasive articles by a publisher, a physician, a lawyer, a university dean, and an editor, all on the usefulness, both long-range and short-range, of English studies.

Dugger, Ronnie. "The Community College Comes of Age." Change 8, no. 1 (February 1976): 32–37.

Appraising the strengths and weaknesses of the community college, Dugger sees a hopeful sign in its emphasis on good teaching.

Dunlop, Elizabeth, et al. Career Opportunities for Liberal Arts Graduates. Ontario, Canada: University and College Placement Association, 1979.

Focusing mainly on Canadian positions, this book offers general principles useful to all liberal arts job-seekers.

Fisher, Francis D. "Educating for Underemployment." Change 8, no. 1 (February 1976): 16, 69.

Fisher, director of Harvard's Office of Career Services and Off-Campus Learning, hails widespread "underemployment" as a symptom of a healthy down-playing of education as the one road to a job, high wages, and material goods.

Freeman, Richard B. The Overeducated American. New York: Academic Press, 1976.

Takes somewhat the same line as Fisher, above.

Gleiser, Molly. "An Obsolescent Life." Harper's Magazine, September 1974, pp. 68–70.

English majors would do well to realize that their chosen career fields are not the only overcrowded ones. In this brief, sardonic autobiography, a chemistry Ph.D., author of four texts and ten published articles, tells of her job search after finding her teaching position phased out for lack of funds.

Harrison, Dorothy. "The Nonacademic Job Market." In Richard I. Brod et al., eds., English and Foreign Languages: Employment and the Profession, a special joint issue of the Bulletin of the Association of Departments of English (no. 50) and the Bulletin of the Association of Departments of Foreign Languages (vol. 8, no. 1), September 1976, pp. 68–70.

Analyzes the implications of the shrinking academic job market and shows the need of further study and development of alternative positions.

* Jacobs, Rita. The Useful Humanists: Alternative Careers for Ph.D.'s in the Humanities. New York: Rockefeller Foundation, 1977.

Survey of possible uses to which the education of Ph.D.'s may be put. A "working paper" based on the premise that "the humanities are not divorced from the concerns of everyday life."

London, Herbert I. "The Case for Nontraditional Learning." *Change* 8, no. 5
    (June 1976): 25–29.
    Examines the claims and implications of such innovative programs as
    "universities without walls."
National Research Council. *National Survey of Doctorate Recipients.* Wash-
    ington, D.C.: NRC, 1980.
    Leaflet giving statistics on employment for Ph.D.'s in all fields; report in-
    cludes distribution by discipline, also median salary.
*———. *Employment of Humanities Ph.D.'s: A Departure from Traditional
    Jobs.* Betty D. Maxfield, Project Director. Washington, D.C.: Commission
    on Human Resources, National Research Council, 1980.
    Gives more detailed data than the item above.
*Orange, Linwood E. *English: The Pre-Professional Major.* Third edition.
    New York: Modern Language Association, 1979.
    Orange's pamphlet deals with the uses of an undergraduate major in En-
    glish and the careers to which it can lead. There is a valuable analysis of
    transferable skills that a student should acquire by majoring in English.
*O'Toole, James. "The Reserve Army of the Underemployed: I—The World
    of Work." *Change* 7, no. 4 (May 1975): 26–33, 63.
———. "The Reserve Army of the Underemployed: II—The Role of Educa-
    tion." *Change* 7, no. 5 (June 1975): 26–33, 60–63.
    A member of the Center for Future Research at U.C.L.A. suggests changes
    in our attitudes toward education, "particularly that we stop implicitly
    and explicitly selling it as an economic investment."
*Rigolot, Carol, ed. *Alternate Careers for Ph.D.'s in the Humanities.* Prince-
    ton, N.J.: Princeton University Press, 1978.
    Report of a conference of academic leaders and executives of life insur-
    ance companies at Princeton University, March 10–11, 1977, sponsored by
    the University Advisory Council of the American Council of Life Insur-
    ance. This pamphlet explores the question whether in the 1980s there is a
    valid role in the business world for humanities Ph.D.'s.
Terkel, Studs. *American Dreams Lost and Found.* New York: Pantheon, 1980.
———. *Working: People Talk About What They Do All Day and How They
    Feel About What They Do.* New York: Pantheon, 1974. Avon, 1975.
    Terkel's books of taped interviews with Americans in a broad spectrum of
    jobs could give academics perspective on their own career problems.
U.S. Department of Labor. *Liberal Arts and Your Career.* Washington, D.C.:
    U.S. Department of Labor, 1978.
    Useful pamphlet.
Wolfe, Gary K., and Carol Traynor Williams. "All Education Is 'Adult Educa-
    tion'." *AAUP Bulletin* 60 (September 1974): 291–95.
    Discusses the recent growth of adult education programs and predicts still
    further expansion.
*Wolfle, Dael, and Charles V. Kidd. "The Future Market for Ph.D.'s." *AAUP
    Bulletin* 58 (March 1972): 5–16.
    Documenting the volume and rate of the recent Ph.D. explosion, Wolfle
    and Kidd make a nationwide survey of overcrowded academia. Every

graduate student should ponder their main conclusion, that "many new doctorates will enter nontraditional jobs and will do work that has not attracted many of their predecessors. . . . Few of them will be unemployed, but few will be employed in college and university teaching and research."

2. On Job-seeking, Being Interviewed, and Related Topics

*Bolles, Richard Nelson. *What Color Is Your Parachute? A Practical Manual for Job-Hunters and Career Changers.* Revised and enlarged. Berkeley, Calif.: Ten Speed Press, 1981. Revised annually.
Job candidates of all ages and both sexes have been discovering since *Parachute's* first edition in 1972 that Bolles has sound, specific advice on how to discover your strongest assets, how to avoid being paralyzed by "rejection shock" and the "numbers game," and how to do substantial homework before having a job interview. Extremely helpful bibliography and appendixes, one of which includes Bolles's "Quick Job-Hunting Map," sometimes published separately.

———. *Tea Leaves: A New Look at Résumés.* Berkeley: Ten Speed Press, 1976.
An iconoclastic view of résumé writing.

———. *The Three Boxes of Life and How to Get Out of Them.* Berkeley: Ten Speed Press, 1978.
Here Bolles offers an "introduction to life/work planning" as he discusses the three periods of life (education, work, and retirement). Interesting expansion of some of the points made in *Parachute.* Helpful appendixes.

Djeddah, Eli. *Moving Up: How to Get High-Salaried Jobs.* Berkeley, Calif.: Ten Speed Press, 1978. New edition.
A cheerful and convincing discussion of setting goals, writing résumés, being interviewed, getting yourself invited back after the first interview, using a referral campaign, answering tough questions, and generally putting yourself in the best light. To Djeddah, the cardinal virtues appear to be chutzpah, imagination, energy; if you can partake of his confidence and put them to work according to his plan, your job campaign could well be successful.

*Figler, Howard. *The Complete Job Search Handbook: All the Skills You Need to Get Any Job and Have a Good Time Doing It.* New York: Holt, Rinehart and Winston, 1979.
Excellent chapters on self-assessment, the personal referral network, interviews, research on job fields, self-marketing, and "the Zen of the career search."

*Fox, Marcia R. *Put Your Degree to Work: A Career-Planning and Job-Hunting Guide for the New Professional.* New York: W. W. Norton, 1979.
Dr. Fox, assistant dean in charge of the placement office at New York University's Graduate School of Public Administration, has sensible things to say about building a dossier, making good use of scholarly conventions for job-seeking, choosing the best kind of fieldwork experience, making intel-

ligent use of your campus placement center, writing effective letters of application, and preparing for a successful interview. Her advice should be useful to both present and former academics in a wide variety of fields.

* Gamble, Richard. "Hitch Your Wagon to a Star: Confessions of a Postacademic Job Seeker." *Profession 80.* Pp. 20–23. New York: Modern Language Association, 1980. (Annual collection of "selected articles from the *Bulletins* of the Association of Departments of English and the Association of Departments of Foreign Languages.")

Gamble, a Ph.D. in English with several years of successful college teaching behind him, describes his job search of over two months in Atlanta. His conclusions: although there is no magic formula, a combination of desperation, unflagging pursuit of every lead, and serendipity *can* lead to satisfying nonacademic jobs for Ph.D.'s, one of which is his position as financial editor of a banking journal.

* Haldane, Bernard. *Career Satisfaction and Success: A Guide to Job Freedom.* New York: AMACOM, 1974.

Haldane, a pioneer in the field of job counseling, tells here how you can discover your "strongest motivated skills," how you can build up a network of contacts that will lead in turn to "referral interviews," and why a standard résumé may not be the best job-seeking tool. Highly recommended by a panelist at a recent MLA session on alternative careers.

Harwood, John T. "From Genre Theory to the Want Ads." *ADE Bulletin* 44 (February 1975): 21–24.

———. "Nonacademic Job Hunting." *AAUP Bulletin* 60 (1974): 3, 3–16.

Harwood's two articles offer advice, mainly on job application letters, résumés, and interviews, from a recent Ph.D. who taught himself to translate his background in English literature into the language of business, and subsequently received numerous job offers.

Holland, John L. *Making Vocational Choices: A Theory of Careers.* Englewood Cliffs, N.J.: Prentice-Hall, 1973.

Based on the premise that "vocational stereotypes have reliable and important psychological and sociological meanings." Categorizes work into six types: "realistic, investigative, artistic, social, enterprising, and conventional." (Dubious logic?)

* Irish, Richard K. *Go Hire Yourself an Employer.* Revised and expanded edition. Garden City, N.Y.: Anchor Press, 1978.

Particularly helpful on résumés, on "interviewing for information rather than for a job," and on working for the government. Dedicated to "everyone who at one time or another is told 'You're too young, old, qualified, unqualified, experienced, inexperienced, beautiful, plain, expensive, or too damn good' for the job," Irish's book should offer encouragement to many "overqualified" graduate students.

———. *If Things Don't Improve Soon I May Ask You to Fire Me.* Garden City, N.Y.: Anchor Press/Doubleday, 1975.

Directed toward holders of or searchers for what Irish calls "judgment jobs," this book attempts to goad people into making the best possible use of their experience even at the risk of security.

*Jackson, Tom. *Guerrilla Tactics in the Job Market*. New York: Bantam Books, 1978.

Offers 78 "tactics" or exercises to carry out as you start on your self-directed job search. By making yourself do them instead of simply rushing through the book, you will have gained considerable understanding of yourself and your chosen field by the time you reach Tactic #78 ("Do not accept the first offer you receive, unless you are certain that it is what you want. Set up a scale of five criteria which the ideal job would have").

Jackson, Tom, and Davidyne Mayleas. *The Hidden Job Market: A System to Beat the System*. New York: Quadrangle/New York Times Book Co., 1976.

"The hidden job market is in people's minds. It is that vast reservoir of job information that people in companies, in associations, and other organizations have about what's happening on their own or on neighboring turf. It is made up of unreleased new plans, emerging new problems. . . ." Jackson and Mayleas undertake to show readers how they can uncover some of these unadvertised opportunities.

Lewis, Adele. *How to Write Better Résumés*. Woodbury, N.Y.: Barron's Educational Series, Inc., 1977.

Many people agree with Lewis (the president of Career Blazers Agency, Inc.), "In the job hunt, the single most important tool is a carefully thought-out, attractively designed, well-written résumé." Those who share this belief may want to look at the more than one hundred sample résumés in this volume, among them résumés for those over forty, minorities, the returning housewife, the handicapped, the foreign-born, and the returning service person. Lewis's book also includes sensible comments on job-seeking and career changing.

Medley, H. Anthony. *Sweaty Palms: The Neglected Art of Being Interviewed*. Belmont, Calif.: Lifetime Learning Publications, a division of Wadsworth Publishing Co., 1978.

Medley, a lawyer who has set up a system of videotaping interviews of job candidates at major law schools, describes various kinds of interviews and suggests ways of preparing for them. His most important point: "Don't think about yourself so much."

* *MLA Guide for Job Candidates and Department Chairmen in English and Foreign Languages*. Revised edition. New York: Modern Language Association, 1978.

Updated every few years. For most readers with a background in English, the pages on "Alternatives to Teaching" should be the starting point in your search for your new career, after which you'll be in a position to use the more specialized resources in the present bibliography. (Be sure to consult the latest edition.)

Pollack, Sandy. *Alternative Careers for Teachers*. The Common, Harvard, Mass.: Harvard Common Press, 1979.

Brief, sensible presentation of the facts you need to know, if you are hoping to switch from teaching to a career in training, administration, personnel, government work, sales, self-employment, publishing, the media, or several others.

3. On Teaching New Clienteles

Angel, Juvenal L. *Directory of American Firms Operating in Foreign Countries.* Ninth edition. New York: Uniworld Business Publications, 1979.
   Useful guide for teachers looking for firms with large overseas cadres of executives and other personnel. Such companies sometimes employ American teachers to staff company-run schools.
   ———. *Directory of International Agencies.* New York: Simon and Schuster, 1979.
   Even more applicable to the needs of readers of this book than the above title.
Bowyer, Carlton H., and Burton B. Fox. *Teaching Overseas: The Carribean and Latin American Area: A Recruitment Handbook.* Second edition. Barranquilla, Colombia: Inter-Regional Center for Curriculum and Materials Development, 1980.
   The only volume of its kind; recommended.
Community and Junior College Journal. Published eight times yearly by the American Association of Junior Colleges, Washington, D.C.
   Articles on such matters as curricular staffing, funding, and new audio-visual technology in the two-year college.
Hellstrom, Ward. "Reaching Nontraditional Students." *Profession 78.* Pp. 22–27. New York: Modern Language Association, 1978.
   Thoughtful article on the value of teaching non-English majors in colleges and universities. Suggests that English departments be increasingly open-minded about interdisciplinary courses and those in film, science fiction, and technical writing.
Kocher, Eric. *International Jobs: Where They Are: How to Get Them.* Reading, Pa.: Addison-Wesley Publishing Co., 1979.
   Includes information about teaching jobs among others.
McIntyre, Pat Kern. *American Students and Teachers Abroad: Sources of Information about Overseas Study, Teaching, Work, and Travel.* Revised edition. Washington, D.C.: U.S. Government Printing Office, 1975. GPO S/N 017-080-013-77-1.
   Helpful pamphlet.

4. On Editing and Publishing

* Appelbaum, Judith, and Nancy Evans. *How to Get Happily Published.* New York: Harper and Row, 1978.
   Although primarily addressed to authors, this lively manual would be useful to anyone who hopes to learn about what editors, copy editors, and literary agents do, and what publishing looks like from the inside.
Bailey, Herbert S., Jr. *The Art and Science of Book Publishing.* New York: Harper and Row, 1970. Austin: University of Texas Press, 1980.
   A thorough description of the various kinds of publishing and the range of jobs within each.

Dessauer, John P. *Book Publishing: What It Is, What It Does.* New York: R. R. Bowker, 1976.
A readable and authoritative discussion.

* *The Editorial Eye: Focusing on Publications Standards and Practices.* Published approximately fifteen times a year by Editorial Experts, Inc., 5905 Pratt Street, Alexandria, Virginia 22310.
Each eight-page issue contains half a dozen brief articles on such points as check lists for copy editors, relations with authors, elimination of jargon and redundancy, proofreading and copy editing tests, or timesaving editorial shortcuts.

Fulton, Len, and Ellen Ferber. *The International Directory of Little Magazines and Small Presses.* Sixteenth edition. 1980–81. Paradise, Calif.: Dustbooks, 1980.
Contains names, addresses, and specialties of over two thousand independent publishers across the United States as well as the more than 175 jobbers, agents, and distributors who handle their books and magazines. For those trying to get a picture of publishing today, this resource offers a wholesome corrective to the idea that every successful book or magazine idea is generated on or near Madison Avenue and carried out by a big publishing house which is subsidiary to an even bigger conglomerate.

Grannis, Chandler B., ed. *What Happens in Book Publishing.* Second edition. New York: Columbia University Press, 1967.
A fascinating collection of articles by specialists in different branches of the book publishing industry. Excellent bibliography.

* Greenfield, Howard. *Books: From Writer to Reader.* New York: Crown, 1976.
Contains eighteen informative chapters on such topics as the literary agent, the editor, the illustrator, the copy editor, the designer, the production supervisor, the proofreader and the indexer, the compositor, and the binder.

† Gross, Gerald, ed. *Editors on Editing.* New York: Grosset and Dunlap, 1962.
A unique collection of articles wherein editors in different branches of publishing (commercial, university press, children's books, and texts) tell not only what they do but how they feel about their jobs.

† Hawes, Gene R. *To Advance Knowledge: A Handbook on American University Press Publishing.* New York: Association of American University Presses, 1967.
The only book-length treatment of how university presses operate; excellent.

Henderson, Bill, ed. *The Publish-It-Yourself Handbook.* Yonkers, N.Y.: Pushcart Press, 1980.
The classic guide on publishing a book without dependence on either commercial publishing houses or "vanity" publishers. Includes essays by Anaïs Nin, Leonard Woolf, Alan Swallow, and others, along with a complete bibliography and "how-to" section.

Joan, Polly, and Andrea Chesman. *Guide to Women's Publishing.* Paradise, Calif.: Dustbooks, 1979.

A comprehensive description of the women's publishing movement.

† Kernaghan, Eileen, Edith Surridge, and Patrick Kernaghan. *The Upper Left-Hand Corner: A Writer's Guide for the Northwest*. Vancouver, B.C.: J. J. Douglas Ltd.; Seattle: Madrona Publishers, 1975.

An invaluable source of names and addresses of Pacific Northwest publishers, periodicals, printers, writers' markets, editors, and sources of financial aid for writers. Also contains sixteen articles about different genres of writing and how to market them.

Literary Market Place. New York: R. R. Bowker Co., 1981. Issued annually.

The directory of and for the book trade; best source of names and current addresses of book publishers both national and regional, as well as of editors, literary agents, printers, and others in the publishing industry. (Not to be confused with *Writer's Market*; see below.)

* Morgan, Roberta. *How to Break into Publishing*. New York: Barnes and Noble, 1980.

On the basis of interviews with publishers and of her own experience in both book and magazine publishing, Morgan describes the range of jobs in the industry and the best preparation for each.

O'Neill, Carol L., and Avima Ruder. *The Complete Guide to Editorial Freelancing*. Revised edition. New York: Barnes and Noble, 1979.

Thorough treatment of what the various kinds of editing and copy editing involve, as well as how to get started. Contains sample copy editing tests.

Pascal, Naomi B. "To Open Publishing Doors." *Scholarly Publishing* 2, no. 2 (January 1971): 195–201.

Account by a university press editor of what students can learn through a well-supervised internship in a publishing house.

* Stith, Mary, Naomi Pascal, et al. "The Out-of-House Editor." *Scholarly Publishing* 3, no. 3 (April 1972): 259–72.

Four university press editors discuss the advantages and disadvantages of using freelance editorial help. Valuable insight into the employer's point of view.

West, Celeste, and Valerie Wheat. *The Passionate Perils of Publishing*. San Francisco: Booklegger Press, 1978.

Detailed information about the economics of the publishing industry, including alternative and feminist presses.

Weyr, Thomas. "Getting into Publishing." *Publishers Weekly*, March 24, 1975, pp. 22–25.

Deals with a random sample of people in publishing and how they found their jobs. Main conclusions: success often stems from "saying the right words on the right day"; moreover, it helps to be young.

Wheelock, John Hall, ed. *Editor to Author: The Letters of Maxwell E. Perkins*. New York: Scribner's, 1950; reprinted 1979.

Although no editor today would have the chance to give as much attention to each of his authors as Perkins did, anyone hoping to get into publishing should read this to get an idea of some of the possibilities and responsibilities of the editor's role.

*Whiteside, Thomas. "The Blockbuster Complex." *New Yorker*, September 29, 1980, pp. 48–101; October 6, 1980, pp. 63–146; October 13, 1980, pp. 52–143.
Anecdotal account of what is happening in publishing today: mergers, conglomerate takeovers, increasing emphasis on the "big book," contracts for which can involve hundreds of thousands of dollars.

5. On Working for Print and Broadcast Media

Audiovisual Market Place. New York: R. R. Bowker, 1980. Revised annually.
Contains names, addresses, and description of product lines for producers and distributors of audiovisual learning material. Lists national professional and trade organizations, as well as educational radio stations and television channels.
Bagdikian, Ben H. "Woodstein U." *Atlantic Monthly*, March 1977, pp. 80–92.
Subtitled "Notes on the Mass Production and Questionable Education of Journalists," this article will give pause to academics who imagine journalism to be a greener field than their own.
Blumenthal, L. Roy. *The Practice of Public Relations*. New York: Macmillan, 1972.
Thorough analysis of the various branches and function of public relations. Excellent bibliography.
Claxton, Ronald H., and B. A. Powell. *The Student Guide to Mass Media Internships*. Boulder, Colo.: Institutional Research Group, University of Colorado, 1980.
Useful information on where to apply.
*Hilliard, Robert L. *Writing for Television and Radio*. Third edition, revised. New York: Communications Arts Books, Hastings House, 1976.
Specific and authoritative.
*Newspaper Fund, *Journalism Career and Scholarship Guide 1981: What to Study in College, Where to Study Journalism and Communications, Where the Jobs Are and How to Find Them*. Princeton, N.J.: The Newspaper Fund, Box 300.
Very comprehensive pamphlet, updated annually. Exceptionally helpful in its sampling of views of newspaper editors from various parts of the country on what they are looking for in applicants for newspaper positions.
*Rivers, William L. *Free-lancer and Staff Writer*. Belmont, Calif.: Wadsworth Publishing Co., Inc., 1972.
Specific and helpful.
*Sandman, Peter M., David M. Rubin, and David B. Sachsman. *Media: An Introductory Analysis of American Mass Communications*. Second edition. Englewood Cliffs, N.J.: Prentice-Hall, 1976.
This thorough and well-documented volume makes a good reference source for anyone considering an entry into the field.
Schramm, Wilbur. *Men, Messages, and Media: A Look at Human Communication*. New York: Harper and Row, 1973.

Very comprehensive survey.

* Smith, Anthony. *Goodbye Gutenberg: The Newspaper Revolution of the 1980's.* New York: Oxford University Press, 1980.
Smith's thesis, which he explores at considerable length, is that "electronics has been summoned to resolve the internal tensions and crises which face the [newspaper] medium today." He sees that "the social function of the newspaper is changing, as is the whole culture of journalism," which will lead the journalist into becoming an "information technician."

6. On Entering the Business World (Finding a Job, or Starting Your Own Concern)

* Channing, Peter C. *The Career Alternative: A Guide to Business Venturing.* New York: Hawthorn Books, 1977.
Not an all-inclusive technical treatise but a very readable attempt to share insights on critical factors that make the difference between entrepreneurial success and failure.

Drucker, Peter. *The Effective Executive.* New York: Harper and Row, 1979.
Drucker, one of the best-known analysts of the American business scene, here undertakes to see what differentiates the effective "knowledge worker" from his or her less effective colleagues. Especially good on time management.

* ———. *Management: Tasks, Responsibilities, Practices.* New York: Harper and Row, 1973.
What better recommendation could this book have than that of Richard Nelson Bolles (of *Parachute* fame): "Should be absolutely required reading for anyone contemplating entering, changing to, or becoming a professional within the business world, or any organization."

Fox, Philip J., and Joseph R. Mancuso. *402 Things You Must Know Before Starting a New Business.* Englewood Cliffs, N.J.: Prentice-Hall, 1980.
Thorough and highly practical.

* Harrison, Dorothy G. "Aristotle and the Corporate Structure." *Change* 8, no. 8 (September 1976): 9, 64.
The author, codirector of a national project funded by the Mellon Foundation to study careers for humanists, finds "much more congruence between graduate training in the humanities and a variety of nonacademic jobs than most people would imagine."

Harrop, David. *Paychecks: Who Makes What?* New York: Harper and Row, 1980.
If you have a craving to know comparative salaries of jobs in banking, advertising, sales, publishing, industry, manufacturing, sports, and the media, Harrop will tell you. This is one of the few books in which even the lists and tables make good reading.

Is Technical Writing Your Career? New York: Society for Technical Communication, n.d. (pamphlet). Available from the SCT office, 815 Fifteenth Street N.W., Suite 506, Washington, D.C. 20005.

Brief explanation of what technical writers do and where you can obtain more information about this growing field.

*Jessup, Claudia, and Genie Chipps. *The Woman's Guide to Starting a Business*. Revised edition. New York: Holt, Rinehart and Winston, 1980.
For anyone of either sex hoping to start an editorial or consulting service, a bookstore, or any other successful small business enterprise, the information and case histories in this book make fascinating and almost essential reading.

Jay, Antony. *Management and Machiavelli: An Inquiry into the Politics of Corporate Life*. New York: Holt, Rinehart and Winston, 1968. Bantam Books, 1978.
Here Jay undertakes, as he explains, to look at the corporations of today "in a new way: looking not through the eyes of the accountant and systems analyst and economist and mathematician, but through those of the historian and political scientist."

Kanter, Rosabeth Moss. *Men and Women of the Corporation*. New York: Basic Books, 1979.
Shows how a corporation works and how it affects the lives of the people in it. Read this before tackling Antony Jay, above.

Personnel Journal. Published monthly. New York.
Typical articles: "The Career Planning Process," "Communicating Company Objectives," "Performance Appraisal," and "Blue-Collar Women."

Personnel: The Management of People at Work. Published bimonthly by AMACOM, a division of the American Management Associations.

Public Relations Quarterly. New York. Deals mainly with issues involving corporate management.

Small Business Association. Publishes pamphlets on financial, marketing, and advertising aspects (among others) of setting up your own business. Check with your local office of the SBA for their latest list.

*Thain, Richard J. *The Managers: Career Alternatives for the College Educated*. Bethlehem, Pa.: College Placement Council, Inc., 1978.
Deals with business fields open to college graduates; offers realistic discussion of employers' prejudices against liberal arts students, career switchers, older job-seekers. Also gives specific examples of what people really do in various managerial jobs—for example, in personnel, planning, public relations, and international business.

*Tichy, Henrietta J. *Effective Writing for Engineers, Managers, Scientists*. New York: John Wiley and Sons, 1966.
If as you consider entering the world of business you think you will have to write nothing but jargon, read this book and take heart. Tichy is both a consultant to several oil and chemical companies and a professor of English at Hunter College. Her book demonstrates how even the most utilitarian writing can achieve clarity, effective organization, forcefulness, and grace.

*Townsend, Robert. *Up the Organization: How to Stop the Corporation from Stifling People and Strangling Profits*. New York: Alfred A. Knopf, 1970.

A classic; worth reading even if you have no intention of venturing into business.

Uris, Auren. *Action Guide for Executive Job Seekers and Employers.* New York: Arco Publishing Co., 1975.

Tries to give to "both the executive looking for a job and the company looking for an executive" insight into the rituals of recruitment, executive search, job advertisements, job counseling, résumés, interviews, reference checking, and "pre-employment investigation."

7. On Government Employment

The Book of the States. Lexington, Ky. Revised annually. This series gives official information on the structure, financing, and activities of each state government. Consult it *before* you write to or visit your state capital in search of a job.

Guide to Federal Career Literature. Washington, D.C.: U.S. Civil Service Commission, GPO, 1975. Comprehensive catalogue up to its publication date; check your nearest GPO bookstore for additions and updates.

Guide to Government Employment in the Midwest (Illinois, Indiana, Iowa, Kansas, Michigan, Minnesota, Missouri, Nebraska, North Dakota, Ohio, South Dakota, Wisconsin). St. Paul, Minn.: Midwest College Placement Association, 1977.

Offers useful guidelines and starting points.

Hawkins, James E. *The Uncle Sam Connection: An Insider's Guide to Federal Employment.* Revised and updated. Chicago: Follett Publishing Co., 1978.

Since the author was formerly deputy assistant secretary in the Department of Commerce, his tips on the federal hiring system are authoritative.

* +Lukowski, Susan, and Margaret Piton. *Strategy and Tactics for Getting a Government Job.* Washington, D.C.: Potomac Books, 1973.

This breezily written book is crammed with information about federal Civil Service exams, job sources, internships, overseas jobs, the foreign language job market, private industry in Washington, and how to get in touch with executive departments and independent agencies. Although focusing mainly on jobs in the Washington, D.C. area, it gives advice about doing groundwork locally and offers leads on a few regional positions.

Pincus, Ann. "How to Get a Government Job." *Washington Monthly,* June 1976, pp. 22–27.

Informative, although less encouraging than Lukowski and Piton.

+Ruemelin, Charles. *A Guide to Government and Public Service Employment.* Cambridge, Mass.: Harvard University, 1975.

Although designed mainly for Harvard undergraduates, this pamphlet would be helpful to anyone looking for any kind of government employment.

The Washington Information Directory. Washington, D.C.: Congressional Quarterly, Inc., n.d. Published annually.

Resource for information, organized by subject, on current governmental issues. Indicates which people and agencies are concerned with which problem.

"Working for the Federal Government." *Occupational Outlook Quarterly* 21, no. 4 (Winter 1977). Order from Superintendent of Documents, U.S. Government Printing Office, Washington, D.C. 20402.

Working for the USA. Washington, D.C.: U.S. Office of Personnel Management, GPO, revised April 1979.

Pamphlet outlining application procedures and general requirements for many classes of federal jobs; supplement it with more detailed information about the field of your interest.

8. For and About Women

Note that many of these titles offer excellent advice to both sexes.

* Berman, Eleanor. *Re-entering: Successful Back-to-Work Strategies for Women Seeking a Fresh Start.* New York: Crown Publishers, 1980.

Suggestions, backed up by case histories, about finding out your true assets, surveying possibilities in several fields, going back to school, writing résumés and cover letters. Recommended to anyone returning to work.

* Catalyst Staff. *Marketing Yourself: The Catalyst Women's Guide to Successful Résumés and Interviews.* New York: G. P. Putnam's Sons, 1980.

Offers a step-by-step guide to selecting your job target, analyzing strengths and talents, writing résumés and cover letters, and being interviewed. (Catalyst, a nonprofit organization dedicated to helping women further their careers, also publishes other books for women job-seekers; a series on Career Options for college undergraduates; a series for the Returning Woman, and more.) They maintain a library, which you can visit at 14 East 60th Street, New York, N.Y. 10022, and they will answer specific questions if you write them. Among the most useful of their pamphlets to liberal arts majors are *Have You Considered Government and Politics?* and others in the series on Banking, Insurance, Retail Management, and Sales.

————. *What to Do with the Rest of Your Life: The Catalyst Career Guide for Women in the 80's.* New York: Simon and Schuster, 1980.

* Fenn, Margaret. *Making It in Management: A Behavioral Approach for Women Executives.* Englewood Cliffs, N.J.: Prentice-Hall, 1978.

Deals with myths and realities of differences in managerial styles based on sex. Attempts to goad women into being aware and active, not simply reactive, as they move from one career stage to another.

†Friedman, Sande, and Lois C. Schwartz. *No Experience Necessary: A Guide to Employment for the Female Liberal Arts Graduate.* New York: Dell, 1971.

Aid and information for that large sector of job-seekers who "have two strikes against them: first, that they are female, and second, that they are liberal arts graduates." Friedman and Schwartz take fourteen fields, from advertising, art, and banking to television/radio and travel, tell exactly what kinds of jobs are typical of each one and what are some of the best paths of entry into them.

Hall, Francine S., and Douglas T. Hall. *The Two-Career Couple*. Reading, Pa.: Addison-Wesley Publishing Co., 1979.
Deals with the problems and strains of this increasingly common marriage pattern; attempts solutions, some conventional, some drastic.

*Harragan, Betty Lehan. *Games Mother Never Taught You: Corporate Gamesmanship for Women*. New York: Warner Books, 1978.
Because of their upbringing, most women take criticism too personally, believe hard work and loyalty are or should be rewarded, try too hard to be liked, and think that one can't have too much of a good thing like education. So argues Harragan, who makes a persuasive case for her thesis that men get along better in their careers and with one another than women do largely because of what they pick up from interaction in team sports and the armed forces. The remedy is not to masculinize women but to teach them to be more observant, analytical, and assertive.

*Higginson, Margaret V., and Thomas L. Quick. *The Ambitious Woman's Guide to a Successful Career*. Revised edition. New York: American Management Associations, 1980.
Although focused primarily on women's careers in business, this volume offers fresh and sensible ideas about job applications, interviews, and résumés applicable to both sexes and a wide variety of positions.

Janeway, Elizabeth. *Man's World, Woman's Place: A Study of Social Mythology*. New York: Dell Publishing Co., 1972.
" 'Woman's place' is a shorthand phrase," says Janeway, "which sums up a whole set of traits and attitudes . . . which we think proper to women, along with the obligations and restrictions that it implies." Janeway's aim here is to challenge such thinking, which she does very persuasively.

Kleiman, Carol. *Women's Networks: The Complete Guide to Getting a Better Job, Advancing Your Career, and Feeling Great as a Woman Through Networking*. New York: Lippincott and Crowell, 1980.
If Kleiman's subtitle pushes the benefits of "networking" a bit too hard, her book nonetheless lists and discusses a fascinating diversity of networks, i.e., informal groups of women sharing a common business, professional, or personal concern who meet to help advance it (and usually their careers as well).

*Modern Language Association. *Careers and Couples: An Academic Question*. Edited by Leonore Hoffman and Gloria DeSole for the MLA Commission on the Status of Women in the Profession. New York: MLA, 1976.
Contributions from sixteen persons representing various new career patterns: the part-time career, the dual career, shared appointments, shared lives, and independent scholars without academic affiliations. Each account raises important questions that as yet have no satisfactory answers.

*Taetzsch, Lyn, and Eileen Benson. *Taking Charge on the Job: Techniques for Assertive Management*. New York: Executive Enterprises Publications, 1978.
Gives the reader the essentials of a course in assertiveness training.

Welch, Mary Scott. *Networking: The Great New Way for Women to Get Ahead*. New York: Harcourt Brace Jovanovich, 1980.

A somewhat more temperate and analytical discussion of women's networks than Carol Kleiman's book (see above).

* Wetherby, Terry, ed. *Conversations: Working Women Talk about Doing "A Man's Job."* Millbrae, Calif.: Les Femmes Press, 1977.
Two dozen women, representing trades, industry, radio, TV, medicine, law, and university administration tell how they arrived at where they are now, and how they overcame various roadblocks along the way.

* Yates, Gayle Graham. *What Women Want: The Ideas of the Movement.* Cambridge, Mass.: Harvard University Press, 1977.
Read this book for an objective and very clear account of the three main strains of thought in the Women's Movement: "the feminist perspective: women equal to men; the women's liberationist perspective: women over against men; and the androgynous perspective: women and men equal to each other."

9. WORKS FOR GENERAL REFERENCE: DIRECTORIES, GOVERNMENT PUBLICATIONS, PERIODICALS, AND NEWSPAPERS

* *Annual Register of Grant Support.* Chicago: Marquis Academic Media, 1980.
Covers over two thousand current grant programs; updated constantly.

* *Black Collegian.* Magazine published five times a year. Devoted to career opportunities for minorities; special annual issues of careers in the media, in the arts, and women's careers have useful points for all. Most campus placement offices have several copies of each issue.

* *A Career Guide to Professional Associations.* Cranston, R.I.: Carroll Press, 1980.
Lists organizations by professional field; indicates which ones offer career information or funding.

Change: The Magazine of Higher Learning. Published eight times a year by the Helen Dwight Reid Educational Foundation.
Contemporary issues in higher education.

* *Chronicle of Higher Education.* Washington, D.C. Published biweekly during the academic year, monthly during the summer.
Provocative articles on academic and professional matters, broadly interpreted. Watch its "Bulletin Board" for academic administrative, and PR positions.

College Placement Annual. Bethlehem, Pa.: College Placement Association.
Valuable information for graduating seniors about current job openings; available in campus placement offices.

* *Dictionary of Occupational Titles.* Fourth edition. Washington, D.C.: U.S. Government Printing Office, 1977.
Describes the usual duties of and qualifications for some twenty thousand jobs, alphabetically listed, ranging from unskilled to managerial and professional.

* *Encyclopedia of Associations.* Fifteenth edition. 3 vols. Detroit: Gale Research Co., 1980.

Annotated alphabetical listing of names, addresses, and functions of American associations of all kinds—professional, business, the arts, and miscellaneous.

Guide for Occupational Exploration. Washington, D.C.: U.S. Government Printing Office, 1979.
Gives information about occupations as classified by general field and job title.

Lefferts, Robert. *Getting a Grant.* Englewood Cliffs, N.J.: Prentice-Hall, 1979.
Very helpful information.

National Trade and Professional Associations of the United States and Canada and Labor Unions. Craig Colgate, Jr., editor. Washington, D.C.
Lists nearly six thousand scientific or technical societies, trade associations, labor unions, and other national organizations.

* *New York Times.* See especially the Sunday edition, section 4, "The Week in Review," which has advertisements of educational positions; also section 3, "Business and Finance," with its articles and ads dealing with career opportunities. Watch too for the Wednesday edition, with Elizabeth Fowler's career column.

Occupational Outlook Handbook. Washington, D.C.: U.S. Department of Labor, 1980–81.
Outlines over three hundred occupations; the nature of work, what its future looks like, training normally required, earnings, working conditions.

Occupational Outlook Handbook for College Graduates. Washington, D.C.: U.S. Department of Labor, 1980.
Version of the above handbook designed for a more highly educated group of readers.

University Affairs: Affaires universitaires. Montreal, Quebec. Published monthly.
Contains articles and news stories on Canadian education and some advertisements of administrative and teaching posts throughout the provinces.

Index

Maslow, Abraham, 21
Master of arts (M.A.) degree, 136,
  266–67n
Master of arts in teaching (M.A.T.) de-
  gree, 194
Master of business administration
  (M.B.A.) degree, 59–60, 169, 177–78,
  266–67n10
Master of fine arts (M.F.A.) degree, 192
Master of library science (M.L.S.) de-
  gree, 58–62 passim
Master of social work (M.S.W.) degree,
  60
Mathematics: courses in, recommended,
  219
May, Ernest, 169
Media. *See* Magazines; Newspapers;
  Radio; Television
Mentor: value of, 36, 232
Messer-Davidow, Ellen, 173, 182–83
Meyer, Carol, 133
Meyer, Charles, 195–98
Michigan, University of, 37, 250–51
Mikkelsen, Norma, 135
Millet, June, 22
Minority affairs counselor, duties of,
  86–87
Minor subjects, 126
Mitchell, Joseph, 7
Mobility: of academic staff, 89; in pub-
  lishing, 130–31, 135–36
Modern Language Association (MLA):
  list of teaching vacancies, 9; role in
  current job crisis, 13, 62; survey of
  Ph.D's in English holding nonteaching
  positions, 13, 18–33 passim, 189, 232,
  263–64n16; annual meetings, 137,
  142
Modern languages: Ph.D's in, as editors,
  16
Moore, John D., 135
Morgan, Roberta, 129, 130, 133
"Moving up," 122–23, 126, 143–44,
  156–60, 218, 219, 223–26
Munford, J. Kenneth, 140
Museums: careers in, 17–18, 86, 211

Nader, Ralph, 166
"Narcissistic fallacy," 39, 232
Needy, Phyllis, 235–36, 239
Networks: circles of personal contacts,
  31–32; women's organizations,
  241–42
Newman, Edwin, 7, 99
Newsletters, 118, 212, 217, 221. *See also*
  House organs

Newspapers: careers on, 145–53
New York University, 39, 169
New Zealand: teaching in, 71–72
Nichols, Luther, 139, 140
Nillson, J. Dexter, 116
Nonprofit agencies: editing and writing
  for, 181, 217

Office of Personnel Management (OPM),
  76, 116, 214–16
Ogilvy and Mather, 165
Oliver, William H., 44, 221–23
Olsen, Fern, 162
O'Neill, Carol, 96, 108, 116
Oral history: careers in, 18, 70, 91–92,
  203, 218; courses in, 18, 217–18
Oral skills, 5, 29, 182, 220–21
Orange, Linwood, 7, 177
Organizational skills, 5, 29, 119, 246
"Overqualification," 91–92, 122–23,
  213, 218
Overseas teaching, 71–73

Pacific Lutheran University (Tacoma,
  WA), 25
Packard, Vance, 166
Part-time work, 55, 79–81, 246
Passivity: avoidance of, in jobseeking,
  35, 46, 230–31, 233
"Perkins, Barbara," 142–44
Perkins, Maxwell, 94, 115
Personnel, Department of (state): exams
  for jobs, 212. *See also* Office of Per-
  sonnel Management
Personnel departments: as hurdles for
  jobseekers, 29, 32, 52, 219
Personnel work: entry into, 171–72, 212
Ph.D. *See* Doctor of philosophy
Photography, 66
Placement and career planning, offices
  of, 36–38, 232–33
Pneuman, Fred, 173
Political organizations and agencies: re-
  search and writing positions in, 207–
  227 passim
Poll-taking experience: as entry into gov-
  ernment work, 207
Portfolios: of writing, 29, 51–53 passim,
  124, 146–47, 161; of speeches written,
  29, 182; of editing, 108–109
Promotion ladder, 136, 222, 243
Proofreading, 96
Publications, consumer, 181–82
Publications office, college or university,
  87
"Public history," 17–18, 92, 217–18, 279n

Dorothy Koch Bestor received her Ph.D. from the Department of
History, the Arts, and Letters of Yale University. She has taught
English at Vassar, Bryn Mawr, and Douglass colleges, the State
University of New York at Albany, and Bellevue Community College
in Washington. She has also held a number of the alternative
positions she describes in this book. She has taught English as a
second language, served as a pollster in public opinion surveys, and
edited books and articles in the health sciences. Formerly a Higher
Education Counselor in the University of Washington Placement
Center, she currently teaches courses in editing, writing, and
literature in the Continuing Education program at the University of
Washington and is a member of a Seattle group of free-lance editors.